Growing points in child language

edited by

KATHARINE PERERA
University of Manchester

GLYN COLLIS
University of Warwick

and

BRIAN RICHARDS
University of Reading

CAMBRIDGE
UNIVERSITY PRESS

PUBLISHED BY
THE PRESS SYNDICATE OF THE UNIVERSITY OF CAMBRIDGE
The Pitt Building, Trumpington Street, Cambridge CB2 1RP
40 West 20th Street, New York, NY 10011-4211, USA
10 Stamford Road, Oakleigh, Melbourne 3166, Australia

© Cambridge University Press 1994

First published 1994

Printed in Great Britain at the University Press, Cambridge

A catalogue record for this book is available from the British Library

Library of Congress Cataloguing-in-Publication Data
Growing points in child language/edited by Katharine Perera, Glyn
Collis and Brian Richards.
  p. cm.
"This volume makes available in book form, complete with index,
the twentieth anniversary issue of the Journal of child language" –
– Cover
  Includes index.
  ISBN 0-521-46906-6 (pbk.)
  1. Language acquisition.   I. Perera, Katharine.   II. Collis,
Glyn.   III. Richards, Brian J.   IV. Journal of child language.
P118. G76 1994   94-10651
401'.93--dc20   CIP

ISBN 0521 46906 6 paperback

CUP

CONTENTS

Preface

It seemed right to celebrate the twentieth anniversary of the founding of the *Journal of Child Language* with a special issue. Therefore, I wrote to all the members of the Editorial Board setting out our ideas for the issue and asking for their suggestions concerning scholars who were doing innovative work who could be invited to submit an article for Vol. 21, No. 1. The enthusiasm of their response reflects the commitment that they consistently show to the *Journal*; I should like to take this opportunity to give public thanks to the members of the Board for their advice, support and encouragement and for the valuable role they play in helping to maintain the academic standard of the *Journal*. The large number of names they suggested testifies to the current vigour of research in the field of child language acquisition.

The *Journal of Child Language* operates a rigorous process of fully anonymous academic peer review (neither author nor referee is made known to the other). The letter inviting scholars to submit their work for possible inclusion in the anniversary issue made it clear that all articles would undergo the normal refereeing process. I am grateful to all those who were willing to contribute on that basis. From the considerable number of articles we received we were fortunate in being able to select those which were highly regarded by at least two experts in that particular area, and which accorded with our editorial view of the overall character of the anniversary issue.

During the nine years that I have been involved in editing the *Journal of Child Language*, I have increasingly come to understand the invaluable contribution that is made by academic referees, and the benefits that accrue to authors, readers and, indeed, to the discipline itself. Many clearly expend a great deal of time and care on the task and are generous with their knowledge and expertise. Their reports may suggest other experimental paradigms, re-work the data using different statistical procedures, show how the data could be more revealingly presented, draw attention to relevant research studies, and provide detailed commentary on textual organization and wording. At the end of each volume we publish the names of those who have acted as referees for us during the preceding year; I am delighted that here I can express more fully the sense of indebtedness that my associate editors and I feel to all those altruistic scholars who are willing to take on the time-consuming and unrewarded task of refereeing.

The *Journal of Child Language* publishes material on all aspects of the scientific study of language behaviour in children, the principles which underlie it and the theories which may account for it. We publish the work of both linguists and psychologists, being open to the range of theoretical standpoints that these disciplines encompass. When we saw how well the anniversary issue reflected the aims of the *Journal*, and how its papers pointed the way to new lines of enquiry, we were keen that it should be published as a book, both so that it could be more widely available, and so that its contents could be indexed. We are grateful to Cambridge University Press for making this possible.

In editing the *Journal*, I am fortunate in having the indispensable help of my associate editors, Glyn Collis and Brian Richards. They both bring the highest standards of scholarship to the academic aspects of the task and unfailing good humour to all the humdrum work that has to be done; for both these qualities I am truly grateful. Finally, I acknowledge with gratitude the secretarial assistance that I have had from Irene Pickford and Steven Sharples, not only for this special anniversary issue but also for the ongoing work of the *Journal*.

University of Manchester, 1994   KATHARINE PERERA

J. Child Lang. **21** (1994), 1–7. Copyright © 1994 Cambridge University Press

Editorial
Child language research: building on the past, looking to the future

Twenty years ago, in 1974, the first volume of the *Journal of Child Language* was published. This special 20th anniversary issue brings together papers by a number of scholars who, coming from various perspectives, present research that not only builds upon the scholarly achievements of the past but also points the way forward to new lines of enquiry.

Over the last 25 years or so a great deal has been achieved descriptively, methodologically and theoretically in the area of child language research. We now know much more than we did at the beginning of the 1970s, for example, about the role of adult input (e.g. Snow, 1986; Shatz, Hoff-Ginsberg & MacIver, 1989; Richards & Robinson, 1993); about individual differences in the course of language acquisition (e.g. Bates, Bretherton & Snyder, 1980; Nelson, 1981; Lieven, Pine & Dresner Barnes, 1992); about children's ability to use language in connected discourse (e.g. Karmiloff-Smith, 1986; Peterson & Dodsworth, 1991); and to adapt their message to the needs of their listener (e.g. Menig-Peterson, 1975; Perner & Leekam, 1986).

The earlier heavy focus on the acquisition of English has been supplemented not only by descriptions of the acquisition of a wide range of the world's languages (e.g. Korean: Clancy, 1989; Tamil: Vaidyanathan, 1991; Turkish: Aksu-Koç, 1988; Warlpiri: Bavin & Shopen, 1985; and see Slobin, 1985 (Vol. I) and 1993 for studies of some 20 languages) but also by cross-linguistic studies which specifically look for comparisons and contrasts in the course of acquisition of languages with differing phonological, morphological or syntactic characteristics (e.g. Slobin, 1985 (Vol. II); MacWhinney & Bates, 1989; Weist, Wysocka & Lyytinen, 1991). This crosslinguistic perspective is particularly important, not just because it helps to prevent the study of language acquisition being too anglocentric but, much more significantly, because of its theoretical value. Since all normally-developing children have the potential to acquire any of the world's languages, regardless of their typology, any theory that seeks to explain the mechanisms of language acquisition must be able to account for ALL the patterns of development that researchers identify, not just those in the world's major languages. These crosslinguistic studies have begun the task of identifying those aspects of acquisition that are universal and those that are language-specific. For example, while studies of English and other Indo-European languages suggest that the passive is a relatively late acquisition (e.g. Maratsos, Kuczaj, Fox & Chalkley, 1979), studies of a number of non-Indo-European langu-

I

ages, such as Turkish, Sesotho and Zulu (Demuth, 1990) show comparatively EARLY acquisition of the passive – highlighting the importance of the interaction between a particular grammatical structure and the linguistic system as a whole, including its pragmatic and communicative aspects.

As far as methodology is concerned, new research paradigms have made it possible to study the neonate's responsiveness to speech sounds (e.g. Moon, Bever & Fifer, 1992). The increasingly widespread use of videotaped data has strengthened the validity of studies of early language which seek to relate grammatical form to communicative function. Crosslinguistically-stimulated work on mean length of utterance – one of the most basic and taken-for-granted yardsticks in language acquisition research – has drawn attention to the limitations of this measure (e.g. Dromi & Berman, 1982; Hickey, 1991). And the establishment of the CHILDES database, with its related computer-coding system for child language data, has enormously enhanced access to the invaluable corpora of data that have been collected by child language researchers around the world (MacWhinney, 1991).

Turning to theoretical advances, the last quarter of a century has seen new and highly productive theories emanate from both linguistics and psychology, e.g. government and binding (Chomsky, 1981, 1986) with its related notion of parameter setting (see, for example, Atkinson, 1992); modularity (e.g. Fodor, 1983); relevance theory (Sperber & Wilson, 1986); semantic boot-strapping (e.g. Pinker, 1984, 1989); and connectionism – or parallel distributed processing (e.g. McClelland & Rumelhart, 1986). Some of these theories have been developed specifically to provide explanations for children's language-learning abilities; others have wider or more abstract aims, such as modelling human learning mechanisms or providing a universally-applicable account of grammatical structure. All these theories have been adduced by various psycholinguists to provide the theoretical underpinning for their investigations into child language, but, interestingly, it is now also the case that the empirical data from acquisition studies are sometimes used to test the validity of linguistic hypotheses that do not have a specifically acquisitionist focus (see, for example, pp. 253–4 below).

Despite all the progress that has been made, it is clear that much more remains to be done. This is partly because the task itself has become more ambitious: the heightened importance of universal grammar within linguistic theory means that many researchers now want language acquisition data to answer questions not only about psycholinguistic mechanisms within the individual learner but also about the inter-relatedness of different linguistic categories within the grammatical system itself. Central, related questions are: how much and what kind of linguistic knowledge is innate? Whatever linguistic knowledge is innate must necessarily be part of universal grammar. So commonalities in the acquisition of languages from typologically different groups are important not just for their intrinsic interest but also for the light they shed on linguistic innateness and universality.

The papers gathered together in this volume all necessarily build on the work of earlier language researchers but they also point the way forward to new research avenues that will be explored during the next decade. A characteristic that they all share is that they open up new lines of enquiry or provide new tools for researchers, pointing the way forward to further productive work in child language.

Competing strands of theory are outlined in the opening contribution by Martin Braine. This paper sets the scene for the rest of the volume because it highlights the kinds of question that descriptive studies need to address, whether the researcher is coming from a nativist or empiricist/interactionist perspective. Braine identifies two tasks of developmental theory: (1) to discover what innate cognitive and linguistic primitives there are – this is the starting point of many linguists; and (2) to provide an account of development within the individual – the starting point of many psychologists. He points out that the second task is a necessary adjunct to the first, since positing a set of cognitive or linguistic primitives and leaving the rest to neurophysiological maturation is not enough. Revealing similarities between Piaget's assimilation–accommodation mechanism and more recent 'bootstrapping' explanations (e.g. Pinker, 1984), he suggests a means by which children can extend their linguistic competence by moving from prototypical exemplars of a category to more peripheral ones. Such a learning mechanism would be economical because it would do away with the need for syntactic primitives and would explain how different mappings between semantic and syntactic categories arise in different languages.

The next two articles deal with aspects of phonology. Oller, Eilers, Steffens, Lynch & Urbano aim to discover the ways in which experience, such as sensory stimulation, interacts with the innate drive to babbling. Their comparisons of the production of canonical syllables in the babbling of infants born either prematurely or at full term into families with either a low or middle socioeconomic background reveal a complex interaction among neurophysiological maturation, perceptual and motoric experience and input from the environment. The authors suggest that in order to expand our understanding of the stages of early vocal development it will be necessary to seek a characterization of the mechanism that might underlie the differences which have been identified in the onset of babbling. In a study of Dutch-speaking children, Wijnen, Krikhaar & den Os draw together two well-known – and apparently universal – facts about early child language: weak syllable omission in polysyllabic words and the omission of grammatical morphemes such as determiners. Using the theoretical framework provided by metrical phonology, they provide a coherent, unified explanation for these two phenomena. They postulate that the strong–weak trochaic stress pattern is a universal of human perceptual and motor performance. If this is the case, the obvious question that arises is how do children move from an innate trochaic stress pattern to the language-specific stress rules of their mother tongue? Research on the acquisition of languages with different stress rules from Dutch and English will be needed to provide answers to this question.

Aspects of vocabulary acquisition are treated in the following two papers. In a large-scale study with over 1,800 children, Bates and seven colleagues take forward the research into individual differences in the style of language acquisition that has been stimulated by Nelson's (1973) distinction between 'referential' and 'expressive' learners. Such differences are of great theoretical interest because they cannot be explained by a maturation account that simply postulates a different RATE of acquisition along the same path. We have to consider what kind of language-learning mechanisms could lead to different language styles. Taking account of Pine & Lieven's (1990) work which suggested that earlier studies had confounded stylistic variation and differential rates of development, Bates *et al.* seek to disentangle the confound and conclude that there is in fact no relationship between early referential style and precocious language development. The period of maximum individual variation in vocabulary size appears to be between 1;4 and 2;0 when children typically have lexicons of between 10 and 50 words. The study reveals a different developmental course for different parts of speech, with changing proportions of common nouns, predicates (verbs and adjectives) and grammatical function words indicating shifts in emphasis in the child's language use from reference to predication to grammar. Systematic relationships – regardless of age – between the size of the lexicon and its composition in terms of word classes provide some evidence for 'critical mass' accounts of vocabulary development. There is now a need for comparable work on other languages to provide information on the extent to which these findings are universal or language-specific. And the task of EXPLAINING the individual differences still lies ahead.

Golinkoff, Mervis & Hirsh-Pasek note that a number of different principles have been proposed in attempts to explain HOW children acquire their vocabularies rapidly and apparently effortlessly. Here, they take six principles and integrate them into a coherent set, organized in two developmental tiers. These principles would allow room for individual differences in learning rate and style. Like Bates *et al.*, Golinkoff *et al.* provide evidence that the composition of the lexicon and the manner of acquiring vocabulary at a given stage might be specifically related to the number of words known at that point. Further studies will be needed to validate the developmental aspects of the set of principles and particularly to establish whether they have a fixed order of appearance.

Morphological and syntactic development feature in the next three papers. All three use evidence from children's speech errors to gain a window into the mechanism of acquisition. A widely-attested type of error is the over-extension of some pronoun case forms. By looking for a phonetic core in English pronouns and determiners and finding it in *he/him/his* and *they/them/their* but not in *I/me/my* or *she/her*, Rispoli provides at least a partial explanation for the asymmetry in the overextension of different pronominal forms. Once again, new research with data from other languages – particularly those where some of the pronouns share a common phonetic core and others in the same paradigm do not – is needed to test this hypothesis further.

Just as Rispoli integrates phonetics and morphology, so Kim, Marcus, Pinker, Hollander & Coppola integrate inflectional morphology and grammar, by showing that children respond differentially to the morphology of irregular nouns and verbs depending upon the identity of the head in the underlying grammatical structure within which the root morpheme is embedded. For example, having first overgeneralized the plural, which leads to forms like *tooths*, children then produce not only *teeth* but also, when appropriate, expressions such as *two sabre-tooths*. Kim *et al.*'s head-based theory provides an economical explanation since only information about the morphology of the root needs to be stored in the lexicon; grammatical structure can be handled by regular grammatical rules which are accessed before the surface morphology. A further advantage of this account is that it is apparently consistent with adults' processing of morphologically irregular forms and so allows for continuity of development.

In a paper that focuses on the errors that children make in their acquisition of interrogatives, Radford reanalyses the data in Klima & Bellugi's classic 1966 article within a government and binding framework. He traces development through Klima & Bellugi's three stages to adult English, attempting to minimize developmental discontinuity. He compares three different GB-based grammatical interpretations of the data: a head analysis, an adjunction analysis, and a specifier analysis. These formulations offer interesting ways forward: it is clear that crosslinguistic accounts of interrogative acquisition will help to show which of these competing theoretical positions has the most universal descriptive and explanatory adequacy.

The final paper by Foster-Cohen examines the interface between syntax and pragmatics by analysing data concerning children's interpretation of pronominal expressions. Binding theory (in Reinhart's 1983 version) gives a unitary account of these, whether they function as anaphors, pronouns or referring expressions. The problem from an acquisitionist point of view is that a number of experimental studies have shown children performing very differently on the three types. Foster-Cohen enlists Sperber & Wilson's (1986) relevance theory to explore how pragmatic characteristics of this single grammatical category might lead to children's erroneous interpretations of pronominal reference. The study suggests a way in which future work in the area might remove the experimental confound between children's syntactic ability and their pragmatic understanding.

The papers gathered together in this volume show how a judicious combination of an appropriate theoretical framework and sensitively-analysed empirical data can provide satisfying answers to issues in child language development. At the same time they stimulate fresh questions. The exploration of these 'growing points' will no doubt contribute to the vitality of research in child language for the rest of the decade.

REFERENCES

Aksu-Koç, A. (1988). *The acquisition of aspect and modality. The case of past reference in Turkish*. Cambridge: C.U.P.

Atkinson, M. (1992). *Children's syntax :* an introduction to principles and parameters theory. Oxford: Blackwell.

Bates, E., Bretherton, I. & Snyder, L. (1980). *From first words to grammar : individual differences and dissociable mechanisms*. Cambridge: C.U.P.

Bavin, E. L. & Shopen, T. A. (1985). Children's acquisition of Warlpiri: comprehension of transitive sentences. *Journal of Child Language* **12**, 597–610.

Chomsky, N. (1981). *Lectures on government and binding*. Dordrecht: Foris.

—— (1986). *Barriers*. Cambridge, MA: MIT Press.

Clancy, P.(1989). Form and function in the acquisition of Korean *wh-* questions. *Journal of Child Language* **16**, 323–47.

Demuth, K. (1990). Subject, topic and Sesotho passive. *Journal of Child Language* **17**, 67–84.

Dromi, E. & Berman, R. A. (1982). A morphemic measure of early language development: data from modern Hebrew. *Journal of Child Language* **9**, 403–24.

Fodor, J. A. (1983). *The modularity of mind*. Cambridge, MA: MIT Press.

Hickey, T. (1991). Mean length of utterance and the acquisition of Irish. *Journal of Child Language* **18**, 553–69.

Karmiloff-Smith, A. (1986). Some fundamental aspects of language development after age 5. In P. Fletcher & M. Garman (eds), *Language acquisition* (2nd edn). Cambridge: C.U.P.

Klima, E. S. & Bellugi, U. (1966). Syntactic regularities in the speech of children. In J. Lyons & R. J. Wales (eds), *Psycholinguistic Papers*. Edinburgh: Edinburgh University Press.

Lieven, E. V. M., Pine, J. M. & Dresner Barnes, H. (1992). Individual differences in early vocabulary development: redefining the referential-expressive distinction. *Journal of Child Language* **19**, 287–310.

McClelland, J. L. & Rumelhart, D. E. (eds) (1986). *Parallel distributed processing: explorations in the microstructure of cognition*. Cambridge, MA: MIT Press.

MacWhinney, B. (1991). The CHILDES project: computational tools for analyzing talk. Hillsdale, NJ: Erlbaum.

MacWhinney, B. & Bates, E. (1989). *The crosslinguistic study of sentence processing*. Cambridge: C.U.P.

Maratsos, M., Kuczaj, S., Fox, D. & Chalkley, M. A. (1979). Some empirical studies in the acquisition of transformational relations: passives, negatives and the past tense. In W. A. Collins (ed.), *Children's language and communications*. Hillsdale, NJ: Erlbaum.

Menig-Peterson, C. L. (1975). The modification of communicative behavior in preschool-aged children as a function of the listener's perspective. *Child Development* **46**, 1015–18.

Moon, C., Bever, T. G. & Fifer, W. P. (1992). Canonical and non-canonical syllable discrimination by two-day-old infants. *Journal of Child Language* **19**, 1–17.

Nelson, K. (1973). Structure and strategy in learning to talk. *Monographs of the Society for Research in Child Development* **38**, No. 149.

—— (1981). Individual differences in language development: implications for development and language. *Developmental Psychology* **17**, 170–87.

Perner, J. & Leekam, S. R. (1986). Belief and quantity: three-year-olds' adaptation to listeners' knowledge. *Journal of Child Language* **13**, 305–15.

Peterson, C. & Dodsworth, P. (1991). A longitudinal analysis of young children's cohesion and noun specification in narratives. *Journal of Child Language* **18**, 397–415.

Pine, J. M. & Lieven, E. V. M. (1990). Referential style at thirteen months: why age-defined cross-sectional measures are inappropriate for the study of strategy differences in early language development. *Journal of Child Language* **17**, 625–31.

Pinker, S. (1984). *Language learnability and language development*. Cambridge, MA: Harvard University Press.

—— (1989). *Learnability and cognition: the acquisition of argument structure*. Cambridge, MA: MIT Press.

Reinhart, T. (1983). *Anaphora and semantic interpretation*. London: Croom Helm.

Richards, B. & Robinson, P. (1993). Environmental correlates of child copula verb growth. *Journal of Child Language* **20**, 343–62.

Shatz, M., Hoff-Ginsberg, E. & MacIver, D. (1989). Induction and the acquisition of English auxiliaries: the effects of differentially enriched input. *Journal of Child Language* **16**, 141–60.

Slobin, D. I. (ed.) (1985). *The crosslinguistic study of language acquisition*. Vols I & II. Hillsdale, NJ: Erlbaum.

—— (ed.) (1993). *The crosslinguistic study of language acquisition*. Vol. III. Hillsdale, NJ: Erlbaum.

Snow, C. (1986). Conversations with children. In P. Fletcher & M. Garman (eds), *Language acquisition* (2nd edn). Cambridge: C.U.P.

Sperber, D. & Wilson, D. (1986). *Relevance: communication and cognition*. Oxford: Blackwell.

Vaidyanathan, R. (1991). Development of forms and functions of negatives in the early stages of language acquisition: a study in Tamil. *Journal of Child Language* **18**, 51–66.

Weist, R. M., Wysocka, H. & Lyytinen, P. (1991). A crosslinguistic perspective on the development of temporal systems. *Journal of Child Language* **18**, 67–92.

KATHARINE PERERA
Editor

J. Child Lang. **21** (1994), 9–31. Copyright © 1994 Cambridge University Press

Is nativism sufficient?*

MARTIN D. S. BRAINE
New York University

ABSTRACT

The past and present state of the empiricism–nativism issue is analysed. Empiricist philosophical doctrine ('no innate ideas') distinguished idea from structure or mechanism. However, Chomsky's conception of innate linguistic universals erased this distinction. The elimination left would-be empiricists without a coherent and defensible position. I argue that the issue remains alive primarily because of tension between two scientific tasks that face students of development. One is to discover what is cognitively and linguistically primitive, a task that encourages nativism. However, nativism is ultimately unsatisfactory because it systematically neglects the other task, which is to account for development, including the emergence of postulated innate primitives. To account for such primitives, it is necessary to relate them to particular central nervous system structures in such a way as to explain how the structure has the particular cognitive effects that define the primitive. That is likely to be difficult, and I show how the study of learning – much neglected in recent years – can help by reducing the number and type of innate primitives whose origin must be explained in that way.

INTRODUCTION

This paper seeks to change perceptions of the nativism–empiricism issue by presenting a fresh meta-theoretical analysis of it. I shall argue that current nativist and empiricist attitudes are rooted in two separate tasks of a developmental theory, tasks that are much more complementary than they are competitive. The tasks are, first, to discover what innate cognitive and linguistic primitives there are, and, second, to provide an account of ontogenetic development, including the origin of primitives. Nativist theories are potential answers to the first task, whereas an empiricist theory would be

[*] This article is revised from a keynote address, entitled 'Whatever happened to empiricism?' given to the Developmental Section of the British Psychological Society in September, 1991. The underlying work was supported by grants from NSF (BNS-8409252) and NICHD (HD20807, Project 2). I am grateful to Patricia Brooks, Jacqueline J. Goodnow, and an anonymous reviewer for comments on previous drafts. David O'Brien was an important colleague in the work on reasoning. Address for correspondence: Martin Braine, Department of Psychology, New York University, 6 Washington Place, 8th floor, New York, NY 10003, USA. Email: mdsb@ xp.psych.nyu.edu.

an answer to the second. Answers to the one task will not normally compete with answers to the other. For many reasons, theoretical thinking over the past 30 years has focused on the first task and neglected the second. However, time is overdue to redress the balance.

I begin by reconsidering the history of the issue with a focus on how what is at stake has changed radically since the English empiricist philosophers confronted Descartes. The changes seem to preclude the possibility of there now existing a coherent intellectual position that is properly called 'empiricism'. Next I consider the present-day intellectual roots of nativist and empiricist inclinations: why does one scientist become a nativist, and another become, if not an empiricist, then at least unsympathetic to nativist views? I shall argue that a primary concern with the first task above, the discovery of primitives, almost inevitably makes one a nativist, and that a concern for the second task almost inevitably makes one dissatisfied with nativism.

Given that there are innate cognitive and linguistic primitives, we (as developmentalists) have the task of explaining how they emerge, ontogenetically speaking.[1] We confront the problem of constructing a developmental theory for each primitive that relates it to available central-nervous-system structures, and that explains how the relevant central-nervous-system structure has the information-processing consequences that instantiate the primitive. The third main section of the paper therefore proposes for discussion a possible schema for explaining the ontogenetic origin of an innate attribute or principle relevant to language.

The difficult problem of accounting for the origin of primitives is significantly reduced if some of them can be explained as derived from others, by learning. To show that this is possible, the final section of the paper discusses a potential learning mechanism that is capable of deriving syntactic categories from semantic ones. I cite some evidence for the existence of the mechanism.

EMPIRICISM AND NATIVISM IN HISTORICAL PERSPECTIVE

Current thinking about language acquisition treats nativist and empiricist explanations as forthrightly opposed, but as potentially varying in degree: language acquisition is mostly a realization of innate principles, or mostly a consequence of learning. When the issue is viewed this way a really radical empiricist position becomes infeasible, because it would confront a basic paradox: the more successful a scientist is in accounting for behaviour in terms of learning, the more powerful the innate learning mechanism that they are forced to posit. Let me amplify a little, in case the point is not obvious. Suppose you are an empiricist trying to explain the development of

---

[1] Of course, there is also a problem for evolutionary biology, of explaining how they evolved. But the phylogenetic problem is very different from the ontogenetic one, and I am only concerned with the latter.

some behaviour, and that you manage successfully to explain it as learned; that is, you find some learning mechanism – call it M_1 – that accomplishes the learning. You are now faced with the task of explaining M_1: is that innate or learned? Suppose again that you are successful: you find that M_1 is itself learned, that is, there is a learning mechanism, M_2, that accomplishes the learning. You now face the task of explaining M_2. Suppose again that you are successful, i.e. you uncover M_3. Now, evidently, M_1, which merely learns, is less powerful than M_2, which not only learns but also learns to learn, and this in turn is less powerful than M_3, which learns to learn to learn, and so on. In short, the more successful your explanations in terms of learning are, the more powerful the innate resources you will eventually be obliged to posit. Any really radical empiricism inevitably faces this paradox.

This paradox never arose for the English empiricist philosophers because they distinguished between mental content (i.e. ideas), on the one hand, and on the other hand, mental structures and learning mechanisms. They claimed that there is no innate mental content, i.e. no innate ideas; what is innate is structure and mechanism only. Thus for them there was no paradox.

However, following the appearance of Chomsky's rationalism about 30 years ago (e.g. Chomsky, 1959, 1965, 1966), a strange thing happened – or rather, what is strange is what failed to happen. Chomsky, it will be recalled, argued that universals of linguistic form are innate: the child had inborn knowledge of the general form of a transformational grammar. That is why children progress so rapidly in acquiring their native language, Chomsky argued – they know in advance the general form of the system to be acquired.

Now, on the face of it, the form of a grammar is hardly mental content. A grammar provides a vehicle, a set of structures or forms, for expressing ideas; it is not itself ideas that are expressed. So it was always open to empiricists to object that grammar was structure, not mental content, and hence that Chomsky's claims contained nothing objectionable to a philosophical empiricism – nothing objectionable to the claim that what is innate is structure and mechanism only.

What may appear strange, and is, indeed, in need of historical explanation, is that no empiricist made this argument.[2] I suspect that there are two reasons for the failure to do so. One stems from the commitment of most empiricists of the early 1960s to simpler mechanisms and structures than those that might be adequate to language learning, namely, the associationist mechanisms of stimulus-response theory.[3] The other reason is a deeper one.

---

[2] Actually, I tried (Braine, 1971: 182–6), but nobody noticed.

[3] I am assuming that empiricism is not to be identified with a claim for the adequacy of the associationist learning mechanisms to account for all learning. The inadequacy of the classical mechanisms was already implicitly conceded by John Stuart Mill with his concept of 'mental chemistry'. The inadequacy of the later S-R versions has been argued by a long line of critics in psychology who were not especially nativist.

Many of the seventeenth century rationalists' 'innate ideas' were propositions – *verités innées* and not just *idées innées* – and often propositions of some philosophical or religious significance. The distinction between content and mechanism is reasonably clear when the 'content' includes propositions, and the denial that there is any innate assignment of truth values to propositions is a philosophically significant – and potentially liberating – claim. The philosophical stakes are different with the late twentieth century rationalism fostered by Chomsky: what is now claimed to be innate are attributes, default tendencies, grammatical principles, and the like. For these sorts of entity the distinction between content and structure/mechanism is not only less philosophically urgent, but also much more difficult to make. Perhaps one should emphasize the latter point: it is hard to see how to draw a general distinction between content and structure/mechanism clearly for the kinds of entities now postulated to be innate, and there appears to be no a priori way of doing so. There are many theoretical systems in which the primitives express an idea through structure; the primitives of logic are an obvious example.

However, once the distinction is dropped, it is no longer clear that anything important is at stake for the would-be empiricist. Empiricism is reduced to a generalized bias against innatist claims, no matter whether they are about structure, content, or mechanism. Essentially, it becomes a plea for a simple organism – which is not what the empiricist philosophers had in mind. It does not appear to make any coherent or significant positive claim of its own, and there is no way to evade the basic paradox I described earlier.

My conclusion from this brief review is that the philosophical basis for the empiricist side of the empiricism–rationalism debate has collapsed. It collapsed when the distinction between mental content and mental structure or mechanism disappeared. In effect, the nativists won by capturing the political centre, so-to-speak, by expanding the term 'idea' so that the distinction between content and structure/mechanism became irrelevant to it, with the result that it covered virtually all the terrain of cognition.

It is consistent with this conclusion that there do not appear to have been any attempts to state an empiricist position written by self-identified empiricists in the last 25 years or so. There have been statements of an empiricist position but these have all been written by nativists (e.g. Matthews, 1989; and several of Fodor's publications include one). Such statements can be interesting, or they may merely serve a rhetorical purpose by breathing some apparent life into a deceased horse called 'empiricism' prior to flogging it; but in either case, they are not statements of an empiricist thesis that the author is trying to persuade a rational reader to subscribe to.

In fact, the major writings by critics of nativism did not restate an empiricist thesis, but, rather, adopted a different thesis, called 'interactionist'. The thesis was expressed primarily in response to the nativist claims of the ethologist, Lorenz. According to interactionism, the development of all relevant phenomena – whether behaviour, structure, mechanism, or mental content – is the consequence of an interaction between genetic and environmental causes. Both nature and nurture are always both causally involved in the ontogeny of species-typical behaviour (including language), and there is no non-arbitrary way of quantifying their relative contributions. If the distinction between content and structure is unavailable, then this interactionist thesis is a very natural one for anyone unsympathetic to nativism to turn to. It became the received doctrine among non-nativists.[4] Even some former nativists, like Tinbergen, were persuaded, I believe, under the influence of arguments of Lehrman and Schneirla (e.g. Lehrman, 1953; Schneirla, 1952, 1966; Tinbergen, 1963. See Hinde, 1966: 315–21 for a textbook summary by an ethologist that is contemporaneous with Chomsky's early arguments; see Braine, 1971, for an interactionist discussion of Chomsky's claims.) However, it seems that many nativists were not persuaded. As a first approximation, one could probably say that what happened was that nativists mostly remained nativist, and former empiricists became interactionist (i.e. they regarded the empiricism–nativism issue as not worth their intellectual attention).

Recent years have seen an important addition to the nativism–empiricism issue, namely the question whether the mind is organized into modules (the 'modularity' thesis: Fodor, 1983), the opposing thesis being that the parts of the mind are highly interactive at all levels. This is a real empirical issue, but it is not clear that it is properly identified with nativism vs. empiricism. It is hard to see a reason for that identification beyond the fact that modularity was first proposed by a nativist (Fodor, 1983), and has been embraced by many nativists. However, from the standpoint of the content-structure distinction, modularity is clearly based on a STRUCTURAL difference. If the distinction between nativism and empiricism is regarded as a matter of degree, then it is not at all clear that a highly interactive mental system, given the complexity of the phenomena it has to handle, would involve less innate apparatus than a modular one. The identification of 'non-modular' with empiricism appears to be another case of nativists defining empiricism, and being able to do so because empiricism no longer has a coherent position that could motivate a would-be empiricist to argue the point.

Why weren't nativists (like Chomsky) converted to interactionism? The more significant reason, I think, is the one discussed in the next section. But a second reason is that the nativist can escape the logical force of interactionism by claiming that the FORM of the knowledge or behaviour to be explained is determined by endogenous factors; that although there may be

---

[4] I say this on the basis of my interactions with people in graduate school in the 1950s, and during the next decade or two.

all sorts of environmental factors necessary for the emergence of the mental phenomena (e.g. a normal human uterine environment, for one), these do not determine the form of the mental phenomena. The constancies of the intra-uterine environment obviously have little directly to do, say, with a primitive notion of causality or with the tree-structure format of a grammar. There may, of course, be experiences that are more intimately related to the character of early causal notions or grammars than coarse-grained constancies like those of the intra-uterine environment. That remains an empirical question, and indeed, it is precisely the kind of question that empirical nature-nurture arguments are about. By redefining the issue as being about the form rather than the existence of representations or behaviour, the same old nature-nurture questions re-emerge within an interactionist framework.[5] Thus interactionism does not really change very much for the would-be empiricist; it makes a logical point, but it does not provide a philosophical position to replace the one that was lost.

THE PRESENT-DAY ROOTS OF NATIVIST AND EMPIRICIST COMMITMENTS

So far we have considered primarily how the issues at stake have changed since the seventeenth and eighteenth centuries. Now I want to consider the present-day intellectual roots of nativist and empiricist preferences. What makes one scientist incline to nativism and another away from it? I want to suggest that the answer largely depends on the investigator's concept of the major scientific task to which they and their like-minded colleagues are committed. That is, in accounting for ontogenetic development, some formulations of the scientific enterprise inevitably incline to nativism, others to empiricism (or, at least, away from nativism).

The roots of nativism. Let us consider first where the impetus to nativism comes from. First of all, it is important that even though there is now plenty of evidence for rich initial cognitive structures in infants, the impetus to nativism does not come primarily from empirical studies of children. That is clear from linguistics: there are many linguists who are staunch nativists who have never done any empirical work with children, and who, moreover, were nativists when child data were very meagre indeed. In linguistics, the main impetus comes from the needs of linguistic theory. The goal of linguistic theory is to describe human languages. Simplicity and generality are gained by a description that minimizes what is specific to each language; one tries to account for as much structure as possible by means of principles and facts that are universal to all languages, and one tries to account for as much

---

[5] The nativist literature occasionally speaks of modelling nativist notions in terms of functions from (broad) sets of environments to (small) sets of mental entities, and such language could be regarded as incorporating interactionist principles.

variation as possible on the basis of variation along well-specified general parameters. The universals and the parameters of variation define what qualifies a language as a 'human' language, which is a component of a definition of 'human'. The assumption that such universals have an innate basis is a natural one, and accounts for why so many linguists are nativists.

The impetus to nativism arises in psychology for basically the same reason as in linguistics – a wish to define what is most basic in human cognition. One sees this in work on number, on causality, on theory of mind; in each case research is involved in seeking out what is cognitively basic. One sees a persistent effort to find a method of eliciting some ability or concept of interest in younger and younger children – an effort to hit cognitive bottom, so-to-speak, to discover what is developmentally primitive. It is assumed, of course, that what is basic will turn out to be universal. The inferential connection between basicness and universality goes in opposite directions in linguistics and psychology: the linguist looks empirically for what is universal and concludes that it is innate, whereas the psychologist searches for what is cognitively primitive and assumes that it is universal – but both equate cognitively primitive with innate and with universal. And in both, the nativist commitment comes from the commitment to the scientific task of discovering what is linguistically and cognitively basic. And it is of course a scientifically vital task of cognitive psychology.

I shall illustrate this confluence of cognitively basic, innate, and universal from my own work on reasoning. Some years ago, investigating how adults reason in ordinary English, I and colleagues found that there is a set of logical inferences that people make routinely and essentially without error (Braine, Reiser & Rumain, 1984). They are simple inferences closely tied to the meanings of words like *or* and *if*; e.g. given that you know that one or the other of two alternatives must hold, and that subsequently you discover that one does not hold, then you infer that the other does; intuitively, if someone cannot make that inference then they really cannot be said to understand *or*. Similarly, given an *if*-statement, when you discover that its *if*-clause is true, you conclude that its main clause must also be true; that inference seems integral to the meaning of *if*. The set of these routine inferences forms a logic defining inferences associated with the meanings of *and, or, if* and *not* (Braine *et al.* 1984; Braine, 1990).

We hypothesized that these inferences are cognitively very basic, on the assumption that they are part of an innate format for representing knowledge that is a precondition for the existence of declarative memory. It seems obvious that in order for a child to be able to represent factual knowledge about the world in memory, there must be some pre-existing format for such representation. If you do not have a format for representing something, you do not have a way of representing it. The format would have to have some logical structure: for instance, it would have to be able to distinguish relations from the things noticed to be related, and properties from the things remembered as having the properties, i.e. it must have some sort of predicate-argument structure. And it would need to be able to represent conjunction, disjunction, and negation, too, because memory needs to be able to record conjunction, to record that there are alternatives, and to record that a given property is not present. These are some of Fodor's arguments for an innate language of thought (Fodor, 1975). One does not have to go along with all Fodor's claims, but surely at least one has to go along with the assumption of an innate format for encoding information.[6] So there are good reasons for expecting a format for representing propositional knowledge together with some kind of mental logic to be cognitively very basic. I return later to the possible role of this innate information format in language acquisition.

Even though the original work was done with adults, the hypothesis of basicness, by its very nature, leads to a set of predictions (Braine, 1993) that the inferences will turn out to be developmentally primitive; i.e. that they will emerge as part of the child's grasp of *or*, *if*, etc., as these words are acquired; that essentially all languages will have expressions roughly equivalent to English *and*, *or*, *if* and *not*, and that the same set of inferences will be associated with them; and finally, that in the children of all these cultures, the expressions and the inferences will emerge together and be available early in development.

The point that this example is intended to illustrate is that once one makes the hypothesis of basicness, then a collection of nativistic claims having to do with developmental primitiveness and universality follow inexorably. They are simply a consequence of the way one does this kind of theory.

The roots of empiricism. Now let us consider where the impetus to empiricism comes from. I think it comes in large part from a concern with the other major scientific task of a developmental psychology – to provide a theory of development, i.e. of change over time. Let us consider the nature of a developmental theory. Its purpose is to explain how an organism develops from one state (at time t_i, say) to a subsequent state (at t_j, say), see Fig. 1. A

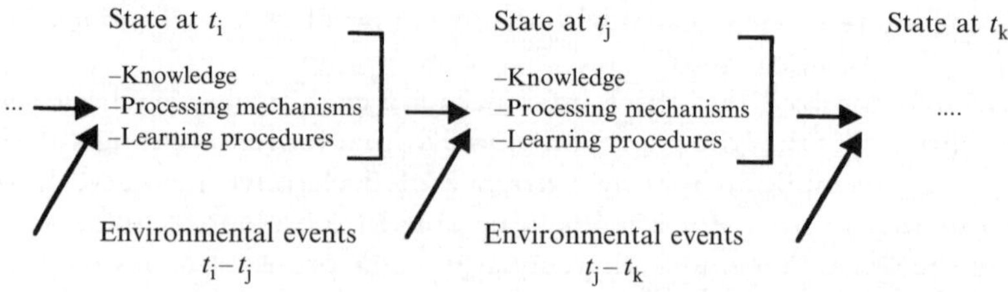

Fig. 1. Schema for an account of developmental change in the state of an organism over time.

[6] In particular, I would not go along with his claim that most lexical concepts are innate.

developmental theory explains the state of the organism at t_j in terms of the state at t_i coupled with environmental events between t_i and t_j. The state at t_i defines the organismic primitives in the account of the change, and the state at t_j the outcome. Obviously, this process of developmental explanation of origins carries indefinitely forward, and also indefinitely backward to the genes laid down at conception. Thus, from a developmental standpoint, when 'innate' is predicated of cognitive or linguistic entities, it merely refers to one stage in the emergence of any particular function. That stage requires developmental explanation like any other stage.

It should be clear now how a concern for development can promote an empiricist outlook. Since one sees oneself as having to account for innate primitives, they do not come free – indeed they are expensive, inasmuch as every time one posits an innate primitive one can see oneself as giving a promissory note which developmental theory will ultimately have to redeem by providing an account of the origin of the primitive. An additional factor that can increase the apparent cost is the fact that the account of development that psychologists best know (or think they know) how to give is via learning, so there is further incentive to minimize innate primitives, since we do not have a schema for how to explain their origins. Note that this cost-benefit situation is quite different from that facing the Chomskyan linguist: there, positing innate primitives (i.e. discovering universals) is not just without cost but comes with a reward, since it achieves an increase in economy in the overall account of human language.

In sum, the empiricism–nativism issue has outlived its original philosophical basis; it still endures because of a tension between two basic scientific tasks in the study of development. The one is to define what is cognitively and linguistically most basic to being human; the other is to provide an account of development. In prosecuting the one task the goal is to discover universal primitives, which, at present, just become problems that drop, like hailstones, on the unprotected heads of proponents of the other task.

I believe that what is left that is valuable about the empiricist tradition is an insistence that the ontogeny of innate primitives has to be explained. What empiricist and other non-nativist positions (e.g. Lehrman, 1953; Schneirla, 1966) have had in common is a refusal to accept 'innate' as an ultimate explanation of the origins of characteristics of postnatal behaviour. All scientific theories rely on intuitive perceptions of theoretical simplicity, but the question of the domain over which simplicity is taken is a metatheoretical one. The valuable remnant core of empiricism insists that the domain over which simplicity is taken must include the account of the origin of postulated primitives – something not now true of current nativistic theory. However, the insistence is clearly scientifically sound, and it requires that intellectual work be put into the task of considering how to explain the ontogeny of innate primitives. It also follows that when no one has the slightest idea how to account for the origin of a postulated primitive, it should count as complex on the intuitive simplicity scale.

If this analysis is correct, suspicion of nativist proposals is made more potent by the lack of a schema for how to construct a developmental account of the origin of innate cognitive or linguistic primitives: we do not know how to carry a developmental theory backwards from the innate stage. So let us consider this problem.

ACCOUNTING FOR THE DEVELOPMENTAL ORIGIN OF COGNITIVE PRIMITIVES

I recently asked a linguist how he imagined that linguistic universals arose developmentally. He said he assumed that they were due to maturation of something in the central nervous system (CNS). He added that such an account did not concern him because it was merely (*sic*) a matter of physical growth. Let us fill out the conception of development that is implicit in this proposal; the idea is probably common and no doubt not altogether wrong. Following the schema of Fig. 1, since the proposal posits maturation of some CNS structure, the states at t_i and t_j will be states of the CNS structure; the environmental events will be whatever events are relevant to the maturation of the CNS structure; the developmental theory will be a growth theory given by developmental neurophysiology. The proposal holds that the CNS structure eventually reaches a threshold of maturation at which it begins to function. At this point, the innate cognitive or linguistic universal springs into being. Subsequent development is then through learning mediated by the new resource. Implicit in this schema is a concept of what is special about the innate stage: it is a point of transition in the nature of developmental theorizing. Prior to the innate stage our account of development is in terms of physical growth; after it, our account is in terms of information processing.

What should one think of this as a schema for accounting for the origin of innate cognitive or linguistic primitives? There is one really important problem that I want to discuss, and there are some other fairly important qualifications that I will mention but otherwise ignore. Let me get the qualifications over first. Clearly, we should be wary of assuming an abrupt transition; new systems have stops and starts and need some exercise to become fully functional. Also, exercise can promote physical growth, even in the nervous system (e.g. Rosenzweig, 1966, 1970). In addition, some environmental events may not be easily classifiable as having their effects through learning or through physical growth. However, these complications I shall ignore. The really important problem is that the schema is seriously incomplete – it needs what I will call a 'bridging theory' at the transition point.

To see the need for a bridging theory, let us pick a claimed linguistic universal and do a thought experiment. Consider the claim that syntactic categories and their embedding relationships are innate – what linguists refer to as the 'X-bar schema' (Jackendoff, 1977). That is, approximately, Nouns are a category within Noun Phrases, Verbs a category within Verb Phrases, Noun Phrases and Verb Phrases jointly compose sentences, etc. Now suppose that a new neurological structure is discovered in the left hemisphere that becomes operational at around 1;3 to 1;6, and suppose further that someone has claimed that syntactic categories and phrase structure emerge as a consequence. Continuing our thought experiment, suppose also – even more remarkably – that within-child temporal correlations between the maturation of the structure and the emergence of syntax make the claim empirically possible. Now, granted all this, observe that we would still need a theory to explain HOW the CNS structure could have the linguistic consequences claimed for it. That is what I mean by a 'bridging theory'.

How could one construct a bridging theory for a linguistic universal or cognitive primitive? Such a theory would need three components. First, one would need a detailed information-processing analysis of how the linguistic universal or cognitive primitive operates in language acquisition or cognitive development – in the syntactic example of our thought experiment, one would need an analysis of the work done by the innate syntactic category organization in the emergence of language, including the kinds of cognitive operations it gives rise to. Second, one would need a description and analysis of the architecture of the physiological system. Finally, one would need an argument – ideally a proof, or demonstration by simulation – that the physiological architecture would have the information-processing effects. The three components together would constitute the needed bridging theory. That is, they would provide a theoretical bridge between the pre-innate growth processes and the post-innate learning events.

If this account of how to explain cognitive primitives is correct, then we have a picture of how the scientific task of discovering primitives fits into the broader task of accounting for development; that is, we have a framework that includes both tasks. Moreover, by making clear that primitives require a developmental explanation and by showing how to construct one, the framework offers the possibility of making tentative assessments of the plausibility or likely parsimony of particular proposals about what is cognitively or linguistically primitive. There is, after all, a fact of the matter about whether or not a proposed cognitive or linguistic primitive is innate. If it is, then there exists some maturing neurophysiological substrate, and there is a bridging theory that explains how the character of the substrate determines the nature of its cognitive effects. Hence, the envisageability of a bridging theory is relevant to assessing the plausibility of a particular proposal. In general, the easier it promises to be to construct a bridging theory, the more attractive a proposal is.

Any attempt to explain cognitive or language development must of course begin by assuming a set of primitives – the child's assumed resources at the starting point. There are three potential influences on the choice of a set of primitives. One is empirical evidence from psychology or linguistics on what is primitive or universal. A second is the constraint that comes from the desire to have a theory that could work – a constraint that promotes rich assumptions about the initial resources. Third is a potential constraint that comes from a need to keep the task of accounting for the origin of the resources manageable: our assumptions about the initial resources must be realistic, that is, a bridging theory must be a realistic possibility. This third constraint has been little discussed or invoked, although, as I just argued, it is the one that fuels current empiricist inclinations. A few years ago (Braine, 1988), advocating a stance that I called 'methodological empiricism', I argued that this kind of constraint entails a preference for learning mechanisms and certain kinds of innate concept as primitives. The kinds of innate concept that the constraint would favour are those that could plausibly be given by innate perceptual, motoric, or affective processing systems, because for these one can most easily envisage a bridging theory.

Many complex and highly abstract primitives that have been proposed, especially in the linguistic literature, need analysis to specify just what kinds of mental operations and structures they are really committed to. For instance, the current Chomskyan linguistic theory offers various universal principles that have arcane-sounding names – the projection principle, the theta-criterion, subjacency, the case filter, the empty category principle, to name a few. However, there has been no discussion of HOW such principles would be embodied in mental operations or structures in the child's mind, so as to constrain the form of the emerging linguistic system. Until we know that, we do not know what innate mental resources are actually being posited, and *a fortiori*, we cannot estimate how feasible a bridging theory would actually be. Intellectual work needs to be done to create a theory of the mental operations and structures that realize each principle, including how they operate to constrain the linguistic system and its acquisition.

FOUR ACTUAL OR POTENTIAL CURRENT STANCES

Before turning to the final topic, which discusses what the study of learning can contribute to the task of accounting for primitives, I conclude the discussion of the metatheoretical issues concerning innateness claims by sketching four positions that can be arranged along a dimension from a radical kind of nativism to a radical kind of neo-empiricism. I do not mean to claim that the positions are categorically distinct; rather, they vary in degree, and intermediate ones are possible. However, for simplicity's sake I shall ignore intermediate positions. It seems to me that the first two are positions actually held (or are quite similar to positions actually held), the third is the one I am advocating, and the fourth seems to me a potential position that some might find attractive.

1. *Maturationism.* This is the most radical kind of nativism. Development of any function consists of stages, each created by the maturation of a new innate system. New CNS structures mature according to a timetable of neurological growth, and developmental changes in the linguistic system are due primarily to this neurological maturation which makes new linguistic competences available (e.g. Felix, 1991). Learning is believed to be practically non-existent and plays no role in explaining transitions between one stage and another. (However, 'triggering' is admitted.[7]) On the differences between this stance and the next, see Borer & Wexler (1987). Since the postulated innate apparatus is maximal in this stance, the ultimate problem of explaining its ontogeny at each stage is also greatest, and has not been a subject of discussion.

2. *Nativism (standard nativism).* The innate principles and constraints are present at the earliest stage of acquisition and continue available throughout acquisition; they are determined by the 'universal grammar' of current linguistic theory. Pinker (1984) refers to this as the 'continuity' hypothesis, as opposed to the 'maturation' hypothesis outlined above. A fairly broad spectrum of such nativist theories is possible, and the role played by learning in accounting for development can be considerable in this kind of theory (e.g. Pinker, 1984, 1989). The potential 'cost' of accounting for the origin of the postulated innate apparatus is not factored into considerations of the economy of the total theory. Rather, it is assumed that internal evidence within linguistics alone will guarantee that linguistic theory is bound to converge on the 'true' set of innate principles; that being so, an account of the origin of the principles will eventually be found when the task is ultimately made the focus of research.[8]

3. *Methodological empiricism.* This is the relatively weak kind of neo-empiricism that I have been arguing for. A rich set of innate primitives is expected, but linguistics cannot be expected to soon deliver a maximally economical set. As noted earlier, the kind of economy now sought in

---

[7] In principle, Stimulus A 'triggers' notion B if the experience of A causes B to become (and stay) mentally available. It is not required that there be a rational (semantic) relation between a notion and its triggers (such as might provide a basis for learning). Without further constraint, this conception allows that a tap on the knee could trigger the setting of a linguistic parameter, or – to take Fodor's (1981: 305) example – the sight of an elephant might trigger the concept 'triangle'! Obviously, a triggering theory needs to include constraints on what can trigger what. In fact, a learning theory can be regarded as a triggering theory that posits only a particular kind of such constraints. The claim that triggering exists that cannot count as learning lacks the support of any empirically well-documented case of triggering that would not count as learning.

[8] I assume that this is the rationale; I never have seen the question of ontogeny of primitives explicitly discussed in the context of this kind of theory.

linguistics is not primarily economy of its primitives, but rather economy in the explanations of other phenomena given the postulated primitives. (In some ideal future age, when linguistics is approaching a state of completion, linguists may give absolute priority to economy of primitives, just as logicians do after a theory is complete – e.g. the primitives of propositional logic were, over time, reduced from three to two to one.) Acquisition theory should proceed with close attention to current linguistic theory (or theories), but not be absolutely bound by it (or them). Primitives should be preferred for which a potential bridging theory is envisageable; an analytic effort is to be made to keep others to a minimum set, and to develop analyses of how they operate mentally which can lead towards a bridging theory.

4. *Radical interactionism.* This is a term I give to an extreme neo-empiricist position that is conceivable. Holders of the position would anticipate that the notion of an innate stage where physical growth processes give way to learning processes is a chimera. It would be expected that development will turn out to be a continuous process of interaction between existing structure and the environment in which it develops and changes form, and that a clean distinction between growth and learning processes will prove impossible to make. This seems fairly close to the position advocated by Lehrman (1953) and Schneirla (1966).

The second and third positions above share the notion of an innate stage where growth processes give place to learning. They would probably tend to converge if the need to account for the origin of innate primitives were included in the domain of concern of the nativist acquisition theorist, and if it motivated the analytic effort needed to work out what mental operations are necessary to realize postulated innate principles. Once that is done, it will be easy to recognize that it is the structures that organize the mental operations that are actually innate, not the principles (which are merely abstract descriptions of the functions of the structures), and we will be some way towards a bridging theory.

One will not be able to tell whether there is any merit to the fourth position until sufficient research has been done that one can envisage what the developmental processes really are. It seems conceivable that the facts might turn out to be such as to make possible a rapprochement between the first and fourth positions.

THE NEED FOR A RETURN TO THE STUDY OF LEARNING

It seems obvious that the more we can reduce the number, and the abstractness or complexity, of apparent primitives by explaining them as learned, the more we reduce the burden of accounting for the developmental origin of primitives. Unfortunately, hardly any empirical work has been done in the last 25-odd years on human learning mechanisms available at an early age that could be relevant to language acquisition and cognitive development.[9] The result is that developmental theory has no inventory of the resources for learning available to children that could be applied to acquiring a language. We do not even have empirically-supported theories for those aspects of language acquisition that almost everyone would agree were probably learned. An inventory of learning resources that a language acquisition theory can draw on is badly needed.

I shall not attempt to provide such an inventory here, but will discuss one particular learning mechanism. It is an instantiation of Piaget's assimilation-accommodation mechanism, and it offers a solution for a common class of problems encountered in the analysis of language acquisition. Let us consider the class of problems first. Syntactic categories often seem to be associated with particular semantic categories, in the sense that words or phrases that represent instances of the semantic categories appear to be privileged or prototypical members of the syntactic category (see, for example, Pinker, 1984, Table 2.1). However, the association is commonly very far from perfect. Thus, words that represent types of material entity are typically nouns, but there are many nouns that do not represent material entities. Similarly, NPs are very often phrases denoting arguments of a verb, often arguments that refer to a material entity. Words for actions are typically verbs, but there are, of course, action nouns, and there are many verbs that do not represent actions. Subjects in English are prototypically associated with two semantic categories – agents of transitive verbs, and the single argument of a monadic predicate (e.g. a predicate adjective or noun, or an intransitive verb). Sometimes there is a cognitive continuum, perhaps with prototypical end-points. For instance, Schlesinger (1979) has shown that there is a continuum between COMITATIVE and INSTRUMENTAL, as illustrated in the following set of sentences:

> George went to the store with his daughter.
> The lieutenant captured the hill with a squad of paratroopers.
> The prisoner won the appeal with a highly-paid lawyer.
> The lawyer won the case with an astutely-constructed brief.
> John cut the meat with a knife.

Some languages use two expressions (e.g. different prepositions) to cover this continuum, one for the more comitative-like meanings, the other for the more instrument-like; however, the different languages partition the continuum at different points. The generic problem is to account for this loose association between semantic and syntactic categories, and define its role, if any, in language acquisition.

---

[9] There has, of course, been a lot of work on learning in connectionist networks in recent years. Although some of it could indeed turn out to be relevant to early learning processes in children, this work studies how certain machine models learn, not how humans, children or adult, learn.

Piaget's assimilation-accommodation mechanism accounted for development by a process in which existing competence became modified by use: when it was applied to (i.e. assimilated) a new stimulus, it necessarily accommodated to the characteristics of the stimulus, with the result that the competence became modified – the particularities of the stimulus left an imprint on it. The mechanism was first proposed to explain sensori-motor development (Piaget, 1952/1936). Thus, in children a few months old, the reach-and-grasp schema might assimilate (be applied to) a new object seen, and in the course of application the schema would accommodate to the distance and particular shape and size of the new object; the accommodation would have an effect on the schema that left the baby more skilled in grasping an object of similar shape and size in the future.

Interestingly, developmental psychology generally has made very little use of this mechanism. However, proposals that are essentially instantiations of Piaget's mechanism have twice been proposed in work on language acquisition to relate semantic and syntactic structure in development – by Schlesinger (1982, 1988) in his SEMANTIC ASSIMILATION theory, and by Pinker (1984) in SEMANTIC BOOTSTRAPPING theory.[10] In a recent article (Braine, 1992), I have shown that semantic bootstrapping and semantic assimilation theories are formally very similar indeed. Both theories posit that the initial state of the semantics/syntax interface is one of perfect correspondence. Moreover, the mechanism that drives semantic and syntactic structure apart – which destroys the perfect initial correspondence – is the same in both types of theory. I have called it the principle that 'old rules analyse new material'. In comprehending each new utterance, existing rules are used to parse (i.e. assimilate) it; in the process, the rule system accommodates to the new utterance by creating new lexical entries for new words and perhaps modifying existing entries for familiar words, so that the grammar changes in the very process of being used to try to understand new input; the changes often complicate the correspondence.

There are several differences between Schlesinger's proposals and Pinker's, the most important being that Pinker posits syntactic categories (Noun, Verb, NP, VP, etc.) as innate primitives in addition to semantic categories. However, I have shown (Braine, 1992) that it is possible to reformulate Pinker's theory (and any theory of the semantic bootstrapping type) without innate grammatical categories that are distinct from the semantic categories. The theory illustrated below is that of Braine (1992). In all theories of this type the nature of the learning process explains both why syntactic categories usually have a semantic nucleus and how they come to gain members that do not instantiate the semantic category that is the semantic nucleus. It also

---

[10] I am indebted to Harry Beilin for drawing my attention to the formal similarity of these theories to Piaget's assimilation-accommodation mechanism.

explains how different mappings between semantics and syntax can arise in different languages. In the case of continuum phenomena like the comitative-instrumental example, it explains how different partitions of the continuum can be acquired in different languages.

To illustrate the mechanism, let us consider first how some initial rules are acquired, and then how a word that does not designate a material entity – *smell* (say) – might become classified as a noun in the child's developing mental lexicon. I argued earlier that children must have some sort of innate format for encoding declarative (factual) information, and that this format would necessarily have some logical properties. These would include a way to record predications; thus, a distinction between PREDICATE and ARGUMENT will be available at the outset of language acquisition. Let us suppose, further, that this 'syntax of thought' makes some classical ontological distinctions, such as between material entities (objects and substances), events, actions, places, and times. Like virtually all recent views of language acquisition, our learning model will assume that the essential input to the child consists of utterances that the child is able to understand based on context and already acquired knowledge of the language. Comprehension involves mapping an utterance into a thought, so to speak, and therefore, at the outset of syntax acquisition (when there are no rules), it includes parsing the utterance in the syntax of thought (the innate format) – that is, labelling the parts of the utterance according to their status in the syntax of thought, by ontological category and predicate-argument status. Thus, as in Pinker's bootstrapping theory, the child uses semantic and pragmatic information to construct a parse-tree, and then reads rules off the tree. Let us take a simplified example. Suppose a child hears *The man kissed the baby*, and has just seen a man kiss a baby, and already knows the words *man, kiss* and *baby*. Using knowledge of ontological categories and assimilating the scene and sentence into the innate predicate-argument format for information – that is, using the knowledge that a man and a baby are objects and kissing-the-baby an action, and perceiving that *the man* and *the baby* are arguments vis-à-vis predicate *kissed*, the child can construct something like the tree of Fig. 2;[11] he or she can then construct the rules shown from the tree.

Suppose now that the child has experienced several sentences like that, so that the rules of Fig. 2 are firmly learned. Then we have the beginnings of a grammar, and now that there exists some knowledge of the language (beyond mere vocabulary), the assimilation-accommodation mechanism comes into play. Possessing the rules of Fig. 2, suppose that our child hears the sentence *The smell grossed out the baby* uttered in suitable context (e.g. a smell present, and the baby wrinkling its nose in apparent disgust). As soon as there are

---

[11] Other trees are theoretical possibilities, but they are irrelevant to the point of the argument; see Braine (1992) for discussion.

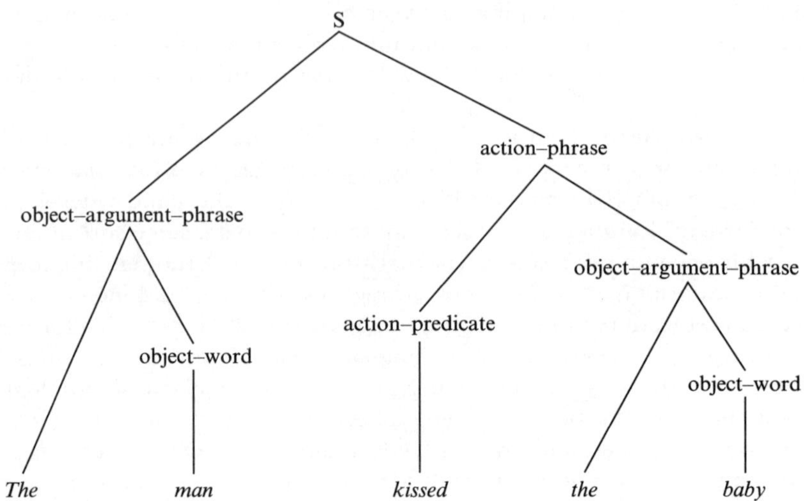

Fig. 2. Parse-tree for *The man kissed the baby*, that a child might construct, given the sentence, the scene, acquired knowledge of the words *man, kiss* and *baby*, and innate syntax-of-thought categories and structure. Rules constructed from the tree: S → object–argument–phrase + action–phrase; action–phrase → action–predicate + object–argument–phrase; object–argument–phrase → *the* + object–word.

rules available, the semantic bootstrapping theory proposes that the child attempts to parse new sentences in terms of the now known rules, using phrase position and function words like *the* to construct a tree. After constructing the tree, the child puts into the lexical entries for the words the category information in the tree. It follows that the child constructs something like the tree of Fig. 3. Having constructed the tree, the child annotates the lexical entries for *smell* and *gross out*: *smell* becomes marked as an object-word, and *grossed out* as an action-predicate. Thus the category object-word, which initially contained just *man* and *baby* and other object names, has expanded to include a word that does not designate an object, *smell*; similarly, *the smell* has been parsed as an object-argument-phrase. As the child encounters other non-material entities in noun positions in sentences (*the wind, the sky, the night, the wish*, etc.), the object-word category will expand further and become co-extensive with noun; similarly, the category object-argument-phrase will become co-extensive with NP, and action-predicate co-extensive with verb. Of course it does not matter what we call the categories – the fact is that the child will have nouns and verbs. Note how this exemplifies the assimilation-accommodation process: the known rules assimilate the new sentence, and then the grammar accommodates to it by marking the class of the new words in the developing lexicon.

This sort of learning mechanism offers a general learning procedure that can, in principle, account for the acquisition of all syntactic categories that

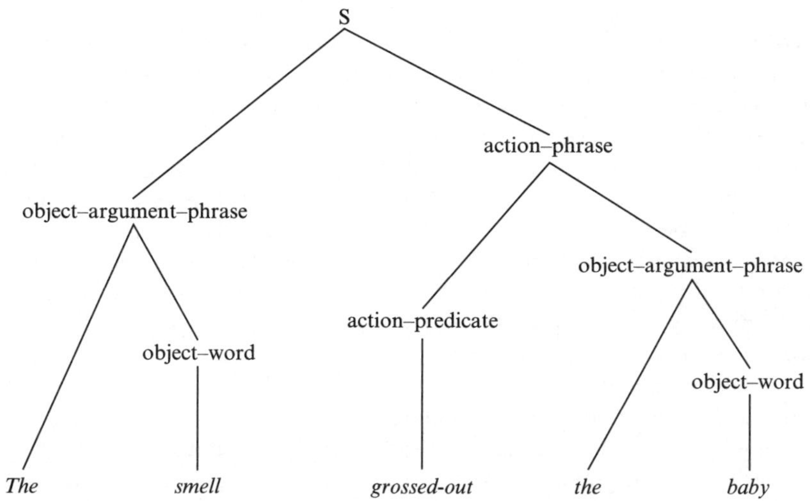

Fig. 3. Parse-tree for *The smell grossed out the baby*, that a child might construct after having learned the rules in Fig. 2.

have a semantic category as nucleus, but whose membership is not co-extensive with that of the semantic category. A slight extension of the same mechanism could account for cases where there is an underlying semantic continuum, like the comitative-instrumental example cited earlier: we may assume that there are two canonical semantic categories – COMITATIVE (or conjunction, perhaps) and INSTRUMENTAL – and that, in languages which associate a different preposition with each, the boundary is determined by the accommodation process. In effect, a child learns what counts as comitative and what counts as instrumental for grammatical purposes in their language. The mechanism can also be extended to account for the acquisition of categories, like Subject, that appear to be based on two different semantic categories (Actor, and being the argument of a monadic predicate): a theory of the basis of Subject that seems to account for cross-linguistic phenomena relating to this category is proposed in Braine (1992), and elaborated with some supporting evidence in Braine, Brooks, Cowan, Samuels & Tamis-LeMonda (in press).

So far, I have only shown what such a learning mechanism COULD do. I have not shown that there is such a mechanism. An existence proof is needed to justify confidence that the theoretical possibilities are more than mere speculation. Unfortunately, it is hard to see how one could obtain convincing evidence from young children learning their native language. However, there is relevant evidence from experimental work on the learning of syntactic classes in miniature artificial languages. An experiment (Braine, 1987) compared the acquisition of gender subclasses of nouns in two artificial languages. In one, half the masculine (M) nouns denoted men in stereotypically-male occupations, and half the feminine (F) nouns denoted women in stereotypically-female occupations; the other nouns denoted inanimate objects that were randomly assigned to the M and F classes. It was anticipated that the class markers (suffixes on the nouns) would be associated with real sex initially, and then extended to the nonsexed objects whose gender would be acquired individually – note that this extension of the gender class beyond its semantic nucleus reflects an assimilation-accommodation mechanism like that postulated. The learning was compared with that for a control language in which the number of exemplars of male- and female-stereotyped occupations was the same in both classes; thus, since there was no obvious semantic nucleus available, assimilation to a class based on a semantic nucleus would be extremely difficult in the control language. As predicted, the experimental language proved significantly easier to learn than the control, providing evidence for a semantic bootstrapping/ assimilation-accommodation mechanism.

Work on gender categories in languages like French, Hebrew, German, etc. has suggested that the initial bases of these categories are more often phonological than semantic (e.g. Karmiloff-Smith, 1978; Zubin & Kopcke, 1981; Levy, 1983). An experiment formally similar to the one described above was conducted in which the common property shared by a subset of the M and F nouns was phonological rather than semantic (Brooks, Braine, Catalano, Brody & Sudhalter, 1993). Again, there was significantly more learning in the experimental language than the control (no class learning occurred in any control subject). The result was shown to hold for nine-year-old as well as adult subjects. The results of Brooks *et al.* indicate that bootstrapping-type learning processes of the kind described do not require that the initial basis of class learning be semantic, nor that it be innate – any salient property marking a common subset of the class can initiate learning.

In sum, there is evidence that assimilation-accommodation (alias bootstrapping – semantic or phonological) is a real learning mechanism, not a hypothetical one.

I now return to the question raised at the beginning of this section – whether it is possible to reduce the burden of putative primitives on a developmental theory by accounting for some of them as learned. I have tried to show that the prospects for doing so are excellent. There exists a learning mechanism that systematically derives syntactic categories by learning based on an initial semantic nucleus (and sometimes, especially in morphology, based on a phonological nucleus – cf. MacWhinney, 1978). Since all major grammatical categories and relations are implicated as having a semantic nucleus, there is reason to suspect that none will be needed as primitives. Thus, it may well turn out that the only primitives needed to account for grammatical categories and relations are those of the syntax of thought (e.g.

notions like predicate and argument and much other logical structure, and ontological categories). Such a reduction would represent an immense gain in theoretical economy, inasmuch as the syntax-of-thought primitives are required anyway, in everybody's theory. This conclusion is consistent with proposals of Jackendoff (e.g. 1990), who has argued that syntactic X-bar theory rests on a foundation of semantic X-bar theory, the latter being, precisely, a hypothesis about the syntax of thought.

As noted earlier, an innate syntax of thought is needed to account for the possibility of the encoding of declarative information into memory, independently of considerations of language acquisition. Thus, the concept is unavoidable, although there is some room for argument about how elaborate this innate syntax of thought is: I would suggest that it is quite elaborate.

SUMMARY AND CONCLUSIONS

I have argued that the historical empiricism–nativism argument depended on a distinction between structure or mechanism, on the one hand, and idea or content, on the other – a distinction which has long disappeared from modern theoretical thinking. Unfortunately, it has not been fully appreciated that without this distinction the classical empiricist position lacks intellectual substance. The fact has apparently been understood implicitly by theorists with empiricist sympathies because, for the last several decades, discussions of nature–nurture questions from the non-nativist side have abandoned the former empiricist position in favour of interactionism, a standpoint that denies theoretical interest to empiricist vs. nativist argument about species-typical behaviours.

Nativism has prospered because discovering what is cognitively and linguistically primitive is one of the fundamental tasks of the study of cognition and development, and great progress has been made on it in recent years. However, nativism is ultimately insufficient because it systematically ignores the other major task of the study of development, which is to account for developmental change, including the ontogeny of primitives. In the last 25 years, that problem has been largely omitted from the scientific agenda. When we put the problem back on the scientific agenda, it becomes clear that we need to attend to two intellectual tasks. One is to develop a schema for how to explain the ontogenesis of innate cognitive and linguistic primitives; I proposed such a schema for discussion. The other task is the study of the learning processes available early to children that could be applied to acquiring a language, or to other achievements of early cognitive development.

To the extent that we can explain the origin of some putative primitives in terms of learning based on others, we reduce the total number of innate primitives and thereby also the burden on a developmental theory of accounting for the origin of cognitive primitives. I showed that there is a possible learning process capable of systematically eliminating syntactic categories from the list of innate primitives, accounting for them in terms of learning based on semantic primitives; these provide the nuclei on which the syntactic categories grow and they have to be postulated anyway for purposes other than language acquisition. This learning process is a version of Pinker's bootstrapping mechanism, itself an instantiation of Piaget's assimilation-accommodation process. It is not completely hypothetical since there is evidence for the existence of a learning process of this sort in miniature artificial language work on the acquisition of gender-like categories. Thus the study of learning processes offers a rich pay-off in reducing the number and kinds of innate primitives required by language acquisition theory.

REFERENCES

Borer, H. & Wexler, K. (1987). The maturation of syntax. In T. Roeper & E. Williams (eds), *Parameter setting*. Dordrecht: Reidel.

Braine, M. D. S. (1971). On two types of models of the internalization of grammars. In D. I. Slobin (ed.), *The ontogenesis of grammar: a theoretical symposium*. New York: Academic Press.

—— (1987). What is learned in acquiring word classes – a step towards an acquisition theory. In B. MacWhinney (ed.), *Mechanisms of language acquisition*. Hillsdale, NJ: Erlbaum.

—— (1988). Introduction. In Y. Levy, I. M. Schlesinger & M. D. S. Braine (eds), *Categories and processes of language acquisition*. Hillsdale, NJ: Erlbaum.

—— (1990). The 'natural logic' approach to reasoning. In W. F. Overton (ed.), *Reasoning, necessity, and logic: developmental perspectives*. Hillsdale, NJ: Erlbaum.

—— (1992). What sort of innate structure is needed to 'bootstrap' into syntax? *Cognition* **45**, 77–100.

—— (1993). The mental logic and how to discover it. In J. Macnamara & G. E. Reyes (eds), *The logical foundations of cognition*. Oxford: O.U.P.

Braine, M. D. S., Brooks, P. J., Cowan, N., Samuels, M. C. & Tamis-LeMonda, C. (in press). The development of categories at the semantics/syntax interface. *Cognitive Development*.

Braine, M. D. S., Reiser, B. J. & Rumain, B. (1984). Some empirical justification for a theory of natural propositional logic. In G. H. Bower (ed.), *The psychology of learning and motivation: advances in research and theory*. Vol. 18. New York: Academic Press.

Brooks, P. J., Braine, M. D. S., Catalano, L., Brody, R. E. & Sudhalter, V. (1993). Acquisition of gender-like subclasses in an artificial language: the contribution of phonological markers to learning. *Journal of Memory & Language* **32**, 76–95.

Chomsky, N. (1959). Review of B. F. Skinner *Verbal Behavior*. In *Language* **35**, 26–58.

—— (1965). *Aspects of the theory of syntax*. Cambridge, MA: MIT Press.

—— (1966). *Cartesian linguistics*. New York: Harper & Row.

Felix, S. W. (1991). Language acquisition as a maturational process. In J. Weissenborn, H. Goodluck & T. Roeper (eds), *Theoretical issues in language acquisition: continuity and change in development*. Hillsdale, NJ: Erlbaum.

Fodor, J. A. (1975). *The language of thought*. Cambridge, MA: Harvard University Press.

—— (1983). *The modularity of mind*. Cambridge, MA: MIT Press.

Hinde, R. A. (1966). *Animal behavior: a synthesis of ethology and comparative psychology*. New York: McGraw-Hill.

Jackendoff, R. (1977). *X-bar syntax: a study of phrase structure*. Cambridge, MA: MIT Press.

—— (1990). *Semantic structures*. Cambridge, MA: MIT Press.

Karmiloff-Smith, A. (1978). The interplay between syntax, semantics, and phonology in language acquisition processes. In R. Campbell & P. Smith (eds), *Recent advances in the psychology of language*. New York: Erlbaum.

Lehrman, D. S. (1953). A critique of Konrad Lorenz's theory of instinctive behavior. *Quarterly Review of Biology* **28**, 337–63.

Levy, Y. (1983). The acquisition of Hebrew plurals: the case of the missing gender category. *Journal of Child Language* **10**, 107–21.

MacWhinney, B. (1978). The acquisition of morphophonology. *Monographs of the Society for Research in Child Development* **43**, No. 1.

Matthews, R. J. (1989). The plausibility of rationalism. In R. J. Matthews & W. Demopoulos (eds), *Learnability and linguistic theory*. Dordrecht: Kluwer.

Piaget, J. (1952). *The origins of intelligence in the child*. London: Routledge & Kegan Paul. (First published 1936.)

Pinker, S. (1984). *Language learnability and language development*. Cambridge, MA: Harvard University Press.

—— (1989). *Learnability and cognition: the acquisition of argument structure*. Cambridge, MA: The MIT Press.

Rosenzweig, M. R. (1966). Environmental complexity, cerebral change, and behavior. *American Psychologist* **21**, 321–32.

—— (1970). Evidence for anatomical and chemical changes in the brain during primary learning. In K. H. Pribram & D. E. Broadbent (eds), *The biology of memory*. New York: Academic Press.

Schlesinger, I. M. (1979). Cognitive structures and semantic deep structures: the case of the instrumental. *Journal of Linguistics* **15**, 307–24.

—— (1982). *Steps to language: toward a theory of language acquisition*. Hillsdale, NJ: Erlbaum.

—— (1988). The origin of relational categories. In Y. Levy, I. M. Schlesinger & M. D. S. Braine (eds), *Categories and processes in language acquisition*. Hillsdale, NJ: Erlbaum.

Schneirla, T. C. (1952). A consideration of some conceptual trends in comparative psychology. *Psychological Bulletin* **49**, 559–97.

—— (1966). Behavioral development and comparative psychology. *Quarterly Review of Biology* **41**, 283–302.

Tinbergen, N. (1963). On aims and methods of ethology. *Zeitschrift für Tierpsychologie* **20**, 410–33.

Zubin, D. A. & Kopcke, K. M. (1981). Gender: a less than arbitrary grammatical category. In R. Hendrick, C. Masek & M. F. Miller (eds), *Papers from the Seventh Regional Meeting*. Chicago: Chicago Linguistic Society.

J. Child Lang. **21** (1994), 33–58. Copyright © 1994 Cambridge University Press

Speech-like vocalizations in infancy: an evaluation of potential risk factors*

D. KIMBROUGH OLLER, REBECCA E. EILERS,
MICHELE L. STEFFENS
University of Miami

MICHAEL P. LYNCH
Purdue University

AND

RICHARD URBANO
University of Miami

ABSTRACT

This work reports longitudinal evaluation of the speech-like vocal development of infants born at risk due to prematurity or low socio-economic status (SES) and infants not subject to such risk. Twenty infants were preterm (10 of low SES) and 33 were full term (16 of low SES), and all were studied from 0;4 through 1;6. The study provides the indication that at-risk infants are not generally delayed in the ability to produce well-formed speech-like sounds as indicated in taperecorded vocal samples. At the same time, premature infants show a tendency to produce well-formed syllables less consistently than full terms after the point at which parents and laboratory personnel note the onset of the canonical babbling stage (the point after which well-formed syllables are well established in the infant vocal repertoires). Further, even though low SES infants produce well-formed speech-like structures on schedule, they show a reliably lower tendency to vocalize in general, as reflected by fewer utterances per minute in recorded samples.

INTRODUCTION

The robustness of speech-like vocal development in humans

Vocal development through the first year of life proceeds along a course that appears strongly influenced by the biological endowment of the species. This conclusion is suggested by the consistency in infant vocal development across

---

[*] This work was supported by NIH/NIDCD grant No. R01 RC00484 to D. Kimbrough Oller. Address for correspondence: D. Kimbrough Oller, Mailman Center for Child Development, P.O. Box 016820, Miami, FL 33101 USA.

33

different environmental and developmental conditions. For example, the onset of the canonical babbling stage (i.e. the stage wherein infants show controlled production of well-formed syllables or syllable sequences such as *baba* or *dada*) appears to occur not later than ten months of age in infants who are (*a*) either full term or preterm (Eilers, Oller, Levine, Basinger, Lynch & Urbano, 1993); (*b*) of middle or low socioeconomic status (Eilers *et al.* 1993), and (*c*) from Spanish or English speaking, or bilingual families (Oller, Lewedag, Umbel & Basinger, 1992). Even Down syndrome infants usually begin canonical babbling within the typical period (Smith & Oller, 1981; Lynch, Oller, Eilers & Basinger, 1990). The robustness of canonical babbling is also reflected in the fact that infants tracheostomized at birth, and consequently unable to vocalize until decannulation during the second year of life or later, commonly show canonical babbling, and/or speech utilizing canonical syllables within a few weeks of decannulation (Locke & Pearson, 1990; Bleile, Stark & McGowan, 1992).

Although considerable stability of infant vocal development in the face of developmental and environmental variation is by now well-recognized, it is important to document the conditions that do affect the topography of infant speech-like sounds. This importance is both theoretical because our understanding of the nature of the human linguistic endowment may be enhanced, and practical because screening for developmental disorders through evaluation of vocalizations requires broad awareness of conditions under which vocal development may vary.

Among the most common risk factors generally associated with abnormal development are premature birth and low socioeconomic status (SES), and both provide special opportunities to assess the robustness of infant vocal development. Although recent work in our laboratories has suggested that there is no delay in the onset of canonical babbling in either low SES or preterm infants, there has emerged a surprising trend in which preterms (at ages corrected for prematurity) actually appear to show somewhat earlier onset than full term infants in two motoric developments, rhythmic hand banging and canonical babbling (Eilers *et al.* 1993). The tentative interpretation of these findings depends on recognition of the fact that preterm infants have a different history of experience from full terms. Being born early, they witness more events 'out in the world', more sound, more sight, more self-generated movement than do full term infants matched for corrected age. Preterm infants may profit from their precocious sensory and motoric experience, and, consequently, certain developmental events that may require experience for activation (among them canonical babbling and hand banging), may occur earlier in development than expected.

Early experience appears to stimulate accelerated vocal development, while inadequate early experience can, in extreme cases, have a retarding effect. Notwithstanding widely publicized claims to the contrary (see Lenneberg, Rebelsky & Nichols, 1965; Lenneberg, 1967), normal human vocal development is markedly hampered by lack of normal auditory experience. Profound hearing impairment has been shown to have a major retarding effect on the onset of canonical babbling (Oller, Eilers, Bull & Carney, 1985; Stoel-Gammon & Otomo, 1986; Kent, Osberger, Netsell & Hustedde, 1987; Oller & Eilers, 1988). The sharp difference between deaf and hearing infants suggests that audition is a requirement of normal vocal maturation, whether by virtue of listening experience or by virtue of self-generated feedback.

Given that hearing is fundamental in infant vocalizations, it is important to explain why deaf infants ever begin canonical babbling. One possibility is that deaf infants acquire auditory experience gradually (because they usually have some residual hearing), and that their delayed onsets are predictable based on the degree of their hearing losses. Although this possibility is still in the process of evaluation, Lynch, Oller & Steffens (1989) have demonstrated that canonical babbling can begin (albeit many months late) in an infant with bilateral cochlear aplasia, a condition which precludes audition of any degree. In this case, the onset of well-formed syllables occurred following intensive speech therapy and experience with a vibrotactile stimulation system, a simple artificial hearing device. Thus, although audition (whether of others' voices or of one's own) seems to be the most effective form of stimulation for the onset of canonical babbling, it appears that other kinds of stimulation (from another sensory modality), in combination with social interaction can be substituted to initiate the process.

Interpreting the body of existing results on the onset of babbling is thus complicated. The following account represents one possible interpretation of the data. Canonical babbling usually begins in response to a certain amount of auditory experience (otherwise deaf infants would not begin late), but the human infant may be responsive even in unusual circumstances to conditions that may stimulate babbling development. Even if experience occurs prematurely (as in the preterm infant), it appears to have a stimulating effect; even if the environment is less vocally stimulating (as may be the case with the low SES infant), the process of development appears to be initiated on schedule; even if there is no auditory experience at all (as in the acochlear infant), other sensory experiences can, with sufficient time, activate the process; and even if the infant is prevented from exercising a canonical babbling ability (as in the case of the tracheostomized infant), there is a broad time window within which completion of required motoric developments is possible. These empirically-based suggestions are consistent with the possibility that our evolutionary histories have provided a capability for vocal development, the robustness of which is reflected in its flexibility. The evolutionary success of our distant ancestors may have depended on the emergence and growth of linguistic abilities, and a key to the power of human language may have been its resilience in the face of changing circumstances.

35

Goals of the present work : effects of prematurity and low socioeconomic status on vocal development

The infant born at risk for developmental delay because of premature birth (Greenberg & Crnic, 1988) represents an especially interesting case where the natural timing relationships of sensory/motoric experience and maturational events may be disrupted. Yet despite such potential asynchronies, most preterm infants seem to develop normally, and, in certain domains, accelerating effects of early experience have been noted. Similarly, the evaluation of vocal development in infants of low SES has produced the suggestion that the onset of babbling is broadly similar to that of more socially and economically advantaged infants. Our previous reports based on a longitudinal study of preterm and full term as well as low and mid SES infants (Eilers *et al.* 1993) focused exclusively on phenomena of vocal stage onset. The present paper focuses instead on the growth of babbling measured quantitatively during the first 18 months of life as well as on the details of the development of other vocal categories in infancy during the emergence of the speech capacity.

The goal of the present study is to evaluate quantitatively a variety of speech-like vocalizations in preterm and full term as well as low and mid SES infants. The work may help to clarify the sense in which human vocal development is robust, and may provide the basis for further understanding of linguistic handicaps that sometimes are presaged by babbling anomalies.

METHODS

Subjects

Twenty preterm infants (13 female) were evaluated in a longitudinal study of infant vocal development and early speech. They were found through a combination of active recruitment and referrals from local hospitals. Their mean birth weight was 1820 g (range = 1446–2070 g), and average gestational age was 33 weeks (range = 3·5–11·5 weeks premature) based on estimation procedures consistent with the recommendations of DiPietro & Allen (1991). The procedure includes evaluation of a combination of data from prenatal examinations and appears to be 'conservative' in that empirical data suggest that estimates of prematurity so obtained tend to be slightly less than the degree of prematurity that would be designated based on procedures that are commonly used with non-at-risk births (in particular, the common procedure based on the mother's indication of date of the last menstrual period). Additional description of the evaluation of prematurity can be found in Eilers *et al.* (1993).

Because a primary goal of the work was to assess the potential effects of premature extra-uterine stimulation, infants with significant health problems were not included in the study. In particular, infants manifesting intra-ventricular haemorrhage, respiratory distress syndrome, severe hyper-bilirubinemia, or any other important complications requiring perinatal medical intervention, were excluded. In addition, five-minute Apgar scores were required to be seven or greater, indicating substantially normal response in the first minutes after birth. All the preterm infants were housed in minimal care nurseries during postnatal hospitalization.

Thirty-three full term infants (11 female) were selected from a pool identified through health department birth records. When the infants were one month old, parents received a letter inviting them to participate in a three-year study of infant vocal development and young child speech. Parents who returned a postcard were then contacted by phone and interviewed regarding the infant's health and the family's employment and educational history. Because of the longitudinal design of the research, a key issue evaluated in the initial phone interview was the likelihood of the family moving out of the metropolitan area within the time frame of the study.

Families whose infants met the study criteria (either preterm or full term) and who planned to stay in the metropolitan area were invited to come in for an initial appointment. During this appointment, the first laboratory re-cording of infant vocalizations was made, and parents filled out an extensive questionnaire about their infant's health and development and the family's educational and social background. The questionnaire data provided the basis for socioeconomic status evaluation. The families were categorized as middle or low SES based on educational level and employment in white-collar or blue-collar occupations. The families were distributed evenly across the middle and lower SES groups (10 vs. 10 in the preterm group, and 17 vs. 16 in the full term group).

Assignment to socioeconomic status. The SES categorizations were based on a synthesis of methods (especially Hollingshead, 1978; Nam & Powers, 1983). The present approach made adaptations to account for the information that was reliably and practically obtainable from the families in the study. Three basic dimensions of SES were taken into account: parental educational background, source of family income and stability of family structure. Each family was assigned to one of five SES levels. No family in the present study was categorized at the fifth or lowest level (no completion of high school, unskilled workers, single parent and highly unstable families). Low SES families in the study were mostly from level 4 (no college, one parent with high school diploma, blue-collar employment), and a few were from level 3 (some college, but no completed degrees, transitional white-collar, non-management employment). Most mid SES families in the study were from level 2 (at least one parent having completed college, white collar, middle-management, teachers, nurses, mid-scale proprietors, two-parent homes), but some were from level 1 (both parents having completed college, professional or high level management employment, stable two-parent homes), and a few from level 3.[1] The mean SES level of mid SES families was 2·04 (S.D. = 0·71) and of low SES families was 3·73 (S.D. = 0·45).

Hearing. In order to document normal hearing sensitivity, both the preterm and full term infants received at least one hearing evaluation during the second half year of life using visual reinforcement audiometry. None of the infants demonstrated a significant sensorineural hearing impairment. Infants who demonstrated a mild conductive hearing impairment with accompanying middle-ear effusion were referred for treatment by primary health care providers.

Procedure

The primary data to be discussed in the present paper, spanning the period from 0;4 to 1;6, were based upon tape recordings made at each visit by the infants and their families to the laboratory. All infants were seen at least monthly in the first year and at least bimonthly thereafter. During the sessions, conducted in a single-walled IAC chamber with a Marantz PMD-221 cassette taperecorder and a Bose condenser microphone mounted on a boom stand, a research assistant and a care-giver (usually a parent) interacted with the infant using quiet toys. Both parent and research assistant made an effort to be silent whenever the infant vocalized and to elicit speech-like vocalization through eye contact, verbal encouragement and playful interaction. Some infants appeared to vocalize most effectively when left to play in a noninteractive fashion, especially after the onset of mobility. The parents' and experimenters' knowledge of the individual children was drawn upon in deciding how best to encourage vocalization in each child at each age. Recording sessions were half-an-hour long.

Data analysis

Selection of samples to be evaluated. In order to keep the data at a manageable size, research assistants selected recorded vocalization samples from each child to represent the ages 0;4, 0;6, 0;8, 0;10, 1;0; 1;2, 1;4 and 1;6. Each selected recording was judged to be typical of the infant's vocal behaviour at the designated age. More than half of the samples chosen fell within two weeks of the designated ages, and samples were not accepted if they did not fall within four weeks of the age for the interval. The average deviation of actual sampling ages from the designated ages was about one week. More than 90 %

---

[1] The boundary between mid SES and low SES was within level 3. The seven highest SES families in level 3 were designated mid SES and the eight lowest were designated low SES.

of the samples chosen included 70 utterances (the maximum number categorized). Samples that contained fewer than 30 utterances were not selected.

Infraphonological categorization. Each selected tape recording was categorized according to the infraphonological model of Oller (1986) and Oller & Lynch (1992). The intent of the model is to provide a basis for assessment of the degree to which vocalizations approximate the characteristics of mature speech. The term 'infraphonological' is intended to invoke the idea that infrastructural properties of speech can be characterized and that pre-linguistic vocalizations of infants can be assessed in terms of the extent to which they incorporate those properties. The framework of description that has resulted from such work specifically notes the extent to which infant utterances possess well-formed nuclei (or vowel-like elements) and well-formed transitions between nuclei and margins (or consonant-like elements).

The definitions of well-formedness that the infraphonological framework entails represent an attempt to provide an explicit characterization of the tacit knowledge of well-formedness possessed by all mature human listeners. It is certain that mature humans have such knowledge because, without it, they would not know the difference between speech and nonspeech. Furthermore, they would be unable to recognize the fact that a person speaking an unfamiliar foreign language is speaking, as opposed to performing some other vocal act.

The goal of infraphonological training is merely to bring the tacit awareness of what is and what is not speech to a conscious level and to provide the trainee with a set of labels by which to characterize varying degrees of speech-sound well-formedness. In keeping with the goals of infraphonological training, research assistants in the project were taught to categorize a nucleus (or vowel-like sound) as well-formed if it included normal phonation (the kind of phonation that typifies speech and is, consequently, not whispered, dysphonated, creaky, falsetto, or characterized by tremor) and a resonance pattern typical of speech, implying a special (not at rest) posturing of the vocal tract. An 'at rest' tract (either closed or in a muscularly lax slightly open state associated with quiet breathing) produces a recognizable resonance pattern in vocalization, and such a pattern is not considered to be well-formed for speech, because the vowels of natural languages (with rare exceptions) are produced in specialized postures. The at rest posture is characterized by primarily low frequency resonances and usually by nasal anti-resonances (see Oller *et al.* 1985). In our experience with research on infraphonological development, adult listeners quickly learn (within a single session) to designate ill-formed nuclei (or quasi-vowels) as being less speech-like than well-formed ones, and, in particular, they easily acquire the ability to designate reliably that a nucleus is a fully resonant vowel (a 'postured' nucleus) or a quasi-vowel (an 'at rest' nucleus). This proves to be an important distinction because infants commonly produce an abundance of quasi-vowels, especially in the first year of life.

Similarly, our experience indicates that trainees quickly learn to bring to conscious awareness their tacit ability to judge well-formedness of transitions between consonants and vowels. Natural speech systems include syllables that are constrained in time, and the pattern of constraint is similar across languages. A formant transition (from a closed vocal tract associated with a consonant to a full vowel posturing) that is from 25 to 120 ms and has no phonation breaks is usually judged by listeners to be appropriate for speech. This time frame encompasses syllables that tend to have relatively short transitions (e.g. stop-vowel sequences such as [ba]) and syllables that tend to have relatively long transitions (e.g. glide-vowel syllables such as [wa]). Even longer transitions ($>$ 120 ms) occur commonly in infant protosyllables (called 'marginal syllables') and are usually judged by listeners to be less speech-like than otherwise analogous syllables with shorter transition durations.

Categories of judgement and measures of infant vocalizations. Vegetative sounds (crying, laughter, sneezes, coughs, hiccoughs, etc.) are taken within the infraphonological model to be special cases of nonspeech vocalization. Consequently, such utterances were not considered in the categorizations to be reported here. Instead, the focus of the study was on those vocalizations that appear to be more indicative of the emerging speech capacity. In particular, the study focused on the following categories: full vowels, quasi-vowels, marginal syllables (which include a consonant and vowel with no well-formed transitions), and canonical syllables (which include at least one well-formed consonant-vowel transition). These categories are all specified directly by the infraphonological model, because they exemplify syllabic units with or without key features of well-formedness.

In addition, in the present work we took note of the occurrence of a series of additional, commonly occurring speech-like vocalizations of infants: squealing (vocalization at high pitch, usually in falsetto, distinctly out of the range that would be typical in speech); growling (vocalization at low pitch, often in creaky voice, distinctly out of the range that would be typical in speech); glottal fricative and glottal stop sequences (wherein vowels or quasi-vowels occur in syllable-like sequences with glottal consonants, which require no formant transition because they require no supraglottal articulation); and raspberries (labial trills or vibrants). These vocal types (and a few other nonvegetative sounds not reported on here) are sometimes referred to as 'precursor' vocalizations because they occur prior to the onset of fully well-formed babbling. Squealing and growling are particularly interesting precursor sounds because they appear to represent an exploration of the pitch parameter by the infant. Glottal stop and fricative sequences are early attempts at primitive syllables (with consonant-like elements, but lacking formant transitions). These utterance types are widely documented in infants during the first few months of life (Zlatin, 1975; Roug, Landberg & Lundberg, 1989; Oller, in press). Glottal stop sequences have been specifically noted as occurring with inordinate frequency in deaf infants (Oller *et al.* 1985). Raspberries are one of the most salient utterance types of the middle of the first year, and preliminary evidence has indicated an inordinate proportion of occurrence in at least one linguistically handicapped group, Down syndrome (Smith & Oller, 1981).

Each vocalization type was assessed as a proportion of the total speech-like (nonvegetative) syllables of the infant. The value is computed as a ratio where the numerator is the total number of syllables, in a given sample of utterances, that fit a given category, and the denominator is the total number of syllables of all categories in the sample. For example, the canonical babbling ratio is the number of canonical syllables divided by the total number of syllables of any kind. Three of the ratio variables so constituted (canonical babbling ratio, full vowel ratio and quasi-vowel ratio) were used to provide an indication of the degree of well-formedness of infant productions along a given dimension. Precursor vocalizations were also evaluated as a proportion of all syllables in the samples in order to provide an indication of the extent of occurrence of the sounds in the general vocal repertoire of the infants. The reader may note that the ratio used here with a 'syllables' denominator differs from the ratio presented in Oller & Eilers (1988) where the denominator was 'utterances'. The change to a syllables denominator began with Carney (1991) and was followed up by Steffens, Oller, Lynch & Urbano (1992) in response to the concern that, as far as possible, numerator and denominator should have comparable potential ranges. Of course the shift of definition produces lower ratio values, but all the trends to be discussed below are similar whether the denominator is syllables or utterances.

In addition to evaluating well-formedness and proportional occurrence of sound types, the present work also examined the 'volubility' of infants, as measured by the rate of vocalization per unit time in the vocalization samples. By considering volubility along with the category measures, it was hoped that a more general perspective could be established on the occurrence of speech-like vocalizations in at-risk infants.

Observer preparations and reliability. As research on infraphonological development proceeds, it is necessary to establish formal methods of categorization and ways to ensure inter-rater reliability. The present research is part of a long-term programme of work to develop the infraphonological framework and its required methodological underpinnings. Consequently, preparations for the research reported here have been extensive. The seven members of the categorization team worked together with six additional trainees in a four-month seminar on infant vocalization, in which the goal was to establish clear definitions and criteria for judgement of infraphonological categories. The topics for the seminar included definitions of the infra-phonological framework as specified by Oller (1986), evaluation of infant vocalization examples from a previous longitudinal study (Oller & Eilers, 1982) dubbed to a training tape to illustrate infraphonological categories occurring at various ages of development, and synthesized (utilizing Klatt, 1980) continua of vowels to quasi-vowels and canonical to marginal syllables. A number of exercises during the seminar required participants to categorize samples of utterances from infants and later to discuss the discrepancies among the various observers' judgements.

Through the course of these sessions, categorizational criteria were set for the group on the quasi-vowel/full vowel distinction, the canonical/marginal babbling distinction, and the utterance count. In order to attain high interobserver reliability on these judgements, it was found useful to establish a group awareness of how to parse the relevant continua. For example, along an eleven-step continuum from an unambiguous quasi-vowel to a mid-central schwa vowel, the listeners were encouraged to categorize synthesized syllables based on a specific boundary (between steps three and four) that appeared to correspond best to the infraphonological definition. Group variance was reduced by adoption of the common criterion. The boundary for individual subjects differed by as much as 7 steps before training but differed by 2 steps or less after one hour of instruction. Later, working with real samples of speech-like vocalizations from infants, the group compared the proportion of quasi-vowel and full vowel judgements obtained from independent categorizations. An effort was made again to adopt a common criterion, and individual observers whose judgements differed most from the mean outcomes were instructed to adjust their criteria appropriately and to recategorize the sample in question.

The same sorts of training were pursued for the canonical/marginal babbling distinction and for the utterance count issue. It appears to have been of particular importance that the group found best reliability (to within 15 % agreement across all observers) on the utterance count factor when they were instructed to count even the least audible nonvegetative sounds. The decision to adopt this sort of utterance count criterion had the advantage of increasing reliability, but it should be remembered that such a procedure may affect the values of measures used to assess the extent of production of individual sound types – the measures used in our studies are based on ratios of particular syllable types to the total syllable count. For example, it appears likely that the utterance count procedure used in the present work has the effect of yielding relatively low canonical babbling ratios (number of canonical syllables divided by total number of syllables) compared to ratios reported in previous studies (e.g. Oller & Eilers, 1988), because the least audible utterances (or syllables) tend to be noncanonical.

Using this sort of definitional training followed by group study of taperecorded continua, then categorization of real vocal samples, followed by recategorization to reduce group variance through adoption of criteria based on mean performance, it was possible to improve reliability and confidence in categorizations. The procedure culminated in formal tests of reliability prior to the beginning of categorization of the data for the study in question. In essence, as described in Steffens *et al.* (1992), 70-utterance samples of vocalizations were transcribed independently by each transcriber on three occasions: just prior to the beginning of categorization for the study, about one-third of the way through the study, and about two-thirds of the way through the study. It was intended that all transcribers should give values on all the key measures that met a preset standard of agreement – no score would differ from the mean score on the measure for the group by more than 10% of a predesignated maximum expected value on the given measure. The maximum expected values were determined empirically for each measure based on data from earlier longitudinal studies on infants ranging in age from 0;2 to 1;2 (Smith & Oller, 1981; Oller & Eilers, 1982). By referencing the reliability score to an expected maximum, it was possible to avoid inflated error percentages in cases where obtained ratios were near zero. It should be noted that these standards were strictly enforced prior to the beginning of categorization data-gathering with regard to canonical babbling ratio, vowel ratio and quasi-vowel ratio. With the marginal babbling ratio, utterance and syllable count, the criterion was relaxed to 15% error. At the reliability check points, it was verified that all transcribers had scores within the designated ranges for the key variables. The remaining measures that were monitored (glottal stop and glottal fricative sequences, squeals, growls, and raspberries) were considered less likely to be of major importance and were categorized without extensive reliability evaluation.

Coding and preliminary analysis software. Entry of data by the transcribers was facilitated by software developed in our laboratories and in use for over five years. The system speeds data entry and includes a variety of error traps to prevent observers from keying in illegal data, and to alert observers to possible errors when they enter especially atypical values.

The preliminary analysis of the data is conducted entirely by the computer. The output of that analysis yields all the necessary ratios and the utterances-per-minute values.

RESULTS

Chronological age analyses

Four mixed ANOVAs for four dependent variables, canonical babbling ratio (CBR), full vowel ratio (FVR), quasi-vowel ratio (QVR) and utterances per minute (U/M) were conducted. Each design had two between-subject factors (SES, term) and one within-subject factor (age). The analyses were conducted with seven samples of data collected from each infant at chronological ages of 0;6 through 1;6 at two-month intervals. An additional sample collected at age 0;4 was not included in this analysis but was used in the corrected-age-matched analyses reported below.

The preterm infants' chronological ages are comparable to those of the full term infants, as indicated in Table 1*a*, where the groups are presented

TABLE 1. *Chronological sample : mean age, standard deviation and number of subjects*

Target age:	0;6	0;8	0;10	1;0	1;2	1;4	1;6
			(*a*) Chronological age (in weeks)				
Preterm	26·78	35·39	43·75	52·29	61·83	69·70	77·93
S.D.	3·08	3·74	2·17	2·08	2·27	2·64	3·03
N	18	18	16	17	18	17	15
Full term	27·91	34·85	43·06	51·75	59·93	69·04	77·86
S.D.	3·16	3·35	3·61	3·34	3·32	2·60	1·56
N	33	33	33	32	28	28	28
			(*b*) Corrected age (in weeks)				
Preterm	19·94	28·56	36·94	45·29	55·22	62·82	71·53
S.D.	3·60	4·09	3·02	2·84	2·86	3·52	2·94
Full term	27·91	34·85	43·06	51·75	59·93	69·04	77·86
S.D.	3·16	3·35	3·61	3·34	3·32	2·60	1·56

collapsed over SES. The number of infants included in each group varies from sample to sample owing to factors such as illness on the part of infants, scheduling difficulties, and subject attrition across the longitudinal study. In Table 1*b* the mean corrected ages of the preterm infants evaluated at each sample are provided.

Results confirm the anticipated main effects for age for the three key well-formedness variables, CBR ($F[6, 259] = 24·87$, $p < 0·0001$); FVR ($F[6, 259] = 8·89$, $p < 0·0001$); and QVR ($F[6, 259] = 9·53$, $p < 0·0001$). These statistically reliable effects support the idea that the measures effectively provide a basis for monitoring infraphonological growth. *Post hoc* analyses of these main effects (Duncan's Range test) are generally consistent with the expectation that CBR and FVR should increase as a function of development over the study period while QVR should decrease significantly over the same period of time. The means and standard deviations for each age and ratio variable are shown in Table 2. For CBR, samples at ages 0;6 and

TABLE 2. *Overall mean ratios and standard deviations for canonical babbling* (CBR), *full vowel* (FVR) *and quasi-vowels* (QVR) (*chronological age sample*)

Target age:	0;6	0;8	0;10	1;0	1;2	1;4	1;6
CBR	0·11	0·20	0·31	0·34	0·35	0·42	0·43
S.D.	0·14	0·18	0·21	0·17	0·19	0·20	0·19
FVR	0·65	0·70	0·77	0·81	0·80	0·82	0·82
S.D.	0·21	0·21	0·17	0·15	0·14	0·19	0·16
QVR	0·34	0·28	0·21	0·17	0·18	0·17	0·17
S.D.	0·21	0·20	0·16	0·13	0·14	0·19	0·16

0;8 differ significantly from one another and from samples at ages 0;10 to 1;2, and all of these differ from the samples at ages 1;4 and 1;6. For both FVR and QR, the 0;6 and 0;8 samples differ significantly from all of the remaining samples.

In the chronological age analyses, main effects are also found for term status for each dependent ratio variable. In each case, full term infants exhibit the more mature behaviour to a reliably greater extent than the preterm infants. Thus, term infants have reliably higher CBRs ($F[1, 39] = 4\cdot28$, $p < 0\cdot05$) and FVRs ($F[1, 39] = 4\cdot95$, $p < 0\cdot05$) and reliably lower QVRs ($f[1, 39] = 5\cdot00$, $p < 0\cdot05$). Means and standard deviations as a function of term status are displayed in Fig. 1 a–c.

In addition to the main effects, reliable interactions between term and age are found for FVR ($F[6, 259] = 2\cdot23$, $p < 0\cdot05$) and QVR ($F[6, 259] = 2\cdot56$, $p < 0\cdot05$). These interactions are reflected in Fig. 1 b and c by the differences between the groups at younger ages and convergence of the groups thereafter. A series of one way ANOVAs were computed to evaluate the interactions. Results of these analyses indicate that the term by age interaction for both FVR and QVR is carried by the reliable differences in the samples from ages 0;8 and 0;10 between preterm and full term infants. After the samples from age 0;10, the ratios of full term and preterm infants converge. It appears that from age 1;0 on, the infants show relatively stable and comparable production of both full vowels and quasi-vowels.

As far as the SES variable is concerned, the three well-formedness variables do not show reliable differences between low SES and mid SES infants. However, the volubility variable, utterances per minute (U/M) does show a main effect for SES ($F[2, 39] = 7\cdot05$, $p < 0\cdot01$). The low SES infants

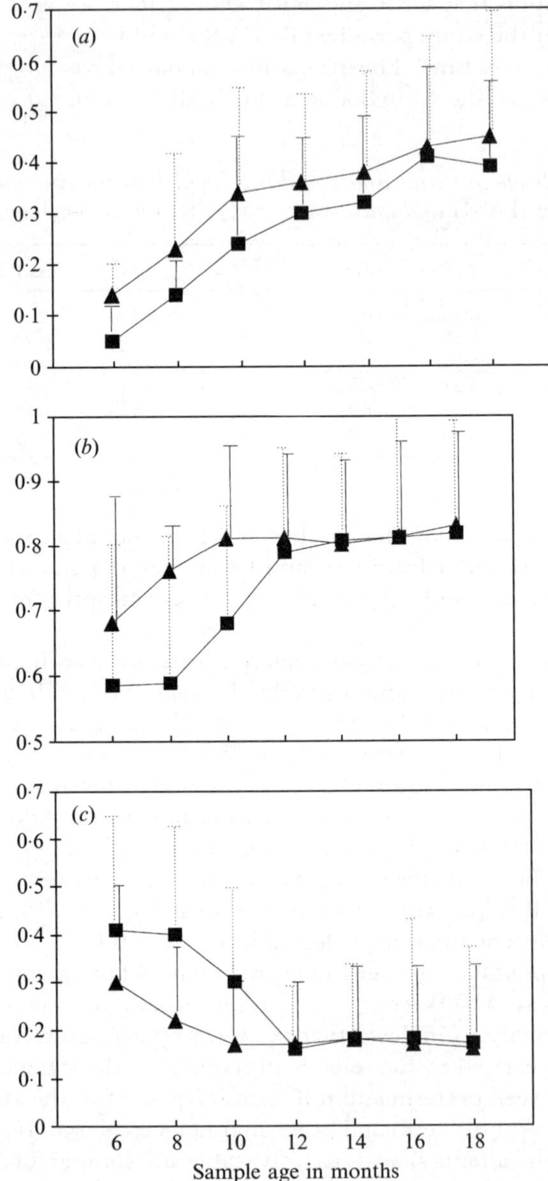

Fig. 1. (*a*) Canonical babbling ratio as a function of age in months in preterm and full term infants for the chronologically matched sample. (*b*) Full vowel ratio for the chronologically matched sample. (*c*) Quasi-vowel ratio for the chronologically matched sample. ■—■, preterm; ▲—▲, full term.

TABLE 3. *Corrected age sample: mean age, standard deviation and number of subjects*

Target age:	0;4	0;6	0;8	0;10	1;0	1;2	1;4
			(a) Corrected age (in weeks)				
Preterm	19·28	28·12	36·87	46·47	56·06	64·50	72·50
S.D.	2·33	2·47	2·26	2·59	2·04	2·31	2·43
N	14	17	15	15	18	14	12
Full term	19·60	28·00	37·63	46·28	55·00	64·88	75·00
S.D.	2·91	2·49	2·22	2·58	1·93	2·77	2·67
N	25	32	30	28	24	25	22
			(b) Chronological age (in weeks)				
Preterm	26·07	34·76	43·40	53·27	62·27	70·86	78·50
S.D.	2·49	3·58	2·29	3·06	2·97	3·25	2·97
Full term	19·60	28·00	37·63	46·28	55·00	64·88	75·00
S.D.	2·91	2·49	2·22	2·58	1·93	2·77	2·67

have reliably fewer utterances per minute (mean = 6·0, S.D. = 3·2) than their mid SES counterparts (mean 7·5, S.D. = 3·7), while preterm and full term infants show similar volubility (preterm mean = 6·7, S.D. = 3·5, full term mean = 6·8, S.D. = 3·6).

Analysis of U/M also shows an age effect ($F[6, 259] = 4·28$, $p < 0·001$), reflective of the comparatively high values of the two SES and term groups on U/M in the samples from ages 1;4 and 1;6 (means 7·8 and 8·3). These values are confirmed through *post hoc* tests to be reliably greater than those seen in samples from the younger ages (means of 6·0, 6·8, 5·9, 6·4, and 6·4 for samples from ages 0;6 through 1;2, respectively).

Corrected age analyses

In order to determine the extent to which the reliable differences found above are a function of the differing gestational ages of the infant subjects at each sampling period, an additional set of parallel ANOVAs was conducted with infants matched for gestational age (corrected age). To obtain the matched samples, new groups of infants were constituted from the same pool so that chronologically younger full term infants could be compared with their preterm counterparts of similar gestational age. The construction of the corrected-age-matched data corpus included restructuring of relationships at every sample, and was done in such a way as to maximize the size of the available data set without violating the principles upon which construction of the chronologically-age-matched samples were based – namely, all samples accepted for the database were required to have been taken within one month of each designated age, and no samples less than 30 utterances were accepted (the great majority of samples were of 70 utterances). Because the preterm infants were born at variable degrees of prematurity and because individual samples were taken at variable points (though within one month) with respect to the targeted ages, the optimal restructuring yielded centres of age that were somewhat variable. For simplicity, they will be indicated in the following discussion and figures by the approximate values: ages 0;4, 0;6, 0;8, 0;10, 1;0, 1;2 and 1;4. Table 3a presents the means and standard deviations for age in weeks for corrected ages of preterm infants included in the samples for the corrected-age-matched analyses. Table 3b includes the chronological ages of the preterm and full term infants at each sample point.

Like the chronological age analyses, the corrected age analyses yield main effects of age for each of the ratio measures, CBR ($F[2, 216] = 30.46$, $p < 0.0001$), FVR ($F[6, 216] = 11.85$, $p < 0.0001$), and QVR ($F[6, 216] = 11.76$, $p < 0.0001$), indicating again that the infraphonological analysis system provides useful developmental data through which infant speech-like vocalizations can be monitored across the early months of life. The means and standard deviations for the age variables are presented in Table 4 for

TABLE 4. *Mean ratios and standard deviations for canonical babbling, full vowel and quasi-vowels (corrected age sample)*

Target age:	0;4	0;6	0;8	0;10	1;0	1;2	1;4
CBR	0.04	0.12	0.27	0.36	0.32	0.39	0.42
S.D.	0.06	0.14	0.19	0.20	0.20	0.20	0.20
FVR	0.58	0.64	0.75	0.82	0.80	0.80	0.80
S.D.	0.23	0.22	0.17	0.15	0.14	0.20	0.16
QVR	0.41	0.34	0.23	0.16	0.18	0.18	0.19
S.D.	0.24	0.22	0.17	0.13	0.14	0.20	0.16

each ratio measure. *Post hoc* analyses for the CBR variable indicate a complex pattern of differences that is generally consistent with the expectation that CBR should increase with age. The age 0;4 and 0;6 samples differ reliably from one another and from all other samples; the following pairs also differ reliably from all other samples: (a) ages 0;8 and 1;0, (b) ages 0;10 and 1;0, (c) ages 0;10 and 1;2, and (d) ages 1;2 and 1;4.

For FVR, the samples from ages 0;4 and 0;6 differ from all other samples. In addition, the samples from age 1;0 to 1;4 differ from the sample from age 0;10. For QVR, the samples from ages 0;4 and 0;6 differ from all other samples. No other main effects or interactions were found.

The reliable differences between full term and preterm infants on well-formedness variables as seen in the chronological age analyses are not present in the corrected age analyses. Fig. 2a–c display the data graphically and

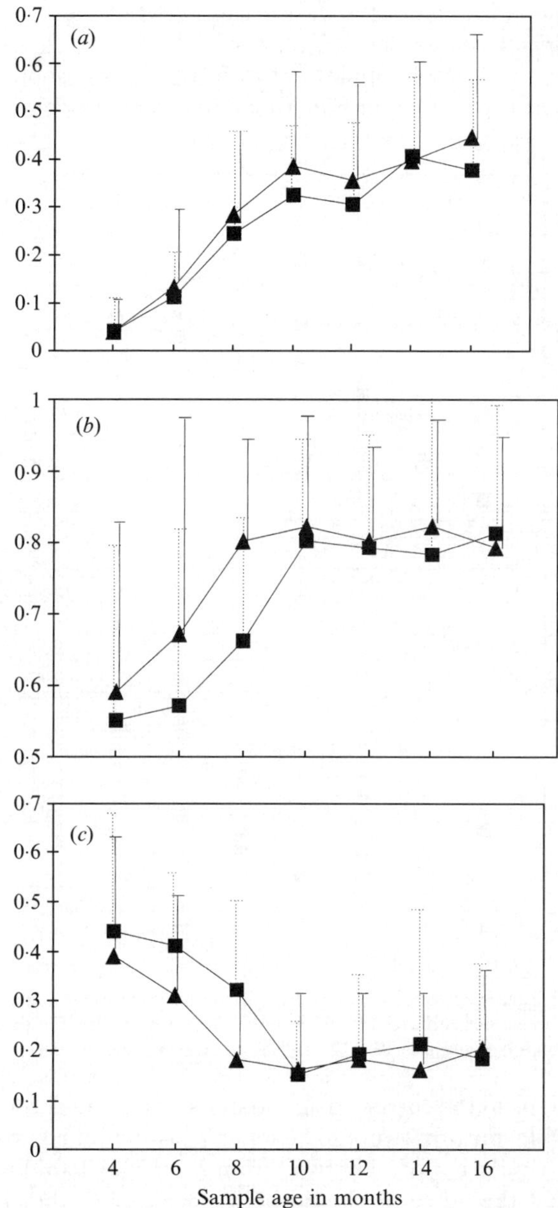

Fig. 2. (*a*) CBR as a function of age in months in preterm and full term infants for the corrected age matched sample. (*b*) FVR for the corrected age matched sample. (*c*) QVR for the corrected age matched sample. ■——■, preterm; ▲——▲, full term.

indicate a notable reduction of the differences between the two groups seen in the chronologically based data (Fig. 1 *a–c*).

A view of the similarity of infants of differing socioeconomic status on vocal development is provided in Fig. 3 *a*, which shows the data on CBR for

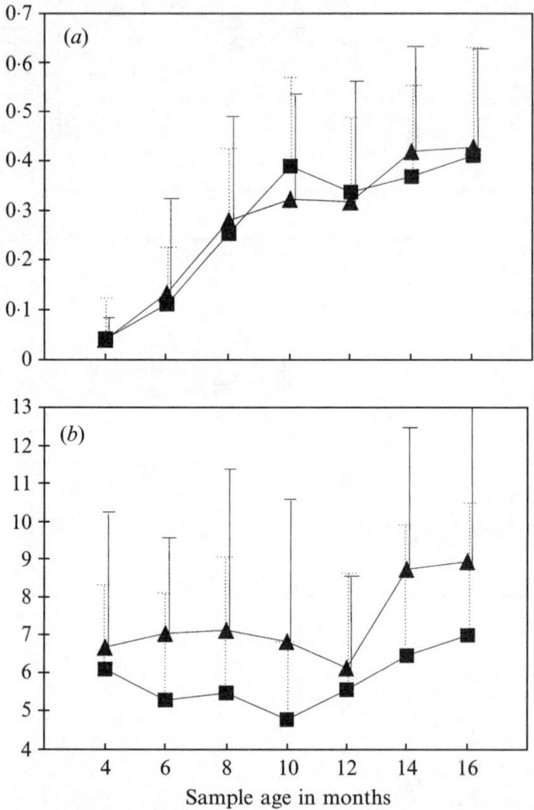

Fig. 3. (*a*) CBR for infants of low and mid SES for the corrected age matched sample. (*b*) Volubility (or utterances per minute) for infants of low and mid SES for the corrected age matched sample. ■—■, low SES; ▲—▲, mid SES.

the two SES groups in the corrected age analysis. As in the chronological age analysis, the SES factor proves not to be reliable, as should be expected given the substantial similarity of the two groups on the babbling measure. Furthermore, that the outcome should be the same as in the chronological age analysis should not be surprising, because it is merely the result of reanalysing the corpus of data after shifting subjects in accord with gestational age – such shifts have little effect because gestational age is more or less balanced across the SES factor. It is similarly expected and confirmed also that both FVR and QVR do not show reliable differences across the SES groups in the corrected age analysis, and that the main effects of SES ($F[1, 27] = 7.61, p < 0.01$) and age ($F[6, 216] = 3.49, p < 0.01$) for volubility (U/M) are maintained in the corrected age analysis. Again, the low SES group produces fewer utterances per minute (mean = 5.7, S.D. = 3.1) than their mid SES counterparts (mean = 7.3, S.D. = 3.6) as indicated in Fig. 3b. And again, the age effect owes to the greater volubility of infants in both SES groups and both term groups in the oldest two age samples (mean = 7.6 and 8.0 utterances per minute) as opposed to the five youngest samples (mean = 6.4, 6.1, 6.3, 5.8, 5.9).

Within-group and session-to-session variability

Examination of the various figures reveals that for both chronological and corrected age analyses, within group variances for the variables evaluated in the study are high – in some cases, one standard deviation at a particular age exceeds the difference between the highest and lowest means for individual age groups. For example, in Fig. 1b, FVR is seen to vary across ages for the full term group from a mean of 0.68 to a mean of 0.83, a difference of 0.15; one standard deviation for either the full term or the preterm group at both ages of 0;4 and 0;6 exceeds this difference. High within-group variances with respect to age or group effects are important to note because they suggest that different infants are developing at different rates; although group summaries of data present the appearance of smooth patterns, in fact, across ages and individual children, the picture is quite complex, and individual subjects may differ greatly from any group mean. For example, the group patterns suggest stabilization of the FVR by about 0;10 corrected age at a value of about 0.80; yet past this age, individual samples continue to occur with FVR's as high as 1.0 or as low as 0.06 (a very extreme case), and many samples are below 0.50. For CBR, it might be imagined that, because all the infants are designated to be in the canonical stage by the 0;10 (corrected age) sample and because the means for the two term groups range from 0.30 to 0.44, all the infants would be producing considerable proportions of canonical syllables in all samples after age 0;10. In fact, however, samples with very few canonical syllables continue to occur until the age 1;6 samples, and the range of individual CBRs at age 1;4 is from 0.90 to 0.02.

The extent of variability on production of well-formed syllables raises questions about the nature of stages of vocal development. It seems possible that different groups of infants may show differences in stage attainment pattern, even if they do not show significant group differences in quantitative values such as the CBR. A previous study from our laboratory on Down syndrome infants (Lynch *et al.* 1990) has indicated that for several months after the designated onset of canonical babbling (based on parent report and verified in the next occurring laboratory evaluation), Down syndrome infants are less likely than their typically developing peers to produce samples of canonical syllables exceeding a criterion of 0·15 CBR, a value that laboratory personnel set early in the study as corresponding to the minimal impressionistically 'fully canonical' sample. Other work (Oller & Eilers, 1988) has also suggested that the canonical stage may begin in deaf infants more gradually and with more fits and starts than in the case of hearing infants.

These suggestions raise the possibility that even though preterm infants at corrected ages do not differ statistically from their full term peers on CBR, they might, like the Down syndrome or deaf infants, show a somewhat different pattern of onset. To evaluate this possibility, infants in the full term and preterm groups were evaluated to determine how many of the four consecutive samples after the designated onset of canonical babbling (as reported in Eilers *et al.* 1993) exceed the criterion of 0·15 CBR. Seventy-five per cent of the samples from the full term group exceed the criterion after the designated onset, but only 57 % of the preterm samples do. A χ^2 analysis of these data reveals that the full term infants are significantly more likely ($\chi^2 = 8\cdot6$, d.f. $= 3$, $p < 0\cdot05$) than the preterm infants to exceed the criterion of 0·15 CBR. No such difference obtains between the low SES and mid SES groups, where the comparisons are 73 % and 71 % respectively exceeding the criterion.

Additional vocal categories

The evaluation of additional categories of vocalization was conducted descriptively, with no statistical analysis of possible group differences, for two reasons: (1) many samples had no vocalizations at all in the particular precanonical categories and (2) no observational reliability data were available.

The descriptive information of primary interest is summarized in Table 5, where the average ratio for each of five precanonical vocal types is presented, broken down by full term and preterm infants for the 0;4 to 1;6 chronological age samples.

The table indicates that there were vast differences between the rates of production of the five sound types, glottal fricative sequences occurring with an average ratio (number of glottal fricative sequences in the sample divided by the total number of syllables in the sample) between 0·15 and 0·18 and raspberries occurring with an average ratio of less than 0·01. The occurrence of no vocalizations in particular categories during particular sessions is of interest because it further illustrates the ubiquitous pattern of variability in vocalizations of infants. The data suggest that infants 'play' with sounds, producing particular elements repetitively for a time, then leaving them and going on to others. Infants in the two term groups and SES groups often tend to focus on a particular precanonical vocal type within a session, but then may not produce that same type again in subsequent sessions. Note for

TABLE 5. *Descriptive statistics for five precanonical vocal types in infants aged 0 ;4–1 ;6 (chronological age sample)*

	Average ratio[a]		Percent samples having ratio = 0		Highest ratio for any sample	
	Full term	Preterm	Full term	Preterm	Full term	Preterm
Glottal fricative sequences	0·19	0·15	2	3	0·65	0·59
Glottal stop sequences	0·07	0·09	25	17	0·46	0·62
Squeals	0·03	0·03	49	45	0·40	0·34
Growls	0·03	0·01	50	69	0·44	0·26
Raspberries	< 0·01	< 0·01	72	75	0·22	0·18

[a] Number of syllables of the indicated type divided by the total number of syllables in the sample.

example that about 50 % of samples show no squeals at all, but that the highest sample ratios (0·4 for the full terms, 0·34 for the preterms) are indicative of repetitive production of squeals in individual sessions. Even glottal fricative sequences, which are rarely absent in individual sessions, sometimes show extremely high values, as high as 0·65 for the highest full term sample, compared to the mean ratio of less than 0·2; raspberries, which are absent in nearly three-quarters of the sessions, show individual sessions where ratios shoot up, with a highest sample ratio of 0·22. Also notable is the fact that while all the precanonical ratios reduce to low levels in the latest recording sessions, there persist occasional occurrences of each of these precanonical vocal types through the samples from age 1 ;6.

The pattern of the production of particular sound types in individual sessions results in extreme variability within child from session to session. Consequently, even if there are reliable differences between full term and preterm infants, or between low SES and mid SES infants on rate of production of precanonical sounds, it would be very difficult given current methods of observation to obtain solid evidence of such differences.

DISCUSSION

The longitudinal research reported here indicates that the measures of infraphonological development employed in the study are sensitive to growth in the production of well-formed speech-like units across the first year of life. Furthermore, the measures of infraphonological well-formedness are sensitive to differences in vocal development of chronologically age-matched infants born at full term as opposed to those born prematurely. The premature infants, especially early in the first year, show reliably less mature vocal patterns than their full term age mates do. However, when premature infants are compared on infraphonological development with full term infants matched for gestational age, the statistically reliable differences in rate of production of well-formed units disappear. Infants from middle and low SES backgrounds also prove statistically indistinguishable in ratios of speech-like vocalizations.

This pattern of results bolsters an emerging perspective on the biological foundations of speech. It appears that infants come to produce well-formed speech-like units in a manner that is notably flexible under changing circumstances. If the infant is born early, the vocal system is adaptable and emerges basically intact. Similarly, if the infant is born into a family of low SES where evidence suggests environmental support for language development may be weak (Hart & Risley, 1989), well-formed vocalizations develop, apparently fully on schedule. The robustness of the development of infraphonological capabilities may reflect the fundamental importance of being able to produce the sounds of speech throughout human history.

At the same time, it is important not to overstate the similarities in at-risk infants and infants born free of such risk. Infants with more ominous risk conditions (e.g. deafness or Down syndrome) clearly show aberrations of vocal development, and evaluation based on adjustments of method may reveal differences that are missed in initial tests even with infants beset by milder risks. The present work also provides evidence of a difference in the nature of canonical babbling in premature infants as opposed to their term counterparts. It has been traditionally assumed (Koopmans-van Beinum & van der Stelt, 1986; Oller, 1986) that the canonical stage begins suddenly and that the ability to produce well-formed syllables is never thereafter lost. This switching-on of the ability to produce speech-like syllables has been presumed to be reflected in substantial consistency of production of canonical syllables, day after day, whenever the canonical-stage infant vocalizes. The present research suggests that the onset of canonical babbling in premature infants may not be as stable as in full term infants. Thus, in four consecutive samples after the onset of canonical babbling, premature infants were reliably less likely to reach a minimum criterion of canonical syllable production than their full term counterparts. How could this be so, given that gestationally age-matched premature and full term infants produced statistically indistinguishable amounts of canonical babbling? We have noted two potential sources of the difference. First, the premature infants actually began the canonical stage (as well as handbanging) somewhat earlier (by about three weeks on the average, as reported in Eilers *et al.* 1993); and second, at gestationally matched ages they produced fewer (though not significantly so) canonical syllables than the full terms. This combination may account for the significant differences between the full term and premature infants on consistency of well-formed syllable productions after the canonical stage was in force.

That the stage of canonical babbling should emerge with some differences in infants of differing risk has been suggested by previous studies as well. Work with hearing-impaired infants (Oller & Eilers, 1988) and infants with Down syndrome (Lynch *et al.* 1990) has suggested that extreme risk of speech disorder may be accompanied by instability in the production of well-formed syllables after the apparent onset of the canonical stage. Such results, of course, raise questions about the meaning of the 'stage' construct. In our view, the notion of stages of vocal development has been intended primarily as a heuristic device, and no strong theoretical claims have been intended. But now that it has been seen that canonical babbling emerges more gradually in some infants than in others, and that gradual emergence may be associated with certain disorders, it becomes more appealing to explore the idea of stages in the hope of establishing a more generally useful perspective.

To expand the perspective on vocal stages it will be important to seek a characterization of the mechanism that might underlie the apparent differences in onset of canonical babbling among at-risk infants and those not at-risk. There are several possible explanations for inconsistency in babbling after the onset of the canonical stage, possibilities that revolve around potential asymmetries in motoric development of premature infants, and which suggest that the production of canonical syllables involves a complex motoric structure, different components of which can come into play at different points of maturation. Premature infants may progress faster than full term infants matched for gestational age, owing perhaps to their greater motoric experience, but only in some subset of the complex motoric structure that drives the production of well-formed syllables. The part of the structure that premature infants develop ahead of schedule may make it possible for them to produce canonical syllables but may not facilitate the productions under as many circumstances as occurs with the full term infant.

Another possible asymmetry that could account for the inconsistency of babbling in premature infants depends on the possibility that the requisite motoric capability develops ahead of the social factors that motivate much vocal activity. Previous research indicates that premature infants function somewhat differently in social interaction than their full term counterparts (less smiling, Goldberg, 1978; less activity, alertness, responsiveness, Bakeman & Brown, 1980; more crying, Friedman, Jacobs & Werthmann, 1982), and that parents respond differently to premature infants (Barnard & Bee, 1982; Stern & Hildebrandt, 1986). These facts encourage the suggestion that preterm infants may show social development that is unique, and perhaps disarticulated from the normally expected pattern of motor development.

That social factors play a role in the performance of vocal acts in infants has been well-known for some time (see in particular Bloom, 1977; Papoušek & Papoušek, 1982; Poulson, 1983; Papoušek, Papoušek & Bornstein, 1984). Although the present study indicates that low SES infants display a rich repertoire of vocalizations, and although well-formed speech-like units seem to make their appearance on schedule and in normal proportions in children born into low SES families, it is notable that low SES conditions appear to produce a depressive effect on the amount of vocalizing of infants. The lower rate of vocalization in the infants of lower SES families may be a reflection of differences in the amount of vocal stimulation through interaction with care-givers. Recent studies of vocal interaction among parents and children in 'disadvantaged' families suggest markedly low rates of conversation (Hart & Risley, 1989), and related studies suggest some impoverishment of the vocal repertoire of children in low SES families, an impoverishment that is reflected not in structural (grammatical) deficiencies, but in vocabulary usage (Hart & Risley, 1981).

The present study has noted differences in the amount of vocalization among infants being reared in differing social circumstances, but has emphasized similarities in the development of infraphonology. To note that infraphonological patterns of production are notably stable does not, of course, deny the possibility of subtle differences in other domains of speech-related abilities. For example, whatever the many global similarities in vocal patterning of infants reared in differing language environments (see, for example, Oller & Eilers, 1982), there may be quantitative differences in articulation of certain phonetic segments (see de Boysson-Bardies, Hallé, Sagart & Durand, 1989), and there appear to be differences in speech perception abilities by 0;6 to 0;9, dependent upon the specific language in the home (Eilers, Gavin & Wilson, 1979; Werker, Gilbert, Humphrey & Tees, 1981; Eilers, Gavin & Oller, 1982; Werker & Tees, 1983). Such results remind us that the emergence of the speech capacity may be multifaceted and may reflect complexities of both biological determination and environmental sensitivity.

REFERENCES

Bakeman, R. & Brown, J. W. (1980). Early interaction: consequences for social and mental development at three years. *Child Development* **51**, 437–47.

Barnard, K. E. & Bee, H. L. (1982). Developmental changes in maternal interactions with term and pre-term infants. Paper presented at the International Conference of Infant Studies, Austin, TX.

Bleile, K. M., Stark, R. & McGowan, J. S. (1992). Evidence for the relationship between babbling and later speech development. Paper presented at International Clinical Phonetics and Language Association 2nd Symposium, London.

Bloom, K. (1977). Patterning of infant vocal behavior. *Journal of Experimental Child Psychology* **23**, 367–77.

Carney, A. E. (1991) Vocal development in hearing-impaired infants. Paper presented at the annual meeting of the Acoustical Society of America, Houston, TX.

de Boysson-Bardies, B., Hallé, P., Sagart, L. & Durand, C. (1989). A cross-linguistic investigation of vowel formants in babbling. *Journal of Child Language* **16**, 1–17.

DiPietro, J. A. & Allen, M. C. (1991). Estimation of gestational age: implications for developmental research. *Child Development* **62**, 1184–99.

Eilers, R. E., Gavin, W. J. & Oller, D. K. (1982). Cross-linguistic perception in infancy: early effects of linguistic experience. *Journal of Child Language* **9**, 289–302.

Eilers, R. E., Gavin, W. J. & Wilson, W. R. (1979). Linguistic experience and phonemic perception in infancy: a cross-linguistic study. *Child Development* **50**, 14–18.

Eilers, R. E., Oller, D. K., Levine, S., Basinger, D., Lynch, M. P. & Urbano, R. (1993). The role of prematurity and socioeconomic status in the onset of canonical babbling in infants. *Infant Behavior and Development* **16**, 297–315.

Foreman, N. & Altaha, M. (1991). The development of exploration and spontaneous alternation in hooded rat pups: effects of unusually early eyelid opening. *Developmental Psychobiology* **24**, 521–37.

Friedman, S., Jacobs, B. & Werthman, M. (1982). Preterms of low medical risk: spontaneous behaviors and soothability at expected date of birth. *Infant Behavior and Development* **5**, 3–10.

Goldberg, S. (1978). Prematurity: effects on parent–infant interaction. *Journal of Pediatric Psychology* **3**, 137–44.

Greenberg, M. T. & Crnic, K. S. (1988). Longitudinal predictors of development status and social interaction in premature and full-term infants at age two. *Child Development* **59**, 554–70.

Hart, B. & Risley, T. R. (1981). Grammatical and conceptual growth in the language of psychosocially disadvantaged children. In M. J. Begab, H. Garber & H. C. Haywood (eds), *Prevention of retarded development in psychosocially disadvantaged children*. Baltimore: University Park Press.

—— & —— (1989). The longitudinal study of interactive systems. *Education and Treatment of Children* **12**, 347–58.

Hollingshead, A. B. (1978). *Two factor index of social status*. New Haven, CT: Yale University Press.

Kent, R. D., Osberger, M. J., Netsell, R. & Hustedde, C. G. (1987). Phonetic development in identical twins who differ in auditory function. *Journal of Speech and Hearing Disorders* **52**, 64–75.

Klatt, D. H. (1980). Software for a cascade/parallel formant synthesizer. *Journal of the Acoustical Society of America* **67**, 971–95.

Koopmans-van Beinum, F. J. & van der Stelt, J. M. (1986). Early stages in the development of speech movements. In B. Lindblom & R. Zetterstrom (eds), *Precursors of early speech*. New York: Stockton Press.

Lenneberg, E. (1967). *Biological foundations of language*. New York: Wiley.

Lenneberg, E. H., Rebelsky, G. F. & Nichols, I. A. (1965). The vocalizations of infants born to deaf and hearing parents. *Human Development* **8**, 23–37.

Lickliter, R. (1990). Premature visual stimulation accelerates intersensory functioning in bobwhite quail neonates. *Infant Behavior and Development* **13**, 487–96.

Locke, J. & Pearson, D. (1990). Linguistic significance of babbling: evidence from a tracheostomized infant. *Journal of Child Language* **17**, 1–16.

Lynch, M. P., Oller, D. K., Eilers, R. E. & Basinger, D. (1990). Vocal development of infants with Down Syndrome. Paper presented at the University of Wisconsin 11th Annual Symposium for Research on Child Language Disorders, Madison, WI.

Lynch, M. P., Oller, D. K. & Steffens, M. (1989). Development of speech-like vocalizations in a child with congenital absence of cochleas: the case of total deafness. *Applied Psycholinguistics* **10**, 315–33.

Nam, C. V. & Powers, N. G. (1983). *Socioeconomic approach to status measurement*. Houston: Cap & Gown Press.

Oller, D. K. (1986). Metaphonology and infant vocalizations. In B. Lindblom & R. Zetterstrom (eds), *Precursors of early speech*. New York: Stockton Press.

—— (in press). Development of vocalizations in infancy. In H. Winitz (ed.), *Human communication and its disorders*.

Oller, D. K. & Eilers, R. E. (1982). Similarities of babbling of Spanish and English learning babies. *Journal of Child Language* **9**, 565–78.

—— & —— (1988). The role of audition in infant babbling. *Child Development* **59**, 441–9.

Oller, D. K., Eilers, R. E., Bull, D. H. & Carney, A. E. (1985). Prespeech vocalizations of a deaf infant: a comparison with normal metaphonological development. *Journal of Speech and Hearing Research* **28**, 47–63.

Oller, D. K., Lewedag, V., Umbel, V. & Basinger, D. L. (1992). The onset of rhythmic babbling in infants exposed to bilingual and monolingual environments. Paper presented at Symposium on rhythmic vocal development at the International Conference on Infant Studies, Miami Beach, FL.

Oller, D. K. & Lynch, M. P. (1992). Infant vocalizations and innovations in infraphonology: toward a broader theory of development and disorders. In C. Ferguson, L. Menn & C. Stoel-Gammon (eds), *Phonological development*. Parkton, MD: York Press.

Papoušek, H. & Papoušek, M. (1982). Vocal imitations in mother-infant dialogues. *Infant Behavior and Development* **5**, 176.

Papoušek, M., Papoušek, H. & Bornstein, M. H. (1984). The naturalistic vocal environment of young infants: on the significance of homogeneity and variability in parental speech. In T. M. Field & N. Fox (eds), *Social perception in infants*. Norwood, NJ: Ablex.

Poulson, C. L. (1983). Differential reinforcement of other-than-vocalization as a control procedure in the conditioning of infant vocalization rate. *Journal of Experimental Child Psychology* **36**, 471–89.

Roug, L., Landberg, I. & Lundberg, L. J. (1989). Phonetic development in early infancy: a study of four Swedish children during the first 18 months of life. *Journal of Child Language* **16**, 19–40.

Smith, B. L. & Oller, D. K. (1981). A comparative study of pre-meaningful vocalizations produced by normally developing and Down's syndrome infants. *Journal of Speech and Hearing Disorders* **46**, 46–51.

Steffens, M. L., Oller, D. K., Lynch, M. P. & Urbano, R. C. (1992). Vocal development in infants with Down syndrome and infants who are developing normally. *American Journal of Mental Retardation* **97**, 235–46.

Stern, M. & Hildebrandt, K. A. (1986). Prematurity stereotyping: effects on mother-infant interaction. *Child Development* **57**, 308–15.

Stoel-Gammon, C. & Otomo, K. (1986). Babbling development of hearing-impaired and normally hearing subjects. *Journal of Speech and Hearing Disorders* **51**, 33–41.

Werker, J. F., Gilbert, J. H. V., Humphrey, K. & Tees, R. C. (1981). Developmental aspects of cross-language speech perception. *Child Development* **52**, 349–55.

Werker, J. F. & Tees, R. C. (1983). Developmental changes across childhood in the perception of non-native speech sounds. *Canadian Journal of Psychology* **37**, 278–86.

Zlatin, M. (1975). Explorative mapping of the vocal tract and primitive syllabification in infancy: the first six months. Paper presented at the American Speech and Hearing Association Convention, Washington, DC.

J. Child Lang. **21** (1994), 59–83. Copyright © 1994 Cambridge University Press

The (non)realization of unstressed elements in children's utterances: evidence for a rhythmic constraint*

FRANK WIJNEN

University of Utrecht

EVELIEN KRIKHAAR

University of Groningen

AND

ELS DEN OS

University of Amsterdam

ABSTRACT

In this study it is argued that the omission of closed class morphemes and of unstressed syllables within words is related to their common characteristic, viz. that they are unstressed, rhythmically weak parts of utterances. Several strands of evidence indicate that it is unlikely that children are unable to perceive these elements in the input speech. The pattern of (non)realization of unstressed syllables within content words and the class of determiners, was analysed in two Dutch children from 1;6 to 2;11. It appeared that polysyllabic words were quite generally truncated in such a way that they fitted a trochaic (strong-weak) pattern, particularly in the early samples. Some observations with respect to the (non)realization of determiners are suggestive of an influence of an SW-constraint on the realization of noun phrases. These findings support the hypothesis that in the course of utterance preparation, words and phrases are mapped onto S(W) templates. Anecdotal evidence suggests that the dissolution of the SW-constraint coincides with the acquisition of specific aspects of stress assignment in Dutch, such as quantity sensitivity.

---

[*] We thank our subjects and their parents for their patient co-operation. Thanks are also due to Tirtsa Huiskamp, for her assistance in judging stress patterns, and to Loekie Elbers, René Kager, Sarah Hawkins, and an anonymous reviewer, for their thoughtful and stimulating comments on earlier versions of this paper. Els den Os and Frank Wijnen were supported by grants from the PSYCHON foundation, which is funded by the Netherlands Organization for Scientific Research (NWO). Address for correspondence: Frank Wijnen, Department of Linguistics & Department of Psychology, University of Groningen, Oude Kijk in 't Jatstraat 26, 9712 EK, Groningen, The Netherlands. E-mail: wijnen@let.rug.nl.

INTRODUCTION

The omission of unstressed syllables from polysyllabic words is widely documented in children acquiring various, divergent languages. It appears to be a virtually universal characteristic of early child language. Several explanations for this phenomenon have been advanced, which represent the classic oppositions in developmental psycholinguistic theorizing: perception vs. production, and performance vs. competence (Clark & Clark, 1977). Not many of these explanations, however, have related syllable omissions to another, fairly wide-spread phenomenon in early child language, viz. the absence of so-called grammatical morphemes (Brown, 1973). In the present study an attempt is made to relate both phenomena, starting from the simple observation that most grammatical morphemes and unstressed syllables within words share the phonological property of being unstressed, or rhythmically weak.

The absence of grammatical morphemes from early (Stage I, or telegraphic) child utterances has been explained by Brown (1973), and others after him, by referring to their semantic complexity. Grammatical morphemes are 'modulators' of meaning. The concepts they express (e.g. determinacy, number) are more abstract than those expressed by the content words, and could, therefore, be more difficult to acquire. In support of this idea, Brown provides evidence showing that the order of appearance of the famous first 14 grammatical morphemes can be explained by their cumulative semantic complexity.

More recently, attempts have been made to relate the absence of these morphemes to the acquisition of syntax. Many of the grammatical morphemes are specifically linked to what syntacticians call functional projections. For instance, articles and other determiners, as well as pronouns, are heads of DET projections, and auxiliaries are heads of INFL projections. It has been argued that functional projections are not yet present in the syntactic representations of Stage I children, so that, even if they knew the morphemes that are linked to them, they would be unable to express them, as they cannot be syntactically licensed (Radford, 1990). It is held that the presence and character of functional categories varies parametrically across languages. Eventually, on the basis of positive evidence, children who are confronted with languages such as English or Dutch will alter their phrase structure representations in order to include the appropriate functional categories. This will be reflected by the appearance of the associated morphemes in language production.

The semantic and syntactic explanations of the absence of grammatical morphemes are challenged by Pye's (1983) observations on the acquisition of Quiché. Pye noted that two-year-old children, in their attempts to use the morphologically complex verb forms of Quiché, often did not produce the verb's root morpheme (i.e. a semantically 'simple' content word), but a syllable consisting of the last consonant of the root morpheme plus a VC-shaped termination suffix, expressing various highly abstract semantic and syntactic features (Pye, 1983: 585ff.). This can be related to the phonological form of the verbs. Morpheme and syllable boundaries do not coincide in Quiché verbs, due to resyllabification. The part that children produce corresponds to the syllable bearing primary stress. Pye argues that stress patterns in the input language are a major determinant of the acquisition and use of words by children. The grammatical morphemes in languages such as Dutch and English are generally unstressed, even unstressable. Thus, although semantic and syntactic factors undoubtedly contribute to the acquisition of the grammatical morphemes (it is hard to see, for instance, how the order of acquisition can be explained by reference to prosodic differences alone), their initial absence from the utterances of children who acquire these languages might be explained by their prosodic characteristics. This explanation suggests a connection to the omission of unstressed syllables within words. The question then is what kind of process or mechanism related to stress might account for the omission of both unstressed syllables and grammatical morphemes.

As a first option, we might look at the perception of speech. In comparison to stressed syllables, unstressed syllables have a shorter duration and a lower amplitude. Moreover, they do not involve the pitch modulations that are associated with intonational accents. Consequently, unstressed syllables may be masked by stressed syllables, and the resulting reduction in perceptibility may be the reason why children omit them in their own speech. There are several arguments against this solution. First, Pye (1983) observed that children acquiring Quiché do also produce verb roots, particularly when the verb occurs sentence-medially. Pye connects this to the variation in stress placement as a function of the verb's sentence position in the input language: the final syllable is stressed when the verb occurs in sentence-final position, whereas the verb root is stressed in sentence-medial position. The children's behaviour indicates that they perceive and store both verb root and suffix. Consequently, the fact that they systematically avoid producing both parts within the same utterance cannot be ascribed to a perceptual problem. It is on the basis of data such as these that Gleitman, Gleitman, Landau & Wanner (1988) suggest that for young speakers, 'word' and 'stressed syllable' are equivalent.

A second argument against the perceptual explanation can be derived from experimental studies of children's sentence comprehension. Shipley, Smith & Gleitman (1969) and Petretic & Tweney (1977) found that children who omit function words from their speech nevertheless are more likely to respond appropriately to utterances containing function words than to utterances without them. Moreover, Gerken, Landau & Remez (1990), using an imitation paradigm with existing and nonsense function words, showed that although stress plays a major role in the tendency to exclude function words from imitative responses, existing function words were responded to differently from nonsense words, which suggests that, despite their relative inconspicuousness, these words were perceived and processed.

Finally, it appears that parts of the syllables that are omitted from multisyllabic words (particularly consonants or consonant features) are retained, and may be substituted for, or added to the segments of one of the realized syllables (Allen & Hawkins, 1980; Fikkert, 1991). Examples from Fikkert's data base of Dutch child phonology are given in (1):

(1 a)   telefoon /ˌteːlə'fon/ 'telephone': [ˌtɔː]   (Tom 1;7.11)
 (b)   ballon   /bɑ'lɔn/   'balloon':   ['plɔm] (Tom 1;7.9)
 (c)   konijn   /ko'nɛin/ 'rabbit':   ['ŋɛi]   (Tom 1;5.28)

In (1 a) the vowel of the realized syllable roughly corresponds to that in the adult model, but it is preceded by the onset of the word's initial (unstressed) syllable. In (1 b) the initial /b/, pronounced as [p] is added to the second (stressed) syllable onset. In (1 c) finally, the initial nasal in the child's realization is velarized, presumably as a result of the velar stop /k/ in the adult form. Examples such as these, which are typical for most children, suggest that the segmental information contained in the unstressed syllables is perceived and stored. Thus, these examples are also hard to reconcile with the hypothesis that listeners tend to consider stressed syllables as word onsets (Cutler & Norris, 1988), which predicts that information preceding the syllable bearing primary stress would be excluded from language learners' initial lexical representations.

If perceptual explanations of children's omissions of unstressed syllables and morphemes fail, as the above overview suggests, the logical next step would be to look for an explanation in the production domain. Allen & Hawkins (1978, 1980) have proposed that the omission of unstressed elements is the result of a condition on the rhythmical structure of utterances. After an initial stage in which only monosyllabic utterances are allowed, children's utterances will tend to meet two requirements: (1) weak (unstressed) and strong (stressed) syllables should alternate; and (2) initial syllables should be strong. Together, these requirements constitute a trochaic bias, which, as Allen & Hawkins surmise, reflects a universal of human perceptual and motor performance.[1] Although in adult speech the universal tendency to alternate between strong and weak syllables in a regular fashion is still discernible (see Kelly & Bock, 1988, and their references), stress and rhythm are largely determined by language-specific stress rules. However, in the speech of children who have not yet acquired language-

---

[1] This idea is traceable to Henry Sweet (1875, cited in Kelly & Bock 1988).

specific rules of stress and rhythm, the trochaic bias is argued to be directly reflected by the widely reported tendency to omit unstressed syllables that either are word-initial $(W_1S(W_2) \rightarrow S(W_2))$, or that precede other unstressed syllables $(SW_1W_2 \rightarrow SW_2)$. Allen & Hawkins' claim has been challenged by Hochberg (1988) on the basis of imitative and naturalistic data from children acquiring Spanish. Hochberg states that a rhythmic bias cannot be discerned in her subjects' speech. It should be noted, however, that she eliminated polysyllabic realizations of monosyllabic target words and truncated realizations of polysyllabic targets – in other words, the data on which Allen & Hawkins' claim is based – from her analyses. Even so, it appears that in Hochberg's data set, children's realizations with final stress are less frequent than those with penultimate stress. Thus, the contrast between Allen & Hawkins and Hochberg seems to be largely superficial.

Allen & Hawkins' trochaic bias may be interpreted as a constraint on phonological (prosodic) representations that is specific to an early stage in the development of language. At least two different conceptions of the level of processing and representation at which this constraint is implemented are possible. First, it might be part of the system by which the stored phonemic or featural information (which is based on auditory input) is transformed into output representations. Traditionally, child phonologists have described this 'transduction system' in terms of rewrite rules (Menyuk, Menn & Silber, 1986). To attain compatibility with modern non-linear phonology, we might assume that the transduction system involves the mapping of 'melodic' (i.e. segmental or featural) information onto phonological representations at various – syllabic and prosodic – levels of description. This seems to provide a natural fit with current models of language production, which assume that planning involves the insertion of information stored in memory (words, segments, features) into planning frames that are derived from the relevant sets of grammatical rules (Dell, 1986; Levelt, 1989; Wijnen, 1990, 1992). Supposedly, the only type of frame that is allowed at the level of prosodic planning during an early stage of language acquisition is one that captures the Strong-Weak structure. We will refer to this hypothetical representation as the 'SW-template'. A question that may be raised is whether it is derived from universal grammar (Dresher & Kaye, 1990), or whether it reflects the child's initial inductive hypothesis concerning the metrical structure of the input language. In the latter case, we would expect to find the trochaic constraint only in children acquiring languages such as English or Dutch, in which 75 % or more of the words are trochaic (Cutler & Carter, 1987; Quené, 1992).

Alternatively, the trochaic constraint might take effect within the lexicon. This would imply that immediately upon acquisition, a new word would be adapted to the trochaic template. This hypothesis leads to predictions that differ from those related to the previous one in two respects. First, we would not expect to find free variation in the realization of word forms. For instance, a word like *banana* [bə'nænə] should always be realized as, e.g. ['nænə], for this would represent the stored form. Secondly, an effect on the realization of phrases and sentences is ruled out. In contrast, the assumption that a trochaic constraint takes effect during transduction (i.e. utterance planning) makes variation in realized forms conceivable. So, for instance ['nænə], ['bænə] and [bə'nænə] might occur as realizations of *banana*. Moreover, not only words, but also phrases and sentences might be adapted to fit the template, so that a particular realization may depend on the rhythmic structure of the surrounding utterance. The complete utterance, however, should agree with the trochaic pattern.

Clearly, only the 'planning' version of the rhythmic constraint hypothesis can account for the omission of both unstressed syllables and grammatical morphemes by utilizing their common phonological characteristic. Some evidence in support of this hypothesis was gathered by Gerken (1990, 1991) in a sentence imitation task with two-year-old children. She found that unstressed closed class words, such as determiners and pronouns, which constituted weak parts of iambic feet were systematically omitted. In a later study (Gerken, 1992), a positive correlation was found between two-year-olds' MLUs and their tendency to preserve weak (unstressed) syllables in the imitation of multisyllabic nonsense words. Since increases in MLU in the stage of development that Gerken studied predominantly reflect the increasing use of closed class morphemes, this correlation corroborates the idea that the omission of both closed class morphemes and unstressed syllables reflects the same underlying mechanism.

In this study, we analyse the patterns of realization and omission of unstressed syllables in content words, and of a particular class of function words, viz. determiners, in two Dutch children's spontaneous utterances, recorded between 1;6 and 2;11. Our aim was to establish whether these children adapt the rhythmic form of words and phrases in such a way that trochaic patterns result. We also wanted to find out whether the subjects only use OMISSION (truncation) as a means to this end, or whether they are also able to deploy other strategies, such as stress shifting or the addition of 'filler' syllables.

In addition to our attempt to establish whether or not children adapt the rhythmic form of words and phrases, we also address the question of whether the composition of early vocabularies reflects a bias towards words that match the rhythmic constraint. Child phonologists have found that the intake of words from the ambient language may be affected by certain segmental biases. Children may avoid words that contain sounds they are unable to pronounce, or they may show a preference for structures that fall within their capabilities (Waterson, 1971; Schwartz, 1988). It is conceivable that a similar 'lexical filtering' occurs with regard to rhythmic forms.

Finally, should the early utterances indeed be bounded by the trochaic constraint, we will examine whether later there are any signs of the abandonment of this early pattern in favour of the stress rules of Dutch.

METHOD

Subjects

This study is based on a longitudinal corpus of utterances produced by two children acquiring Dutch: Daan (male) and Marloes (female). Both are first-born children, growing up in middle-class families. At age 2;0, Marloes was enrolled in a daycare centre.

At the start of the observation period, Daan was 1;7, Marloes 1;6. At the end, their ages were 2;11 and 2;10, respectively. Daan's MLUs were 1·0 and 3·6 in the first and last samples, respectively. The values for Marloes were 1·0 and 3·2. The average length of words (in syllables) in the first sample were 1·69 for Daan and 1·49 for Marloes. These figures indicate that both children were capable of producing multisyllabic words.

Data collection

The children were recorded in their homes, at monthly intervals (one session with Marloes, at age 2;8, was missed due to a holiday). Each recording session lasted for approximately 60 minutes. Usually, the children were interacting with their mother. Mother and child were often engaged in play. Also, picture books were used to stimulate naming. In some of the later recordings of Marloes, her father was present. Furthermore, two researchers (the second and third authors) were present, one handling the recording equipment, the other observing and taking notes. The subjects were recorded on both video- and audiotape. The audio equipment was of high quality (Marantz CP-430 cassette recorder and two Sennheiser MD21 microphones), so as to allow for acoustic analysis of the children's speech (see Den Os, 1990a, b).

Transcription and coding

The first 100 child utterances in each session were fully transcribed, both orthographically and phonetically. The rhythmic form of all content words (nouns, verbs and adjectives) was coded, in terms of strong (S) and weak (W) syllables. The syllable bearing primary stress was coded as S, all other syllables were coded as W. It appeared that the data set thus obtained contained too few tokens of W-initial words and words longer than two syllables to allow for quantitative analyses. Therefore, we added all tokens of W-initial and multisyllabic S-initial words that occurred in the remaining utterances to the data base. We did not distinguish between morphologically simple and complex words, since this appeared unnecessary for our purposes.

Generally, all words that were obviously imitated were discarded from the analyses.

The assignment of stress in the children's speech was evaluated perceptually by a phonetically trained person (the second author). To check for reliability, a sample of 314 word tokens taken from the two corpora (95 from Marloes, 219 from Daan) was evaluated by a second judge, a speech therapist. The rhythmic classifications assigned by the two judges agreed in 84 % of the cases.

For all noun phrases in the first 100 utterances of each sample, we decided whether, according to adult standards, a determiner would have been obligatory, and we registered the appearance of a determiner or filler syllable (schwa).

RESULTS

The composition of the early lexicon: filtering?

If a rhythmic constraint affects the intake of lexical items, it may be expected that words with initial S-syllables are preferred to words with initial W-syllables, and that words in which strong and weak syllables alternate are preferred to words with a non-alternating pattern. To test these predictions, we classified all content words in our subjects' speech according to their rhythmic pattern in adult usage (irrespective of the actually realized forms). Thus, in this section and throughout the paper, classifications of words (and phrases) in terms of rhythmic structure refer to their appearance in adult speech. Fig. 1 is a cumulative graph of the absolute numbers of S, SW, SWW, WS, WSW and WWS words (types) in the children's corpora as a function of age. Note that SW and WS, and SWW, WSW and WWS, constitute a minimally different pair and triplet, respectively, with respect to the position of the stressed syllable and the presence or absence of alternation, while the number of syllables, which might have an additional influence on the intake of words from the ambient language, is constant. If lexical filtering in accordance with the trochaic constraint occurs, we would expect a predominance of SW over all other word types. Moreover, we would not expect a clear difference between WS and WSW, except for a possible preference for the shorter words. Finally, we suspect that initial stress is more important than stress alternation, so that SWW should be preferred to WSW, which, in turn would be preferred to WWS.

The patterns in Fig. 1 show a close correspondence to these predictions. SW-words are predominant in both children, throughout the period of observation, except for the very first sample of Marloes, they even outnumber monosyllabic words. The proportions of WS- and WSW-words are quite low, but, apparently, approximately equal. SWW-words are more frequent than WSW-words, and, finally, WWS are only marginally present at best.

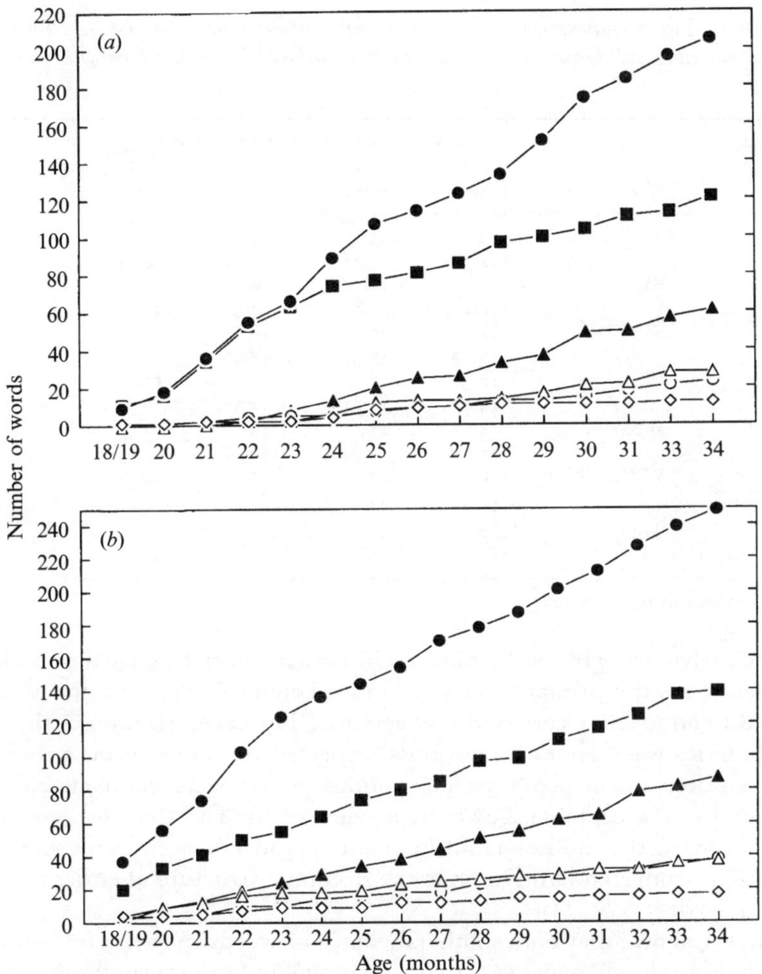

Fig. 1. Cumulative graphs of vocabulary growth. (*a*) Marloes, (*b*) Daan. Solid squares, circles and triangles = S, SW and SWW words respectively; open circles, triangles and diamonds = WS, WSW and WWS words respectively.

In order to conclude, however, that these trends reflect rhythm-based filtering in lexical acquisition, we are required to show that the children's proportions of rhythmic types differ from the pattern that is prevalent in the speech addressed to them. Hence, we classified and tallied all content words in the speech addressed to the subjects by their mothers in the first four samples, and compared the resulting numbers to the distributions of rhythmic types in the children's corpora up to 1;11. We chose these samples because we suspected that a putative lexical learning bias would present itself

67

3-2

TABLE 1. *The numbers and percentages of content words in six rhythmic form classes as derived from the speech of the subjects' mothers in the first four samples*

	Marloes' mother		Daan's mother	
Word type	Types	Tokens	Types	Tokens
S	102	245	54	121
	(42·5)[a]	(45·5)	(25·6)	(20·6)
SW	97	209	100	351
	(40·4)	(38·8)	(47·4)	(59·8)
SWW	21	37	18	39
	(8·8)	(6·9)	(8·5)	(6·6)
WS	10	26	9	13
	(4·2)	(4·8)	(4·3)	(2·2)
WSW	4	11	23	41
	(1·7)	(2·0)	(10·9)	(7)
WWS	6	10	7	22
	(2·5)	(1·9)	(3·3)	(3·7)
Total	240	538	211	587
	(100)	(100)	(100)	(100)

[a] Percentages in parentheses.

most clearly during the early stages. Additionally, until this age the children's mothers were the primary source of input language. Marloes, for instance, started to go to a day care centre at age two. The categorization of the input vocabularies was based on the words' expected rhythmic form, rather than transcriptions of the actual pronunciations, which were not available. This appears to be acceptable, however, in view of the fact that the researchers who recorded the mother–child interactions did not notice any systematic deviations from standard Dutch in the rhythmic structure of either mother's speech.

Table 1 shows that both mothers' choice of words in their child-directed speech quite closely matches the composition – in terms of rhythmic patterns – of their children's vocabularies. Chi-squared tests do not yield significant differences between the distributions of rhythmic types in the children's corpora and those in their respective mother's speech. In contrast, the children's distributions differ significantly from those in the speech of their COUNTERPART's mother. Thus, the proportions of rhythmic types in Daan's corpus differ significantly from the proportions in Marloes' mother's speech ($\chi^2(5) = 27\cdot08$, $p < 0\cdot001$), and Marloes' proportions differ from those of Daan's mother ($\chi^2(5) = 21\cdot96$, $p < 0\cdot005$).

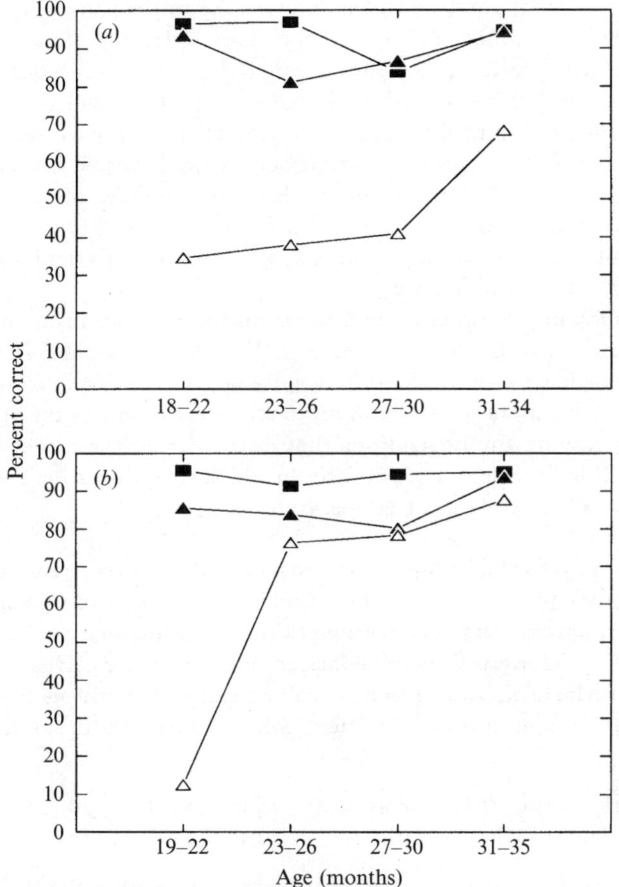

Fig. 2. Percentages of correct (= adult-like) realizations of rhythmic form of S, S-initial and W-initial words, as a function of age. (*a*) Marloes, (*b*) Daan. Solid squares, S; solid triangles, S-initial; open triangles, W-initial

Realizations of content words

Chi-squared tests indicate that the overall proportion of correctly realized monosyllabic S tokens (94 %) is significantly higher than the proportion of correctly realized polysyllabic, S-initial words (Marloes: 88 %; $\chi^2(1) = 13\cdot15$, $p < 0\cdot001$; Daan: 86 %; $\chi^2(1) = 21\cdot20$, $p < 0\cdot001$). The graphs in Fig. 2 suggest that the first two (Marloes) or three (Daan) sections of the observation period are largely responsible for this difference.

Polysyllabic S-initial tokens appear to be significantly more often correct than W-initial tokens (Marloes: 46 %; $\chi^2(1) = 203\cdot41$, $p < 0\cdot001$; Daan:

68 %; $\chi^2(1) = 53.63, p < 0.001$). Fig. 2 gives the impression that the effect in Daan is brought about mainly by the data from the first four months (1;7–1;10). In Marloes, on the other hand, the difference is present throughout the full period of observation. In other words, the children appear to show different developmental trends. In Marloes, we see a rather gradual increase of correct production of W-initial words, but she does not reach the level of 70 % correct in the last four months of the observation period (2;7–2;10). Daan, on the other hand, shows a rather abrupt course of development, with below 20 % scores at ages 1;7 to 1;10, and a jump to the near 80 % level around age two.

In the following sections we will focus on the realizations of words that – in adult usage – can be described as S, SW, SWW, WS, WSW and WWS. Although words with more than three syllables (in the target form) occurred as well, their numbers were too small to allow for quantitative analyses. We will concentrate on the realizations that deviate from the target form, since these will allow us to gain insight into the child's rhythm rules; particularly, whether a trochaic constraint is operative.

Words with an initial S-syllable. All correct and incorrect realizations of S- and SW-content words in the first hundred utterances of all samples were tallied. Throughout the observation period, the majority of the S-words (94 %) were correctly produced. Marloes made 33 errors, Daan 27. Most of these (24 in Marloes; 19 in Daan) involved schwa epenthesis in the context of a liquid and a non-coronal obstruent, which is practically standard in child Dutch:

(2a) jurk /jœrk/ 'dress': ['jœrək] (D 2;3)[2]
 (b) melk /mɛlk/ 'milk': ['mɛlək] (M 1;10)

In a few cases (4 in each child), a schwa was appended at the end of a word:

(3a) oom /om/ 'uncle': ['omə] (M 2;3)
 (b) bal /bɑl/ 'ball': ['bɑlə] (D 1;9)

And, finally, in the remaining cases (9 in all), we see the insertion or addition of a schwa at the beginning of a word, analogous to the cases of word-final epenthesis, resulting in a WS-structure.

(4a) klok /klɔk/ 'clock': [kə'lɔk] (M 1;10)
 (b) trein /trɛɪn/ 'train': [tə'rɛɪn] (D 2;7)

Of the 1531 SW words (tokens), 94 % were realized in a rhythmically correct way. The majority of errors (67 %) were deletions of the final (unstressed) syllable:

---

[2] The codes following the examples indicate the child (**Daan** or **Marloes**) and his/her age.

(5 a) centjes /ˈsɛncjəs/ 'coins':   [sɛ]   (M 1;10)
 (b) meisje /ˈmɛɪʃə/ 'girl':   [mɛɪs] (M 1;10)
 (c) molen /ˈmoːlə/ 'windmill':   [moːl]   (M 1;10)
 (d) koffie /ˈkɔfi/   'coffee':   [kɔf]   (D 1;10)
 (e) puzzel /ˈpœsəl/ 'puzzle':   [pœs]   (D 1;10)
 (f) onder /ˈɔndər/ 'under':   [ɔn]   (D 1;10)

Other errors, in order of frequency, involved epenthetic schwa-insertion, resulting in SWW or WSW structures (26%, ex. 6), and stress shift (7%, ex. 7).

(6 a) varken /ˈfɑrkə/ 'pig':   [ˈxɑʀəkə] (M 2;0)
 (b) vlinder /ˈflɪndər/ 'butterfly': [xəˈlɪnə] (M 1;10)
 (c) zebra /ˈsebra/ 'zebra':   [ˈsebəra] (D 1;11)

(7 a) baby /ˈbebi/ 'baby':   [beˈbeː] (M 1;10)
 (b) ijsbeer /ˈɛɪsbeːʀ/ 'polar bear': [ɛɪsˈbeːʀ] (M 1;10)

All SWW word tokens were included in the data base, 126 for Marloes, and 169 for Daan. Correct realization was considerably less frequent in these words than in the two categories described above; the overall scores were 64·3% for Marloes and 62·1% for Daan. However, performance improved with increasing age. Approximately one quarter (25·4% in Daan, 23% in Marloes) of all renditions involved deletions of one of the two weak syllables, which results in an SW structure. The words from which one weak syllable is deleted can be divided into two types: those in which both weak syllables are equivalent in terms of stress (both contain schwas), and those in which one of the two weak syllables is stronger than the other. In the second type of word (ex. 8), it is mostly the weakest syllable (usually containing a schwa) that is omitted (88% of all cases). The other weak syllable, which in fact bears secondary stress, is retained. In the first type of word (ex. 9), it is not possible to tell which of the two weak syllables is lost, because both contain schwas. A reasonable interpretation is that either syllable 2 or 3 can be dropped, or that the two are conflated.

(8a) ziekenhuis /ˈsikəˌhʌys/ 'hospital':   [ˈsikhʌys] (M 1;10)
 (b) olifant   /ˈoliˌfant/   'elephant':   [ˈoːxant]   (M 1;11)
 (c) kangoeroe /ˈkaŋxuˌru/ 'kangeroo':   [ˈkɑxʀu]   (D 1;11)
 (d) stofzuiger /ˈstɔfˌsʌyxər/ 'vacuum cleaner': [ˈkɔkhʌyx] (M 1;11)
 (e) vrachtauto /ˈfrɑxtˌauto/ 'lorry':   [ˈfrɑxau]   (M 1;11)
 (f) neushoorn /ˈnøːsˌhɔːrən/ 'rhinoceros': [ˈnøːshɔːr] (D 1;11)

(9a) poppetje /ˈpɔpəcjə/ 'doll':   [ˈpɔpə]   (D 1;8)
 (b) andere   /ˈandərə/   'other':   [ˈanʀə]   (D 2;4)

(c) andere   /'andərə/   'other':   ['andə]   (M 2;4)
(d) Janneke   /'janəkə/   :   ['zaŋkə] (M 2;3)

Words with initial W-syllables. From all samples in both children, all words that, according to their target form, have initial W-syllables were extracted. Table 2 summarizes the various realizations of WS-words as a function of

TABLE 2. *Realizations of WS words*

Age*	Marloes				Daan			
	Cor[a]	Trn	S-s	Tot	Cor	Trn	S-s	Tot
A	9	10	0	19	4	11	1	16
	(47·4)[b]	(52·6)	(0)	(100)	(25)	(68·8)	(6·3)	(100)
B	3	5	11	19	21	1	1	23
	(15·8)	(26·3)	(57·9)	(100)	(91·3)	(4·3)	(4·3)	(100)
C	10	4	22	36	32	6	0	38
	(27·8)	(11·1)	(61·1)	(100)	(84·2)	(15·8)	(0)	(100)
D	11	1	9	21	53	3	0	56
	(52·4)	(4·8)	(42·9)	(100)	(94·6)	(5·4)	(0)	(100)
Total	33	20	42	95	110	21	2	133
	(34·7)	(21·1)	(44·2)	(100)	(82·7)	(15·8)	(1·5)	(100)

* Age codes: A, 1;6–1;10; B, 1;11–2;2; C, 2;3–2;6; D, 2;7–2;11.
[a] Cor, correct; Trn, truncation of initial syllable; S-s, stress shift.
[b] Percentages in parentheses.

age. Aggregated over all samples, Marloes produces considerably more incorrect realizations than Daan (65 % vs. 17 %). This difference is primarily related to a difference in the pattern of development parallel to the one noted before. The percentage of Marloes' correct realizations barely increases over age. Daan, by contrast, shows an abrupt improvement: from 25 % correct realizations in the first period to around 90 % after age 1;11. Most of Marloes' incorrect realizations are stress-shifts of the type WS→SW. However, all of these cases concern the same word, viz. the child's own name. The reason for this idiosyncracy is not clear. Daan most frequently truncates (ex. 10); his stress-shifts affect only two words, *lawaai* ('noise') and *Ireen*. Overall, 19·2 % of the WS tokens in both corpora are realized with an SW rhythm, and 17·9 % are realized as monosyllables. Monosyllabic realization is predominant in the first four months of the observation period (Daan: 68·8 %, Marloes: 52·6 %).

(10a) ballon /ba'lɔn/ 'balloon': [lɔn] (D 1;7)
   (b) papier /pa'pi:r/ 'paper': [pi:ʀ] (D 1;10)
   (c) konijn /ko'nɛin/ 'rabbit': [nɛin] (D 2;5)

A sudden increase in the amount of correct realizations in Daan's corpus, similar to the one observed for the WS words, is present in the WSW words, as Table 3 shows. In Marloes' data, again, the improvement appears to be

TABLE 3. *Realizations of WSW words*

Age*	Cor[a]	Ts	Tsw	Rst	Tot
		Marloes			
A	0	1	2	0	3
	(0)[b]	(33·3)	(66·7)	(0)	(100)
B	5	0	13	0	18
	(27·8)	(0)	(72·2)	(0)	(100)
C	10	0	14	1	25
	(40)	(0)	(56)	(4)	(100)
D	17	0	1	0	18
	(94·4)	(0)	(5·6)	(0)	(100)
Total	32	1	30	1	64
	(50)	(1·6)	(46·9)	(1·6)	(100)
		Daan			
A	1	0	19	0	20
	(5)	(0)	(95)	(0)	(100)
B	17	0	6	0	23
	(73·9)	(0)	(26·1)	(0)	(100)
C	11	0	3	1	15
	(73·3)	(0)	(20)	(6·7)	(100)
D	17	0	3	2	22
	(77·3)	(0)	(13·6)	(9·1)	(100)
Total	46	0	31	3	80
	(57·5)	(0)	(38·8)	(3·8)	(100)

* Age codes as in Table 2.
[a] Cor, correct; Ts, truncation to S; Tsw, truncation to SW; Rst, rest.
[b] Percentages in parentheses.

more gradual. Overall, 54 % of all word tokens are incorrectly realized. Most of these cases involve deletion of the initial weak syllable (ex. 11). It should be noted that truncations to WS do not occur. Furthermore, the frequency of monosyllabic realization is nearly zero. Overall, 42·4 % of all WSW words in both children are realized as SW. During the first four months, this percentage is higher, 66·7 % in Marloes and 95 % in Daan.

(11*a*) kastanje /ˌkɑsˈtɑnjə/ 'chestnut': [ˈtɑnə] (M 1;10)
  (*b*) pantoffel /ˌpɑnˈtɔfəl/ 'slipper': [ˈtɔfət] (M 2;1)
  (*c*) giraffen /ˌʃiˈrɑfə/ 'giraffes': [ˈsɑfə] (D 1;11)
  (*d*) verwarming /fərˈʋɑrˌmɪŋ/ 'heater': [ˈfʋɑmɪŋ] (D 2;6)

As can be seen in Table 4, the percentages of incorrectly realized WWS

TABLE 4. *Realizations of WWS words*

Age*	Cor[a]	Ts	Tws	S-s	Rst	Tot
			Marloes			
A	0	0	3	1	0	4
	(0)[b]	(0)	(75)	(25)	(0)	(100)
B	17	0	4	8	0	29
	(58·6)	(0)	(13·8)	(27·6)	(0)	(100)
C	11	0	7	3	0	21
	(52·4)	(0)	(33·3)	(14·3)	(0)	(100)
D	10	0	2	1	0	13
	(76·9)	(0)	(15·4)	(7·7)	(0)	(100)
Total	38	0	16	13	0	67
	(56·7)	(0)	(23·9)	(19·4)	(0)	(100)
			Daan			
A	3	13	3	1	0	20
	(15)	(65)	(15)	(5)	(0)	(100)
B	12	1	2	2	1	18
	(66·7)	(5·6)	(11·1)	(11·1)	(9·6)	(100)
C	10	0	0	3	1	14
	(71·4)	(0)	(0)	(21·4)	(7·1)	(100)
D	7	1	1	2	0	11
	(63·6)	(9·1)	(9·1)	(18·2)	(0)	(100)
Total	32	15	6	8	2	63
	(50·8)	(23·8)	(9·5)	(12·7)	(3·2)	(100)

* Age codes as in Table 2.
[a] Cor, correct; Ts, truncation to S; Tws, truncation to WS; S-s, Stress shift; Rst, rest.
[b] Percentages in parentheses.

words in the two children do not differ very much: 43 % in Marloes and 49 % in Daan. One-syllable truncations (ex. 12) make up 55 % of all incorrect renderings in Marloes' corpus and 19 % in Daan's corpus. In most of these cases, the syllable bearing secondary stress is retained (12*a, b, c*). In some other cases, it was impossible to determine which syllable was removed (cf. 12*d, e*). Daan produces relatively many two-syllable truncations (ex. 13). Stress shifts, with or without syllable deletions, occur more often in Marloes than in Daan (ex. 14). Overall, 11·5 % of all WWS words are realized as monosyllables, and 3·8 % as SW patterns.

(12*a*) paraplu /ˌparaˈply/ 'umbrella': [paˈply] (M 2;1)
  (*b*) boerderij /ˌburdəˈrɛɪ/ 'farm': [buˈrɛɪ] (D 2;0)
  (*c*) Marjolijn /ˌmɑrjoˈlɛɪn/ : [mɑˈlɛɪn] (D 2;11)
  (*d*) microfoon /ˌmikroˈfon/ 'microphone': [miˈkʀon] (M 1;9)
  (*e*) Mickey Mouse /ˌmɪkiˈmɑus/ : [miˈjʌys] (M 2;0)

(13*a*) Evelien /ˌefəˈlin/ : [liːn] (D 1;7)
  (*b*) chocola /ˌʃokoˈla/ 'chocolate': [la] (D 1;7)

(c)	papegaai	/ˌpɑpə'xaj/	'parrot':	[pɑːj]	(D 1;7)
(14a)	telefoon	/ˌtelə'fon/	'telephone':	['teːteː]	(M 1;7)
(b)	Sinterklaas	/ˌsɪntər'klas/ :		['sɪntəklas]	(M 1;7)
(c)	Zwarte Piet	/ˌsʋɑrtə'pit/ :		['sʋɑrtəpit]	(D 2;2)
(d)	krokodil	/ˌkroko'dɪl/	'crocodile':	['kʀokədɪl]	(D 2;6)

The proportions of correct and incorrect realizations presented thus far all refer to TOKENS. Thus, it is not yet revealed whether words (types) are consistently realized in a particular way, or whether there is variation. Particularly, in order to decide at which level of representation a putative rhythmic constraint takes effect (lexical representations or phonological representations constructed during utterance planning), it is relevant to decide whether there is free variation. Free variation is defined as the appearance of different rhythmic forms – either correct or incorrect – throughout the period of observation, without a discernable approximation towards the adult form. If the latter should occur, it would be labelled systematic variation.

To explore this issue, we looked at instances of polysyllabic words (other than SW) which were used throughout the whole observation period. To minimize the effect of putative speech errors or other transitory problems, as well as misperceptions on the part of the transcribers of our data set, we added the criteria that at least two different types of realization should be present, and that each of these should be represented by at least two tokens. We found 13 words in Daan's corpus, and 9 in Marloes' corpus that met these criteria. Fourteen of these words showed free variation, which is illustrated by the examples in Table 5. These findings appear to contradict the conjecture that it is the lexical representations that are rhythmically constrained.

Determiners

In order to decide whether the rhythmic form of a putative phrase affects the (non)realization of unstressed, closed-class words, we took stock of all locations in the children's first 100 utterances in each sample where a determiner (usually an article) would have been obligatory in adult speech. We determined the proportion of cases in which a determiner was present under two conditions: (i) the post-determiner content word had an initial S-syllable, or (ii) the content word had an initial W-syllable.

This analysis was complicated by two problems. First, as we have seen above, the realized forms of nouns and other content words may (often quite regularly) deviate from the target form. Hence, the question arises whether we should consider the realized form of the post-determiner content word, or the target form. In the ensuing analysis we have opted for the former, to avoid possibly ill-grounded assumptions about underlying forms in the

TABLE 5. *Examples of free variation of the rhythmic structure in successive renderings of words*

Target form	Word	Age	Utt.no.	Realized form
		Marloes		
WS	*banaan*	1;10	36	maːn
	'banana'	1;10	37	maːn
		1;10	38	maːn
		1;10	39	naːn
		1;10	40	mə'naːn
		1;10	42	maːn
		1;10	43	mə'naːn
		1;10	44	maːn
		1;10	47	naːn
WWS	*microfoon*	1;9	8	mi'krɔːn
	'microphone'	1;9	12	mə'kʀoːn
		1;10	159	mə'xoːn
		2;2	1	miko'xoːn
		2;2	3	mɪko'xoːn
		2;2	86	kɪŋ'xoːn
		2;2	87	miko'xoːn
		2;2	88	mikə'xoːn
		2;2	89	miko'xoːn
		2;9	87	miko'foːn
		2;9	88	miko'foːn
		Daan		
WS	*kapot*	1;7	130	pɔt
	'broken'	1;7	134	dɑ'bɔt
		1;9	38	pot
		2;0	151	kə'pɔt
		2;0	152	ka'pɔt
		2;1	127	ka'pɔt
		2;1	128	ka'pɔt
SWW	*olifant*	1;8	35	'ojəf…fɑnt
	'elephant'	1;9	46	'oːfɑnt
		1;9	55	'oːlifɑnt
		1;11	129	oːlə'fɑnt
		1;11	135	oːlə'fɑnt
		2;0	40	'oːləfɑnt
		2;0	41	oːlə'fɑnt
		2;0	52	'oːləfɑnt
		2;1	155	oːlə'fɑnt
		2;1	161	oːlə'fɑnt

child's mental lexicon. A parallel analysis was also performed on the – much smaller – subset of noun phrases in which the realized rhythmic form of the content word (noun or adjective) corresponded to the adult model. However, the results of this analysis do not differ from those presented below.

A second problem is that our subjects (particularly Marloes) often produce filler sounds (schwas) at putative determiner positions, which cannot be

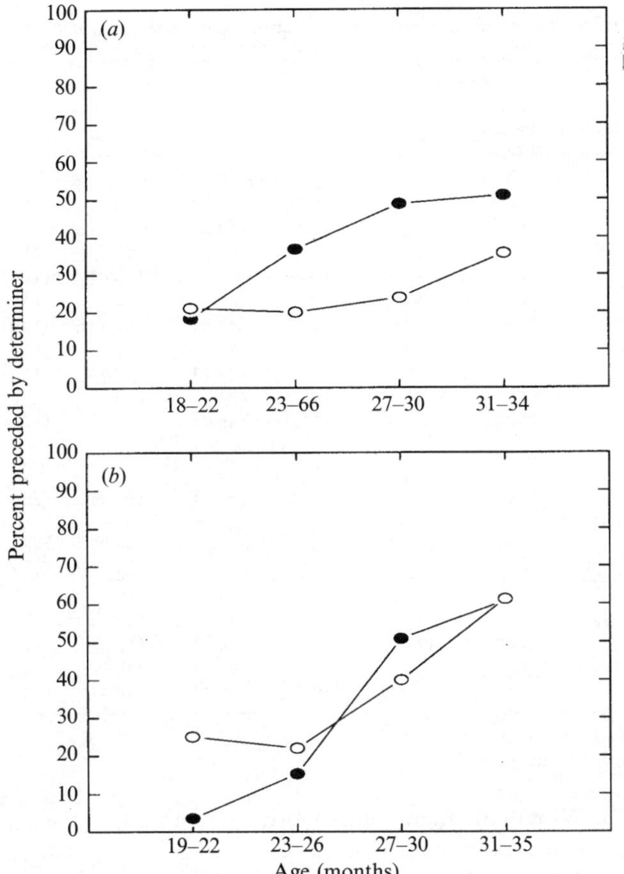

Fig. 3. The percentages of realized determiners (including schwa) as a function of age and rhythmic form of the subsequent content word. (*a*) Marloes, (*b*) Daan. Solid circles, S-initial words; open circles, W-initial words.

readily identified as one of the Dutch article forms. However, on the basis of our impression that the distribution of these fillers equals the distribution of determiners in corresponding adult sentences, we decided to count them as determiners. A preliminary analysis of the much smaller number of cases in which the determiner was phonetically distinct yielded the same pattern of results as the one reported below.

Fig. 3 depicts the percentage of cases in which a determiner was produced where it would have been obligatory according to adult standards. It is obvious that the proportion of realized determiners increase over age. If the rhythmic constraint determines the form not only of words, but also of noun phrases, it can be expected that fewer articles will be produced before words

TABLE 6. *Articles in sentence-initial and non-sentence-initial positions*

	Initial positions			Other positions		
Age*	Absent	Present	Tot	Absent	Present	Tot
			Marloes			
A	225	50	275	60	13	73
	(81·8)[a]	(18·2)	(100)	(82·2)	(17·8)	(100)
B	119	46	165	105	79	184
	(72·1)	(27·9)	(100)	(57·1)	(42·9)	(100)
C	58	39	97	66	69	135
	(60)	(40)	(100)	(48·9)	(51·1)	(100)
D	30	26	56	51	67	118
	(53·6)	(46·4)	(100)	(43·2)	(56·8)	(100)
Total	432	161	593	282	228	510
	(72·8)	(27·2)	(100)	(55·3)	(44·7)	(100)
			Daan			
A	279	4	283	25	9	34
	(98·6)	(1·4)	(100)	(73·5)	(26·5)	(100)
B	137	16	153	57	22	79
	(89·5)	(10·5)	(100)	(72·2)	(27·8)	(100)
C	80	33	113	48	93	141
	(70·8)	(29·2)	(100)	(34)	(66)	(100)
D	61	31	92	42	129	171
	(66·3)	(33·7)	(100)	(24·6)	(75·4)	(100)
Total	557	84	641	172	253	425
	(86·9)	(12·1)	(100)	(40·5)	(59·5)	(100)

* Age codes as in Table 2.
[a] Percentages in parentheses.

with an initial W-syllable than before words with an initial S-syllable. In the former case the article-content word string would involve two adjacent W-syllables, whereas in the latter case, the article (W) and the first syllable of the content word would constitute an alternating pattern, which follows the requirement of rhythmic alternation. Marloes' results agree with this prediction: there are significantly more determiner omissions before W-initial words than before S-initial words ($\chi^2(1) = 4\cdot3$, $p < 0\cdot05$). This result is not replicated for Daan.

The figures in Table 6 show that for both children, articles are significantly less often realized in sentence-initial positions than in sentence-medial positions (Marloes: $\chi^2(1) = 188\cdot33$, $p < 0\cdot001$; Daan: $\chi^2(1) = 254\cdot77$, $p < 0\cdot0001$). This finding suggests that it may be difficult for these children to start an utterance with an unstressed word, which may be a sentence-level parallel of the tendency to delete word-initial weak syllables shown before.

DISCUSSION

We have studied two children's language production in terms of rhythmic patterns, i.e. the alternation of weak (unstressed) and strong (stressed) syllables. Our aim was to determine whether the realized forms of words and noun phrases meet the requirements that constitute a trochaic constraint, as proposed by Allen & Hawkins (1978, 1980). Furthermore, we examined whether the intake of words showed signs of a rhythmically based 'lexical filtering'. With regard to the latter point, we found that our subjects' early lexical inventories appear to be dominated by S-initial words. Moreover, WS and WSW words are quite infrequent, and words with an alternation of weak and strong syllables (i.e. SW, WS, and WSW) are preferred to words with a non-alternating pattern, so that, as a result, WWS words are marginal. However, we could not decide whether a rhythmical bias was effective in the intake of words from the input, since we were unable to show that the proportions of rhythmic types differ from those of the mothers' input vocabularies. Additionally, we observed that the children's vocabularies – in terms of rhythmic patterns – diverge from those of their counterparts' mothers. Taken together, the results may mean that the composition of the children's vocabularies simply reflects the statistical properties of the input. That is, since words that are frequently heard presumably have a higher chance of being acquired than words that are infrequently heard, the distribution of rhythmic types in the child's lexicon will reflect that of the input vocabulary. On the other hand, the structure of the mother's speech might encourage the child to focus on particular types of words. To decide empirically between these two interpretations appears to be rather difficult, however, At any rate, both assumptions may explain why monosyllabic words are considerably more frequent in Marloes than in Daan, since Marloes' mother uses more monosyllabic words than Daan's mother.

As regards the realizations of words, some rather systematic tendencies were observed. SW-words are nearly always produced correctly. SWW-words are considerably more often deformed, and incorrect realizations of W-initial words are very frequent, particularly in the early samples. Generally, the observed deformations agree with the patterns reported by Allen & Hawkins (1978, 1980): SWW words lose one of their weak syllables (though not necessarily the first), or the weak syllables may be conflated. WS and WSW words most often lose their initial syllable. The trochaic constraint does not appear to be all-embracing, however, which also corresponds to Allen & Hawkins' (1980) observations. Marloes, for instance, shows a preference to delete only one weak syllable from WWS words (which produces WS). Moreover, neither of the children shows a tendency to append filler syllables to monosyllabic words (S → SW), and the pattern of truncations also indicates that monosyllables are acceptable renderings.

Nevertheless, the tendency toward the trochaic pattern is quite clear. During the first four months of observation, 30% of the words that (in their adult form) have a structure other than S or SW are realized as monosyllables, and 31% are realized with an SW-pattern. In sum, the data suggest that the children do adapt the word forms to a SW-template, in which, however, the weak part is optional. Truncation appears to be the preferred strategy by which this adaptation is effected. Stress shifting is observed, but appears to play a minor and presumably idiosyncratic role (but see Fikkert, 1993, who claims that stress-shifting becomes more important in a later stage of development). It appears that the adaptation of words to the trochaic pattern is a stochastic process. In particular, the data suggest that one target word may be associated with various alternating realizations. Similar observations have been made in the segmental domain (Ferguson & Farwell, 1975).

Unfortunately, Dutch is not the ideal testing ground for the hypothesis that a trochaic rhythm in speech reflects a prosodic developmental universal. In view of the preponderance of trochaic patterns in Dutch, our subjects' tendency to produce trochaic patterns may very well be the result of their initial hypothesis concerning the metrical structure of Dutch (see Demuth 1992, for an elaboration of this idea). To gain more insight into the issue of universality, one should look at the behaviour of young children who acquire languages in which S-initial patterns are infrequent, such as French.

The results with regard to the realization of determiners suggest that rhythmic requirements may affect the form of phrases, as well as words, in production. We found that Marloes more often produced determiners before S-initial words than before W-initial words, which may be ascribed to the fact that the WS...-string resulting in the former case meets the requirement of alternation, whereas a WW...-string does not. Unfortunately, this result was not replicated in Daan, which, however, may be ascribed to Daan's faster abandonment of the rhythmic constraint, as indicated by the abrupt increase of correct realizations of W-initial words around age two. Nevertheless, in both children a tendency to omit sentence-initial determiners was observed, which accords with Gerken's (1990, 1991) experimental findings regarding the omission of sentence-initial closed class words. This pattern appears to be a sentence-level parallel of the omission of word-initial weak syllables. This finding corroborates the suggestion that particular phenomena in child language that are traditionally associated with syntactic or semantic immaturity, such as the omission of sentence-initial subject pronouns (Hyams, 1986), or, for that matter, the optionality of grammatical morphemes, may in fact be the result of a phonological mechanism.

The determiner results, as well as the observed free variation in the realization of word forms are compatible with the suggestion that the rhythmic constraint is implemented in the 'transduction' mechanism, rather than in the lexicon. We surmise that the observed behaviour can be understood as the result of a process by which 'melodic' information, stored in the lexicon, is associated with representations that encode metrical rhythm. This process can be seen as a part of the utterance planning mechanism (see also Gerken, 1990, 1991). The results of this and related studies appear to give some clues as to the details of this process.

First, the 'merging' of segments or features from two neighbouring syllables (see, for instance, examples 1, 11*c*, 11*d*, 12*d*, 12*e*, 13*c*), seems to rule out a mechanism proposed by Gerken (1990, 1991), in which the mapping of melodic information onto syllabic templates, and the mapping of syllables onto prosodic templates are distinct. Such a mechanism would predict the omission/preservation of COMPLETE syllables, rather than syllable constituents. Rather, it appears that syllabic and prosodic mapping are conflated, as is suggested by some versions of nonlinear phonology (Fee, 1991). We could speculate that the melodic (segmental or featural) information from the lexicon is associated with the independently addressable onset, peak and coda slots of disyllabic templates, of which the leftmost peak slot is marked 'strong', and the rightmost 'weak'. Second, the order in which melodic information is mapped onto this template seems to be correlated with relative prominence. Of course, the clearest instantiation of this principle is that primary-stress-bearing vowels are systematically preserved in children's productions. Furthermore, we have observed, as others have before us (Lohuis-Weber, 1991), that if a multisyllabic word containing a non-reducible vowel as well as a reducible vowel or schwa is truncated, the non-reducible vowel is retained. These observations suggest that relative prominence is an attribute of vowels as they are stored in the lexicon. This hypothesis may explain why stress-shifting is only a marginal phenomenon in our subjects' output. It would entail the alteration of inherent attributes of the stored information, whereas truncation appears to be the 'coincidental' outcome of a mechanism whereby as much melodic information as possible is linked to the most appropriate slots in a restricted template (but see Fikkert 1993, for a competing view).

Given these – speculative – hypotheses, the attainment of the specific rhythmic structures of the target language would imply the gradual dissolution of the rhythmic restrictions on output representations, or rather, the acquisition of rhythm and stress rules that allow for the construction of other than SW-templates. Thus, we would expect to find a connection between the acquisition of language-specific metrical rules and the disappearance of the SW-constraint. One of the characteristics of the Dutch stress system is quantity sensitivity: a heavy syllable, i.e. a syllable with a branching rime, cannot occupy a weak position in a metrical foot. Some of our observations are suggestive of the acquisition of this knowledge, viz. Daan's successive renderings of the word *olifant* /'oli̯fɑnt/ ('elephant', see Table 5). The nice thing about *olifant* is, that it is an exception to the rule of quantity sensitivity.

The final syllable /fant/ is heavy (superheavy, in fact), and since Dutch stress is assigned from right to left (Kager, 1989), it should have had primary stress (compare *ledikant* /ledi'kant/ 'bed'). Daan's mispronunciations of *olifant* as [oli'fant], which begin to occur at age 1;11, seem to imply that he has acquired the quantity sensitivity rule and is actually overregularizing. At approximately the same time, the proportion of correct productions of W-initial words, WWS among them, shows a sudden increase. This observation provides some support for our assumption that the trochaic patterns in child speech are the outcome of a grammar-based restriction on phonological representations. Furthermore, it agrees with Dresher & Kaye's (1990) suggestion that quantity sensitivity is one of the first subsystems to be grasped by the child in the course of acquiring language-specific stress rules.

REFERENCES

Allen, G. D. & Hawkins, S. (1978). The development of phonological rhythm. In A. Bell & J. B. Hooper (eds). *Syllables and segments*. Amsterdam: North Holland.

—— & —— (1980). Phonological rhythm: definition and development. In G. H. Yeni-Komshian, J. F. Kavanagh & C. A. Ferguson (eds). *Child Phonology*: Vol. I. *Production*, New York: Academic Press.

Brown, R. (1973). *A first language: the early stages*. Cambridge, MA: Harvard University Press.

Clark, H. H. & Clark, E. V. (1977). *Psychology and language: an introduction to psycholinguistics*. New York: Harcourt Brace Jovanovich.

Cutler, A. & Carter, D. M. (1987). The predominance of strong initial syllables in the English vocabulary. *Computer Speech and Language* **2**, 133–42.

Cutler, A. & Norris, D. (1988). The role of strong syllables in segmentation for lexical access. *Journal of Experimental Psychology: Human Perception and Performance* **14**, 113–21.

Dell, G. S. (1986). A spreading-activation model of retrieval in sentence production. *Psychological Review* **93**, 283–321.

Demuth, K. (1992). On the 'underspecification' of functional categories in early grammars. In B. Lust (ed.), *Syntactic theory and first language acquisition*. Hillsdale: Erlbaum.

Den Os, E. (1990a). The development of prosody. Poster presented at the Fifth International Congress for the Study of Child Language, Budapest, July.

—— (1990b). Development of temporal properties in the speech of one child between one and three years of age. *Proceedings of the Institute of Phonetic Sciences of the University of Amsterdam* **14**, 39–52.

Dresher, B. E. & Kaye, J. D. (1990). A computational learning model for metrical phonology. *Cognition* **34**, 137–95.

Fee, E. J. (1991). *Segments and syllables in early language acquisition*. Paper presented at the Boston University Conference on Language Acquisition, October.

Ferguson, C. A. & Farwell, C. B. (1975). Words and sounds in early language acquisition. *Language* **51**, 419–39.

Fikkert, P. (1991). Child phonology from a theoretical perspective. Paper presented to the OTS Linguistics Colloquium, November.

—— (1993). The acquisition of Dutch stress. In M. Verrips & F. Wijnen (eds), *Amsterdam Series in Child Language Development*, Vol. 1.

Gerken, L. A. (1990). Performance constraints in early language: the case of subjectless sentences. *Papers and Reports in Child Language Development* **29**, 54–61.

—— (1991). The metrical basis for children's subjectless sentences. *Journal of Memory and Language* **30**, 431–51.

—— (1992). Young children's representations of prosodic phonology: evidence from English-speakers' weak syllable omissions. Unpublished paper, State University of New York at Buffalo.

Gerken, L. A., Landau, B. & Remez, R. E. (1990). Function morphemes in young children's speech perception and production. *Developmental Psychology* **26**, 204–16.

Gleitman, L. R., Gleitman, H., Landau, B. & Wanner, E. (1988). Where learning begins: initial representations for language learning. In F. J. Newmeyer (ed.), *Linguistics: the Cambridge survey*. Cambridge: C.U.P.

Hochberg, J. G. (1988). First steps in the acquisition of Spanish stress. *Journal of Child Language* **15**, 273–92.

Hyams, N. (1986). *Language acquisition and the theory of parameters*. Dordrecht: Reidel.

Kager, R. W. J. (1989). A metrical theory of stress and destressing in Dutch. Unpublished doctoral dissertation, University of Utrecht.

Kelly, M. H. & Bock, J. K. (1988). Stress in time. *Journal of Experimental Psychology: Human Perception and Performance* **14**, 389–403.

Levelt, W. J. M. (1989). *Speaking: from intention to articulation*. Cambridge, MA: MIT Press.

Lohuis-Weber, H. (1991). Kinder-Stress: een onderzoek naar de rol van klemtoon bij moedertaalverwerving. Unpublished M.A. Thesis, University of Utrecht, Dept. of Dutch Language and Literature.

Menyuk, P., Menn, L. & Silber, R. (1986). Early strategies for the perception and production of words and sounds. In P. Fletcher & M. Garman (eds), *Language acquisition* (2nd ed.). Cambridge: C.U.P.

Petretic, P. A. & Tweney, R. D. (1977). Does comprehension precede production? The development of children's responses to telegraphic sentences of varying grammatical adequacy. *Journal of Child Language* **4**, 201–209.

Pye, C. (1983). Mayan telegraphese: intonational determinants of inflectional development in Quiché Mayan. *Language* **59**, 583–604.

Quené, H. (1992). Integration of acoustic-phonetic cues in word segmentation. In: M. E. H. Schouten (ed), *The auditory processing of speech: from sounds to words*. Berlin: Mouton-De Gruyter.

Shipley, E. F., Smith, C. S. & Gleitman, L. R. (1969). A study in the acquisition of language: free responses to commands. *Language* **45**, 322–42.

Radford, A. (1990). *Syntactic theory and the acquisition of English syntax*. Oxford: Blackwell.

Schwartz, R. G. (1988). Phonological factors in early lexical acquisition. In M. D. Smith and J. L. Locke (eds), *The emergent lexicon: the child's development of a linguistic vocabulary*. New York: Academic Press.

Waterson, N. (1971). Child phonology: a prosodic view. *Journal of Linguistics* **7**, 179–211.

Wijnen, F. (1990). The development of sentence planning. *Journal of Child Language* **17**, 651–75.

—— (1992). Incidental word and sound errors in young speakers. *Journal of Memory and Language* **31**, 734–55.

J. Child Lang. **21** (1994), 85–123. Copyright © 1994 Cambridge University Press

Developmental and stylistic variation in the composition of early vocabulary*

ELIZABETH BATES
University of California, San Diego

VIRGINIA MARCHMAN
University of Wisconsin

DONNA THAL
San Diego State University and *University of California, San Diego*

LARRY FENSON
San Diego State University

PHILIP DALE
University of Washington, Seattle

J. STEVEN REZNICK
Yale University

JUDY REILLY
San Diego State University

AND

JEFF HARTUNG
University of California, San Diego

ABSTRACT

Results are reported for stylistic and developmental aspects of vocabulary composition for 1,803 children and families who participated in the tri-city norming of a new parental report instrument, the *MacArthur Communicative Development Inventories*. We replicate previous studies with small samples showing extensive variation in use of common nouns between age 0;8 and 1;4 (i.e. 'referential style'), and in the proportion of vocabulary made up of closed-class words between 1;4 and 2;6 (i.e. 'analytic' vs. 'holistic' style). However, both style dimensions are confounded with developmental changes in the composition of the

[*] Address for correspondence: Elizabeth Bates, Center for Research in Language, University of California at San Diego, 9500 Gilman Drive, La Jolla, CA, 92093-0526, USA.

lexicon, including three 'waves' of reorganization: (1) an initial increase in percentage of common nouns from 0 to 100 words, followed by a proportional decrease; (2) a slow linear increase in verbs and other predicates, with the greatest gains taking place between 100 and 400 words; (3) no proportional development at all in the use of closed-class vocabulary between 0 and 400 words, followed by a sharp increase from 400 to 680 words. When developmental changes in noun use are controlled, referential-style measures do not show the association with developmental precocity reported in previous studies, although these scores are related to maternal education. By contrast, when developmental changes in grammatical function word use are controlled, high closed-class scores are associated with a slower rate of development. We suggest that younger children may have less perceptual acuity and/or shorter memory spans than older children with the same vocabulary size. As a result, the younger children may ignore unstressed function words until a later point in development while the older children tend to reproduce perceptual details that they do not yet understand. Longitudinal data show that early use of function words (under 400 words) is not related to grammatical levels after the 400-word point, confirming our 'stylistic' interpretation of early closed-class usage. We close with recommendations for the unconfounding of stylistic and developmental variance in research on individual differences in language development, and provide look-up tables that will permit other investigators to pull these aspects apart.

INTRODUCTION

Of all the individual differences described to date in the literature on early child language, variations in rate present the least interesting challenge to traditional 'universalist' models of development. If it can be shown that all children go through the same basic sequence, activating a common set of structures and processes, then small variations in the onset time for specific language milestones might represent little more than a minor perturbation to a maturational theory (like variations in the onset of puberty). Putative variations in style of development are more problematic, because they raise questions about the order in which structures are acquired, and the mechanisms used to acquire those structures.

Consider the widespread claim that some children evidence an 'analytic' approach to language learning, while others display a 'holistic' or 'Gestalt' style (Peters, 1977; Plunkett, 1993; for a detailed review, see Bates, Bretherton & Snyder 1988). It has been argued that these stylistic contrasts hold up across traditional linguistic domains, including phonology, lexical semantics and grammar. In phonological development, some children reportedly 'learn the tune before the words', picking up suprasegmental cues (intonation, phrasal packaging) before they tackle the problem of segmenting the speech input into phonemic or syllable units. Other children start with phonemic or syllabic segments and work their way up to the use of larger and longer units. At the lexical semantic level, some children reportedly start their linguistic careers by emphasizing the referential functions of language, mapping strings of sounds onto their most obvious real-world correlates (usually common objects); other children start learning words from a different point of view, emphasizing the social and instrumental functions of language, imitating and reproducing strings of sounds for their social effects without a clear understanding of word-referent relations. At the level of first word combinations, some children reportedly begin by producing telegraphic utterances, strings of uninflected content words (including use of proper names to refer to speaker and listener); others use inflections and function words from the very beginning, although there is reason to believe that these functors are initially embedded in memorized routines or formulae (resulting in, for example, pronoun errors like *Carry you!* to mean *Carry me!*, presumably derived from a rough segmentation of adult strings like *Do you want me to carry you?*).

In each of these domains, the extreme types stand at opposite ends of a unimodal distribution, with most children occupying a middle ground. However, the existence of such extreme types lends support to the notion that children can vary in their choice of tools for language learning, with some children relying heavily on strategies for the segmentation, extraction and generalization of relatively small units, while others rely on storage and retrieval of relatively large but 'underanalysed' input strings. This variation in choice of tools leads, in turn, to qualitative variations in the order of acquisition of basic linguistic structures (e.g. syllables vs. phonological phrases; nominal vs. non-nominal forms; content words vs. functors). If this kind of variation is confirmed on a relatively large scale, it raises serious problems for any theory based on the Modal Child (cf. Fenson, Dale, Reznick, Thal, Bates, Hartung, Pethick & Reilly, 1993).

There are, however, at least two reasons not to abandon the Modal Child quite yet. The first has to do with questions about the reliability of data on individual variations in style. The second has to do with the possibility that variations in style are confounded with variations in rate.

With regard to the first point, most studies of stylistic variation have been carried out on relatively small samples. Some of the most influential studies have involved individual cases that illustrate exceptions to an expected 'textbook' pattern of development, e.g. the extreme holistic style evidenced by Peters' subject Seth (Peters, 1977), the extreme analytic style evidenced by Bates' daughter Julia (Bates *et al.* 1988), or the four children discussed in a rich array of studies by Lois Bloom and her colleagues (Bloom, Lightbown & Hood, 1975; see also Bloom, 1991). Group studies investigating the generality and/or long-term stability of this stylistic variation are typically based on samples ranging in size from 10 (Ferguson & Farwell, 1975; Vihman, 1986; Vihman, Ferguson & Elbert, 1986; Vihman & Greenlee, 1987; Vihman & Miller, 1988) to 18 (in Nelson's pioneering study of lexical style in the one-word stage – Nelson, 1973), to 27 (Bates *et al.* 1988), topping out in sample sizes between 30 and 40 (e.g. Dixon & Shore, 1992). Although it is useful to point out that certain kinds of variation are POSSIBLE, they fall well short of the demonstrations we would need to establish the incidence and prevalence of target variations in the general population.

The second problem revolves around alternative interpretations for the style variations that have been demonstrated to date. In some studies, there appears to be a correlation between style and rate of development. For example, a number of studies have reported that 'referential style' (i.e. a high proportion of common nouns early in the one-word stage) is associated with faster rates of development. When age is held constant, there is a significant positive correlation between overall vocabulary size and percentage of nouns as a function of total vocabulary (Bates *et al.* 1988). However, in recent reviews of the Bates *et al.* (1988) study, Lieven & Pine (1990) and Pine & Lieven (1990) have provided evidence suggesting that there is also a monotonic increase in percentage of nouns as a function of total vocabulary when the SAME children are followed longitudinally across the period from 1 to 50 words. Hence the apparent correlation between precocity and referential style may reflect developmental rather than stylistic variation in noun use.

In their critiques, Lieven & Pine do not dispute the existence of stylistic variations; instead, they are simply trying to point out that expressive or holistic style is not necessarily 'bad' for children. However, this apparent confound between developmental variance and measures of style could pose a serious challenge to the literature on individual differences. If Lieven & Pine are correct, it is possible that the entire body of evidence for qualitative variation in language learning reflects nothing more than a 'snapshot' look at children who are developing at an abnormally fast or slow pace – reducing putative qualitative variations to a familiar unifactorial theory of development.

There are already a few psychometric studies that weaken this unifactorial interpretation. In their longitudinal study of individual differences, Bates *et al.* (1988) conducted confirmatory factor analyses to determine the number of factors needed to account for variations in lexical and grammatical performance within and across age levels (at 1;1, 1;8 and 2;4). Depending on the age level in question, at least three factors were needed to account for the variance: a comprehension factor, a rote production factor, and an 'analysed production' factor that overlapped in part with measures of comprehension. Dixon & Shore (1991) have used confirmatory factor analysis in studies of lexical and grammatical ability at 1;8; they report that at least two factors are needed to fit the data, reflecting something very like the analytic/holistic contrast described in the individual difference literature. Hence there does appear to be more going on than global maturation, or a developmental version of Spearman's g. Nevertheless, our characterization of dimensions like 'analytic/holistic style' is still distressingly vague, and the possibility of a confound between quantitative and qualitative variation remains at many different points on the developmental landscape.

In this paper, we will present results from a study of individual differences in vocabulary development in 1,803 English-speaking children. These results are based on a parental report instrument that has been under development in our laboratories for more than 15 years (see Fenson *et al.* 1993 for details). A variety of studies have demonstrated the reliability and validity of this instrument (Dale, Bates, Reznick & Morisset, 1989; Dale, 1991; Camaioni, Caselli, Longobardi & Volterra, 1991; O'Hanlon, Washkevich & Thal, 1991; Jackson-Maldonado, Marchman, Thal, Bates & Gutierrez-Clellen, 1993) – enough to give us considerable confidence in the generality of these results. For example, the vocabulary checklists correlate positively and significantly with laboratory observations of vocabulary (from standard tests and free speech), with coefficients ranging from $+0.40$ to $+0.80$, depending on the study. The grammar measures obtained in Part II of the Toddler Scale (see Method, below) are also strongly correlated with laboratory measures of grammar. For example, Dale has shown that the grammatical complexity scale correlates with a laboratory measure of Mean Length of Utterance at $r = +0.88$ at age 1;8, and $r = +0.76$ at age 2;0. Despite these successes, there are marked limitations in the kind of information that can be obtained with parental report. For example, we can say nothing here about phonological development (e.g. segmental vs. suprasegmental approaches to the analysis of speech), nor about the frequency with which children use particular vocabulary types (i.e. type/token relations). We cannot distinguish between imitations and spontaneous speech, nor can we specify the range of contexts in which individual lexical items are used (e.g. flexible and productive use vs. memorized frames). However, we can provide an exceptionally clear view of developmental changes in the composition of vocabulary from 0;8 to 2;6, and we can establish the boundaries of variation in vocabulary composition within and across levels of development. This will permit us to disentangle variations in rate and style of development in the first stages of language learning.

One final cautionary note before we proceed. We will be carrying out a combination of developmental analyses (across vocabulary levels) and stylistic analyses (holding vocabulary level constant), using dependent variables like 'percentage of total vocabulary comprising common nouns', 'percentage of total vocabulary comprising verbs' and 'percentage of total vocabulary comprising grammatical function words'. In all of these analyses, the child's reported vocabulary will be analysed from the point of view of adult part-of-speech categories. That is, we will call an item a 'noun', 'verb' or 'function word' if that item functions as a noun, verb or function word in the adult language. And yet, we already know that small children often use words in ways that deviate from usage by adults. For example, detailed case studies have shown that a given child may use the adjective *hot* as a name for stoves, lightbulbs and other heat-bearing objects. *Pretty* may function as the name for jewellery, flowers and buttons. *Up* may be used in a fashion that bears more resemblance to an action verb than a preposition (e.g. used exclusively in contexts in which the child is asking to be picked up). And so forth. Because there is no necessary one-to-one relationship between adult part-of-speech categories and the way that words are used by individual children, what can we learn from a study of vocabulary composition that relies on adult classifications?

Our answer to this question is that adult part-of-speech categories are excellent INDEPENDENT VARIABLES. We do not assume that children in this age range necessarily represent or recognize categories like noun, verb, or grammatical function word. Instead, we treat these categories as a summary or short-hand grouping of many large-scale differences in the nature of the child's linguistic INPUT, including differences in the phonological, semantic, morphological and syntactic properties of words. To the extent that children treat nouns differently from verbs, content words differently from grammatical function words, and so forth, we can assume that they have been affected by these differences in the input characteristics of words. Developmental differences in the acquisition of part-of-speech types may be taken to reflect changes in the child's ability to deal with these types. In the same vein, individual differences in vocabulary composition (with developmental level held constant) can be taken to reflect qualitative variations in the child's sensitivity to the various characteristics that define part-of-speech categories in the adult language. Of course this kind of part-of-speech mapping can only take us so far. A great deal of additional work remains before we can determine which ASPECTS of the input have driven these developmental and/or stylistic patterns (i.e. whether these variations are tied to the phonological, semantic, morphological and/or syntactic characteristics that separate nouns, verbs, function words and other word types). Nevertheless, we are convinced that this is a reasonable place to begin.

METHOD

Subjects

Subjects were 1,803 infants aged between 0;8 and 2;6 whose parents participated in a tri-city norming study of the MacArthur Communicative Development Inventories, conducted in San Diego, Seattle and New Haven

(Fenson *et al.* 1993). Families of 673 children completed the CDI:Infants when their children were between 0;8 and 1;4; families of another 1,130 children completed the CDI:Toddlers when their children were aged between 1;4 and 2;6. Parents also filled out a basic information sheet, with information on sex and birth order, the child's medical history, exposure to languages other than English, and parental education and occupation. The education and occupation statistics were used to calculate a modified version of the Hollingshead social class inventory (Hollingshead, 1965). A minimum of 30 males and 30 females are represented at each one-month age level in both the Infant and the Toddler samples. Middle- to upper-middle-class families are overrepresented in the sample as a whole, and approximately 79 % of the mothers who participated in the study had at least 12 years of formal education. Children with serious health problems or extensive exposure to a language other than English were excluded from the study, based on the basic information sheet (the above numbers represent the total sample after these exclusionary criteria were applied).

Parents of 217 children in the Infant sample also completed the CDI:Toddlers an average of 6·8 months after participating in the cross-sectional study (S.D. = 0·68 months). The average age of these children was 1;1.14 at Time 1 (S.D. = 1·72 months), and 1;8.5 at Time 2 (S.D. = 1·86 months). Parents of another 228 children in the Toddler sample completed the CDI:Toddlers a second time approximately 6·5 months after the initial administration (S.D. = 1·25 months). The average age of these children was 1;8.12 at Time 1 (S.D. = 2·56 months) and 2;2.26 at Time 2 (S.D. = 2·42 months).

Materials

The CDI:Infants is composed of two sections. Part I is a checklist of 396 words that are among the first to appear in the vocabularies of young English-speaking children. Next to each word, the parent is asked to indicate if the child (*a*) understands that word, and (*b*) understands and produces that word.[1] The checklist is divided into 19 (broadly) semantic categories: sound effects (e.g. *moo, vroom*), animal names, vehicle names, toys, food items, articles of clothing, body parts, furniture, household objects, outside things and places to go, people (including proper nouns), routines and games (e.g.

---

[1] In earlier versions of the parent questionnaire, we tried to distinguish between words that the child understands and says, vs. words that the child says in a rote or imitative fashion with little or no comprehension. It became quite clear to us that most parents are unable to make this distinction; indeed, many rejected the distinction altogether, assuming that the child is able to understand any word that he or she can produce. For this reason, we decided to 'go with the parents' theory', assuming that production presupposes the ability to comprehend that word. Obviously this decision must be taken into account in interpreting results from this checklist.

peekaboo), verbs, words for time, adjectives, pronouns, question words, prepositions, and quantifiers. All forms are presented in their 'citation form' (e.g. verbs are listed as stems). Part II is a checklist of 63 communicative and/or symbolic gestures that also develop in this age range. Data for Part II of the Infant Scale will not be discussed in this paper.

The CDI:Toddlers is also composed of two sections. Part I is a checklist of 680 words (including the 396 words from the Infant list). In contrast with the Infant form, the Toddler form only asks about word production (previous research in our laboratories has shown that most parents of normally developing children are unable to track word comprehension after the age of 1;4. The Toddler list is divided into 22 (broadly) semantic categories. In addition to the 19 categories from the Infant checklist, the Toddler list also contains separate sections for 'helping verbs' (auxiliaries and modals) and conjunctions, and the Infant category 'outside things and places to go' is divided into two separate sections, 'outside things' and 'places'.

Part II of the Toddler Scale looks at early grammar, from several different points of view (for a detailed discussion, see Dale, 1991; Fenson *et al.* 1993; Marchman & Bates, 1994). It begins with a single question regarding the onset of word combinations, where parents are asked to check 'not yet', 'sometimes' or 'often'. If the child is reportedly producing any word combinations at all, parents are asked to continue to a series of questions about the nature of word combinations and grammatical forms. These include a checklist of verbs and nouns in regular and irregular inflected forms, a section in which parents are asked to write in the three longest utterances that their child has produced in the last few weeks, and a separate section on grammatical complexity. The complexity section is made up of 37 sentence pairs, each reflecting a minimal contrast in grammatical complexity (e.g. *Kitty sleeping* vs. *Kitty is sleeping*). Parents are asked to indicate which alternative within each pair 'sounds most like the way that your child is talking right now'. The minimal contrasts tapped by this subscale include the presence or absence of copulas, auxiliaries, modals, possessives, plurals, tense markers, prepositions and articles in obligatory contexts. It also includes a few items in which both items are grammatically correct but vary in complexity (e.g. *Lookit me!* vs. *Lookit me dancing!*). Scores can vary from 0 (parents always check the simpler alternative) to 37 (parents always check the more complex alternative). As noted earlier, this scale is highly correlated with laboratory measures of Mean Length of Utterance. In the present study, we will make use of only two measures from Part II: the three-point word combination item, and the grammatical complexity scale.

Procedure

Parents of the children in the norming study were contacted through local doctors' offices and day care programs, and were asked to complete the inventory and return it in a postage-paid envelope. Because the Infant and Toddler Scales are both printed on machine-scannable forms, all returned questionnaires were first subjected to visual analysis (to ensure that parents had followed directions and that the forms were appropriate for machine scanning), and then scored mechanically. The one exception is the section in which parents are asked to describe the three longest utterances their children have produced in the last few weeks. These were scored manually, according to procedures of the Child Language Data Exchange System (MacWhinney, 1991) for calculation of mean length of utterance in morphemes. These MLU counts were not used in the present study, and will not be discussed further.

RESULTS AND DISCUSSION

Results will be presented in three parts: (1) an examination of developmental changes in lexical composition, as a function of overall vocabulary size; (2) an examination of individual differences in lexical composition within vocabulary levels; and (3) a quick look at the correlates of stylistic variation when developmental variance is controlled, including some limited evidence on continuity in style (or lack thereof) in a subset of children whose parents filled out a second report approximately six months after the norming study. As we shall see, there is strong evidence for BOTH developmental and stylistic variation, but there are also clear confounds between the two that should be kept separate in future studies.

Developmental changes in vocabulary composition

In this section, we will describe developmental changes in productive vocabulary (using both the CDI:Toddler and the CDI:Infant data). As background for these analyses of VOCABULARY COMPOSITION, we will start by examining the range of variation that can be observed in VOCABULARY SIZE.

Within the Infant data for ages 0;8 to 1;4 there is (not surprisingly) a significant positive correlation between age and the number of words that children reportedly produce ($r = +0.46$, $p < 0.001$). However, there is also a remarkable amount of variability in vocabulary size within most of the age groups between 0;8 and 1;4. From 0;8 to 0;11, most children are producing little or no meaningful speech (i.e. between 0 and 3 words). This result is compatible with the long-standing claim that language production starts around the end of the first year (e.g. Gesell, 1925; Lenneberg, 1967). However, the variance in word production starts to spread dramatically after that point. At 1;0, the median number of words reported is 6, with a range from 0 to 52. By 1;4 (when our data for the infant scale end), the median number of words produced is 40, but the range extends from a low of 0 words to a high of 347. Because these are parental report data, there are sound reasons to be sceptical about individual reports that are several standard deviations from the mean. But the variance looks enormous even when we adopt a more conservative view, focusing on the 10th and 90th percentiles instead of the minimum and maximum score. At 1;4, 10% of the children were reported to have productive vocabularies below 8 words, while the top 10% were reported to have vocabularies of 179 words or more. We have seen some children who fall at these extremes in our laboratories, and we are now convinced that this level of precocity does in fact exist (Thal & Bates, 1990). It is not necessarily the product of wishful thinking by an overly enthusiastic parent.

Individual differences in word production are even more marked in the period from 1;4 to 2;6. Data from the CDI:Toddlers (based on a list of 680 possible words) show a steady linear increase in vocabulary size as a function of age (reflecting a linear correlation of $r = +0.68$, $p < 0.001$). However, the most striking aspect of our toddler data is the massive variability that can be observed at every age level. The range at 1;4 already extends from 6 to 357 words, with a median of 44. These numbers are very close to estimates from the 1;4 group on the CDI:Infants (see preceding paragraph), and hence can be viewed as a replication (despite the fact that the Infant scale contains 396 possible words while the Toddler scale contains 680 possible words). At 1;8, the range extends from 3 to 544 words, with a median of 170. By 2;0, the median number of words has reached 311, but the range is still extraordinarily large: 10% of the sample is reported to produce 534 words or more, while the bottom 10% is still producing fewer than 57 words. When data for the CDI end at 2;6, the median is 574, with a range from 208 to 675. Hence the bottom 10th percentile has begun to catch up (with a range from 208 to 262), while the top 10th percentile has reached ceiling (with a range from 654 to 675).

It is apparent from these numbers why any analysis of vocabulary composition as a function of age would necessarily collapse across children who are at very different points in lexical development. Indeed, the period of maximum variation in lexical size appears to lie between 1;4 and 2;0 – precisely the range in which most work on individual differences in lexical and grammatical style has concentrated. Hence there are sound reasons to expect a confound between developmental and stylistic variance. To avoid these confounds, all our remaining analyses will divide children by developmental level instead of chronological age.

Starting with results from the Toddler Scale, the full sample of 1,130 children was divided into eight levels of vocabulary size (in number of

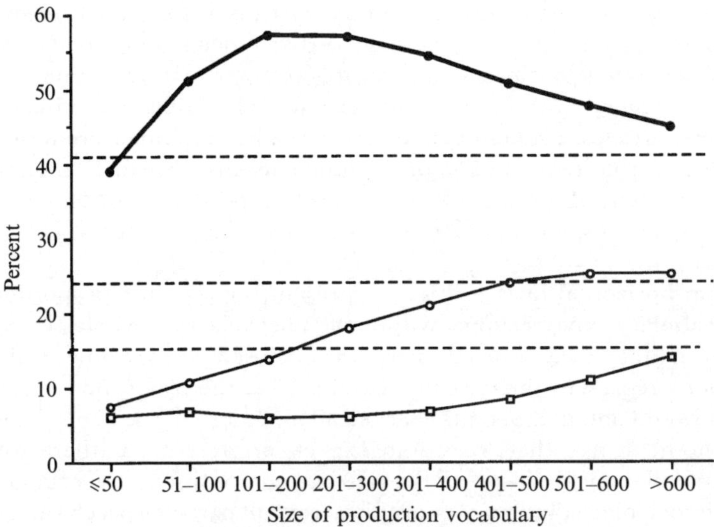

Fig. 1. Vocabulary composition from 1;4 to 2;6: proportion of common nouns, predicates and closed-class words at each vocabulary level. (Flat horizontal lines represent the percentage that each vocabulary type occupies within the checklist as a whole.) ●, common nouns; ○, predicates; □, closed class.

words): 0–50 ($N = 153$), 51–100 ($N = 130$), 101–200 ($N = 177$), 201–300 ($N = 133$), 301–400 ($N = 153$), 401–500 ($N = 155$), 501–600 ($N = 145$), and 601–680 ($N = 84$). Although most of these levels represent 100-word increments, we kept the data separate for the periods between 0 and 50, and 51 and 100, because previous studies have suggested that the 50-word point may represent a developmental watershed.

Fig. 1 summarizes developmental trends in vocabulary composition for three variables: percentage of common nouns, percentage of predicates, and percentage of closed-class items. COMMON NOUNS were defined to include the following categories from the CDI: animal names, vehicles, toys, clothing, body parts, small household items, food and furniture (280 possible items, 41·3% of the total checklist). Potential nominals that were excluded from this category include games and routines (e.g. *pattycake*), sound effects (e.g. *meow, vroom*), names for people (e.g. proper nouns and items like *babysitter*), and places to go (a category which included some common nouns but also included adverbials like *outside* and gerunds like *camping*). These items were excluded because previous studies have suggested that they may follow a different developmental course from 'true nominals' (Snyder, Bates & Bretherton, 1981; Bates *et al.* 1988). PREDICATES were defined as the sum of two categories: verbs (referred to on the CDI as 'action names': 103 items, 15·2% of the total checklist) and adjectives (referred to on the CDI as 'descriptive words': 63 items, 9·3 % of the checklist). The verb category only included words that are used as main verbs; modals and auxiliaries were analysed separately as closed-class vocabulary items. In the same vein, the adjective category was designed to exclude closed-class modifiers (e.g. quantifiers, articles, pronominal adjectives). The combined predicate category contains 166 items, 24·4 % of the total checklist. Finally, CLOSED-CLASS ITEMS were defined to include pronouns, prepositions, question words, quantifiers, articles, auxiliary verbs and connectives (102 items, 15 % of the checklist).

The flat horizontal lines in Fig. 1 represent the absolute proportion that each vocabulary type occupies within the checklist as a whole (i.e. 41·3 % common nouns, 24·4 % predicates, 15 % closed class). These absolute proportions represent the checklist baseline, i.e. the proportion scores that children would obtain if parents checked all or almost all the items. They also represent the scores that we would expect, on average, if there were no systematic relationship between the size and composition of vocabulary (i.e. if growth took place randomly or evenly across all part-of-speech categories). Examination of Fig. 1 shows that this is not the case. Instead, common nouns, predicates and closed-class items each follow a different developmental course.

Starting with common nouns, a one-way ANOVA by vocabulary level yielded no significant linear term ($F(1, 1121)$ for weighted linear term = 0·0958, $p > 0·75$). However, the deviation from linearity was highly reliable ($F(6, 1121) = 92·72$, $p < 0·0001$), reflecting the inverted-U pattern that is so evident in Fig. 1. In the period from 1 to 200 words, common nouns occupy an increasing proportion of total vocabulary, in line with the traditional idea that the first stages of lexical development in English-speaking children are dominated by the learning of new names for common objects. However, this increase in 'nouniness' peaks at a mean of 55·2 % in children with vocabularies between 101 and 200 words (the point at which other categories start to expand), and eventually drops to a mean of 41·9 % (just above the 41·3 % figure that common nouns occupy within the checklist as a whole, i.e. the checklist baseline).

This inverted U-shaped function helps to explain longitudinal findings reported earlier by Bates *et al.* (1988). In their sample of 27 children, the relationship between speed of development and 'referential style' (percentage of common nouns) changed in direction as well as size between age 1;1 and 2;4. At 1;1, referential style (computed from parental report) was significantly and POSITIVELY correlated with overall vocabulary size, and with a number of other indices of progress in receptive and productive language ability. At 1;8 this was no longer true; referential style was entirely UNCORRELATED with other measures of language development. By 2;4, referential style (computed from free speech) was NEGATIVELY associated with measures of language ability. Bates *et al.* interpreted these changes in the 'meaning' of referential style to reflect changes in the nature and function of the lexicon – from a concentration on reference, to an emphasis on predication, culminating in an increased emphasis on the closed class. In fact, their longitudinal data (and their interpretation) map onto the cross-sectional data in Fig. 1 exceptionally well. Referring back to the age-based statistics reported earlier, we know that vocabulary size for most children aged 1;1 falls well within the 1–200-word range. Fig. 1 shows that this is the period in which common nouns are still expanding (in proportional as well as in absolute terms). Hence there should be a positive correlation between 'nouniness' and rate of development at this age. We also know from the age-based statistics cited earlier that vocabulary size for most children aged 1;8 falls between 100 and 300 words – straddling the rise and fall in the percentage of common nouns illustrated in Fig. 1. It should be clear why there is no linear correlation between 'nouniness' and vocabulary size in a sample of children that falls within this range. Finally, we know that most children aged 2;4 have vocabularies between 300 and 600 words. This is the developmental range in which there is a systematic drop in the percentage of common nouns, as other categories continue to expand. Hence we should expect a negative correlation between 'nouniness' and vocabulary size for most samples of children aged 2;4. In other words, by following the same sample of children longitudinally, Bates *et al.* were tapping into different parts of the non-linear developmental function that governs the rate of noun growth (relative to other items) from 1;1 to 2;6.

A very different developmental pattern occurs for predicates (i.e. verbs + adjectives). A one-way ANOVA on these proportion scores by vocabulary level yielded a large and significant linear component ($F(1, 1121)$ for weighted linear term $= 1808.38$, $p < 0.00001$); there was also a significant deviation from linearity ($F(6, 1121) = 11.42$, $p < 0.00001$), although this non-linear deviation is considerably smaller than the linear component. Inspection of Fig. 1 shows a steady linear increase in the expansion of the predicate category, from a low of 7.6 % in children with vocabularies between 1 and 50 words, to a peak of 25.2 % in the highest vocabulary group (i.e. just above the 24.4 % checklist baseline). The small non-linear component in the one-way ANOVA probably represents a slight deceleration in the rate of expansion as predicate scores move toward the baseline proportion.

Yet another pattern appears in our analysis of closed-class proportion scores. A one-way ANOVA across the full developmental range yielded a significant linear component ($F(1, 1121)$ for weighted linear term $= 330.98$, $p < 0.00001$) and a significant deviation from linearity ($F(6, 1121) = 22.52$, $p < 0.00001$). At first glance, this looks similar to the statistical results obtained above for the predicate category. However, the exact pattern of development differs markedly, and can be divided into two distinct epochs. Closed-class scores start out very low in children with 50 words or less

97

(occupying 5·9 % of total vocabulary, on average). Furthermore, there is no significant linear or non-linear increase in closed-class proportion scores until total vocabulary passes the 400-word point (determined through a separate one-way ANOVA for the five vocabulary groups under 400 words). After 400 words, closed-class vocabulary starts to expand at the (proportional) expense of other lexical types (determined through a separate one-way ANOVA across the three vocabulary levels above 400 words). This late increase has a significant linear component (F (1, 381) for weighted linear term $= 260·04$, $p < 0·00001$), with no significant deviation from linearity (F (1, 381) $= 0·89$, $p > 0·65$). Hence we can view 400 words as the 'take-off point', suggesting that development of closed-class vocabulary may require the presence of a certain critical mass of nouns, verbs and other content words (see Marchman & Bates, 1994, for supporting evidence).

To summarize so far, there are linear and non-linear changes in lexical composition across the 1;4 to 2;6 age range, reflecting distinct patterns of growth for nouns, verbs, adjectives and closed-class words as a function of total vocabulary size. Nouns accelerate early (relative to other types), and level off around 200 words. Predicates start off slowly but show a constant linear expansion up to the checklist baseline. Closed-class words represent a small and unchanging proportion of total vocabulary in the period between 1 and 400 words; after that point, they accelerate sharply relative to other lexical types. This pattern could be summarized in fairly traditional terms, as follows:

> Changes in the composition of the lexicon across this developmental range reflect a shift in emphasis from REFERENCE, to PREDICATION, to GRAMMAR.

Before we accept this sensible but relatively strong conclusion, some control analyses are in order. Common nouns, predicates and closed-class items each represent a different absolute proportion of the vocabulary checklist. That is, there are many more nouns on the checklist than predicates, and more predicates than grammatical function words. We composed the vocabulary checklist in this fashion for two reasons: (1) there are equivalent differences in the absolute size of these categories within the adult language; and (2) these were the proportions that have shown up in previous studies using a more 'open-ended' format (including live observations as well as parental report). A comparison between the flat horizontal lines in Fig. 1 and the observed developmental trends should make it clear that vocabulary composition really is changing over time (i.e. it is not an artefact of the checklist itself). Nevertheless, this result is important enough for our understanding of early lexical development that we thought it would be useful to examine these growth rates in vocabulary types from several points of view.

First, although the literature on individual differences has emphasized the proportion of common nouns and other terms within vocabulary as a whole (as indicated in Fig. 1), the raw growth functions within each category are also of some interest. Fig. 2 presents the absolute number of common nouns,

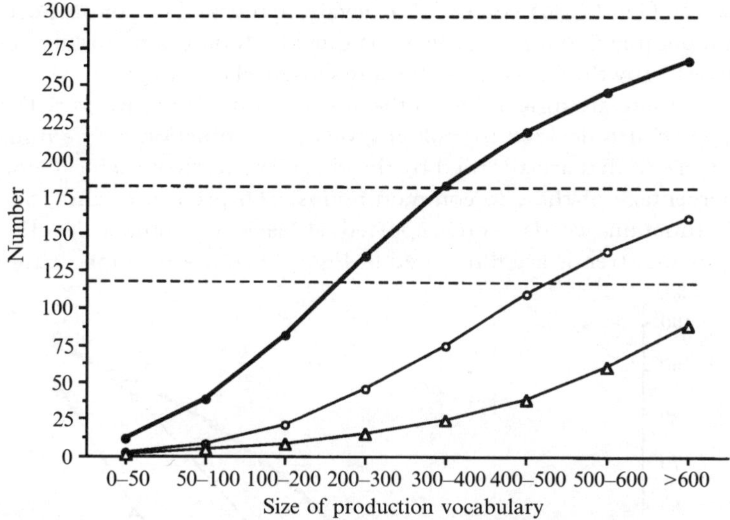

Fig. 2. Absolute number of common nouns, predicates and closed-class items reported. (Horizontal lines represent the absolute number of common nouns, predicates and closed-class terms available on the checklist as a whole.) ●, common nouns; ○, predicates; △, closed class.

predicates and closed-class terms at each vocabulary level. The flat horizontal lines in Fig. 2 represent another kind of point of comparison: the total number of common nouns (280), predicates (166) and closed-class terms (103) that are available on the checklist as a whole (i.e. the respective ceilings for each vocabulary type). As we might expect when children are grouped by total vocabulary size on a finite checklist, all three categories show positive growth and all three converge on their respective ceilings in children with more than 600 words. However, it is also clear from Fig. 2 that the growth curves differ for these three lexical types. To obtain more information about the shape of each curve, we carried out three one-way ANOVAs (common nouns, predicates and closed-class words as a function of vocabulary level). Of course we knew that all three analyses would yield huge between-group effects, because the three category totals are contained within (and hence dependent on) vocabulary size. The real purpose of these analyses was to determine which polynomials reached significance (i.e. linear, quadratic, cubic). In fact, there were enormous between-group effects of vocabulary grouping on all three variables, and the linear, quadratic and cubic functions all reached significance in every case (with F-values ranging from 50·00 to

4 2

more than 20,000, all at $p < 0.00001$). This finding is compatible with independent analyses of vocabulary growth over age conducted by Fenson *et al.* (1993), who showed that early vocabulary growth is best fitted by a logistic function – a function that contains linear, quadratic and cubic components (see also van Geert, 1991; Bates & Carnevale, in press). For our purposes here, the main point is that nouns grow most quickly, followed by predicates, with the slowest growth observed within the closed-class category.

Because there are differences in the absolute number of items within each category, we also decided to look at growth as a function of the number of OPPORTUNITIES that are afforded by the checklist, WITHIN each category (e.g. what percentage of the 280 common nouns, 166 predicates and 102 grammatical function words were reported at each vocabulary level? These developmental trends are illustrated in Fig. 3. From this graph, it should be

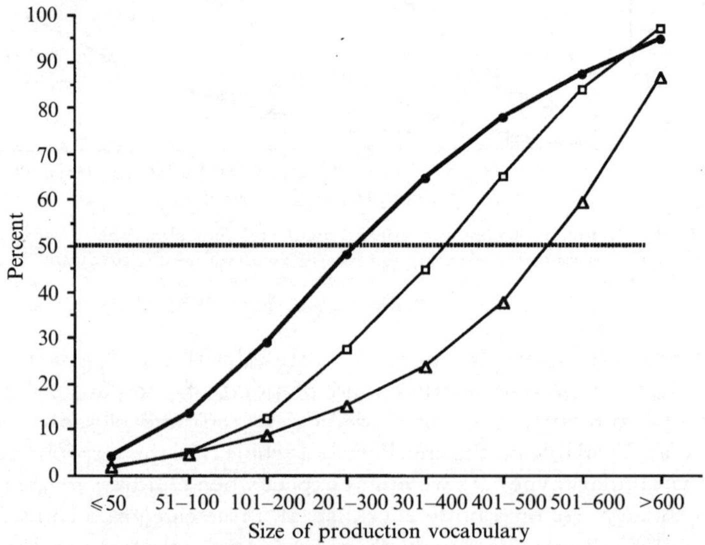

Fig. 3. Proportion of total common-noun, predicate and closed-class items on checklist that were reported at each vocabulary level from 1;4 to 2;6. ●, common nouns; □, predicates; △, closed class.

clear that children begin to 'fill up' the common-noun opportunities first, followed by the predicates, with closed-class opportunities 'filling up' much later in development. For example, 50 % of the nouns have been checked (on average) when total vocabulary stands between 200 and 300 words. 50 % of the predicates have been checked (on average) when overall vocabulary size falls between 300 and 450 words. Closed-class opportunities do not reach the 50 % mark until total vocabulary falls between 500 and 600 words. The reliability of these trends was verified in a mixed 8×3 ANOVA treating vocabulary level as a between-subjects variable, with part-of-speech category treated as a within-subject variable. All three effects reached significance: a main effect of vocabulary size ($F(7, 1122) = 7068.7$, $p < 0.0001$), a main effect of category ($F(2, 2244) = 2390.5$, $p < 0.0001$), and an interaction between size and category ($F(14, 2244) = 165.70$, $p < 0.001$).

A somewhat different perspective on the same data comes from an examination of the RATE OF CHANGE from one vocabulary level to another. Of course we cannot calculate rate-of-change statistics for individual children, because these are cross-sectional data. However, some insights into the average rate of growth can be obtained by comparing group means. For example, the mean number of common nouns for children with vocabularies between 1 and 50 is 11.58; the mean number for children between 51 and 100 is 37.86. The difference between these two means is 26.28, which represents an increase of 227 % (26.28/11.58). Fig. 4 graphs the percentage increase that

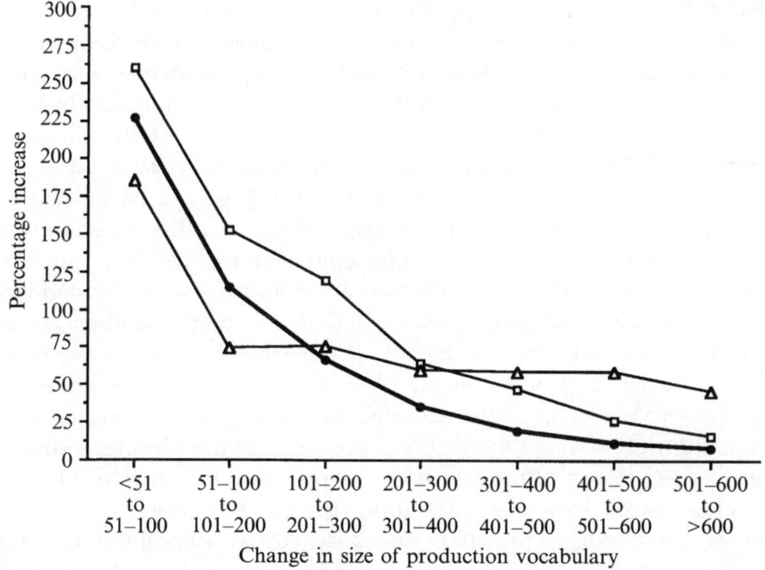

Fig. 4. Percentage increase in number of common nouns, predicates and closed-class items reported, from one vocabulary level to another. ●, common nouns; □, predicates; △, closed class.

is observed for each category, from one vocabulary level to another. All three categories show huge growth at the first comparison (i.e. the difference between children with vocabularies under 50 words, and children with vocabularies between 50 and 100 words). This is what we should expect, since many children in the < 50 group have just begun to talk. For the same reason, all three categories also show a sharp drop in rate of growth after this point. Most interesting for our purposes are the growth rates that are observed between 100 and 600 words. For common nouns, there is a steep and constant deceleration in rate of growth across all vocabulary levels after the 50-word point; furthermore, common nouns grow more slowly than any other category after the 100-word point. Predicates also show a steady decline in rate of growth across the period from 100 to 600 words; nevertheless, predicates are growing faster than nouns or closed-class words in the period between 50 and 400 words. Finally, as we might expect from our earlier analyses, closed-class words are the fastest growing category for all children with vocabularies that exceed 400 words.

In short, no matter how we look at these effects, they appear to be extremely lawful, suggesting that there are indeed 'three waves' or 'three moments' in the composition and recomposition of the lexicon between ages 1;4 and 2;6, when total vocabulary grows from under 50 words to more than 600. In particular, we confirm the proposed shift in rate of growth (or relative emphasis) from reference, to predication, to grammar.

These results confirm and extend earlier suggestions by Lieven & Pine (1990), showing that measures of 'referential style' (defined as 'percentage of common nouns') may be heavily confounded by developmental changes that presumably affect all children. However, a great deal of the literature on referential style has focused on the period between 0 and 50 words – a single point on the developmental curves illustrated in Figs 1–4. What happens in the very first stages of lexical development? To answer this question, we turn to analyses of vocabulary composition in our data for the CDI Infant Scale.

Data for the 659 children aged between 0;8 and 1;4 were divided into the following six developmental levels (based on total number of words produced): 0 words ($N = 134$, 20·3 % of the sample), 1–5 words ($N = 180$, 27·3 % of the sample), 6–10 words ($N = 85$, 12·9 % of the sample), 11–20 words ($N = 106$, 16·1 % of the sample), 21–50 words ($N = 92$, 14 % of the sample) and more than 50 words ($N = 62$, 9·4 % of the sample, representing a range from 51 to 347). Proportion scores for common nouns, predicates and closed-class words were calculated following the definitions outlined above. Out of the 396 words on the infant checklist, 182 were common nouns (46 % of the total checklist), 92 were verbs or adjectives (23·2 % of the checklist) and 36 were closed-class items (9·1 % of the checklist). Obviously such proportion scores have no meaning for children at the zero-word level. Hence all our one-way ANOVAs were conducted over the five vocabulary levels from 1 to 347. Results of these analyses are illustrated in Fig. 5 (where the three flat horizontal lines represent the checklist baselines for common nouns, predicates and closed-class items, respectively).

Results for the common-noun category suggest that the early linear trend observed in our Toddler analyses holds all across the range from 1 to 50 words. A one-way ANOVA for common-noun proportion scores yielded a

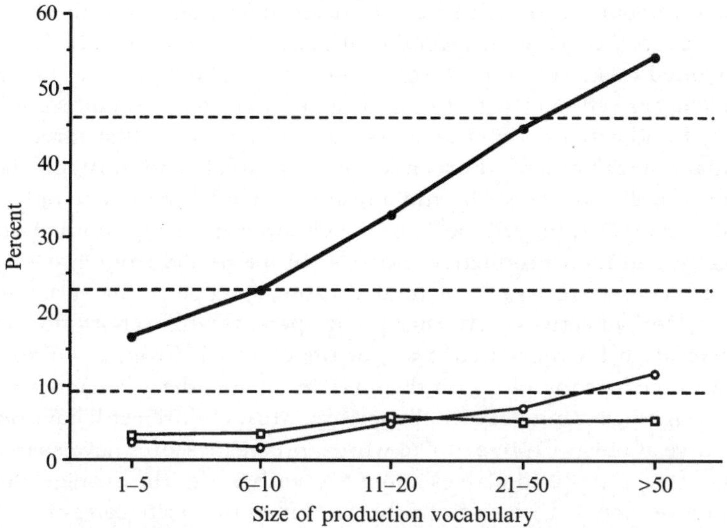

Fig. 5. Vocabulary composition from 0;8 to 1;4: percentage of common nouns, predicates and closed-class words at each vocabulary level. (Horizontal lines represent the percentage that each vocabulary type occupies within the checklist as a whole.) ●, common nouns; ○, predicates; □, closed class.

large linear component (F (1, 520) for weighted linear term = 212·81, $p <$ 0·00001), with no significant deviation from linearity (F (3, 520) = 0·63, $p >$ 0·60). In the relatively unstable period between 1 and 5 words, common nouns represent only 16·4% of total vocabulary, on average (far below the 46% baseline). These percentages climb steadily, from 22·9% in children with 6–10 words, to 32·9% in children with 11–20 words, to 44·5% in children with 21–50 words, to a peak of 54·1% in children with more than 50 words (well above the 46% baseline, suggesting an overrepresentation of common nouns). Remember that we have defined the category 'common noun' to exclude sound effects, names for people, and other items that are typical in the first naming acts performed by one-year-old children (e.g. *Daddy*; *woowoo* for dog; *vroom* for car or airplane). Hence these results may actually UNDERESTIMATE the extent to which early lexical development revolves around the naming function. We conclude that the 'discovery' and expansion of referring terms dominates the first stage of lexical development, from 1 to 100 words (but see individual differences in the section on stylistic variation, below).

Results for the predicate category support this conclusion. Within the Infant data, a one-way ANOVA over developmental levels yielded a large linear component (F (1, 520) for weighted linear term = 75·33, $p <$ 0·00001). In contrast with the steady linear trend observed for common nouns, the predicate category also yielded a significant deviation from linearity (F (3, 520) = 4·21, $p < 0·01$), with a significant quadratic component (F (1, 520) for the weighted quadratic term = 10·59, $p < 0·01$). The non-linear component in this analysis reflects the fact that most children in the Infant sample have no verbs or adjectives at all (i.e. a floor effect) across the first three levels of vocabulary development. For children with small and unstable lexicons between 1 and 5 words, verbs and adjectives together comprise only 2·25 % of total vocabulary; indeed, 90 % of the children in this group had no verbs or adjectives in their productive lexicons. In the period from 6 to 10 words, predicates constitute 1·54 % of total vocabulary (1·08 % for verbs and less than 1 % for adjectives). At this point, parents still report no verbs or adjectives at all for more than 85 % of the children. From 11 to 20 words, predicates account for 4·81 % of the total (2·7 % for adjectives and 2·12 % for verbs), a significant but very small increase. Most children still have one verb or adjective at most. From 21 to 50 words, predicate scores have soared to an average of 7 % (4·3 % adjectives and 2·7 % verbs). But the average child still has no more than 2–3 items from the combined predicate category. Finally, predicate scores for children with vocabularies over 50 words reach an average of 11·8 % (4·8 % adjectives and 7·0 % verbs), still well below the 23·2 % that predicates represent within the checklist as a whole. We may conclude that verbs and adjectives develop very slowly in the first stages of lexical development, at least for this English-speaking sample (cf. Bates, Caselli & Casadio, 1990; Gopnik & Choi, 1990). These predicate terms do not 'take off' for most children until they achieve a critical vocabulary size of at least 50 words. (For further evidence of such 'critical mass' effects in lexical organization, see Marchman & Bates, 1994; for simulations of language learning that rely on a similar 'critical mass' mechanism, see Plunkett, Marchman & Knudsen, 1993.)

Finally, closed-class items constitute a negligible proportion of total vocabulary throughout the Infant range. A one-way ANOVA over developmental levels yielded a significant but relatively small linear component (F (1, 520) for weighted linear term = 4·39, $p < 0·04$), with no significant deviation from linearity (F (3, 520) = 0·58, $p > 0·63$). Grammatical function words constitute an average of 3·2 % of vocabulary for children with vocabularies between 1 and 5 words, and most children (90 %) reportedly have no items from this category. Between 6 and 10 words, the average is still only 3·6 %. By the period between 11 and 20 words, the average has reached 5·8 %, but the mean drops slightly to 5·15 % between 21 and 50 words. Finally, for children with vocabularies over 50 words, closed-class items still average only 5·4 % of total vocabulary. These scores replicate and extend the findings reported for older children in our analyses of the Toddler Scale: closed-class items undergo no real growth (relative to other items) until a much later stage in language development. The handful of closed-class items produced by children between 0;8 and 1;4 include the occasional preposition or locative adverbial (e.g. *up!*), a few pronouns and pronominal modifiers (e.g. *that*, *mine*), some quantifiers (e.g. *more*) and negatives (e.g. *no*). All of these are of course terms that can be used in single-word speech, to indicate states and relations that are best considered 'pre-grammatical'.

To summarize, the Infant data support our earlier conclusion regarding a shift in the focus of lexical expansion from reference, to predication, to grammar. The Infant data do give us a more detailed picture of the earliest stages in lexical development, showing that (1) verbs, adjectives and closed-class words are very rare in English-speaking children with vocabularies under 50 or 100 words; and (2) the proportional expansion of common nouns begins with the first word and continues up to the 100-word point. Hence there appears to be a CONFOUND BETWEEN DEVELOPMENTAL AND STYLISTIC ASPECTS of 'referential style' at every point in the one-word stage.

Stylistic variation in vocabulary composition

We have shown that there are clear-cut developmental changes in lexical composition from age 0;8 to 1;4. In this section, we want to determine whether there is any evidence left for variations in lexical style when developmental levels are held constant.

Starting with common-noun proportion scores (our best estimate of 'referential style'), Fig. 6 displays the 10th, 25th, 50th, 75th and 90th percentile scores for this variable in the Toddler data, across the eight vocabulary levels described above. Although it is clear from Fig. 6 that the developmental trends in common-noun usage are evident across the entire sample (i.e. a curvilinear function that peaks between 100 and 200 words), there is also enormous variability within vocabulary levels, particularly in the early stages of development. For children with vocabularies under 50 words, the median 'referential style' score is 40·65%. However, the absolute range extends from 0% to 75%. If we use the 10th and 90th percentiles as a more conservative estimate of the outer limits for variation in referential style, we find that children in the bottom 10th percentile have scores under 15·5%, while children in the top 10th percentile have scores of 56·8% or greater. The standard deviation in this developmental range is also an impressive 15·9%. From this point on, the standard deviation for common-noun scores grows smaller, but absolute proportion scores reach their peak at Level 3 (101–200 words), where the median is 72·7%. The range at this level of development goes from a low of 53·6% to a high of 98·7%. In other words, there is at least one child in this large sample with a vocabulary larger than 100 words, consisting almost exclusively of names for common objects! Once again, parental reports that are as extreme as this should perhaps be viewed with caution. However, if we use the more conservative 10th and 90th percentiles, we find that children in the bottom 10th percentile for Level 3 have

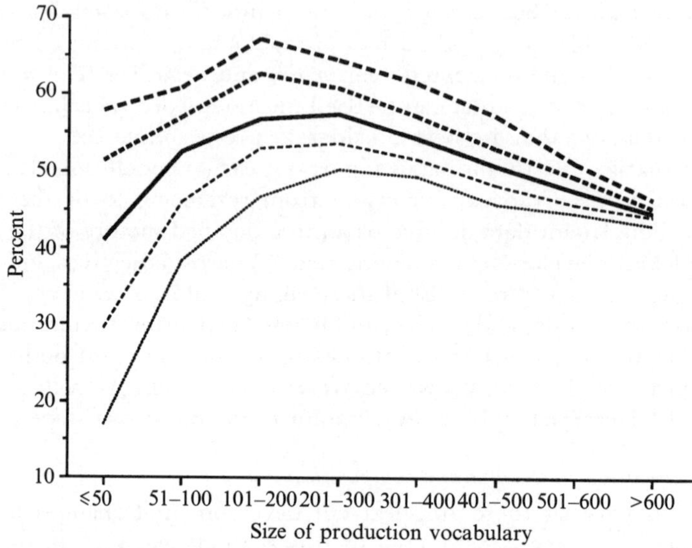

Fig. 6. Referential style from 1;4 to 2;6: percentage of common nouns over total vocabulary at each vocabulary level. – – –, 90th percentile; – – –, 75th percentile; ———, 50th percentile; – – –, 25th percentile; ⋯⋯, 10th percentile.

vocabularies with fewer than 45 % common nouns, while children in the top 10th percentile have referential style scores of 65·9 % or greater. By the time vocabularies reach 500 words or more, Fig. 6 shows that variation in 'nouniness' has all but disappeared; this is due to the fact that most children have settled into the checklist baseline for this particular measure.

It should be clear from these analyses that there is ample variation in referential style, over and above the developmental effects that we documented earlier. This variation is most marked in the early stages of development, particularly in children with vocabularies in the 1–50-word range. To examine this early variability in more detail, we turn to common-noun proportion scores for the Infant data, illustrated in Fig. 7. This Figure also illustrates the 10th, 25th, 50th, 75th and 90th percentile scores, for each of the five vocabulary levels described earlier (1 = 1–5 words; 2 = 6–10 words; 3 = 11–20 words; 4 = 21–50 words; 5 = > 50 words). For children with very small vocabularies (1–5 words), the median common-noun proportion score is 0 (i.e. no object names at all), but the range extends from 0–100 %, and the standard deviation is a full 25 %. The picture is still quite extreme if we use the 10th and 90th percentile scores as a more conservative estimate of the range (0 for children in the bottom 10th percentile, 50 % for children in the top 10th percentile). However, because these proportion scores are based on very small denominators, their internal stability is questionable. A more reliable and informative view of variation in 'referential

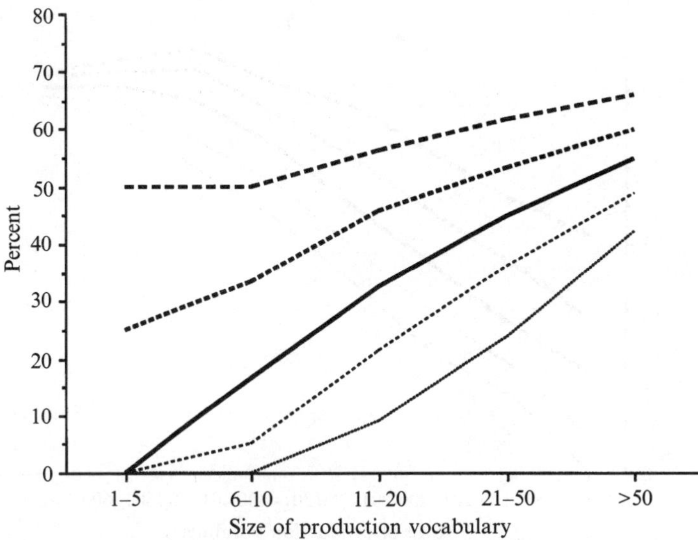

Fig. 7. Referential style from 0;8 to 1;4: percentage of common nouns over total vocabulary at each vocabulary level. Key as for Fig. 6.

style' comes between Level 3 (11–20 words) and Level 4 (20–50 words). This is the vocabulary range that has been the focus of most previous work on referential style (e.g. Nelson, 1973; Snyder *et al.* 1981). At Level 3, we find a range from 0 to 79%, with a standard deviation of 17·2%. Children in the bottom 10th percentile have vocabularies in which common nouns represent less than 10% of the total; children in the top 10th percentile have vocabularies that are at least 56·3% common nouns. At Level 4, the variation is only slightly smaller: a range of 12–100%, with a standard deviation of 15·1%; children in the bottom 10th percentile have 'referential style' scores under 24%, while children in the top 10th percentile average 61·8% or greater. By Level 5 (when vocabularies go over 50 words), variation in referential style starts to drop markedly. The outer range extends from 36% to 72%, with a standard deviation of 8·6%; scores for the bottom 10th percentile fall at 41·8% or lower; scores for the top 10th fall above 66%.

We may conclude that variation in referential style is a real and robust phenomenon, one that persists after we have controlled for variation that is due to developmental change. This variation is most apparent (and most reliable) in children with vocabularies in the 10–50 words range – right where Katherine Nelson and her colleagues discovered it more than 15 years ago! Later on we will look at some of the concurrent and predictive correlates of referential style when developmental confounds are removed in this way. Meanwhile, our data also permit us to examine individual differences in the distribution of other lexical categories, most notably predicates and gram-

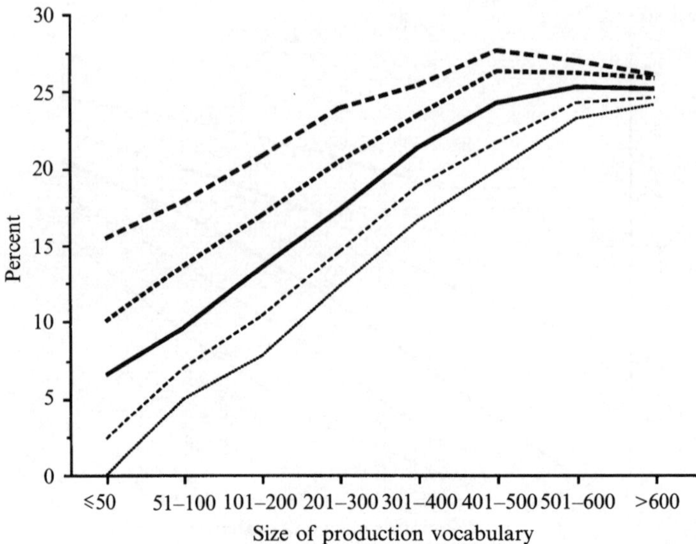

Fig. 8. Variation in production of predicates as a proportion of total vocabulary from 1;4 to 2;6. Key as for Fig. 6.

matical function words. (We will restrict ourselves to the Toddler data for these analyses, because there are so few predicates or function words before age 1;4.)

Fig. 8 illustrates the variation observed in predicate proportion scores in our Toddler data (the 10th, 25th, 50th, 75th and 90th percentiles within each of the eight vocabulary levels described above). These results can be summarized fairly quickly: in contrast with the broad variation observed in referential style, predicate scores show relatively little variation. The largest range (0–79 %) is observed in the data for children with vocabularies under 50 words; the extreme high scores all come from children with very small and unstable total vocabularies (under 10 words), and are never observed again across the entire developmental range. If we use the top and bottom 10th percentiles as a more conservative estimate of the range at Level 1, we find that children in the bottom 10th percentile have no verbs or adjectives at all, while children in the top 10th have predicate scores of 15·4 % or greater. After this developmental level, variation in predicate scores is even more constrained. Standard deviations decrease slowly from 8·72 % at Level 1, to less than 1 % at Level 8 (when most children are at the checklist baseline). In short, although there is some variation in predicate growth around the developmental trends described earlier, predicates do not show the same kind of quantitative and (perhaps) qualitative variation that we observed with common nouns.

A somewhat different story emerges when we examine variation in the closed class, holding vocabulary size constant. The developmental analyses presented earlier revealed that closed-class growth in toddlers can be divided into two distinct developmental epochs: for children with vocabularies under 400 words, there is no linear or non-linear relation between vocabulary size and closed-class proportion scores; after the 400-word level, these items start to 'take off', occupying an increasing proportion of reported vocabulary totals. This finding raises the possibility of a change in the distribution and meaning of closed-class proportion scores when vocabulary size is controlled. Fig. 9 illustrates the 10th, 25th, 50th, 75th and 90th percentiles for this

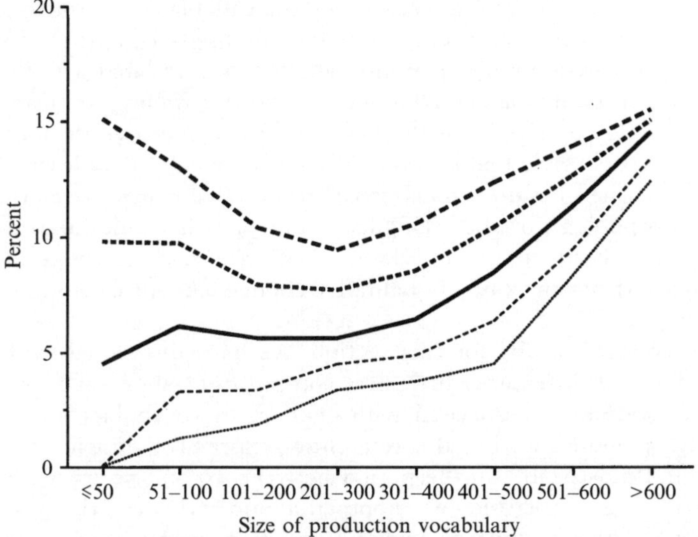

Fig. 9. Variation in production of closed-class words as a proportion of total vocabulary from 1;4 to 2;6. Key as for Fig. 6.

variable, across all eight vocabulary levels in the Toddler data. This graph shows substantial individual variation in the contribution of the closed class for children within the 1–400-word range. Hence there appears to be NO confound between developmental and stylistic variance in closed-class usage in children with vocabularies under 400 words. After 400 words, there is a linear increase in closed-class proportion scores for the entire sample, a change that is visible from the lowest 10 % to the highest 10 % of the sample. Hence there clearly IS a confound between developmental and stylistic variance in closed-class usage after total vocabulary reaches the 400-word mark.

This finding is quite consistent with previous reports on the timing and nature of 'nominal/pronominal style'. For example, in the pioneering study by Bloom and her colleagues (Bloom *et al.* 1975), variation in the use or non-use of subject pronouns was restricted to the stage of first word combinations (roughly corresponding to Roger Brown's Stage I – Brown, 1973). After that point, all four children started to use nouns and pronouns in comparable ways. In the same vein, Bates *et al.* (1988) reported a marked change between 1;8 and 2;4 in the statistical effects associated with closed-class proportion scores. At 1;8, these scores are correlated with a variety of 'rote style' measures, but they are essentially unrelated to overall rate of development; at 2;4, the same closed-class proportion scores are correlated with many different indices of progress in lexical and grammatical development, including Mean Length of Utterance and total vocabulary size (based on free speech only, since parental reports were not available at 2;4 for the Bates *et al.* sample). Bates *et al.* also reported that 1;8-closed-class proportion scores (for free speech) are significantly and NEGATIVELY correlated with the 'same' measure eight months later! They interpreted this finding to mean that the early use of closed-class items derives from reliance or overreliance on rote memory, a lexical style that is apparently not very helpful (at least not in the short term) when children must attain productive control over the grammatical morphology of their language. Fig. 9 tells us nothing about the advantages or disadvantages of 'closed-class style' in the early period, but it does suggest that some kind of qualitative change takes place around the 400-word boundary.

To summarize results for this section, we have uncovered evidence for large individual differences in lexical composition, above and beyond the systematic variations associated with changes in vocabulary size. Stylistic variation in noun use (i.e. the referential/expressive dimension) is most evident and most stable in the period between 10 and 50 words, although there is a confound between developmental and stylistic variations at every point beyond the first word. Stylistic variation in the use of closed-class morphemes (i.e. the analytic/holistic dimension) is most apparent in children with vocabularies under 400 words – a period in which there is no discernible relation between closed-class proportion scores and overall vocabulary size. We are now in a position to disentangle developmental and stylistic effects, examining some of the concurrent and longitudinal associates of referential style, and closed-class proportion scores.

Correlates of stylistic variation in lexical composition when vocabulary level is controlled

(i) Correlates of referential style
In previous studies using percentage of nouns as a measure of referential style (without controlling for overall vocabulary size), children who are high in referential style appear to be more precocious (i.e. they reach the same levels of lexical development at a younger age). They are also more likely to be girls,

first born, and/or higher in social class. What happens to these demographic 'fellow travellers' of referential style when developmental variance is controlled? To ask these questions, we calculated percentile scores for each child in the Infant sample with a vocabulary size of at least 10 words (yielding a total sample size of 274 children). The look-up table on which these calculations were based is included in the Appendix. Correlational analyses were conducted comparing results for these adjusted scores with the results obtained using unadjusted percentage scores. Table 1 summarizes the

TABLE 1. *Correlations of adjusted and unadjusted referential style scores with vocabulary size and demographic variables (for children with vocabularies of 10 words or more)*

	Unadjusted: raw % common nouns	Adjusted: percentile score for % common nouns
Total vocabulary	0·35***	0·02
Age	0·31***	0·15**
Gender	0·02	0·11*
Birth order	−0·12*	−0·08
Socioeconomic status	0·09	0·18**
Mother's education	0·11*	0·18**
Father's education	0·11*	0·19***
Mother's occupation	0·01	0·11*
Father's occupation	0·10*	0·14*

$* = p < 0.05$; $** = p < 0.01$; $*** = p < 0.001$.

correlations of these two referential style measures with total vocabulary size, age, gender, birth order, and five demographic variables (socioeconomic status (SES), maternal education and occupation, paternal education and occupation).

As we might expect from the results presented earlier (see especially Figs 5 and 7), the raw measure of referential style was significantly correlated with age ($r = +0.31$, $p < 0.001$) and total vocabulary size ($r = +0.35$, $p < 0.001$). There was also a small but reliable correlation with birth order, indicating that later-born children have lower scores for referential style ($r = -0.12$, $p < 0.05$). Finally, there were small but statistically significant correlations with maternal education ($r = +0.11$, $p < 0.05$), paternal education ($r = +0.11$, $p < 0.05$) and paternal occupation ($r = +0.10$, $p < 0.05$). In short, results obtained with the unadjusted scores for referential style replicate other reports in the literature using this measure.

The picture changes slightly when we look at correlations involving the developmentally adjusted percentile scores. The correlation with total vocabulary disappeared (a natural by-product of the fact that these percentile scores were calculated within vocabulary levels). The correlation with age was still significant ($r = +0.15$, $p < 0.01$) – but notice that this is a positive correlation, suggesting that children high in referential style are actually somewhat older than children with proportionally fewer common nouns. In other words, they are NOT precocious (i.e. they are not arriving at their respective vocabulary levels at a particularly early age). On the contrary, they tend to be slightly older – which may mean that we have not succeeded in removing all the developmental variance contained within scores for referential style. With the adjusted scores, a sex difference emerged that was not visible with the raw style measure ($r = +0.11$, $p < 0.05$, indicating slightly higher referential scores for girls). On the other hand, the birth order correlation dropped below significance ($r = -0.08$, n.s.). Finally, all of the correlations between referential style and social class were reliable when adjusted scores are used – and they were somewhat stronger than the two significant correlations obtained using unadjusted scores.

Because we have controlled here for the child's level of productive vocabulary, we know that these associations between parental variables and referential style are not due to a global correlation between social class and rate of development. In this respect, our results are compatible with a variety of studies suggesting a more specific link between parental style and 'nouniness' early in the one-word stage (e.g. Nelson, 1981; Goldfield & Snow, 1985; Hampson & Nelson, 1993). However, these effects should be interpreted with caution. These demographic measures are responsible for relatively little of the variation in referential style evidenced in these data. Because these effects are small, and because they bear a very indirect relation to parental style, our results can only be taken as weak support for environmental accounts of variation in referential style.[2]

Finally, we looked at the long-term predictability of referential style, using the adjusted scores (for children with a minimum of 10 words at Time 1 – leaving a total sample of 169). Results at Time 2 (approximately 6.5 months

---

[2] In a sample as large as this one, it is possible to obtain effects that are statistically reliable even though they actually account for less than 2 % of the variance. Obviously one is entitled to conclude that such effects are statistically significant, but theoretically trivial – or, at the very least, impossible to study without a sample of more than a thousand children. On the other hand, a small effect can be contributed by a critical subsection of the population that is quite interesting from a theoretical point of view (e.g. the kind of problem faced by epidemiologists who are trying to determine which individuals are likely to be the one in 10,000 to suffer from a particular disease). One strategy for dealing with this problem is to use the kind of large-scale information reported here to search for a small sample of extreme cases (e.g. to find 10 children who are extremely high in referential style, matched to 10 children who are very low in referential style but similar in many other respects). If the effect in question proves to be robust in these extreme cases (e.g. if the parents of the 10 high-referential children behave in a manner that is reliably different from the parents of the 10 low-referential children), then we may conclude with some confidence that the effect is interesting and real, even though it would be difficult to detect in an unselected sample.

later) come from the Toddler Scale, providing scores for total vocabulary, vocabulary composition (percentage of common nouns, percentage of predicates, and percentage of closed-class words), and grammatical complexity. The longitudinal correlations can be summarized succinctly:

> There were no significant effects of referential style at Time 1 on any of the Time 2 measures, including total vocabulary, percentage of common nouns, percentage of predicates, percentage of closed-class words, or grammatical complexity.

This was true even when we restricted ourselves entirely to children with Time 2 vocabularies under 400 words (i.e. the period in which we are sure that there are no confounds between 'closed-class style' and overall vocabulary size).

Our failure to find a longitudinal correlation between early referential style and later closed-class use is particularly important, since it has been claimed that referential children adopt a telegraphic style in their first word combinations, while 'expressive children' (i.e. children with low proportions of common nouns early in the one-word stage) tend to adopt a pronominal/holistic/formulaic approach to early grammar. Our results suggest that such claims were contaminated by developmental variance in measures of referential vs. expressive style. At first glance, this also appears to contradict reports by Bates *et al.* (1988) on continuity in lexical style in children aged 1;1 to 2;4. However, their conclusions were not based on simple scores for the percentage of common nouns. In fact, their measure of the percentage of common nouns at 1;1 showed relatively little continuity with 1;8 and 2;4 language measures. The style measure that did show continuity across this age range in their study was a factor score called 'analytic production', a composite of interview and observation measures that loaded highly on comprehension as well as referential production. This measure was contrasted with another composite score called 'rote production', reflecting (among other things) a tendency for the child to repeat or produce words that he or she does not appear to understand on a separate comprehension test. These measures seem to have more in common with the so-called analytic/holistic dimension than referential style *per se*. This brings us to concurrent and longitudinal predictions involving closed-class proportion scores, another candidate for a measure of analytic/holistic style.

(ii) Correlates of closed-class proportion scores

For our measure of referential style, the confound between developmental and stylistic variance extends across every point in development from the first word. To disentangle the two forms of variance, we had to use some fairly complex scoring procedures. By contrast, variation in closed-class proportion scores can be neatly divided into two epochs. For children with

TABLE 2. *Demographic correlates of closed-class percentage scores*

	Size of total vocabulary		
	All ($N = 1130$)	< 400 ($N = 744$)	> 400 ($N = 386$)
Age	0·36***	0·12**	0·36***
Birth order	0·01	0·02	0·01
Socioeconomic status	−0·01	0·00	−0·01
Mother's education	0·13**	0·01	0·13**
Father's education	−0·06	−0·03	−0·06
Mother's occupation	−0·03	0·03	−0·03
Father's occupation	0·01	−0·04	0·01

* $= p < 0.05$; ** $= p < 0.01$; *** $= p < 0.001$.

vocabularies under 400 words, there is no linear or non-linear association with lexical level. For children with vocabularies over 400 words, there is a strong linear relationship with vocabulary size that includes all children from the bottom to the top 10th percentiles. Hence it seems fair to conclude that stylistic variance dominates in the period from 0 to 400 words, while developmental variance dominates after vocabulary reaches 400 words. In this section, we can explore the stylistic and developmental correlates of closed-class proportion scores within the < 400-word epoch, where there is no conflict between stylistic and developmental factors, and compare those results with those for children in the > 400-word epoch. The main point of these analyses is to determine whether early 'stylistic' variance in closed-class usage is continuous with productive control over grammar, or whether this 'style' measure taps into sources of variance that are unrelated to later grammar (in line with claims by Bates *et al.* 1988). We will begin with results for the full cross-sectional sample, and then present results for a subsample whose parents filled out the CDI:Toddlers twice, with a separation of approximately 6·5 months between administrations.

Table 2 summarizes the concurrent correlations of closed-class style with age, gender, birth order and the same five measures of social class described in the previous section. These correlations were conducted three ways: for the total sample ($N = 1130$), for children with vocabularies under 400 words ($N = 744$), and for children with vocabularies above 400 words ($N = 386$). In all three analyses, age was significantly correlated with closed-class style – although, as we shall see later, there is reason to believe that these correlations may have a different cause before and after the 400-word point. In contrast with the above analyses of referential style, there is very little evidence here for a link between closed-class style and demographic variables. The only correlation that reaches significance is a $r = +0.13$ relationship with maternal education ($p < 0.05$). As can be seen from Table 2, this correlation is due entirely to children with vocabularies over 400 words – the period in which closed-class words are starting to develop in a systematic way.

In our previous work (see especially Bates *et al.* 1988), we have argued that early use of closed-class words reflects a 'rote' or 'holistic' approach to language – one that is discontinuous with productive use of grammar later on. Another test of this hypothesis comes from the 228 children whose parents filled out the Toddler Scale for a second time, approximately 6·5 months after the first administration. We correlated closed-class proportion scores at Time 1 with two concurrent measures of language (total vocabulary and grammatical complexity), and with three longitudinal measures at Time 2 (total vocabulary, grammatical complexity, and closed-class percentages). The same correlations were conducted four times: for the sample as a whole ($N = 228$), for children whose vocabularies exceed 400 words at both time points ($N = 37$), for children whose vocabularies fell below 400 words at both time points ($N = 83$), and for children who made the passage from vocabularies below 400 words at Time 1 to vocabularies over 400 words at Time 2 ($N = 108$). These four groupings are based directly on our earlier results (see especially Fig. 9) suggesting that variance in closed-class use is purely stylistic before 400 words, while it comes under systematic developmental control after that point. Results of these analyses are summarized in Table 3.

TABLE 3. *Concurrent and longitudinal correlations between Time 1 closed-class percentage scores and other language measures*

	Size of vocabulary at Time 1 and Time 2			
	T_1 All T_2 All ($N = 228$)	$T_1 > 400$ $T_2 > 400$ ($N = 37$)	$T_1 < 400$ $T_2 < 400$ ($N = 83$)	$T_1 < 400$ $T_2 > 400$ ($N = 108$)
Time 1				
Total vocabulary	0·16**	0·60***	−0·01	−0·18*
Complexity	0·31***	0·80***	0·01	0·01
Time 2				
Total vocabulary	0·07	0·45**	−0·19*	−0·05
Complexity	0·13*	0·52**	−0·07	−0·03
% Closed class	0·34***	0·48**	0·46***	0·07

$* = p < 0.05$; $** = p < 0.01$; $*** = p < 0.001$.

For the group as a whole, the early closed-class scores are significantly and positively correlated with vocabulary and grammar at Time 1, and with grammatical complexity and closed-class usage at Time 2. However, the remaining analyses show that there are really three distinct patterns underlying these correlations.

For children who are already into the productive range at Time 1 (with vocabularies over 400 words) it is fair to conclude that 'everything correlates with everything else'. That is, their use of closed-class items is strongly related to concurrent vocabulary and grammar, and to all three measures later on. This is what we would expect if closed-class usage reflects 'true grammar' in children with vocabularies as large as this, and it also suggests that grammar and vocabulary are very tightly linked during this phase of development (see also Marchman & Bates, 1994).

For children who are still below the 400-word mark at both time points, early closed-class usage bears no relationship at all to concurrent vocabulary or grammar. It bears a weak relationship to later vocabulary – but in the negative direction ($r = -0.19$, $p < 0.05$), suggesting that heavy reliance on closed-class items in the early stages of development may be associated with a slower rate of development overall. And yet, interestingly enough, there is clear continuity between closed-class usage at Time 1 and the same measure at Time 2 for this particular group of children ($r = +0.48$, $p < 0.01$), suggesting that they are still (for better or for worse) taking the same general approach to language learning. If (as we have assumed) the early appearance of closed-class words before the 400-word point actually reflects a rote or holistic approach to language learning, then we may conclude that this approach is stable (at least for some children) between the second and third year of life.

The most important finding comes from the largest group of children, those who are below the 400-word mark at Time 1 but beyond that point at Time 2. These children are not particularly slow for their age (a vocabulary under 400 words is quite normal at Time 1), nor are they particularly fast (i.e. a vocabulary above 400 words is not unusual at Time 2). However, if we assume that variation in closed-class scores is STYLISTIC in the < 400 range and DEVELOPMENTAL in the > 400 range, then our conclusion is clear:

> The early appearance of closed-class words bears no relationship at all to the later acquisition of grammar.

Furthermore, because this group shows a significant negative correlation between closed-class scores at Time 1 and vocabulary size at Time 1 ($r = -0.18$, $p < 0.05$), it seems fair to conclude that this dimension of style is associated with a slight disadvantage in overall rate of lexical development. Of course this does not mean that closed-class usage is bad for children in the early stages. Indeed, there is nothing that we can conclude about direction of causation from the pattern of correlations in Table 3. Some possible interpretations for these patterns are proposed below.

SUMMARY AND CONCLUSIONS

We have provided evidence for developmental changes in the composition of the lexicon, reflecting a shift in emphasis from reference, to predication, to grammar. Each of these transitions takes place within a particular vocabulary range: 1–100 words for common nouns: 50–200 words for verbs and adjectives; 400 words for closed-class morphemes. These systematic relationships between size and composition of vocabulary (despite wide variations in age) provide evidence for recent 'critical mass' accounts of early lexical and grammatical development (e.g. Plunkett *et al.* 1991; Marchman & Bates, 1994). At the same time, they prove that the study of QUALITATIVE variation in lexical style is confounded by QUANTITATIVE variation in rate of lexical development – in line with recent criticisms by Lieven & Pine (1990).

We examined the range of individual differences that can be observed in 'referential style' (percentage of common nouns) and 'closed-class style' (percentage of grammatical function words), when individual differences in rate of lexical development are controlled. There does indeed appear to be substantial individual variation in lexical composition within vocabulary levels. For referential style, the variance is maximal between 10 and 50 words (in line with Katherine Nelson's original findings – Nelson, 1973). However, stylistic and developmental variances co-exist across this range, requiring some kind of multivariate approach and/or the use of percentile scores based on vocabulary size if we want to pull apart these two distinct sources of variation in early noun use. By contrast, variation in closed-class proportions is characterized by two distinct developmental epochs. For children with vocabularies under 400 words, there is no linear or non-linear relationship between vocabulary size and closed-class scores. And yet there are still substantial individual differences across this lexical range – stylistic variation that appears to be independent of vocabulary size. After 400 words, the picture changes: there is a strong linear relationship between lexical development and closed-class use that affects all children from the bottom to the top tenth percentile. Hence stylistic variance (if any remains) is now obscured by developmental effects. Given these distributions, it seems that we can use straightforward linear statistics to study variation in closed-class usage before the 400-word point. After that point, developmental confounds have to be controlled, by parcelling out vocabulary size and/or by assigning percentile scores based on vocabulary levels (a look-up table for the calculation of closed-class style is provided in the Appendix).

Finally, we followed these recommendations in studying the correlates of lexical style. First, we looked at the correlates of referential style in children with vocabularies between 10 and 50 words. When vocabulary levels are controlled, the oft-cited association between referential style and precocity seems to disappear. However, modest correlations with social class and maternal education remain, suggesting that environmental factors may contribute some of the variance in early 'nouniness' (but see footnote 2). With the measures that are available to us in this study, we find little evidence for long-term associates of referential style. It is not the case, for example, that referential children invariably 'turn into' children with low levels of closed-class use 6–7 months later (i.e. telegraphic style), nor do expressive children 'turn into' children with exceptionally high levels of closed-class use (i.e. pronominal, holistic or formulaic style). Previous demonstrations of continuity in 'nouniness' from single- to multiword speech may have reflected continuity in the developmental variance that is also contained in such measures. To uncover the earliest manifestations of analytic/holistic style, we may need a very different set of lexical and/or phonological measures (e.g. the 'rote production' variables described by Bates *et al.*, or the phonological style variables described by Vihman and her colleagues). The simple proportion scores provided by this vocabulary checklist are not enough.

In analysing the correlates of closed-class style, we found some limited evidence in support of a link between rate of development (i.e. precocity) and closed-class proportion scores. Even when we restrict our attention to children with vocabularies under 400 words (when there is no developmental relation between closed-class scores and vocabulary size), a small but reliable correlation with age remains. Specifically, children at the high end of the closed-class continuum tend to be slightly older; children at the low end tend to be a little bit younger. This is compatible with the argument that 'holistic' children detect and reproduce function words in rote frames because they have more mature memories and/or better-developed perceptual abilities. This information-processing account is buttressed by the fact that we found no correlations between closed-class style and the 'fellow travellers' of precocity (e.g. gender, birth order, social class, maternal education). The same hypothesis can be used to explain the negative correlations between rate of vocabulary development and closed-class style when we restrict our attention to children in the < 400-word range. That is, we need not assume that early use of function words is 'bad for children'. Instead, we suggest that children who are developing slowly (for reasons that we do not yet understand) arrive at the 'same' stage of lexical development with an information-processing system that is somewhat more mature in other respects than that of younger lexically matched controls. This fact permits them to pick up perceptual details that younger children cannot detect, or choose to ignore. As a result, they try to reproduce those details (e.g. *Uh wan' dat*), whether they understand them or not.

We also considered a 'grammar module' explanation for the independence of closed-class variance and vocabulary size in children under the 400-word boundary. To test this hypothesis, we examined correlations between closed-class style at Time 1 (in the < 400-word range) and measures of lexical and grammatical development at Time 2 (in the > 400-word range). These analyses showed that the Time 1 measure of closed-class usage was completely unrelated to later advances in language (including later measures of grammar). We conclude from these longitudinal analyses that early usage of closed-class words does NOT reflect the early emergence of productive grammar.

At this point, we can only speculate about the basis of the closed-class style dimension. As we noted at the outset, many important sources of information about early language development cannot be obtained through parental report – including phonological factors, perceptual factors, measures of child memory and cognitive style, type/token ratios and other frequency-sensitive measures of input and output, and sensitive indices of parent–child interaction. All these variables (and others as well) will need to be explored if we want to understand the causes of individual variation in early language development. Nor should we fall into the trap of treating these causal variables as mutually exclusive, competing explanations. We have argued elsewhere (e.g. Bates *et al.* 1988; Bates & Thal, 1991; Bates, Thal & Marchman, 1991) that variations and dissociations of the kind described here provide clues to the underlying mechanisms that can 'come apart' in the first stages of development. But these mechanisms may 'come apart' for a variety of reasons, including differential rate of maturation within and across components, child temperament, and variations in parental style and linguistic input.

In this paper, we have provided evidence for robust individual differences in the early stages of language development, although these differences often reflect a complex interplay of developmental and stylistic variation. Most of the hard work that will be required to explain these differences still lies ahead of us. Furthermore, most of this research will require more costly and labour-intensive sources of information than we can obtain with parental report. However, the parental report data that we have provided here can be used to place children on the developmental and stylistic landscape, identifying subjects for participation in more intensive studies. To assist in that effort, we have provided an Appendix with percentile scores for referential style (percentage of common nouns) and closed-class style (closed-class proportion scores) within vocabulary levels.

As a final note, we should stress that all our conclusions pertain to children who are learning English as their native language. It remains to be seen whether the same developmental and stylistic patterns hold up across structurally distinct language types. For example, Gopnik & Choi (1990) have reported earlier use of verbs and slower growth for nouns for infants who are learning Korean (an SOV language in which parents often use sentences consisting of a single inflected verb). Their results are based on a different methodology (i.e. free speech in a controlled situation), so it is still unclear whether the apparent difference between English and Korean reflects methodological factors or a cross-linguistic finding with important consequences for theories of lexical and grammatical development during the second year of life. At present (1993) versions of the MacArthur CDI are available for Spanish (Jackson-Maldonado *et al.* 1993), Italian (Caselli & Casadio, 1992), Japanese (Ogura, Yamashita, Murase & Dale, 1992), and American Sign Language (Reilly, Provine, Anderson & Bellugi, 1992). In a relatively short time, we may learn a great deal about language universals and language-specific patterns of variation during the passage from first words to grammar.

REFERENCES

Bates, E., Bretherton, I. & Snyder, L. (1988). *From first words to grammar: individual differences and dissociable mechanisms.* New York: C.U.P.

Bates, E. & Carnevale, G. F. (in press). New directions in research on language development. *Developmental Review.*

Bates, E., Caselli, M. C. & Casadio, P. (1990). A crosslinguistic study of early lexical development using parental report. In C. Rovee-Collier (ed.), *Abstracts of the Seventh International Conference on Infant Studies. Special issue of Infant Behavior and Development* **13**, 258. Norwood, NJ: Ablex.

Bates, E. & Thal, D. (1991). Associations and dissociations in language development. In J. Miller (ed.), *Research on child language disorders: a decade of progress.* Austin, TX: Pro-Ed.

Bates, E., Thal, D. & Marchman, V. (1991). Symbols and syntax: a Darwinian approach to language development. In N. Krasnegor, D. Rumbaugh, R. Schiefelbusch & M. Studdert-Kennedy (eds), *Biological and behavioral determinants of language development.* Hillsdale, NJ: Erlbaum.

Bloom, L. (1991). *Language development from two to three.* New York: C.U.P.

Bloom, L., Lightbown, L. & Hood, L. (1975). Structure and variation in child language. *Monographs of the Society for Research in Child Development* **40**, Serial No. 160.

Brown, R. (1973). *A first language: the early stages.* Cambridge, MA: Harvard University Press.

Camaioni, L., Caselli, M. C., Longobardi, E. & Volterra, V. (1991). A parent report instrument for early language assessment. *First Language* **11**, 345–59.

Caselli, M. C. & Casadio, P. (1992). *Fondazione MacArthur: lo sviluppo comunicativo nella prima infanzia.* Rome: Istituto di Psicologia, Consiglio Nazionale delle Ricerche.

Dale, P. S. (1991). The validity of a parent report measure of vocabulary and syntax at 24 months. *Journal of Speech and Hearing Sciences* **34**, 565–71.

Dale, P., Bates, E., Reznick, S. & Morisset, C. (1989). The validity of a parent report instrument of child language at 20 months. *Journal of Child Language* **16**, 239–49.

Dixon, W. & Shore, C. (1991). A confirmatory factor analysis of language style. Paper presented at the Society for Research in Child Development, Seattle, WA.

—— & —— (1992). Confirming linguistic styles. Paper presented at the International Conference on Infant Studies, Miami Beach, FL.

Fenson, L., Dale, P., Reznick, J. S., Thal, D., Bates, E., Hartung, J., Pethick, S. & Reilly, J. (1993). *The MacArthur Communicative Development Inventories: user's guide and technical manual.* San Diego: Singular Publishing Group.

Ferguson, C. A. & Farwell, C. B. (1975). Words and sounds in early language acquisition. *Language* **51**, 419–39.

Gesell, A. (1925). *The mental growth of the preschool child: a psychological outline of normal development from birth to the sixth year, including a system of developmental diagnosis.* New York: Macmillan.

Goldfield, B. & Snow, C. (1985). Individual differences in language acquisition. In J. Gleason (ed.), *Language development.* Columbus, OH: Merrill.

Gopnik, A. & Choi, S. (1990). Do linguistic differences lead to cognitive differences? A cross-linguistic study of semantic and cognitive development. *First Language* **10**, 199–215.

Hampson, J. & Nelson, K. (1993). Relation of maternal language to variation in rate and style of language acquisition. *Journal of Child Language* **20**, 313–42.

Hollingshead, A. (1965). *Two-factor index of social position*. New Haven: Yale University Press.

Jackson-Maldonado, D., Thal, D., Marchman, V., Bates, E. & Gutierrez-Clellen, V. (1993). Early lexical development in Spanish-speaking infants and toddlers. *Journal of Child Language* **20**, 523–49.

Lenneberg, E. H. (1967). *Biological foundations of language*. New York: Wiley.

Lieven, E. & Pine, J. M. (1990). Review of E. Bates, I. Bretherton & L. J. Snyder, *From first words to grammar: individual differences and dissociable mechanisms*. In *Journal of Child Language* **17**, 495–501.

MacWhinney, B. (1991). *The CHILDES project: tools for analyzing talk*. Hillsdale, NJ: Erlbaum.

Marchman, V. & Bates, E. (1994). Continuity in lexical and morphological development: a test of the critical mass hypothesis. *Journal of Child Language* (in press).

Nelson, K. E. (1973). Structure and strategy in learning to talk. *Monographs of the Society for Research in Child Development* **38**. (1–2, Serial No. 149).

—— (1981). Individual differences in language development: implications for development and language. *Developmental Psychology* **17**, 170–87.

Ogura, T., Yamashita, Y., Murase, T. & Dale, P. (1992). Some preliminary findings from the Japanese Early Communicative Development Inventory. Unpublished abstract, Shimane University.

O'Hanlon, L., Washkevich, D. & Thal, D. (1991). MacArthur Communicative Inventory – Toddlers: validation for language-impaired children. Poster presented at the Annual Convention of the American Speech-Language-Hearing Association, Atlanta.

Peters, A. (1977). Language-learning strategies: does the whole equal the sum of the parts? *Language* **53**, 560–73.

Pine, J. M. & Lieven, E. (1990). Referential style at 13 months: why age-defined cross-sectional measures are inappropriate for the study of strategy differences in early language development. *Journal of Child Language* **17**, 625–31.

Plunkett, K. (1993). Lexical segmentation and vocabulary growth in early language acquisition. *Journal of Child Language* **20**, 43–60.

Plunkett, K. & Marchman, V. (1993). From rote learning to system building: acquiring verb morphology in children and connectionist nets. *Cognition* **48**, 21–69.

Reilly, J., Provine, K., Anderson, D. & Bellugi, U. (1992). Does modality influence lexical development? Parent report data on the emergence of American Sign Language. Unpublished abstract, San Diego State University.

Snyder, L., Bates, E. & Bretherton, I. (1981). Content and context in early lexical development. *Journal of Child Language* **8**, 565–82.

Thal, D. & Bates, E. (1990). Continuity and variation in language development. In J. Colombo & J. Fagen (eds), *Individual differences in infancy: reliability, stability, prediction*. Hillsdale, NJ: Erlbaum.

Van Geert, P. (1991). A dynamic systems model of cognitive and language growth. *Psychological Review* **98**, 3–53.

Vihman, M. (1986). Individual differences in babbling and early speech: predicting to age three. In B. Lindblom & R. Zetterstrom (eds), *Precursors of early speech*. Basingstoke, Hampshire: Macmillan.

Vihman, M., Ferguson, C. & Elbert, M. (1986). Phonological development from babbling to speech: common tendencies and individual differences. *Applied Psycholinguistics* **7**, 3–40.

Vihman, M. & Greenlee, M. (1987). Individual differences in phonological development: age one and age three. *Journal of Speech and Hearing Research* **30**, 503–28.

Vihman, M. & Miller, R. (1988). Words and babble at the threshold of language acquisition. In M. D. Smith & J. L. Locke (eds), *The emergent lexicon*. New York: Academic Press.

APPENDIX

Tables for determining referential style and closed-class style, corrected for vocabulary level

TABLE A1. *Table for determining referential style (percentage of common nouns adjusted for vocabulary size) between age 0;8 and 1;4 on CDI : Infants*

Percentile for percentage of common nouns	Production level (total words)				
	1–5[a]	6–10	11–20	21–50	> 50
5	0	0	1·94	20·72	37·47
10	0	0	9·09	23·61	42·20
15	0	0	14·34	26·87	44·70
20	0	0	18·91	30·62	46·38
25	0	5·00	21·43	36·09	48·83
30	0	11·11	25·00	37·50	50·00
35	0	12·68	26·67	40·41	50·38
40	0	14·28	27·78	41·83	51·27
45	0	16·67	30·77	43·48	53·08
50	0	16·67	32·46	44·91	54·61
55	0	21·50	33·33	45·85	55·47
60	0	27·14	36·46	46·93	56·58
65	20·00	28·57	38·70	50·00	57·66
70	20·00	33·33	40·00	51·77	59·00
75	25·00	33·33	45·63	53·13	59·76
80	33·33	40·00	47·25	55·56	62·57
85	40·00	50·00	52·79	58·56	65·01
90	50·00	50·00	56·25	61·77	65·82
95	100·00	59·14	62·90	69·11	66·63

[a] Because most children with vocabularies between 1 and 5 words have no common nouns at all, this table should only be used to assign scores for relatively HIGH common-noun percentage scores in this vocabulary range (i.e. scores in the top quartile, from 25 to 100 % common nouns).

TABLE A2. *Table for determining referential style (percentage of common nouns) between age 1;4 and 2;6 (or linguistic equivalent)*

Percentile for percentage of common nouns	Production level (total words)[a]		
	0–50	50–100	100–200
5	9·48	34·41	42·45
10	15·50	37·59	44·74
15	20·00	40·98	47·57
20	22·81	42·01	49·15
25	28·78	43·67	50·23
30	30·77	45·46	51·61
35	33·33	46·21	52·22

TABLE A2.—*cont.*

40	35·79	47·29	52·84
45	38·65	49·18	53·72
50	40·65	51·30	54·67
55	41·93	52·00	55·55
60	42·86	52·67	56·56
65	45·11	53·67	57·66
70	48·04	54·20	59·55
75	50·00	55·88	60·54
80	51·56	56·89	61·17
85	53·36	58·00	62·80
90	56·80	59·29	65·87
95	59·52	61·24	68·80

[a] Because variance in referential style (i.e. percentage of total vocabulary consisting of common nouns) changes shape and meaning after 150–200 words, we are only providing tables for children with vocabularies under 200 words.

TABLE A3. *Table for determining levels of closed-class use (holding vocabulary level constant) between age 1 ;4 and 2 ;6*

Percentile for percentage of closed class	Production level (total words)							
	0–50	50–100	100–200	200–300	300–400	400–500	500–600	> 600
5	n.a.	0·60	0·96	2·52	2·62	3·11	6·81	10·19
10	n.a.	1·28	1·80	3·31	3·73	4·39	8·28	11·64
15	n.a.	2·39	2·64	3·73	4·14	5·21	8·62	12·60
20	n.a.	3·06	3·06	4·05	4·49	5·88	9·07	13·02
25	n.a.	3·23	3·36	4·37	4·87	6·25	9·46	13·13
30	n.a.	4·01	3·59	4·68	5·28	6·91	9·84	13·40
35	0·0	4·40	4·24	5·12	5·55	7·45	10·31	13·59
40	2·29	4·76	4·77	5·35	5·97	7·81	10·46	13·83
45	2·92	5·10	5·34	5·50	6·16	8·07	10·75	14·02
50	4·08	6·03	5·59	5·86	6·45	8·33	11·24	14·22
55	4·80	6·33	5·75	5·97	6·82	8·75	11·42	14·45
60	5·88	6·93	6·07	6·44	7·32	9·12	11·59	14·54
65	7·36	7·58	6·68	6·93	7·82	9·39	11·98	14·65
70	8·87	8·52	7·14	7·34	8·22	9·88	12·38	14·85
75	9·64	9·50	7·88	7·75	8·45	10·35	12·54	15·02
80	11·77	10·53	8·20	7·97	8·74	10·91	12·90	15·12
85	12·93	11·38	9·01	8·56	9·40	11·35	13·39	15·20
90	14·79	12·92	10·09	9·36	10·45	12·31	13·95	15·45
95	19·20	16·31	12·28	10·73	11·37	13·55	14·60	15·78

J. Child Lang. **21** (1994), 125–155. Copyright © 1994 Cambridge University Press

Early object labels: the case for a developmental lexical principles framework*

ROBERTA MICHNICK GOLINKOFF

University of Delaware

CAROLYN B. MERVIS

Emory University

AND

KATHRYN HIRSH-PASEK

Temple University

ABSTRACT

Universally, object names make up the largest proportion of any word type found in children's early lexicons. Here we present and critically evaluate a set of six lexical principles (some previously proposed and some new) for making object label learning a manageable task. Overall, the principles have the effect of reducing the amount of information that language-learning children must consider for what a new word might mean. These principles are constructed by children in a two-tiered developmental sequence, as a function of their sensitivity to linguistic input, contextual information, and social-interactional cues. Thus, the process of lexical acquisition changes as a result of the particular principles a given child has at his or her disposal. For children who have only the principles of the first tier (REFERENCE, EXTENDIBILITY, and OBJECT SCOPE), word learning has a deliberate and laborious look. The principles of the second tier (CATEGORICAL SCOPE, NOVEL NAME – NAME-LESS CATEGORY' or N3C, and CONVENTIONALITY) enable the child to acquire many new labels rapidly. The present unified account is argued to have a number of advantages over treating such principles separately

[*] A version of this paper was presented at the Society for Research in Child Development meetings in 1993. The research described herein was supported by a fellowship from the John Simon Guggenheim Memorial Foundation and a James McKeen Cattell Sabbatical Award to Golinkoff, and grant No. HD19568 from the National Institute of Child Health and Human Development awarded to Golinkoff and Hirsh-Pasek. Mervis's participation also was supported by grants from that Institute (HD27042 and HD26892) and from the National Science Foundation (BNS84-19036). We wish to thank Jacquelyn Bertrand, Lois Bloom, Bill Frawley, Gaby Hermon and our long-standing MLU group for their helpful comments on various drafts of this manuscript. Address for correspondence: Roberta Golinkoff, Department of Educational Studies, College of Education, University of Delaware, Newark, Delaware, 19716, USA. Email: CXC04599@UDELVM.BITNET.

and non-developmentally. Further, the explicit recognition that the acquisition and operation of these principles is influenced by the child's interpretation of both linguistic and non-linguistic input is seen as an advance.

INTRODUCTION

Rapid word acquisition, beginning in the second year of life, is the norm for human children. Before children can tie their shoes they have learned approximately 14,000 words, an average of nine new words a day (Carey, 1982). To account for this prodigious feat, a line of research on the 'principles' or 'constraints' which guide lexical acquisition has emerged. This paper examines the following claim which characterizes the general rationale behind that research: lexical acquisition proceeds in the rapid, relatively effortless way that it does because the child operates with a set of principles that guide the task of word learning. These principles enable the child to avoid the Quinean (1960) conundrum of generating limitless, equally logical possibilities, for a word's meaning. For example, Quine (1960) raised the issue of how one could know the meaning of a simple term, such as 'rabbit'. 'Rabbit' could mean the whole rabbit or the left ear or the fur, etc. Yet, children do not appear to weigh these alternatives for a new word's meaning. Rather they seem to operate with what have been called 'biases', 'constraints', or 'principles' to circumvent these blind alleys.

Researchers have made important theoretical and empirical contributions to lexical acquisition by positing several principles (some of which compete) and by conducting research to validate the existence of these principles (e.g. Barrett, 1978; Markman, 1989; Merriman & Bowman, 1989; Clark, 1990; Waxman & Kosowski, 1990), many of which will be discussed below. However, no unified account of these principles exists. Thus, two challenges face this area: first, can some combination of old and new principles be systematized into a story that coheres?; and second, can the research in lexical acquisition be used to evaluate competing principles?

This paper is designed to meet these challenges. Six principles have been organized into a developmental framework which is represented in Fig. 1. Three of the principles appear in each of two tiers. Principles within a tier are predicted to emerge within a short time of each other and to be linked conceptually. Treating these principles as a two-tiered set has the following three advantages: first, principles which were previously presupposed emerge in bas relief. For example, before the child can know the KINDS of categories object words label (a presupposition in Markman & Hutchinson's (1984) 'taxonomic assumption'), the child must know that words do not label only individual exemplars (this is the principle of extendibility). Second, embedding the principles in a developmental framework highlights the question of

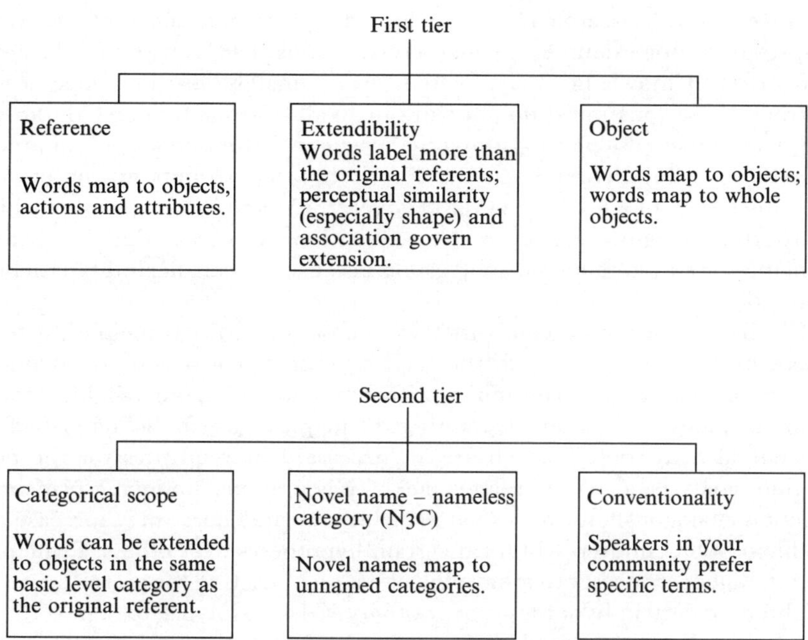

Fig. 1. Principles of lexical acquisition – a summary.

whether they are unique to language or rest on collateral cognitive achievements. This treatment may also have practical implications for understanding children who have difficulty acquiring language (Mervis & Bertrand, 1993). Third, when the principles are organized developmentally, possible explanations emerge for the changing character of the lexical acquisition process across the second year of life. The fact that lexical learning starts off slowly and deliberately and then enters a period of rapid growth (Dromi, 1987) may be partially explained by changes in the child's store of word learning principles.

'Principles' versus 'constraints' and problems common to both

It should be noted at the outset that the case for constraints or principles of word learning is not universally accepted (Nelson, 1988; Kuczaj, 1990). Arguments against the constraints position are sometimes rooted in terminological confusion since the term 'constraint' has two senses. In the first sense, constraints LIMIT the learner, making certain information impossible to learn. In the second sense, constraints POTENTIATE learning by limiting hypotheses that the learner considers (Carey & Gelman, 1990). Using the first sense, Nelson (1988) argued that constraints operate in an all-or-none fashion, are universal and innate, and do not allow for individual differences.

However, most researchers have adopted the second sense of the term 'constraint'. For example, Gelman (1990) states that 'constraint' does not imply that all knowledge in a domain is given innately; learning must occur. Further, these constraints do not work in an all-or-none fashion (Markman, 1989) and they do permit individual variation throughout development (Waxman, 1989; Behrend, 1990). Thus, these constraints are unlike the principles, say, of Chomsky's (1981) government and binding syntax which (purportedly) tightly constrain the acquisition of syntax. Further, lexical principles are more biologically feasible because of their flexibility (Lieberman, 1991).

To alleviate semantic confusion, we adopt the term 'principle', a term whose meaning overlaps with the second sense of constraint. In addition, 'principle' maintains a continuity with previous theorizing. Slobin (1985: 1159) generated a set of 'Operating Principles' which he described as '…general heuristic[s]' which are '…necessary prerequisites for the perception, analysis, and use of language…' His grammar-inducing principles function analogously to the lexical principles posited here: they increase the likelihood that children will form certain hypotheses over others. Principles are intelligent strategies that have the effect of restricting the search space by heightening certain hypotheses over others (Glass, Holyoak & Santa, 1979). The principles are themselves byproducts of cognitive and linguistic development.

Treating lexical principles as byproducts of other developments raises issues about the necessity of positing the principles altogether. Indeed, Bloom, Tinker & Margulis (1993) and Nelson, Hampson & Shaw (1993) have argued that lexical principles are merely convenient descriptions of behaviour rather than rules in the child's head that enable word learning. Further, principles are not needed because children are so adept at utilizing non-linguistic cues to word meaning. Children can focus on their mental representations of the well-worn routines (e.g. eating) in which they hear words to help them 'narrow the range of possible meanings any particular word could have' (Bloom *et al.* 1993: 25). This is Bloom *et al.*'s principle of 'relevance'. Yet relevance still begs the question of how the mapping between mental representations and words occurs. Children's mental representations of events are multifaceted; somehow they must decide exactly WHICH facet of their representation is being commented on. Thus, relevance by itself is too vague, although surely cues from context and social interaction play an important role in delimiting word meaning.

What is needed in addition are specific lexical principles which bring certain hypotheses for the meanings of words to the 'top of the stack'. If this is true, the next question is where do these principles come from? Unfortunately, this has not been a productive debate since it has been cast as a nature-nurture issue. Yet there are a number of possible curves which describe the emergence of knowledge or processes which have innate underpinnings (Aslin, 1981). The fact that the principles are not all present from the start neither confirms nor disconfirms the role of *a priori* factors. Since some elements used by children in the construction of these principles may well be innate, and since our present state of knowledge in this area does not permit us to disentangle what is innate from what is learned, the emphasis herein will be on how children might CONSTRUCT these principles, utilizing linguistic input and cues from social interaction. However, not all principles are constructed in the same way. The construction of some principles relies on children's early sensitivity to non-linguistic cues and suprasegmental (prosodic) information in the speech stream; the construction of others relies more heavily on children's sensitivity to linguistic information. For this reason, we propose that the principles are acquired in two-tiers, with the principles of the first tier serving as the output on which the second tier principles build. Principles come 'on-line' as the child becomes increasingly capable of utilizing the available linguistic and non-linguistic input. Further, once the child constructs these principles, they become enabling devices to spur further word learning in a way not possible before their construction.

Having cleared the terminological waters and raised some of the problems which face this line of research, we next present the principles themselves. Any allusions to the age of appearance of these principles, or indeed to their order of appearance within a tier, should be taken as only tentative. It may well be the case that as our knowledge of lexical acquisition increases, the proposed principles will be modified.

PRINCIPLES FOR LEARNING OBJECT LABELS: DESCRIPTION AND
EVIDENCE

The focus here is on object labels for three reasons.[1] First, since prior research has focused on object label acquisition (e.g. Clark, 1983), there is an abundance of descriptive and empirical research to draw upon to formulate and evaluate the principles. Second, while all languages have a category 'noun' which maps to 'concrete object' (Maratsos, 1991), they may lack other word classes. Third, labels for objects make up the largest proportion of any word type in children's early lexicons (Gentner, 1983) – even in

---

[1] We fully recognize that object labels are generally count nouns in English. However, keeping in mind that the principles are formulated for young language learners who may not start out with the category 'noun,' and not for adults who can readily assign a novel word to a form class, we often use the phrases 'object label' or 'object word'. Further, by 'object' we mean 'discrete solid object' although, as will be seen later in the paper, these principles are also meant to work for the acquisition of other open class words.

languages like Japanese which permit noun ellipsis (Fernald & Morikawa, 1993). Thus, the acquisition of object labels seems a good place to start to see if the principles approach has any validity.

The examination of this issue for object labels can provide a backdrop against which to evaluate whether the nature of the mapping between words and other kinds of ontological categories is similar or different. For example, the mapping of words to objects could then be compared to the mapping of words to substances (Soja, Carey & Spelke, 1991) or actions (Golinkoff, Hirsh-Pasek, Mervis, Frawley & Parillo, in press). In what follows, six lexical principles are presented along with (*a*) speculations about their origins and (*b*) evidence to support them. The principles which are suggested cohere on two developmental tiers designed to capture children's increasing linguistic sophistication.

The principle of reference

The principle of reference is the first and most fundamental insight children must attain and the principle on which all other principles rest. As Brown (1958: 7) wrote, 'The use of language to make reference is the central language function which is prerequisite to all else'. While children must learn exactly which words people use to refer to which objects or events, they first must know THAT people use words to refer. As Terrace (1985: 1014) wrote, 'a strong case can be made for the hypothesis that the deceptively simple ability to communicate via words required a cognitive advance in the evolution of human intelligence that was at least as significant as the advance(s) that led to grammatical competence.'

The principle of reference states that words can be mapped onto the child's representations of objects, actions, events or attributes in the environment. Obviously, this definition hinges crucially on the meaning of 'word' and 'map'. Both philosophers and linguists have had a difficult time defining the concept 'word'. Equally mysterious is the nature of the mapping relation between words and referents in the environment. As Gauker (1990) pointed out, a word does not refer just because presentation of a specific object or event elicits its production. For example, one can say 'yikes!' each time one sees a particular cat, but that is not necessarily the same thing as referring to the cat. 'Yikes' could merely be an emotional reaction; it could also be a trained associate (as in paired associate learning).

For us to claim reference as a first principle, however, requires a commitment to some definition of these historically troublesome terms. Suffice it to say that a word which is used to make reference is a phonological shape which bears no iconic relationship to the concept it represents, although a word is surely many other things as well (Lyons, 1977). 'Mapping' refers to the symbolic relationship between the word (be it oral or sign) and the event or object it represents. The problem is figuring out how the form gets 'hooked up' with the meaning. Said in another way, how does the form come to symbolize, or 'stand for', the referent and not just 'go with' the referent, as in a paired-associate relationship? It is very difficult, indeed virtually impossible, to diagnose a clear-cut case of linguistic reference.

Possible origins of the principle of reference. Note that reference is not a property of words *per se*. As Lyons (1977: 177) pointed out, something in the environment can be referred to in any number of ways (e.g. *Fido* or *dog*). It is '...the person who refers [or who comprehends a referring expression] who invests the expression with reference'. Consider what the child must do to recognize an act of referring on the part of another. Following Macnamara (1982), the child must know that the sounds emanating from the speaker's mouth are about something in the environment and are not just designed to soothe or to comment, as in *Let me see....* This presumes that the child can (1) distinguish the intention to refer from other intentions; (2) isolate the word or words (the phonological shape in the input) doing the referring, and (3) using non-linguistic cues, find the item or event being referred to in the environment. Macnamara (1982) takes reference as a 'primitive'. Such a position appears to presume that the infant is born with a 'theory of mind' (Wellman, 1990), or the recognition that people possess thoughts and beliefs different from the infant's own. By the time children are producing their first words (at around 1;0) they may indeed have a primitive theory of the mind of the other (Golinkoff, 1992). However, it seems likely that the cognitive and communicative achievements of the preverbal period are the source of the principle of reference.

Infants' appreciation of communicative intention. When infants (at about 0;9) start to follow a pointed index finger to a distal object (as opposed to staring at the finger), it can be argued that they have interpreted the point as 'referring' to something in the distal field (e.g. Lock, 1978). Infants also engage in 'cross-checking' at about 0;8 (Scaife & Bruner, 1975), or looking back and forth between the distal array and the parent's point. It is as if the infant is saying, 'Did I get the point of the point?' Such behaviours suggest that the infant already has an idea that people can use gestures to refer (broadly speaking) to something in the environment. Not only do infants come to apprehend the meaning of consistently used gestures to focus their attention, they also begin to emit gestures for this purpose (Bates, Camaioni & Volterra, 1975) and to 'cross-check' to see if the parent is looking at the object they have indicated (Franco & Butterworth, 1991).

In sum, the intention to direct others' attention to things in the environment, as well as the ability to understand others' communicative intentions, is a primitive, non-verbal precursor of the act of referring using words. Babies know about the underlying, intentional structure of acts of referring before they can utter their first words. While the case for prelinguistic reference seems compelling, preverbal reference does not equate to verbal reference. This is because the same nonverbal gesture (such as a point) can be used to refer to any number of referents in the same or different ontological categories; verbal referring expressions map uniquely to particular categories of object referents.

The 'missing link' between preverbal reference and verbal reference may be seen in the case of children who use phonetically consistent non-words to indicate particular meanings before they begin to use words *per se* (e.g. Halliday, 1975). Here a non-standard phonological shape appears to take on the status of a symbol. Once standard words appear, researchers split on whether they believe they are used pre-referentially (Nelson, 1988) or referentially from the start (Huttenlocher & Smiley, 1987; Mervis, Mervis, Johnson & Bertrand, 1992). The explanation for this discrepancy may be a function of two factors: the particular input a child receives for a word, i.e. whether it is used for a single or multiple exemplars (Harris, Barrett, Jones & Brookes, 1988), and whether or not the child has generalized the word to new exemplars. A classic example of a child using a word in a situation-bound way, comes from Bloom's (1974) daughter, Allison. Before her first birthday, Allison recognized *birds* only in connection with the mobile over her dressing table. She did not recognize this word in any other situations, or with other exemplars, for many months. When the word and object are in a 'one word to one exemplar in one situation' mapping relationship, it is even unclear what aspect of the situation is serving as the referent for the word, *birds*. The referent that the child has in mind could differ from the adult's. Perhaps for Allison the referent was the coloured string which attached the birds to the mobile. Cases similar to Allison's use of *birds* were documented by Dromi (1987) who reported that many of her daughter's early words were not extended to other exemplars. In fact, Dromi concluded that, '...pairing a word with a single referent might be an operative strategy that the child follows in acquiring meaning' (1987: 141).

As soon as these children appear capable of recognizing (or producing) the words they know in situations other than the original context, researchers are more likely to agree that they are functioning with the principle of reference. Such episodes shows evidence of EXTENSION, and not just context-bound recognition. The difference between imputations of reference in the literature appears to hinge on this distinction. Only decontextualized word usage is accepted as adequate evidence of reference by some researchers since, except for proper names, words label categories of objects.

Evidence for the principle of reference. If infants operate with the principle of reference, it should be possible to show that words affect their attention, perception, categorization, and memory for events differently from other acoustic stimuli. This is because if words bear a 'stands for' rather than a 'goes with' relationship to referents, they should make referents more distinct and promote categorical thinking. In general, the research supporting the principle of reference is sparse and contradictory. For example, Baldwin & Markman (1989) found that infants (age 0;10) looked more at an object that an adult had labelled than at an object the adult had not labelled. However, this result may not be specific to labels; ANY sort of auditory stimulus coincident with the presentation of a novel object may recruit relatively more attention.

Waxman & Balaban (1992) pitted words against sine wave tones of the same duration and amplitude in a categorization task with infants aged 0;9. Only when a word, and not a tone, accompanied slides of animals did infants appear to form a category by watching an out-of-category object longer at test. On the other hand, Roberts & Jacobs (1992) pitted music against linguistic stimuli in a categorization task with older infants (age 1;3). Category formation was in evidence under both words and music but not in the absence of auditory input (Roberts & Cuff, 1989). Overall, these results provide mixed support for the contention that words have special status for the infant.

Perhaps better evidence that infants know that words refer are reports that infants as young as 1;0 to 1;2 name objects for the sheer pleasure of naming (Mervis, 1987). Further, some infants at this age have a non-standard but phonologically consistent form that they use to request object labels before they begin to produce any words (Halliday, 1975). Reference can also be invoked to help explain symbol use in the absence of input, as in deaf individuals who have not been exposed to sign language and invent 'home signs' to refer (Goldin-Meadow & Mylander, 1984). Reference also remains relatively robust in the face of brain injury. While expressive aphasics may struggle or fail to retrieve the correct name for a referent, all but the most globally impaired aphasics never lose the insight that naming exists (Saffran & Schwartz, personal communication, 1990).

The best evidence for the principle of reference is reviewed below under the principle of extendibility. This is because we have taken the decontextualized use of words to be the hallmark of reference.

Why reference is not enough. The process of word learning begins when infants recognize that people use words to make reference. However, children still need to work out exactly what people use a word to refer TO. Except for the case of proper names, much of the power of reference would be lost if children thought that words referred only to the original exemplar. Perhaps early in lexical development infants do believe that words are tied exclusively to their original context – as Bloom (1974) and Dromi (1987) indicate. Evidence for the fact that children do not interpret all words as context bound comes when children use one word for multiple exemplars, extending a word to tokens they had not previously heard labelled. This behaviour exemplifies the principle of extendibility and gives researchers more confidence in concluding that the principle of reference is present. Thus, extendibility comes in contemporaneously with or shortly after reference is in place.

In short, the principle of reference by itself leaves infants with a number of unanswered questions about exactly how people use words to refer. Unless coupled with a principle such as extendibility, the evidence for reference as here construed is virtually non-existent.

The principle of extendibility

The principle of extendibility is that a word can be used to label referents other than exemplars which someone else has previously labelled. Under extendibility, the criteria for extension are either similarity to the original referent or a common thematic relationship. 'Similarity' can be defined in any number of ways: shape is most frequently used, but sound, smell, texture and taste are also bases for extension (Clark, 1983). The fact that extension initially occurs on a myriad of bases is not surprising; after all, when a word is uttered in the presence of a novel object, there is no accompanying indication as to whether it is to be extended based on shape, or colour, or size, or thematic relations. Despite the fact that the child will need to refine extendibility, this principle captures an important insight into the way words work: they do not label unique referents. Even when words function as proper names, as Brown (1958) pointed out, they label people and places that continually undergo change and transformation. Thus, even a proper noun is in some sense extended. In fact, extendibility may also be explained as an outgrowth of a generalization process.

Under the principle of extendibility a word is seen as labelling a fuzzy set of exemplars, bound together most often by common shape, but sometimes by common usage or association (thematically). For example, Guillame's (1927) son said the French word for breast at 0;11. He used this word not only to ask for the breast but to ask for a biscuit, to refer to a red button, to the point of an elbow, to an eye in a picture, and to his mother's face in a photograph (cited in Bloom & Lahey, 1978). Some of these extensions appear to be shape-based (e.g. the red button), while others appear more thematic in nature (e.g. mother's face). Over time, shape will predominate in extension as the child notes that words tend to pick out objects which share shape. However, extension at this point is still not based on taxonomic category membership *per se* (as it will be in the second tier) but on shared perceptual features (most often shape) which are highly correlated with category membership.

Three predictions follow from this principle. First, prior to extendibility, children should extend only those words which, in the input, have been used to multiple referents. Second, after extendibility, extension based on shape and from the adult perspective, non-standard criteria such as smell, taste, and thematic relations, should be observed. This prediction is supported in the literature. When extension based on shape occurs, it may appear to be taxonomic extension at the child's basic level (Mervis, 1987). However, tests should show (this is the third, as yet untested prediction) that until the advent of the second-tier principle of 'categorical scope', extension which appears to be on the basis of taxonomic category membership is really only on the basis of shared perceptual features. That is, extension is not as much on the KIND of object something is as on how it APPEARS – a more superficial basis for extension.

Possible origins of the principle of extendibility. Reliance on shape as the main basis for extension is presumably rooted in the primacy of shape for object identification. However, the young child is also capable of perceptual discriminations along dimensions such as smell, sound, touch, etc., and it is therefore not surprising that occasional extensions will occur on the basis of shared perceptual features other than shape. As the child gains more experience in observing that words label objects which share shape (as opposed to other perceptual features), extension by shape will come to predominate.

Evidence for the principle of extendibility. Once children have the principle of extendibility, they should extend an object label to other related objects, even if they have never heard a label for these objects. Diary studies support this claim: instances of restriction of word extension to a single object or a very small set of previously named objects are limited to the child's first words (e.g. Bloom, 1973; Barrett, 1978; Dromi, 1987; Mervis *et al.* 1992).[2] The majority of extensions are shape-based but extensions based on other types of similarity, e.g. taste or sound (Clark, 1983), probably rooted in associations, occur as do extensions based on thematic relations. An example is when an item used in conjunction with the original referent is given that label, e.g. the Hebrew word *niyar* for 'paper' said of a pencil (Dromi, 1987).

The importance of shape *per se* for novel word extension has been shown in studies by Smith, Jones & Landau (1992) who pitted the dimension of

---

[2] Huttenlocher & Smiley (1987) suggest that unusual extensions (like saying *cookies* to a cupboard) are children's attempts to fulfil a range of communicative functions with limited lexicons (in this case, as a request). In our view, it is unlikely that all non-taxonomic extensions can be explained in this way.

shape against the dimension of colour using novel artefactual objects. Children aged three used shape for extension when the task involved novel count nouns. Baldwin (1989) conducted a similar study with children aged 2;0 and 3;0. When an adult did not provide a label but simply asked children aged 2;0 to, 'Find another one,' from among two choices, children selected the object which shared either shape or colour with the target. However, when the adult asked the child to select another object by NAME, e.g. 'Find another zom,' selections were based on shape significantly more often than on colour. Children aged 3;0 responded on the basis of shape with and without a label. In addition, young children prefer to extend new words on the basis of shape rather than material (Au, 1985; Dockrell & Campbell, 1986; Heibeck & Markman, 1987) or function (Tomikawa & Dodd, 1980).

Thus, a key prediction of extendibility is upheld: extensions of object labels occur to more than just the original referent. Extension is based on shared perceptual features (e.g. taste, smell) and thematic relations. Extensions come to be dominated by shape as children recognize that, of the perceptual features available for extension, shape is the most frequently used in the input. Eventually, however, the child must conclude that shape is just one highly correlated aspect of category membership and that it is the latter which determines extension. At that point, shape *per se* will lose its potency as the sole basis for extension. In sum, the principle of extendibility enables children to use a word to refer to more than just a single item, although some extensions will be on non-taxonomic bases.

Are the principles of reference and extendibility sufficient for word learning? Knowing that a word can be used to refer to something in the environment and that a word refers to more than exemplars that someone has previously labelled for the child is not sufficient. Children need to have more specific hypotheses about WHAT in the environment words label and HOW they are extended. The next principle, object scope, reduces much of the ambiguity about what words label.

The principle of object scope
The principle of object scope has two parts. First, it states that words label objects. Second, it states that words refer to the whole object as opposed to its parts or attributes. Gleitman's (1990) example of a mother and child observing a jumping rabbit demonstrates the utility of this principle. Part 1 of object scope has the effect of predisposing the child in Gleitman's example to assume that the mother's utterance has to do with some object in the event. Part 2 enables the child to assume that the utterance is about the object as a whole and not its parts or other attributes. Macnamara (1982: 190) stated this principle when he noted that infants '...automatically take the word as

applying to the object as a whole'. Mervis (1987) and Markman & Wachtel (1988) also discussed a whole object principle, although they did not distinguish between its two parts.

Possible origins of the principle of object scope. The reason that infants assume object scope is by no means obvious. Why should the label not apply to the object's movement, or moving parts, or its brightly coloured, highly textured surface?

Gentner (1983) noted that object labels constitute the largest single class of children's earliest words across many languages. Although in her analysis object PARTS were not distinguished from names for objects as a whole, Mervis's (1990) analysis buttresses Gentner's arguments: names of object parts are rarely produced among children's earliest words. One hypothesis for the abundance of whole object labels is that whole objects are perceptually salient for infants, who know about the permanence and solidity of objects early in the first year (Spelke, 1990). Counter to this hypothesis, however, infants can also perceive object parts and properties (e.g. Younger & Cohen, 1986). A second hypothesis for the preponderance of whole object labels is that language may predispose the child to note whole objects because of the prosodic emphasis given to object names in infant-directed speech. A testable prediction follows from this strong claim: hearing a word in the presence of an object with an interesting part should promote discrimination and memory for the whole object. Conversely, seeing that object without a word should lessen the likelihood that the child will focus on the object as a whole.

Is there any way in which child-directed speech might promote attention to the class of object words or to whole objects rather than to their parts or attributes? Gentner (1983) argued that nouns are not uniquely marked in the world's languages; nor that they are particularly salient in speech. In contrast, Goldfield (1993) provided evidence of the salience of object words compared to action words in child-directed speech. Among English-speaking mothers, nouns (as compared to verbs) are produced with higher frequency, greater stress, more often in last position in the sentence, and with fewer inflections. Turkish mothers even violate canonical word order (Turkish is verb-final) to place nouns in the final position in child-directed speech (Aslin, 1992). Thus, in child-directed speech, nouns may indeed receive a kind of 'underscoring' which might facilitate their segmentation in the speech stream and heighten infants' attention to them. Western parents may not only highlight object labels, but labels for whole objects rather than for object parts. Ninio (1980) found that in a book-reading situation parents labelled whole objects before they labelled parts or attributes of objects. Further, parents embedded labels for parts of objects in sentences which highlighted their secondary status relative to the whole object, as in, *See the bunny's nose?*

In sum, the principle of object scope biases the infant to assume that a word labels (1) an object in an observed event; and (2) the whole object as opposed to its parts. Input may support the acquisition of this principle since parents appear to highlight labels for whole objects in their child-directed speech.

Evidence for the principle of object scope. According to part 1 of object scope, the child should interpret a new term as a label for the object involved in an event rather than for, say, the action the object is undergoing. Data for this claim come from a study by Echols (1992) in which infants (0;9 and 1;2) were shown one of two displays accompanied by the same linguistic message. Either a novel object was seen undergoing three different MOTIONS (namely, a straight movement across a plane, a wave-like movement, or an angular movement) or three different OBJECTS were seen undergoing the same motion (namely, the wave-like movement). Infants were also divided into groups depending on whether or not they heard a label (*That's a danu*) as they watched these events. At test, infants in both conditions were shown the same stimuli: an old object undergoing a novel motion and a novel object undergoing an old motion. The outcome was as predicted by object scope. When they had heard a label (...*danu*), the older infants (whether in the consistent motion or the consistent object condition) watched the novel object/old motion combination more than the old object/new motion combination. This result suggests that by 1;2, infants are predisposed to connect a label with an object rather than the object's motion.

For part 2 (words label whole objects), there is evidence that young children who do not have a name for an object construe a label for a part or attribute of the object to be the label for the whole object. For example, Mervis & Long (1987) found that children age 1;6 and 2;0 interpreted a label for a part as the label for the whole object. Infants heard a label for a prominent part of a novel object. When tested for comprehension of the new word in the presence of similar but not identical objects, the object usually selected had the same overall shape as the original object but did not include the labelled part. Importantly, the object which included the same part in the same location but had a different overall shape was generally rejected by the children. Golinkoff, Kenealy & Hirsh-Pasek (1993) used a no-label control condition in a study with five-year olds and adults. With a label, children never selected the part alone as another exemplar of the object; without a label they did so about a quarter of the time. Taylor & Gelman (1988) also report that two-year-olds will construe a label for a novel object to be a label for the whole object and not for a salient attribute (in this case, a bright pattern). Children selected other referents in the same taxonomic class as the named novel object, as opposed to selecting referents outside the class that shared the same salient pattern (e.g. a different type of toy with the same plaid pattern).

It is probably the case that the principle of object scope can be overridden by linguistic input once the child knows something of the syntactic reflexes associated with the different form classes. For example, at 2;0 Taylor & Gelman's (1988) subjects gave both category and property responses when the novel term they heard was an adjective. Thus, an adjective clearly disrupted categorical responding even if it did not move children all the way to property extensions. Arguably then, the object scope principle may be maximally useful to the infant just breaking into the lexicon; knowledge of syntax may later allow mappings outside the class of nouns.

Are the principles of reference, extendibility, and object scope sufficient for word learning? The principles just described comprise the first tier of the model and are sufficient to get the infant's word learning 'off the ground'. None of these principles requires much linguistic sophistication. Rather, infants who have the principles of the first tier but who do not yet have the principles of the second tier primarily pay attention to social cues as they co-occur with the prosodic aspects of linguistic input. As infants sort out the relationship between language and other sources of information, they begin to construct the principles of tier two that will guide their future word learning. Until that time, however, new vocabulary acquisition has a distinctly deliberate look. Children begin to produce a new object word only after they have heard it multiple times and they do not learn all, or even many, of the new object words that they hear. Learning appears to be restricted to names for objects that the child finds particularly interesting.

The second tier of principles will be much more dependent on sensitivity to syntax and will further constrain the basis for extension (categorical scope); it will help children readily map new words to objects in the environment (novel name – nameless category); and it will encourage children to adopt conventional names for things (conventionality). These more advanced principles enable word learning to proceed rapidly and efficiently, in contrast to the first tier principles which simply allow word learning to begin. Further, the principles of the second tier are increasingly shaped by the child's observations of the way language works.

The principle of categorical scope

Under categorical scope, the extension of novel object words occurs mainly on the basis of basic level category membership. According to Rosch, Mervis, Gray, Johnson & Boyes-Braem (1976), as summed up in Lakoff (1987: 47), the 'basic level' is basic in four respects:

(1) perception (including overall perceived shape); (2) function (same general motor program involved in interaction with members of the category; (3) communication (shortest, most commonly used words;

contextually neutral; first learned by children); and (4) knowledge organization.

In addition, parental input appears to be mostly at the basic level (e.g. Brown, 1958; Blewitt, 1983) and children focus their attention at the basic level (Mervis & Crisafi, 1982; Mervis, 1983).

Markman & Hutchinson (1984: 20) captured a related insight when they suggested that, 'words refer mainly to objects that share some property or function rather than to objects united by thematic relations' (their 'taxonomic assumption'). We adopt the principle of categorical scope instead of the taxonomic assumption for two important reasons. First, the statement that extension is based on 'shared properties or function' could include such things as taste or sound. In the present framework, this is the earlier principle of extendibility. Second, the taxonomic assumption implies that extension applies equally well at the basic and at the superordinate levels of categorization. The evidence to be reviewed below, however, indicates that extension occurs mainly at the basic level (Golinkoff, Shuff-Bailey, Olguin & Ruan, 1993).

The major strength of categorical scope is that it makes a clear prediction which is disconfirmable. As reviewed under extendibility, prior to categorical scope, children should attempt to extend a novel object word on the basis of shared perceptual features (especially shape) or thematic links. Once categorical scope is present, however, extension should occur based on membership in the same basic level category – sometimes as defined from the child's perspective (Mervis, 1987). That is, extension should be based on whether the object is considered to be the same kind as the original. This argument is similar to one made by Soja *et al.* (1991) and Keil (1989) who argue that ontological category (or kind of object) carries great weight for extension. Further, as Gelman & Markman (1986) have shown, even young children can override perceptual similarity, making inductions on the basis of deeper, biological or structural commonalities which animate objects or inanimate artefacts share. In practice, however, since items in the same basic level category share shape, Smith *et al.*'s (1992) shape bias accounts for most of the extensions that occur.

Possible origins of the principle of categorical scope. Initially, under the principle of extendibility, children extend object labels to items that are perceptually similar to the original, most often relying on shape (e.g. Smith *et al.* 1992). However, objects that are the same shape are not always in the same category. For example, a 'piggy bank' can be shaped like a ball and yet it is not designed to be thrown. As children have experiences where they realize that extension may be based on features other than shape, they begin to sort out the fact that shape is only one basis for category membership (e.g.

someone shows the child that pennies go in the bank's slot, thereby demonstrating the object's function). At first, they allow the object in question to be in the original (incorrect) category (e.g. calling a bank *ball*) and the new category (*bank*) (Banigan & Mervis, 1988) simultaneously. Eventually, objects come to be assigned to a single category based on basic level category membership, probably from developments in understanding category structure, as well as in observing how language works.

Evidence for the principle of categorical scope. Support comes from diary studies of four children (Barrett, 1982; Dromi, 1987; Mervis *et al.* 1992). By the time a productive vocabulary of about 50–60 words was attained, words were extended to items in the same child basic level category (Mervis, 1987) as the original. The few object words that were not extended on basic-level category membership were used to name categories at either the superordinate or subordinate levels. (In these latter cases, the child already knew the basic level name for the relevant objects.)

Experimental support comes from studies that show that, once a label is introduced, children attend to categories at the basic level. Hall & Waxman (in press) and Hall, Waxman & Hurwitz (in press), for example, found that children who do not yet have a label for an object tend to interpret a novel word (regardless of whether it is a count noun, a proper noun, or an adjective) as though it was referring to a basic level object category. Furthermore, Hall & Waxman found that three-year-olds preferred terms akin to 'person' (a basic-level kind) rather than context-restricted terms such as 'passenger' or what they called 'life-phase-restricted' terms such as 'puppy'. Additional support for categorical scope comes from Markman & Hutchinson (1984) who reported that children from 2;5 to 5;0 preferred to extend a novel noun to an item in the same basic level category as opposed to extending it to a thematically linked item.[3]

Golinkoff *et al.* (1993) also found that children of 4;0 prefer to extend novel object words at the basic level in a forced-choice triad task with three alternatives. For instance, one stimulus set included a banana (the target), a quarter moon (the perceptual choice), a monkey (the thematic choice), and another banana not identical to the target (the basic level choice). (Independent ratings showed that the perceptual and basic level distractors were of equivalent similarity to the target.) Children were either asked to, 'Find another "dax"' or 'Find another one', referring to the target. Children made significantly more basic level than perceptual or thematic choices in the

---

[3] Bauer & Mandler (1989) claimed that words do not promote taxonomic responding since they found that infants of 1;4 made taxonomic selections with and without a novel word. However, this study had two design flaws: first, children received reinforcement for their responses; and second, the correct choice was presented in a strictly alternating order (namely left-right-left, etc.)

presence of a word than in the no-word condition. The fact that shape is but one cue to category membership once something is known of the category is shown by the finding that children did not extend words on the basis of perceptual similarity but on common basic level category membership. An as yet untested prediction is that when children have only extendibility, they should select the perceptual alternative as often as the basic level choice.

Golinkoff *et al.* also failed to find extension at the superordinate level once the similarity between the superordinate alternative and the target was minimized – even when children knew the superordinate category of the stimulus items. This finding, then, suggests that children only spontaneously extend at the basic level. When previous studies (e.g. Markman & Hutchinson, 1984; Waxman & Gelman, 1986; Waxman & Kosowski, 1990) found extension at the superordinate level it was probably due to perceptual similarity (the principle of extendibility) and not category membership.

Summary of the categorical scope principle. The principle of categorical scope follows its necessary precursor, the principle of extendibility. Children first learn THAT words can be extended without being completely clear about the BASIS for extension, although shape is the favoured basis. Categorical scope restricts the basis for the extension of novel object labels to basic level category membership. Now the child can go beyond perceptual similarity to extend object labels on the basis of basic level object kind. Additional tests of this distinction beg to be conducted.

Are the principles posited thus far sufficient for word learning? A principle is needed which will enable the child to accumulate new words swiftly. We next describe a new principle intended for this purpose – the 'novel name-nameless category' principle – and show how it differs from its three competitors (contrast, mutual exclusivity, and fill-the-gap).

The novel name – nameless category principle (N3C)

Here is the phenomenon: a child hears a new label in the presence of some named objects and an unnamed object. The speaker does not make an explicit link between the new name and the unnamed object. Yet, after hearing the novel name once, the child appears to have learned that the unnamed object is the referent for the novel name. If children are to acquire words with the rapidity which is seen to begin in the middle of the second year of life, a principle is needed which will allow children to 'hook-up' novel names with previously unnamed objects with only one or two exposures to the novel name. Three prior principles have been posited to serve this function: Clark's (1983) 'contrast' and 'fill-the-gap' and Markman's (1989) 'mutual exclusivity' (hereafter ME) (see also Merriman & Bowman, 1989). The principle posited here – N3C – also facilitates rapid lexical acquisition and avoids some of the pitfalls of the prior principles.

The N3C principle states that novel terms map to previously unnamed objects. Thus, N3C predicts that the child will map the new term to a whole object (given the object scope principle) without a name. Prior to the appearance of N3C, children may ignore many of the new terms they hear or require repeated exposures to the same word-referent pair (Mervis & Bertrand, 1993). After N3C, the child will readily infer that a novel term maps to an unnamed object, requiring only a single pairing to do so and without the speaker providing an explicit nonverbal link (e.g. a point) between the name and the object (Golinkoff, Hirsh-Pasek, Bailey & Wenger, 1992; Mervis & Bertrand, 1993). N3C is a heuristic that moves a single hypothesis for what the novel word might mean to the top of the stack: the novel term maps to an unnamed object. Note that N3C is NOT simply a restatement of Clark's (1983) principles of contrast or fill-the-gap; nor of ME (Markman, 1989). The following discussion critically analyses these alternatives and makes clear how they differ from N3C.

Clark's principle of contrast. Contrast states that, 'Every two forms contrast in meaning…any difference in FORM in a language indicates that there is a difference in meaning' (Clark, 1983:318). Contrast, then, is a pragmatic principle, rooted in Gricean conversational maxims (Clark, 1990). The child, hearing a new term, assumes that the speaker means something different from what has already been said. The main problem with contrast is where it leaves the word learner. If the child does not mind overlaps in reference, so long as terms differ in meaning, why should the child assume that a new term maps to an unlabelled object? The new term might just as easily be a name for an already named object (e.g. *sofa* and *couch*) as for the unlabelled object. On the principle of contrast, the child could continue to affix new labels to the same object, as long as the child thought there were slight variations in extension or intension. Contrast then, gives insufficient guidance since it does not provide the child with any strategic advantage for the rapid learning of new terms (Gathercole, 1989; Markman, 1989; Merriman & Bowman, 1989).

Mutual exclusivity. ME (Markman, 1989) is the claim that young children are biased to assume that an object can have only a single name. Thus, children should expect, for example, that a creature called a 'dog' could not be called a 'cat' (a correct expectation), or an 'animal' (an incorrect expectation). This single-name bias leads the child to map a novel label to an unnamed object since the child AVOIDS attaching a second label to already named objects (Markman, 1989). Without positing that the child eschews second labels, N3C makes the same prediction as ME when an unnamed object is present – that the novel name 'hooks up' to the unnamed object. We next discuss evidence which contradicts the predictions of ME.

ME should be stronger in younger than in older subjects given that it is needed to get the child's word learning off the ground (Markman, 1989). Further, 'comprehension data [from young bilinguals] would provide a stronger test of…ME' than production data (Markman & Wachtel, 1988: 125). Mervis & Ramos (1990) tested seven infants (1;5–1;6) acquiring English and Portuguese (their production vocabularies ranged from 3 to 50 words) for their comprehension of 11 common object names, none of which were cognates. The proportion of words comprehended in the nondominant language that were also comprehended in the dominant language ranged from 0·83 to 1·00. Thus, even early in acquisition when it should be most rigidly adhered to, ME is violated.

What happens when a monolingual child hears a novel label, but already knows a name for each of the objects present? On Markman's account, this situation should lead to a conflict between ME and her 'whole object' principle. That is, on 'whole object,' children should treat the novel word as a name for the whole object, even though they already have another name for the object. On ME, they should treat the word as the name for a part or attribute of the object, rather than as a second label for the object. In such cases, ME takes precedence over whole object (Markman & Wachtel, 1988; Markman, 1989). Thus, the new word would most likely be treated as the name for a salient, as yet unnamed, part of the object.

On the other hand, N3C could not apply in this situation since there is no object available for which the child does not already have a name. Here, there are a number of alternative possibilities for how to interpret a novel term and, all things being equal, they are given approximately equal weight. However, children need not thrash around in an unconstrained manner, sifting through these alternatives, since they can rely on linguistic and non-linguistic INPUT to determine the referent of the novel label. N3C is a second tier principle; its ability to account for only the situation where an unnamed object is present is balanced out by children's increased (and continually increasing) sophistication in interpreting the input. For example, as Baldwin (1993) has shown, by 1;7 children are very sensitive at reading non-verbal cues to reference. It is likely, then, that if they hear a label while observing someone manipulating an object part, the label will be taken as the name for that part. Or, if the carrier phrase included the words, *a kind of*—they might take the novel term to be a superordinate label. Are there data which speak to these divergent predictions?

Markman & Wachtel (1988) found that three-year-old children sometimes, but not always, favoured ME over the whole object principle when the two were in conflict. In some experiments, almost half the responses conformed to the whole object principle (novel word = name for whole object) even though the children already had a name for that object. This finding is in conflict with the claim that ME routinely takes priority over the whole object principle. Other evidence which may be inconsistent with the priority of the ME principle include both observational (e.g. Mervis, 1987) and experimental data (e.g. Banigan & Mervis, 1988; Waxman & Senghas, 1992). In addition, Mervis, Golinkoff & Bertrand (1994) explicitly tested the above predictions in three experiments in which children heard a novel word in the presence of an object for which they already had a name. Two alternative responses were most likely. First, children (age 2;0) could interpret the second term as a label for a salient part for which they did not have a name, a response predicted if ME has priority. Second, children could interpret the second term as a second name for the basic level category – the response consistent with the present framework which contains no strictures about avoiding second labels in the presence of already named objects. Results consistent with our framework and in clear violation of ME were found. Children showed by their object selections in comprehension tests that, for example, 'truck' and 'lorry' were taken as names for the same exemplars in the same basic level category. 'Lorry' was not taken as a label for truck parts, or as a sub- or superordinate level term.

In sum, N3C and ME make similar predictions in the circumstance where a novel name is offered in the presence of a novel object. Where ME fails to predict what children will do is in the situation where a novel term is heard in the presence of already named objects. Here, ME does not win out over the whole object principle and cause children to take the novel term to be a label for an object part. Instead, young children allow the already named object to be the referent for the novel term. Further, ME is often violated, even at the beginning of word learning when children are relatively less sensitive to the mitigating effects of input.

How N3C differs from Clark's fill-the-gap axiom. 'Fill-the-gap' (Clark, 1983) was proposed as a motive for word learning which covers all sorts of cases, including children's limiting of overextensions and their use of all-purpose words such as *that*, as well as their coinage of new words. Two assumptions are part of the word learner's general motive to 'fill' lexical gaps. First, when children want to talk about something and don't have a word for it, they look for or invent a word to fill that gap. N3C makes no prediction about this case. Clark's (1983) research on the neologisms children create suggests that this part of the fill-the-gap assumption captures an important generalization. It is the second part of fill-the-gap which is problematic. It states that when children hear a new word, they assume (by invoking contrast) that the meaning of the new word differs from the meaning of the known word and map the new word to an unnamed category. The same criticism that was used earlier against contrast then, can be used against fill-the-gap: since on the contrast principle the child could continue to affix new labels to the same object (with only slight variations in meaning), contrast gives the child insufficient guidance about how to find a referent for the novel term.

In sum, while the first part of fill-the-gap makes a useful contribution to our understanding of the general motive behind word learning, fill-the-gap fails – unlike N3C – to make a clear prediction in the situation where a new term is heard in the presence of an unlabelled object. Having argued that the principles of contrast, ME, and fill-the-gap work less well than the proposed N3C principle, we next go on to present additional evidence in support of N3C.

Possible origins of the N3C principle. As stated previously, although the principle of reference (words map to objects, actions, and attributes) precedes N3C and is essential to word learning, reference does not allow the child to map novel object names to their referents with ease. How do children get to the point where they can rapidly learn the names of objects WITHOUT being provided with an explicit connection between the referent and its name? In other words, how do they acquire the N3C principle? It appears that they go through a three-step sequence. First, in order to learn the name of an object, the link between the referent and its name must be explicit and provided on multiple occasions. Without having N3C, sometimes even multiple exposures to objects explicitly linked with their names (e.g. parents repeatedly labelling an object within the child's focus of attention) will not guarantee word learning. Second, the link between the label and the referent may be somewhat more indirect but the speaker must be looking at or manipulating the referent even if the child cannot see it. Baldwin (1993) has shown that by 1;7, infants can discern which of two objects an adult is labelling even when they cannot see the referent being discussed and there is another, already named object present. Finally, when N3C has been attained, the speaker need not look at or manipulate the referent while saying its name. As long as an unnamed object is present, the child will form a hook-up between it and the novel name. Thus, the ability to map novel object names to their referents rests partially upon the ability to infer the focus of the speaker's attention (e.g. Baldwin, 1993). It may further rest on the child's implicit belief that all objects have names (see Gopnik & Meltzoff, 1987).

Evidence for the N3C principle. The main prediction of N3C is consistently upheld: presented with an unnamed object and a novel word, the child will guess that the new word maps to the unnamed object (e.g. Merriman & Bowman, 1989; Mervis & Bertrand, 1993, in press). For example, Golinkoff *et al.* (1992) tested whether children age 2;4 would assume a new term mapped to an unnamed object without having the connection between the new term and new object explicitly pointed out to them. Subjects were shown four objects on each of 12 trials, of which either one or two were unfamiliar objects (e.g. a black plastic tube for the bottom of a chair leg) and asked, in counterbalanced order, to give the experimenter either a known or an unknown object (e.g. 'May I have the glorp?'). Children picked the novel object in response to the novel word whether they were asked for the original (the black tube) (78%) or another token (a white tube) (69%). Thus, without any explicit directive to do so, children mapped the unnamed object to the novel noun, as predicted by N3C.

Evidence that N3C emerges in the second tier of principles and that it may facilitate the rapid acquisition of vocabulary, comes from Mervis & Bertrand (1993). These authors asked 32 children (age 1;4–1;7) to indicate a known and an unknown object (e.g. 'Is there a nup?') (in counterbalanced order). All of the children were able to select the known objects. However, only the children who consistently selected the unknown object had had a vocabulary spurt according to maternal report. The two groups of children did NOT differ in age. Mervis & Bertrand monitored the vocabulary acquisition of the 16 children who had been unable to use the N3C principle. Once these children had attained a vocabulary spurt, they were retested using a different set of objects. This time, the children were successful at selecting the unknown objects and at extending the novel word to another appropriate referent.

These results provide strong evidence that the N3C principle is not available at the start of language learning, but is part of the second tier of principles. N3C enables rapid word learning because, even when the link between a referent and a label is not explicit, children are able to make the link on their own. N3C contributes to the even more rapid rise in vocabulary learning that occurs sometime after the relatively modest criteria found in the literature for the vocabulary spurt (e.g. 10 new words in two weeks) have been met.[4]

Summary of the N3C principle. N3C states that novel names are mapped to unnamed referents. By the time children have N3C, they may be able to distinguish between novel NAMES and novel words from other form classes (e.g. Waxman & Kosowski, 1990). However, the desire to have a basic level name for an unnamed category is so strong, that if presented with a choice, two-year-old children often ignore the form class of the novel word in order to interpret it as a basic level label (Hall *et al.* 1994). Thus, N3C works in concert with both linguistic and non-linguistic input and, unlike other

---

[4] Criteria for the spurt vary in three ways: whether there must be a certain minimum number of words before the spurt; the minimum number of words required; and the time span during which this increase should be observed. For example, Gopnik & Meltzoff's (1987) criterion for the spurt requires a minimum of 10 new words acquired over three weeks.

principles, neither disallows second labels for named objects (ME), nor leaves the child to wonder what the best referent for a novel name might be (contrast and fill-the-gap). N3C only requires that the child's first guess at the referent of a novel term be an as-yet-unnamed object.

Are the principles posited thus far sufficient to account for lexical learning? To this point, children are well on their way to acquiring many lexical items rapidly. However, if they occasionally form incorrect word/object hook-ups, a mechanism is needed which motivates them to discard these incorrect usages and to learn the correct term. Furthermore, children should not be so flexible that the name of an object can change with the day and the speaker. Clark's (1983) principle of conventionality will be offered to solve these problems.

The principle of conventionality
Conventionality, according to Clark (1983), is the assumption that speakers expect certain meanings to be expressed by conventional forms within their language community. To use Clark's example, one had better use the conventional word *dog* (and not *horse*), to talk about dogs if one's intentions are to be understood. When children recognize this fact, they become motivated to match their lexical usages to those of the surrounding community. Prior to the emergence of conventionality, children appear less concerned with matching the adult phonological model, as indicated by the use of 'protowords' (Halliday, 1975) or 'phonetically consistent forms' (Dore, Franklin, Miller & Ramer, 1975). Even as late as 1;4, Halliday's son, Nigel, had many non-standard but consistent phonological forms (such as *na*, used to mean 'give me that'). Thus, some children may begin word learning by inventing their own forms which they use with consistent meaning. Conventionality, a principle which is part of the second tier, may be part of what motivates children to adopt adult forms. While children will continue to coin new words beyond the appearance of conventionality to fill lexical gaps, they will eventually replace a neologism with a conventional word (Clark, 1983). As Pinker (1984) argued, distributional evidence must eventually rule the day since children must allow adult input to determine the proper use of linguistic terms. Under conventionality and under Pinker's (1984) uniqueness principle, words coined by children as well as their over- and under-extensions, are pre-emptable by adult input. Conventionality allows children to correct their overextensions even when the only input is the adult provision of the correct label. That is, in contrast to the earlier phases of lexical acquisition, neither explicit correction nor demonstration nor description appears to be required for children to abandon overextensions (Mervis *et al.* 1992).

Possible origins for the principle of conventionality. Golinkoff (1986) studied communicative episodes in which mothers and infants went to great pains to clarify the infant's unclear messages. Conventionality must be born of children's realization that the contents of their minds can be better shared – especially with individuals outside the immediate family – if they use the same forms that others use to express themselves. Thus, conventionality may have its origins in infants' desire to be readily understood.

Evidence for the principle of conventionality. Clark (1983) reviewed three kinds of evidence. First, young children adopt adult word forms and use them consistently across occasions. Second, they request the names of things from adults. And finally, they make spontaneous repairs of their own word choices. As Dromi (1987: 163) noted, it was only after her daughter Keren had acquired more than 150 words that conventional meanings predominated in her lexicon and only then that she started to give up her non-conventional meanings and idiosyncratic forms. Thus, children can know that words refer (the principle of reference), and many other things about how words work, before they realize that their own usage of words must match that of the surrounding linguistic community.

Strong evidence of conventionality is found when speakers distinguish between using term A to family members and term B to the outside community. For example, one of us (Mervis) noticed that her younger son Ethan at first called pacifiers *pops* whether he was addressing members of his family or not. Then, for non-family members only, he began to refer to pacifiers as *pacifiers*. At this point he showed that he had discriminated between different listeners' conventional uses by taking their knowledge into consideration in selecting a lexical item.

Summary of conventionality. Conventionality motivates children to pre-empt their idiosyncratic names for the standard names for objects. That is, when children recognize that they have invented a term (say, *to broom*) for a situation already covered by a standard term (*to sweep*), the standard term will replace the idiosyncratic term created to fill a lexical gap. In the case of overextensions, conventionality enables children to rely on minimal input for their correction. Without this principle, once children had filled a lexical gap, there would be no reason for them ever to adjust their solution in the direction of the adult model.

SUMMARY AND REFLECTIONS

Having just described six principles for the acquisition of object labels, we must first ask what this effort has accomplished. This seems a clear case of 'the whole is greater than the sum of the parts' – despite the fact that the pieces which compose the whole may yet require further revision. That is, by bringing these principles together into a developmental framework, a picture of lexical development emerges which was not possible when each principle was treated separately. The fact that the principles cluster into two tiers and reflect cumulative insights, 'builds' a more complex lexical learner than emphases on single principles allow. Further, by examining lexical acquisition through the lens of the principles approach, principles which were previously presupposed (such as reference and extendibility) stand out in bas relief. For example, take the first principle of reference. If children did not appreciate that consistent phonological forms mapped to their representations of objects in the world, the entire lexical learning enterprise would fail. They would be reduced to functioning like dogs, remembering the phonological form of a few specific commands, but having no general notion that forms map to representations of objects in the world. Though there has been much discussion of reference (e.g. Macnamara, 1982), this crucial principle had not been integrated into accounts of children's lexical learning. Thus, the organization of these principles into a developmental framework makes a package which has more power than any of the principles taken singly. Additional support for the present approach comes from the discovery that these principles are not limited to the class of object words. Golinkoff *et al.* (in press) have argued that the acquisition of action words (verbs) can be covered by these principles with some minor adjustments.

Furthermore, describing the principles in two tiers captures the changing character of the lexical acquisition process and may offer some explanatory force. The first tier was roughly estimated to be present by the beginning of the second year of life; the second tier by the middle of the second year. (The exact sequence of appearance of each principle and the ages are of little importance as there are large individual differences in word learning.) When the child has only the first tier principles of reference, extendibility, and object scope, lexical acquisition proceeds in a piecemeal, one-word-at-a-time fashion. Although these principles are sufficient to permit word learning to occur, none of them assists the child in acquiring new words with ease. Reference and extendibility prime the child to comprehend many and produce some words as applied to diverse exemplars; object scope leads the child to assume that the words heard are mostly, although not exclusively, about objects. The principles of the second tier (categorical scope, N3C, and conventionality) refine the word learning processes started in the first tier. Whereas extendibility, for example, allowed the child to apply newly learned words to non-identical exemplars which share either perceptual similarity or thematic relationship with the original referent, the principle of categorical scope removes doubts about the bases for extension, making category membership at the basic level paramount. Whereas object scope allowed the child to map new terms to objects (as opposed to actions) and to whole objects at that, N3C has the effect of causing the child to search out a 'nameless' object referent as soon as a novel word is heard. And whereas reference meant that consistent phonological forms (words) could map to entities in the environment (via the child's representation of those entities), the appearance of conventionality makes clear that for communication to proceed successfully, those consistent phonological forms need to match the ones used by others in your environment. Thus, the principles of the first tier are honed by those of the second tier. The latter are built upon children's increasing sophistication in interpreting non-linguistic and linguistic cues.

We have tried to speculate on the origins of these principles, having made a commitment to the position that children construct them. We have argued that after a principle is constructed the child's word learning advances to the next level. In order to give the principles explanatory force, we have suggested behavioural interactions which should occur before and after children use a particular principle. The developmental framework implies then, that the same linguistic input will have a differential impact on word learning depending on the particular tier a child is in. For example, if children hear a word used without a clear referent, they will respond differentially depending upon whether or not they have N3C. Before N3C, they are unlikely to map the new word to any referent. After N3C, children are likely to map the novel term to the appropriate referent (Mervis & Bertrand, in press).

In addition, the developmental lexical principles framework raises the further question of whether the principles are unique to word learning or are a more general part of cognitive functioning. After all, collateral cognitive changes (e.g. in categorization, Gopnik & Meltzoff, 1987; Mervis & Bertrand, 1993) are occurring at the same time that these principles are coming on-line.

In sum, the developmental lexical principles framework presented here seems to describe word learning – at least with respect to object words – in a richer way than non-developmental accounts that focus on one or two principles. This developmental perspective also serves to raise additional issues about the applicability of these principles to other form classes and the relationship between the principles and general cognitive functioning.

To recapitulate then, the paper has put forward four main arguments:

(1) Lexical acquisition is guided by a set of six principles, some previously suggested and some proposed here for the first time. These principles have the effect of prioritizing children's hypotheses for what a novel word might mean.

(2) The principles appear in a two-tiered order partially determined by the child's ability to interpret non-linguistic and linguistic input. As these principles emerge they alter the character of the lexical acquisition process. Thus, the tiers serve as both a descriptive and an explanatory tool.

(3) These principles were developed for the class of object labels but may

also apply across other early-appearing word classes such as verbs and adjectives.

(4) Future research may modify the posited principles by exploring the conditions surrounding their acquisition and use.

REFERENCES

Aslin, R. N. (1981). Experiential influences and sensitive periods in perceptual development: a unified model. In R. N. Aslin, J. R. Alberts & M. R. Petersen, M. R. (eds), *Development of perception*. Vol. 2. New York: Academic Press.
—— (1992). Segmentation of fluent speech into words: learning models and the role of maternal input. In B. de Boysson-Bardies, S. de Schonen , P. Jusczyk, P. MacNeilage & J. Morton (eds), *Developmental neurocognition : speech and face processing in the first year of life*. Dordrecht: Kluwer.
Au, T. K. (1985). Children's word-learning strategies. *Papers and Reports on Child Language Development* **24**, 22–9.
Baldwin, D. A. (1989). Priorities in children's expectations about object label reference: form over color. *Child Development* **60**, 1291–306.
—— (1993). Infants' ability to consult the speaker for clues to word reference. *Journal of Child Language* **20**, 377–94.
Baldwin, D. A. & Markman, E. M. (1989). Establishing word-object relations: a first step. *Child Development* **60**, 381–9.
Banigan, R. L. & Mervis, C. B. (1988). Role of adult input in young children's category evolution: II an experimental study. *Journal of Child Language* **15**, 493–504.
Barrett, M. D. (1978). Lexical development and overextension in child language. *Journal of Child Language* **5**, 205–19.
—— (1982). Distinguishing between prototypes: the early acquisition of the meanings of object names. In S. A. Kuczaj (ed.), *Language development*. Vol. I. *Syntax and semantics*. Hillsdale, NJ: Erlbaum.
Bates, E., Camaioni, L. & Volterra, V. (1975). The acquisition of performatives prior to speech. *Merrill Palmer Quarterly* **21**, 205–26.
Bauer, P. J. & Mandler, J. M. (1989). Taxonomies and triads: conceptual organization in one-to two-year-olds. *Cognitive Psychology* **21**, 156–84.
Behrend, D. A. (1990). Constraints and development: a reply to Nelson (1988). *Cognitive Development* **5**, 313–30.
Blewitt, P. (1983). Dog versus collie: vocabulary in speech to young children. *Developmental Psychology* **19**, 602–9.
Bloom, L. (1973). *One word at a time : the use of single word utterances before syntax*. The Hague: Mouton.
—— (1974). Talking, understanding and thinking: developmental relationship between receptive and expressive language. In R. L. Schiefelbusch & L. Lloyd (eds), *Language perspectives – acquisition, retardation and intervention*. Baltimore: University Park Press.
Bloom, L. & Capatides, J. B. (1987). Expression of affect and the emergence of language. *Child Development* **58**, 1513–21.
Bloom, L. & Lahey, M. (1978). *Language development and language disorders*. New York: John Wiley.
Bloom, L., Tinker, E. & Margulis, C. (1993). The words children learn. *Cognitive Development* (in press).
Brown, R. (1958). *Words and things*. Glencoe, IL: Free Press.
Carey, S. (1982). Semantic development: the state of the art. In E. Wanner & L. R. Gleitman (eds), *Language acquisition : the state of the art*. Cambridge: C.U.P.
Carey, S. & Gelman, R. (1990). Description of their forthcoming edited book, *Biology and knowledge : structural constraints on development. The Genetic Epistemologist*, Fall issue, p. 7.
Chomsky, N. (1981). *Lectures on government and binding*. Foris: Dordrecht.

Clark, E. V. (1983). Meanings and concepts. In J. H. Flavell & E. M. Markman (eds), *Handbook of child psychology*. Vol. III. *Cognitive development*. New York: John Wiley.
—— (1990). On the pragmatics of contrast. *Journal of Child Language* **17**, 417–31.
Dockrell, J. & Campbell, R. (1986). Lexical acquisition strategies in the preschool child. In S. Kuczaj & M. Barrett (eds), *The development of word meaning*. Berlin: Springer-Verlag.
Dore, J., Franklin, M., Miller, R. & Ramer, A. (1975). Transitional phenomena in early language acquisition. *Journal of Child Language* **3**, 13–28.
Dromi, E. (1987). *Early lexical development*. Cambridge: C.U.P.
Echols, C. H. (1992). Developmental changes in attention to labeled events during the transition to language. Paper presented at the International Conference for Infant Studies, Miami Beach, FL.
Fernald, A. & Morikawa, H. (1993). Common themes and cultural variations in Japanese and American mothers' speech to infants. *Child Development* **64**, 637–56.
Franco, F. & Butterworth, G. (1991). Infant pointing: prelinguistic references and co-reference. Paper presented at meeting of Society for Research in Child Development, Seattle, WA.
Gathercole, V. C. (1989). Contrast: a semantic constraint. *Journal of Child Language* **16**, 685–702.
Gauker, C. (1990). How to learn a language like a chimpanzee. *Philosophical Psychology* **3**, 31–53.
Gelman, R. (1990). Structural constraints on cognitive development. *Cognitive Science* **14**, 3–10.
Gelman, S. & Markman, E. (1986). Categories and induction in young children. *Cognition* **23**, 183–209.
Gentner, D. (1983). Why nouns are learned before verbs: linguistic relativity versus natural partitioning. In S. Kuczaj (ed), *Language development*. Vol. 2. *Language, cognition, and culture*. Hillsdale, NJ: Erlbaum.
Glass, A. L., Holyoak, K. J. & Santa, J. L. (1979). *Cognition*. Reading, MA: Addison-Wesley.
Gleitman, L. (1990). Structural sources of verb meaning. *Language Acquisition* **1**, 3–55.
Goldfield, B. A. (1993). Noun bias in maternal speech to one-year-olds. *Journal of Child Language* **20**, 85–99.
Goldin-Meadow, S. & Mylander, C. (1984). Gestural communication in deaf children: the effects and non-effects of parental input on early language development. *Monographs of the Society for Research in Child Development* **49** (3–4, Serial No. 207).
Golinkoff, R. M. (1986). 'I beg your pardon?': the preverbal negotiation of failed messages. *Journal of Child Language* **13**, 455–76.
—— (1993). When is communication a 'meeting of minds'? *Journal of Child Language* **20**, 199–207.
Golinkoff, R. M., Hirsh-Pasek, K., Bailey, L. M. & Wenger, R. N. (1992). Young children and adults use lexical principles to learn new nouns. *Developmental Psychology* **28**, 99–108.
Golinkoff, R. M., Hirsh-Pasek, K., Mervis, C. B., Frawley, W. & Parillo, M. (in press). Lexical principles can be extended to the acquisition of verbs. In M. Tomasello & W. Merriman (eds), *Beyond names for things: young children's acquisition of verbs*. Hillsdale, NJ: Erlbaum.
Golinkoff, R. M., Kenealy, L. & Hirsh-Pasek, K. (1993). Object scope: labels promote attention to whole objects. Unpublished manuscript, University of Delaware.
Golinkoff, R. M., Shuff-Bailey, M., Olguin, K. & Ruan, W. (1993). Young children extend novel words at the basic level: evidence for the principle of categorical scope. Unpublished manuscript, University of Delaware.
Gopnik, A. & Meltzoff, A. (1987). The development of categorization in the second year and its relation to other cognitive and linguistic developments. *Child Development* **58**, 1523–31.
Guillaume, P. (1927). Les débuts de la phrase dans le language de l'enfant. *Journal de Psychologie* **24**, 1–15.
Halliday, M. A. K. (1975). *Learning how to mean: explorations in the development of language*. London: Edward Arnold.

Hall, D. G. & Waxman, S. R. (in press). Assumptions about word meaning: individuation and basic-level kinds. *Child Development*.

Hall, D. G., Waxman, S. R. & Hurwitz, W. M. (in press). How two- and four-year-old children interpret adjectives and count nouns. *Child Development*.

Harris, M. B., Barrett, M., Jones, D. & Brookes, S. (1988). Linguistic input and early word mappings. *Journal of Child Language* **15**, 77–94.

Heibeck, T. & Markman, E. M. (1987). Word learning in children: an examination of fast mapping. *Child Development* **58**, 1021–34.

Huttenlocher, J. & Smiley, P. (1987). Early word meanings: the case of object names. *Cognitive Psychology* **19**, 63–89.

Keil, Frank, C. (1989). *Concepts, kinds, and cognitive development*. Cambridge, MA: MIT Press.

Kuczaj, S. A. (1990). Constraining constraint theories. *Cognitive Development* **5**, 341–4.

Lakoff, G. (1987). *Women, fire, and dangerous things*. Chicago: University of Chicago Press.

Lieberman, P. (1991). *Uniquely human*. Cambridge: Harvard University Press.

Lock, A. (1978). (ed.) *Action, gesture and symbol: the emergence of language*. New York: Academic Press.

Lyons, J. (1977). *Semantics*. Vol. I. Cambridge: C.U.P.

Macnamara, J. (1982). *Names for things*. Cambridge, MA: MIT Press.

Maratsos, M. (1991). How the acquisition of nouns may be different from that of verbs. In A. Krasnegor, D. M. Rumbaugh, R. L. Schiefelbusch & M. Studdert-Kennedy (eds), *Biological and behavioral determinants of language development*. Hillsdale, NJ: Erlbaum.

Markman, E. M. (1989). *Categorization and naming in children*. Cambridge, MA: MIT Press.

Markman, E. M. & Hutchinson, J. E. (1984). Children's sensitivity to constraints on word meaning: taxonomic vs. thematic relations. *Cognitive Psychology* **16**, 1–27.

Markman, E. M. & Wachtel, G. F. (1988). Children's use of mutual exclusivity to constrain the meaning of words. *Cognitive Psychology* **20**, 121–57.

Merriman, W. E. & Bowman, L. (1989). The mutual exclusivity bias in children's word learning. *Monographs of the Society for Research in Child Development* **54** (Serial No. 220).

Mervis, C. B. (1983). Acquisition of a lexicon. *Contemporary Educational Psychology* **8**, 210–36.

—— (1987). Child-basic object categories and early lexical development. In U. Neisser (ed.), *Concepts and conceptual development: ecological and intellectual factors in categorization*. Cambridge: C.U.P.

—— (1990). Operating principles, input, and early lexical development. *Communicazioni Scientifiche di Psicologia Generala* **4**, 31–48.

Mervis, C. B. & Bertrand, J. (in press). Acquisition of the novel name – nameless category (N3C) principle. *Child Development*.

—— & —— (1993). Acquisition of early object labels: the roles of operating principles and input. In A. P. Kaiser & D. B. Gray (eds), *Enhancing children's communication: research foundations for interventions*. Vol. II. Baltimore, MD: Brookes.

Mervis, C. B. & Crisafi, M. A. (1982). Order of acquisition of subordinate, basic and superordinate level categories. *Child Development* **53**, 258–66.

Mervis, C. B., Golinkoff, R. M. & Bertrand, J. (1994). Two-year-olds readily learn multiple labels for the same basic level category. *Child Development* (in press).

Mervis, C. B. & Long, L. M. (1987). *Words refer to whole objects: young children's interpretation of the referent of a novel word*. Paper presented at the biennial meeting of the Society for Research in Child Development, Baltimore, MD.

Mervis, C. B., Mervis, C. A., Johnson, K. E. & Bertrand, J. (1992). Studying early lexical development: the value of the systematic diary method. In C. Rovee-Collier (ed.), *Advances in infancy research*. Vol. 7. Norwood, NJ: Ablex.

Mervis, C. B. & Ramos, E. (1990). *Non-mutual exclusivity in early comprehension vocabularies of bilingual children*. Unpublished manuscript, Emory University.

Nelson, K. (1988). Constraints on word learning? *Cognitive Development* **3**, 221–46.

Nelson, K., Hampson, J. & Shaw, L. (1993). Nouns in early lexicons: evidence, explanations and implications. *Journal of Child Language* **20**, 61–84.

Ninio, A. (1980). Ostensive definition in vocabulary teaching. *Journal of Child Language* **7**, 565–73.

Pinker, S. (1984). *Language learnability and language development*. Cambridge, MA: Harvard University Press.

Quine, W. V. O. (1960). *Word and object*. Cambridge: C.U.P.

Roberts, K. & Cuff, M. (1989). Categorization studies of 9- to 15-month-old infants: evidence for superordinate categorization? *Infant Behavior and Development* **12**, 265–88.

Roberts, K. & Jacobs, M. (1992). Linguistic versus attentional influences on nonlinguistic categorization in 15-month-old infants. *Cognitive Development* **6**, 355–75.

Rosch, E., Mervis, C. B., Gray, W. D., Johnson, D. M. & Boyes-Braem, P. (1976). Basic objects in natural categories. *Cognitive Psychology* **8**, 382–439.

Scaife, M. & Bruner, J. S. (1975). The capacity for joint visual attention in the infant. *Nature* **253**, 265–6.

Slobin, D. I. (1985). Cross-linguistic evidence for the language making capacity. In D. I. Slobin (ed.), *The cross-linguistic study of language acquisition*. Vol. 2. *Theoretical issues*. Hillsdale, NJ: Erlbaum.

Smith, L. B., Jones, S. S. & Landau, B. (1992). Count nouns, adjectives, and perceptual properties in children's novel word interpretations. *Developmental Psychology* **28**, 273–86.

Soja, N., Carey, S. & Spelke, E. (1991). Ontological categories guide young children's inductions of word meaning: object terms and substance terms. *Cognition* **38**, 179–211.

Spelke, E. S. (1990). Principles of object perception. *Cognitive Science* **14**, 29–56.

Taylor, M. & Gelman, S. A. (1988). Adjectives and nouns: children's strategies for learning new words. *Child Development* **59**, 411–19.

Terrace, H. S. (1985). In the beginning was the 'name'. *American Psychologist* **40**, 1011–28.

Tomikawa, S. A. & Dodd, D. H. (1980). Early word meanings: perceptually or functionally based? *Child Development* **51**, 1103–9.

Waxman, S. R. (1989). Linking language and conceptual development: linguistic cues and the construction of conceptual hierarchies. *The Genetic Epistemologist* **17**, 13–20.

Waxman, S. R. & Balaban, M. T. (1992). The influence of words vs. tones on 9-month-old infants' object categorization. Paper presented at International Conference for Infant Studies, Miami Beach, FL.

Waxman, S. R & Gelman, R. (1986). Preschoolers' use of superordinate relations in classification. *Cognitive Development* **1**, 139–56.

Waxman, S. R. & Kosowski, T. D. (1990). Nouns mark category relations: toddlers' and preschoolers' word-learning biases. *Child Development* **61**, 1461–90.

Waxman, S. R. & Senghas, A. (1992). Relations among word meanings in early lexical development. *Developmental Psychology* **28**, 862–73.

Wellman, H. M. (1990). *The child's theory of mind*. Cambridge, MA: MIT Press.

Younger, B. A. & Cohen, L. B. (1986). Developmental change in infants' perception of correlations among attributes. *Child Development* **57**, 803–15.

J. Child Lang. **21** (1994), 157–172. Copyright © 1994 Cambridge University Press

Pronoun case overextensions and paradigm building*[1]

MATTHEW RISPOLI

Northern Arizona University

ABSTRACT

Pronoun case errors, or overextensions, like *me want it* are characteristic of English child language. This paper explores a hypothesis that the morphological structure of a pronoun influences the pattern of these errors. The Language Acquisition Device (LAD) attempts to analyse English pronoun case forms into stems and affixes, but cannot because of their irregularity. Nevertheless the LAD extracts a phonetic core for each pronoun (e.g. /m-/ for the 1st sg., /h-/ for the 3rd masc. sg.). The phonetic core blocks the overextension of suppletive nominative forms like *I* and *she*. This hypothesis predicts strong differences in the frequency and types of errors between pronouns with suppletive nominatives and those without. Evidence for this hypothesis was found in a transcript database of twelve children, with data collected in one hour samples every month from 1;0 to 3;0. 20,908 pronouns were examined, 1347 of which were errors. Statistical analyses of these data provide support for this hypothesis.

INTRODUCTION

Young children acquiring English err in their use of pronoun case, producing sentences like those in (1):

(1) *Her crashed. (= She crashed) (Brown, 1973: 142)

The existence of these errors has long been noted (Menyuk, 1969). Tanz (1974) using data from Huxley (1970), analysed one child's production of

---

[*] This research was supported in part by a grant (HD 03144) from the National Institute of Child Health and Human Development to the Bureau of Child Research and the Department of Human Development of the University of Kansas. The author would like to thank Tessa Fouquet and Jennifer Lane for their contribution in the analysis of the English data; Robin Chapman, Diane Frome Loeb, Pamela Hadley, Richard Ingram and Anne Vainikka for discussion and criticism; and last but not least, Betty Hart for her selfless labour in developing the JGLP database. Address for correspondence: Matthew Rispoli, Department of English, PO Box 6032, Northern Arizona University, Flagstaff, AZ 86011-6032, USA.

[1] The forms studied as pronouns in this paper are the personal pronouns *I, me, he, him, she, her, they, them,* together with the related determiners (or possessive adjectives) *my, his, her, their.*

subject pronouns from age 2;3 to 3;8, and found an identical developmental pattern for each pronoun. The nominative forms of each pronoun (*he, she, they,* and *I*) were first used correctly for the sentence subject. The objective forms (*him, her, them,* and *me*) were then used in place of the nominative forms (as in (1) above). Errors continued until nominative forms were reintroduced as the subjects of tag questions, producing sentences such as (2):

(2) *Him did get stung, didn't he?

After being reintroduced in tag questions, the nominative forms were reintroduced to the subject (preverbal) position. Finally, the objective forms disappeared from the subject position, although occasional error persisted for third person pronouns as late as 3;8 (Tanz, 1974: 275). Tanz's focus was on the production of subject pronouns, and she did not treat other case errors that may have been occurring during this developmental period.

A more recent approach has been offered by Radford (1988, 1990). Using the Government and Binding (GB) framework, Radford proposes that early child grammars, roughly below the age of 2;2, are lexical in nature. That is, sentence structure emerges from aspects of the words themselves. At this 'lexical' stage, the child lacks (*inter alia*) the Inflectional (I-) system, which has as its elements, tense and agreement inflections (e.g. *-s* 3rd person singular, *-ed* regular past tense), the modal auxiliaries (e.g. *can, will, may*) and the infinitival *to*. From Radford's GB-based perspective, a child without an operative I-system could not systematically assign nominative case to a pronoun, since nominative case is assigned to the NP that is in the specifier position of the Inflectional Phrase (IP). Developmentally, the child is expected to make pronoun case errors in the earlier, lexical stage. As the I-system becomes operative (at some time approximately after 2;2) the child should begin to produce elements in the I-system (listed above). Simultaneously, pronoun errors should begin to disappear.

Research that seems to support Radford's approach was reported in Loeb & Leonard (1991), in which a correlation between pronoun case errors and verb agreement errors was found in a group of eight children with Specific Language Impairment (SLI) and an equal number of MLU-matched normally developing children. However, Loeb & Leonard looked only at errors in the third person pronouns. It remains to be seen whether such a correlation would stand if the first person singular pronoun were also to be used in such correlations. Findings that run counter to Radford's hypothesis were reported in Ingham (1992). In a longitudinal observation of one child between the ages of 2;5 and 3;0, it was found that the emergence of modals at 2;8 did not trigger a decline in pronoun case errors. In fact, Ingham found that *me* for *I* errors increased, rather than decreased, after the modal *can* was used in subject-auxiliary inversion.

A very different approach to pronoun case errors is found in Budwig (1989). Budwig concentrated totally on errors of *my* and *me* for *I*. Her main hypothesis was to explain the distribution of *I*, *my* and *me* in subject position by recourse to the Hopper & Thompson (1980) transitivity scale and an additional speech act distinction between assertives (sentences that assert a proposition) and control acts (direct and indirect requests, imperatives, etc.). Hopper & Thompson's (1980) Transitivity Hypothesis stated that transitivity was a matter of degree, some sentences in a language being more transitive than others. Budwig found that the *my* and *me* for *I* errors were more likely if the sentence was high on the Transitivity Scale. Sentence (3*a*) is an example of such a child error with an action predicate, ranked high on the Transitivity Scale. Sentence (3*b*) is a correct child sentence ranked lower on the Transitivity scale, because it has a state predicate. The correlation, however, was far from perfect, and another factor was posited. Errors were also more likely if the sentence was used in a control act.

(3*a*) *My taked it off. (Budwig, 1989)
 (*b*) I like Anna. (Budwig, 1989)

Budwig's (1989) research is limited to the first person singular pronoun. One proposed motivation, control act, might work well as an ego-orientated motivation, but it is hard to imagine this pragmatic distinction working as a motivation for pronouns other than first person.

To summarize, two recent approaches to these errors come from very different perspectives. This does not mean that the two approaches result in truly competing hypotheses. In fact, the two may very well be compatible. Radford's hypothesis attempts to explain why the errors occur, while Budwig's research describes what children do once the errors begin. Neither of these hypotheses makes any predictions concerning a very prominent aspect of pronoun case errors: their formal systematicity. It is well known that while the overextensions of *me* for *I* are legion in the child language literature (Menyuk, 1969; Tanz, 1974), the reverse overextensions are rare. It is also known that overextensions of *I* for *my* are exceptionally rare, but the overextension of *my* for *I* is well attested (Brown, 1973: 210; Budwig, 1989). This paper explores a hypothesis that the morphological structure of a pronoun influences the pattern of these errors.

The basic premise behind this approach is that the Language Acquisition Device (LAD) builds paradigms to express a finite stock of grammatical notions (Pinker 1984, Slobin 1985). In the natural course of building a paradigm, the child will search for phonological consistency. A regular paradigm, with a phonologically consistent stem will aid this process. From this perspective, Turkish would be 'child friendly'. As one can see from Table 1, each of the Turkish cases are consistently marked: -$\emptyset$ nominative, -*i/u* accusative, -*a* dative. The one exception here is that -*m* not -*n* is used to

TABLE 1. *Singular personal pronouns in Turkish*

Case	1st person	2nd person	3rd person
Nominative	ben	sen	o
Accusative	beni	seni	onu
Genitive	benim	senin	onun
Dative	bana	sana	ona

mark the genitive for the first person pronoun. Each of the Turkish pronouns has consistent phonetic material identifiable with person and number: *ben/ban-* first person singular, *sen/san-* second person singular and *o(n)-* third person singular. It is important to note at this juncture that the acquisition of Turkish has received a considerable amount of attention from developmental psycholinguists (Aksu-Koç & Slobin, 1985); nevertheless, pronoun case errors of the type found in English have never been reported. We will discuss this point further in the final section of this paper.

In comparison to Turkish, English is certainly not 'child friendly.' If we look at the paradigm of English pronoun case forms (Table 2), we see

TABLE 2. *Personal pronouns and determiners in English*

Case	1st sing	2nd sing	3rd sing Masc	3rd sing Fem	3rd sing Neut	1st plu	2nd plu	3rd plu
Nominative	I	you	he	she	it	we	you	they
Objective	me	you	him	her	it	us	you	them
Genitive	my	your	his	her	its	our	your	their

immediately that there is no phonetic material which consistently signals any of the three cases. We can identify some phonetic consistency for person and number in four of the pronouns. The initial consonant *y-* is used consistently for the second person pronoun, *h-* for the third singular masculine pronoun, *th-* consistently for the third plural pronoun, and the sequence *it* is found for all three forms of the third person neuter singular pronoun. Let us hypothesize that the child establishes minimal phonetic consistencies for these pronouns. That is, the child extracts common phones or phonetic sequences for each of these pronouns. Let us call such a minimal phonetic consistency a phonetic core.

What happens for the other three pronouns which are not as consistent? For the first person singular and the third person feminine, the nominative form is suppletive. Let us hypothesize that the child will extract the phonetic material held in common by the objective and genitive forms as the phonetic core. For the first person singular, then, the phonetic core is *m-*, while for the third feminine the core is the whole sequence *her*. It is not quite clear if there is a phonetic core in the first person plural pronoun. This is because it is not known how abstract the phonetic material in a phonetic core might be. The objective *us* and genitive *our* of the first person plural do not begin with exactly the same vowel, but these initial vowels bear at least some resemblance to each other, neither being front or high vowels.

What connection exists between this rudimentary morphological structure and pronoun case errors? Because English pronoun case forms are irregular they must be learned by rote memorization and produced by direct accessing of the specific pronoun case form; that is, there is no general paradigm to aid in production. While children are still learning these pronoun case forms, they may fail to produce a pronoun case form by direct access. At this point, other forms of the pronoun may be accessed by mistake, leading to what the observer sees as a pronoun case error, or as we shall call them in this paper, an overextension. It is at the point when direct access fails that the phonetic core plays an important role. Only forms sharing in the phonetic core will be accessible after direct access fails. Therefore, suppletive nominative forms, *I* and *she*, will be blocked from this form of secondary access. We can state this consequence of paradigm building and the extraction of phonetic cores in the following manner:

> CONSEQUENCE PB (paradigm building). Only pronoun case forms sharing the phonetic core will be overextended. Therefore, suppletive nominative forms will not be overextended.

The following empirical predictions are based on Consequence PB. These predictions treat only four pronouns: first person (1P) singular, third person (3P) masculine, feminine, and plural. The second person pronoun and the third person singular neuter pronouns do not fall within the scope of these predictions because their nominative and objective forms are identical. Since it is not clear whether the first person plural pronoun is to be treated as having a phonetic core or not, the pronoun will be set aside for the present, and will be discussed subsequently. Consequence PB translates into the following predictions concerning the types of pronoun case overextensions that a child will produce in the course of acquisition.

Prediction 1. The proportion of nominative case overextensions will be greater for the 3P masculine and 3P plural than for the 1P singular and 3P feminine.

Prediction 2. When the proportion of oblique overextensions is compared with the proportion of nominative case overextensions, there will be a large bias in favour of the oblique overextensions for the 1P singular and 3P feminine, in contrast to a significantly smaller bias for the 3P masculine and 3P plural pronouns.

To understand these predictions, several terms should be defined. The 'proportion of nominative case overextensions' is defined as the proportion of pronoun case forms which, according to the adult grammar, should be oblique but are in fact overextensions of the nominative case form, such as the use of *he* for *him* or *his*. The 'proportion of oblique overextensions' is defined as the proportion of pronoun case forms which, according to the adult grammar, should be nominative but are in fact overextensions of oblique forms (where oblique is itself defined as being either an objective or genitive case form). A child's use of *him* for *he* or *my* for *I* would be examples of oblique overextensions.

Prediction 1 follows from Consequence PB in the following manner. Because suppletive nominatives are 'blocked' from overextension, we should see lower proportions of nominative overextensions for the 1P singular pronoun and the 3P feminine singular pronoun than we do for the 3P masculine and 3P plural pronouns. In fact, if phonetic cores truly act as a block, nominative overextensions of *I* and *she* should be extremely rare. This is not a claim that the phonetic core forms an absolute block, but rather a substantial and statistically discernible one.

Prediction 2 follows from Consequence PB in the following way. Because phonetic cores increase the likelihood that pronoun case forms sharing in the phonetic core will be mistakenly accessed when direct access fails, over-extended forms should be more evenly distributed across nominative and oblique categories for the 3P masculine and 3P plural pronouns than for pronouns with suppletive nominatives. Moreover, because *he* and *they* share in the phonetic cores of their respective pronouns, they will have a 'second chance' at being accessed after their direct access fails. Therefore, the proportion of oblique overextensions should be close to the proportion of nominative overextensions for the 3P masculine and 3P plural pronouns, when compared with the difference between oblique overextensions and nominative overextensions for the 1P singular and 3P feminine pronouns.

Note that neither of these predictions is developmental. This is because the effects of morphological structure on pronoun case error patterns has been conceived of largely in synchronic terms. Therefore, in this paper, speculation about longitudinal aspects of pronoun case form acquisition are reserved for the discussion.

METHOD

Having stated these predictions, we will proceed to test them with child language data. Naturalistic, observational methods were used because of the young age at which pronoun case errors begin to appear regularly in English.

Subjects

The subjects for this study were twelve children, six boys and six girls, from a large urban centre in the United States. They and their families spoke standard American English. They were audiotaped at home for one hour every month, from 1;0–3;0, as part of a larger project on language development (Hart, 1991). Transcripts were made from the audiotapes. A reliability check was performed for 48 one-hour tapes, four for every child, two from the first year and two from the second year of observation. A second observer checked every word in the transcript. In these 48 hours of tape there was an average 98% confirmation rate for words. All non-spontaneous utterances, such as imitations of interlocutor utterances, self-repetitions, songs and routines were eliminated from the corpora.

Mean length of utterance (MLU) was calculated for the 2;0 and 3;0 samples, following procedures outlined in Brown (1973: 54). At 2;0, the MLUs of nine children were within one standard deviation of the mean MLU, 1·92 (see Miller, 1981). Two of the children had MLUs that fell slightly below one S.D. (1·35, 1·41), and a third child, child 3, had an MLU that fell above one S.D. (2·82). At 3;0, the MLUs of all of these children was within or above one S.D. of the average MLU, 3·16, reported in Miller (1981). Nine of the children had MLUs between 2·47 and 3·85. Three children had MLUs greater than 3·85 at 3;0 (3·97, 4·30 and 4·62). Thus, we can be reasonably confident that none of the 12 children was delayed in language production. Only one child, child 3, seemed 'precocious', having an MLU one S.D. greater than the average MLU reported in Miller (1981) at both 2;0 and 3;0.

Coding

For this study only sentences produced by the children that had one of four pronouns were analysed: 1P singular, 3P masculine, 3P feminine, and 3P plural. Pronoun errors were defined as the use of a different case form where a nominative (*I, he, she, they*), an objective (*me, him, her, them*), or a genitive (*my, his, her, their*) pronoun was expected on the basis of the surface syntactic environment of the child's sentence. The expected environment for a nominative pronoun was defined as pre-verbal or pre-adjectival, and for an objective pronoun, post-verbal or post-prepositional. The expected environment for a genitive pronoun was defined in a somewhat more complex fashion: (*a*) the pronoun had to be pre-nominal, and either (*b*) there had to be a verb in the utterance (e.g. *go he house*), or (*c*) the pronoun was pre-nominal in a prepositional phase (e.g. *in he house*), or lastly (*d*) the pronoun was self-corrected as a genitive pronoun. This series of conditions insured that utterances like *he house* could not be coded as genitive errors, because such utterances might be the result of verb omission.

Confusions of gender among the 3P singular pronouns were not analysed in this study; thus substitution of *he* for *she* was not considered a pronoun case error. If, in fact, a child used *he* for *her*, the error would still constitute a case error. It is unclear how gender errors would be related theoretically to case errors (but see Loeb & Leonard, 1991, for a possibly differing opinion), because they logically represent different grammatical features from case and because gender only applies for one person (3rd) and one number (singular) (i.e. it is not a general condition on pronominal paradigms). Analysis was limited only to pronoun case errors in finite clauses. Errors in the case of pronouns that were the 'subjects' of infinitival clauses were not counted, since these errors might stem from a very different mechanism than the one of interest here.

RESULTS

A total of 19,561 correct uses of pronouns, and 1347 pronoun case overextensions were identified. Table 3 presents the frequency of correct

TABLE 3. *Correct production of pronouns* ($N = 12$)

Case	1P sing	3P Fem	3P Masc	3P Plu
Nominative	11,791	232	831	444
Objective	1765	233	211	592
Genitive	3186	109	141	26

production of pronoun forms across three cases (nominative, objective, and genitive) and the four pronouns (1P singular, 3P feminine, 3P masculine and 3P plural). The frequencies in each cell are pooled from all twelve children. While these data are not of immediate importance in testing Predictions 1 and 2, they form a backdrop against which the overextension data can be more easily understood. One fact that can be readily seen from Table 3 and that will also bear on the tests of Predictions 1 and 2, is the huge difference in baseline frequency between the 1P singular pronoun and the others. The 1P singular was the pronoun most produced by these children, 16,742 correct 1P pronouns were produced. As can be seen from Table 3, most of these (11,791) were tokens of the nominative pronoun *I*. The 1P singular pronoun clearly plays an important role in the communicative needs of the child, and as such it is produced much more frequently than the other pronouns. This fact bears on the child's learning of the correct pronoun forms, and should be kept in mind when interpreting the results of this study.

A total of 1347 pronoun case overextensions were found: 1037 1P singular overextensions, 195 3P feminine overextensions, 72 3P masculine overextensions, and 43 3P plural overextensions. The greater number of 1P singular pronoun overextensions is understandable given the 1P singular pronoun's importance for the expression of the young child's needs. We will now proceed to the testing of Predictions 1 and 2.

Prediction 1 concerns the overextension of nominative case forms. If the suppletive nature of the nominative pronouns blocks erroneous retrieval, the proportion of overextension for *I* and *she* should be demonstrably smaller than that of *he* and *they*. The average proportion (and standard deviation) of nominative overextension for each of these four pronouns is reported in Table 4. The proportion of nominative overextensions is defined as the

TABLE 4. *Proportion of nominative overextensions*

Child subject	1P sing *I*	3P fem *she*	3P masc *he*	3P plu *they*
1	·00 (506)	·03 (61)	·02 (54)	·00 (33)
2	·00 (762)	·00 (37)	·03 (34)	·02 (93)
3	·00 (440)	·00 (19)	·04 (25)	·05 (40)
4	·00 (202)	·00 (10)	·07 (30)	·00 (32)
5	·00 (306)	·00 (19)	·15 (13)	·03 (29)
6	00 (573)	·00 (38)	·03 (61)	·02 (58)
7	·00 (433)	·02 (64)	·00 (21)	·01 (108)
8	·00 (258)	·00 (46)	·09 (54)	·06 (63)
9	·00 (155)	·00 (15)	·00 (37)	·02 (63)
10	·00 (375)	·00 (11)	·11 (19)	·05 (22)
11	·00 (465)	·00 (12)	·38 (34)	·03 (73)
12	·00 (517)	·00 (13)	·20 (5)	·17 (24)
Mean (*N* = 12)	·00	·00	·09	·04
S.D.	·00	·01	·11	·04

Note. These proportions were calculated according to the following formula:

$$\frac{\text{Nominative overextensions}}{\text{Total oblique (objective + genitive) targets}}$$

All proportions are based on a denominator of 5 tokens or more. Denominator is given in parentheses.

number of nominative overextensions divided by the total number of oblique targets. All proportions in Table 4 are based on denominators of five or more oblique targets (the actual denominators are given in parentheses). The pronouns in Table 4 are grouped to reflect morphological structure: the suppletive nominatives *I* and *she* are to the left, while the non-suppletive nominatives, *he* and *they* are to the right. Visual inspection of the means at the bottom of Table 4 shows that, as predicted, the proportions of over-extension of *I* and *she* are on average lower than the proportion of overextension of *he* and *they*. The proportions of overextension for *I* and *she* were practically zero for each child. No child produced an overextension of *I*, and only two children each produced one overextension of *she*. In comparison, higher averages were found for the overextension of *he* and *they*, as predicted. The average proportion of overextension of *he* was 9%, and the average proportion of overextension of *they* was 4%. Ten of the twelve children produced overextensions of *he*. Ten children produced over-extensions of *they*, as well. Examples of the overextensions of *he* and *they* are found in (4) and (5) respectively:

(4a) I got he out. (child 8: 2;4)
　(b) He got back in he house. (child 10: 2;11)

(5a) I'll put they in. (child 3: 2;11)
　(b) They stay with they mothers. (child 8: 2;10)

Since the range in the proportion of nominative overextensions varied so widely across pronouns (as can be seen from the standard deviations in Table 4), a non-parametric statistic was used to test Prediction 1. A Friedman two-way ANOVA by ranks was performed on the proportion of nominative overextension for each pronoun (Siegel, 1956). The result was significant, $\chi^2 = 16\cdot9$, $p < 0\cdot001$. Clearly, there are wide differences in the amount of overextension across the pronouns, conforming to a large extent with the difference between suppletive nominatives and non-suppletive nominatives.

Prediction 2 is concerned with the comparison of the proportion of oblique pronoun overextension to the proportion of nominative overextension. The value of interest is the difference between the proportion of oblique overextension and nominative overextension. This difference score should be large for pronouns with suppletive nominatives and small for non-suppletive nominatives.

Table 5 presents the proportion (and standard deviations) of oblique overextensions across the four pronouns. This proportion is defined as the number of oblique overextensions for nominative targets, divided by the total number of nominative targets. The proportions in Table 5 are all based on denominators of at least five nominative targets (the actual denominators are given in parentheses). Note that one child, child 4, did not produce the required minimum number of nominative targets for the 3P feminine pronoun. Therefore, her data were dropped from this analysis. The average proportions reported at the bottom of Table 5 are based on an N of 11 children.

Visual inspection of the means and standard deviations at the bottom of Table 5 reveals that the 3P masculine and 3P plural pronouns were very similar, as expected based on their morphological structure. The 3P mas-culine had an average proportion of oblique overextensions of 5%, and the 3P plural pronoun showed an average proportion of oblique overextensions

TABLE 5. *Proportion of oblique overextensions*

Child subjects	1P sing *me* *my*	3P fem *her*	3P masc *him* *his*	3P plu *them* *their*
1	·02 (1585)	·46 (94)	·04 (126)	·04 (49)
2	·06 (1527)	·60 (35)	·08 (37)	·18 (60)
3	·02 (1422)	·11 (19)	·00 (31)	·00 (15)
4	·02 (773)	— (2)	·01 (83)	·00 (9)
5	·05 (726)	·50 (12)	·14 (14)	·08 (24)
6	·04 (1167)	·33 (27)	·02 (128)	·00 (55)
7	·01 (1488)	·12 (58)	·03 (104)	·01 (94)
8	·06 (1180)	·74 (85)	·02 (85)	·03 (33)
9	·15 (687)	·10 (42)	·05 (88)	·02 (58)
10	·06 (696)	·64 (14)	·05 (62)	·14 (7)
11	·15 (849)	·70 (20)	·08 (86)	·07 (55)
12	·55 (688)	·88 (16)	·14 (22)	·22 (9)
Mean ($N = 11$)	·10	·47	·05	·06
S.D.	·15	·27	·05	·08

Note. These proportions were calculated according to the following formula:

$$\frac{\text{Oblique (objective + genitive) overextensions}}{\text{Total nominative targets}}$$

All proportions are based on a denominator of 5 tokens or more. Denominator is given in parentheses. '—' represents a denominator of fewer than 5 tokens.

TABLE 6. *Average difference scores: oblique minus nominative overextensions* ($N = 11$)

	1P sing	3P fem	3P masc	3rd plu
Mean	·11	·47	−·03	·03
S.D.	·15	·28	·10	·06

of 6%. The 3P singular feminine pronoun had a very different average proportion, 47%. On the basis of morphological structure alone, we might expect the 1P singular pronoun to have an average proportion of oblique overextension approximately equal to that of the 3P feminine. However, the average proportion of oblique overextension for the 1P singular pronoun was 10%. The comparatively low proportion of the 1P singular pronoun is understandable if we realize that because the 1P singular pronoun is the most important to children for their communicative needs, they may have learned it during the two-year period which is collapsed in the synchronic view of these data. We will pursue this point further in the discussion.

Examples of 3P oblique overextensions are shown in (6). Overextensions of oblique forms for the 1P singular pronoun appear in (7).

(6*a*) Him's a boy. (child 6: 2;9)
  (*b*) Her cries a lot. (child 2: 3;0)
  (*c*) No, them ain't right. (child 11: 2;11)

(7*a*) Now can me do it? (child 3: 3;0)
  (*b*) My can do this. (child 7: 2;9)

There are two types of error which contribute to the proportion of oblique overextension: (1) objective for nominative overextensions, and (2) genitive for nominative overextensions. It is impossible to distinguish these two types of overextension for the 3P feminine pronoun (*her* in both cases), but it is for the other three pronouns. 798 *me* for *I*, and 191 *my* for *I* overextensions were found. In the 3P pronouns, *his* was never overextended for *he*, and *their* was overextended for *they* only once. A general trend seems to be that the objective forms were overextended more often than the genitive forms. However, at least one point should be borne in mind with regard to this apparent bias, and that is that *their* for *they* overextensions may be disguised by the contraction *they're*. Unfortunately, there is no simple, direct way to separate out possible disguised overextensions. For the present, we shall accept the apparent lack of *their* for *they* overextensions at face value, since this characteristic of the data makes a coherent pattern with the minority of *my* for *I* errors, and the absence of *his* for *he* overextensions.

Of primary interest in testing Prediction 2 is Table 6, which displays the average difference between the proportion of oblique pronoun overextension and the proportion of nominative overextension. The difference scores were computed by subtracting the proportion of nominative overextension (see Table 4) from the proportion of oblique overextension (see Table 5). Below the mean difference scores are the standard deviations in these difference scores. Since child 4 did not produce the minimum number of nominative targets for the 3P feminine pronoun (see Table 5), her data were dropped from the analysis presented in Table 6, and the averages reported in Table 6 are based on an *N* of 11. Visual inspection of Table 6 shows that these differences are greater for the pronouns with suppletive nominatives than they are for pronouns with non-suppletive nominatives. The difference between the proportions for the 3P masculine singular pronoun was -3%, which means that on average, the proportion of nominative overextensions was greater than the proportion of oblique overextensions. The data reported in Tables 4 and 5 show that five children had negative difference scores: children 3, 6, 8, 11 and 12. The difference between the proportions for the 3P plural pronoun was 3%, and Tables 4 and 5 show that three children had negative difference scores: children 3, 6 and 8. In contrast, no negative difference scores were found for either the 1P singular or the 3P feminine pronoun. The average difference between the proportions for the 3P feminine pronoun was 47%, and for the 1P singular pronoun, 11%. Admittedly, the difference between these two averages is very large. Again, it is not unreasonable to suspect that the average for the 1P singular pronoun reflects learning, a fact that cannot be handled by this synchronic view of the data. Overall, the direction of these averages is congruent with Prediction 2. The 3P feminine and the 1P singular pronouns had higher average difference scores than the 3P masculine and the 3P plural pronouns.

Because the range in the difference scores varied so widely across pronouns (as can be seen from the standard deviations in Table 6), it was thought best to use a non-parametric statistic to test Prediction 2. Once again, a Friedman two-way ANOVA by ranks was performed on the difference scores between the proportion of oblique overextensions and the proportion of nominative overextension for the four pronouns. The result was significant, $\chi^2 = 21\cdot8$, $p < 0\cdot001$, providing statistical support for Prediction 2.

As the data provide support for Predictions 1 and 2, the results establish the plausibility of the proposal that morphological structure affects the overextensions children make with pronoun case forms. It would appear that suppletion blocks overextension. This in turn, suggests the possibility that children extract a phonetic core out of a set of highly irregular pronoun case forms.

DISCUSSION

These seems to be good evidence for Prediction 1. There were statistically significant differences between the proportion of nominative overextension across the four pronouns. The average proportion of overextension for *I* and *she* was approximately zero, with very little variation. The average proportions of overextension for *he* and *they* were evidently above zero, although these proportions were prone to more variation (see Table 4). The fact remains that none of the twelve children overextended *I*, and two children overextended *she* (only one overextension for each child), whereas ten children overextended *he* and ten children overextended *they* (see Table 4). The observed differences correspond well to the suppletive/non-suppletive classification of the nominative pronouns, and so provide support for Prediction 1.

The support for Prediction 2 is somewhat weaker (see Table 6). Although the observed trend in average difference scores between the proportion of nominative overextension and oblique overextension is congruent with Prediction 2, there was a large discrepancy between the 1P singular and the 3P feminine pronouns. Prediction 2 is dependent on both the proportion of nominative and oblique overextension. There is no reason to suggest that the suppletive block changes with learning, but the proportion of oblique overextension must decrease with the learning of the nominative forms. It is quite possible that the proportion of oblique overextension for the 1P singular observed here is somewhat low because of the effects of this learning. Further consideration of this suggestion is beyond the scope of the present paper, but can be found in recent research by Rispoli (1993), which indicates that pronoun case overextensions for 3P pronouns become most frequent after the 1P pronoun case forms have been learned.

There are several well documented patterns of pronoun case errors in English. First and foremost is the overextension of objective forms for nominative forms. Secondly, the use of *my* for *I* is a well established finding. Other error patterns are extremely rare or non-existent in the literature. This study has presented evidence that these particular asymmetries exist because of the role that morphological structure plays in the production of pronoun case overextensions. Because the LAD extracts a phonetic core for each pronoun, and because a phonetic core limits retrieval after direct access of a pronoun case form fails, suppletive nominatives are blocked from overextension. The effect of this casual sequence was stated in the opening of this paper as Consequence PB (repeated here for convenience):

CONSEQUENCE PB. Only pronoun case forms sharing the phonetic core will be overextended. Therefore, suppletive nominative forms will not be overextended.

Further evidence for Consequence PB can be found in the literature. In Ingham's (1992) study of one child, it was found that *he* was overextended for *him* at age 3;0, when the child was just beginning to use the 3P masculine pronoun. Predictably, this same child was reported to have had an overwhelming bias toward overextending *me* for *I*, and *her* for *she*, but the uses of *I* for *me* and *she* for *her* were not observed.

In the current study, no predictions were made regarding error patterns of the first person plural pronoun, because it was unclear whether *us* and *our* shared a phonetic core. In reviewing the literature, no reports of the overextension of *we* are found. Reference to the overextension of both *us* and *our* for *we* can be found in the literature. The overextension of *us* for *we* is documented in Huxley (1970). Similarly, the systematic overextension of *our* for *we* is reported by Ingham (1992). These data suggest that at least for some children, the first person plural pronoun has a phonetic core, and that *us* and *our* share this core. These data also suggest that the nominative form, *we* is suppletive and so blocked from overextension in accordance with Consequence PB.

CONCLUSION

In our review of the literature on pronoun case overextensions in the acquisition of English, we outlined two recent hypotheses that originate from two quite different perspectives, Radford (1988, 1990) and Budwig (1989). In essence, Radford's hypothesis is simple. The syntax of young children is too immature to motivate case assignment. Therefore children overextend pronoun case forms. Budwig's hypothesis is that children use three different pronoun case forms, *I*, *me*, *my*, in a systematic way, reflecting semantic and pragmatic distinctions. Despite the radically different perspectives from which these recent hypotheses have been generated, these hypotheses remain compatible. Radford attempted to explain why pronoun case overextensions occur, while Budwig attempted to articulate how the pronoun case forms were used once overextensions began to occur.

In this paper, we have expressly avoided these two questions: (1) What causes pronoun case errors? and (2) Does the use of different pronoun case forms reflect semantic and pragmatic distinctions, other than those normally assumed to be concomitant with nominative, objective and genitive case? Rather, we have pursued a separate question: (3) What affects patterns of pronoun case overextensions? It should not be surprising that distinctly separate questions can be posed and investigated when dealing with a phenomenon as complex as pronoun case overextension. It would be wrong to assume that the proposed explanation for the findings of this paper formed a logical or necessary alternative to either Radford's (1990) or Budwig's (1989) hypothesis.

This study has revealed evidence that the morphological structure of a pronoun will have an effect on the patterns of its overextension. There seems to be good evidence that suppletive nominative forms, *I* and *she* are blocked from overextension in a way that is not true of *he* and *they*. This difference is understandable if the LAD extracts a phonetic core for each pronoun that limits overextension. The extraction of a phonetic core may be a by-product of the LAD's thwarted attempt to build a general paradigm for pronoun case.

The veracity of the current hypothesis must be tested on the basis of its explicit predictions. When we move to other languages, we find some counterevidence to Prediction 1. In Dutch, there are nominative pronouns, *ik* 'I' etc., objective pronouns, *mij* 'me' etc. and unstressed objective pronouns *me* 'me' etc. Kaper (1976) reports that his two children occasionally replaced *mij* with *ik*. However, it is not at all clear how systematic this error pattern is, since Kaper used diary data exclusively, and did not present a quantitative analysis of the production of these pronoun case forms. Earlier in this paper we compared English pronoun case forms with those of Turkish, and found that Turkish pronoun case forms are highly regular. If pronoun case overextensions in English are related to the irregularity of the pronoun case forms, then we should expect little in the way of pronoun case error in Turkish. Given the prevalence of zero anaphora in Turkish, this prediction may be difficult to test without a very large sample. Practical considerations aside, however, the course of future research points in the direction of crosslinguistic comparison.

REFERENCES

Aksu-Koç & Slobin, D. (1985). The acquisition of Turkish. In D. Slobin (ed.), *The crosslinguistic study of language acquisition*. Vol. 1. *The data*. Hillsdale, NJ: Erlbaum.

Brown, R. (1973). *A first language*. Cambridge, MA: Harvard University Press.

Budwig, N. (1989). The linguistic marking of agentivity and control in child language. *Journal of Child Language* **16**, 263–84.

Hart, B. (1991). Input frequency and children's first words. *First Language* **11**, 289–300.

Hopper, P. & Thompson, S. (1980). Transitivity in grammar and discourse. *Language* **56**, 251–99.

Huxley, R. (1970). The development of the correct use of subject personal pronouns in two children. In G. Flores d' Arcais & W. Levelt (eds.), *Advances in psycholinguistics*. Amsterdam: North Holland.

Ingham, R. (1992). The optional subject phenomenon in young children's English: a case study. *Journal of Child Language* **19**, 133–51.

Kaper, W. (1976). Pronominal case-errors. *Journal of Child Language* **3**, 439–41.

Loeb, D. & Leonard, L. (1991). Subject case marking and verb morphology in normally developing and specifically language-impaired children. *Journal of Speech and Hearing Research* **29**, 481–93.

Menyuk, P. (1969). *Sentences children use*. Cambridge, MA: MIT Press.

Miller, J. (1981). *Assessing language production in children*. Austin, TX: Pro Ed.

Pinker, S. (1984). *Language learnability and language development*. Cambridge, MA: Harvard University Press.

Radford, A. (1988). Small children's small clauses. *Transactions of the Philological Society* **86**, 1–43.

—— (1990). *Syntactic theory and the acquisition of English syntax: the nature of early child grammars of English*. Cambridge, MA: Blackwell.

Rispoli, M. (1993). The acquisition of pronoun case. Unpublished manuscript, Northern Arizona University.

Siegel, S. (1956). *Nonparametric statistics for the behavioral sciences*. New York: McGraw-Hill.

Slobin, D. (1985). Crosslinguistic evidence for the language-making capacity. In D. Slobin (ed.), *The crosslinguistic study of language acquisition*. Vol. 2. *Theoretical issues*. Hillsdale, NJ: Erlbaum.

Tanz, C. (1974). Cognitive principles underlying children's errors in pronominal case-marking. *Journal of Child Language* **1**, 271–6.

J. Child Lang. **21** (1994), 173–209. Copyright © 1994 Cambridge University Press

Sensitivity of children's inflection to grammatical structure*

JOHN J. KIM, GARY F. MARCUS, STEVEN PINKER

Massachusetts Institute of Technology

MICHELLE HOLLANDER

University of Michigan

AND

MARIE COPPOLA

Massachusetts Institute of Technology

ABSTRACT

What is the input to the mental system that computes inflected forms like *walked, came, dogs,* and *men*? Recent connectionist models feed a word's phonological features into a single network, allowing it to generalize both regular and irregular phonological patterns, like *stop-stopped, step-stepped* and *fling-flung, cling-clung*. But for adults, phonological input is insufficient: verbs derived from nouns like *ring the city* always have regular past tense forms (*ringed*), even if they are phonologically identical to irregular verbs (*ring the bell*). Similarly, nouns based on names, like *two Mickey Mouses,* and compounds based on possessing rather than being their root morpheme, such as *two saber-tooths,* take regular plurals, even when they are homophonous with irregular nouns like *mice* and *teeth*. In four experiments, testing 70 three- to ten-year-old children, we found that children are sensitive to such nonphonological information: they were more likely to produce regular inflected forms for forms like *to ring* ('to put a ring on') and *snaggletooth* (a kind of animal doll with big teeth) than for their homophonous irregular counterparts, even when these counterparts

[*] We would like to thank Sandeep Prasada, Annie Senghas, Fei Xu and two anonymous reviewers for helpful suggestions. We would also like to thank the Bowen After School Care Program, Inc. in Newton Center, Bright Horizons Children's Center in Boston, Bright Horizons Children's Center in Kendall Square, Children's Village in Cambridge, the Dandelion School in Cambridge, and the Lotus Children's Center in Cambridge, the MIT Summer Day Camp, and the Newton-Wellesley Children's Corner in Newton Lower Falls for participating in our studies. This research was supported by NIH Grant HD 18381 and NSF Grant BNS 91-09766 to Steven Pinker. The first and second authors were supported by NDSEG Fellowships. Address for correspondence: John J. Kim, Institute for Research in Cognitive Science, University of Pennsylvania, 3401 Walnut Street, Room 407c, Philadelphia, PA 19104-6228, USA.

were also extended in meaning. Children's inflectional systems thus seem to be like adults': irregular forms are tied to the lexicon but regular forms are computed by a default rule, and words are represented as morphological tree structures reflecting their derivation from basic word roots. Such structures, which determine how novel complex words are derived and interpreted, also govern whether words with irregular sound patterns will be regularized: a word can be irregular only if its structure contains an irregular root in 'head' position, allowing the lexically stored irregular information to percolate up to apply to the word as a whole. In all other cases, the inflected form is computed by a default regular rule. This proposal fits the facts better than alternatives appealing to ambiguity reduction or semantic similarity to a word's central sense. The results, together with an analysis of adult speech to children, suggest that morphological structure and a distinction between mechanisms for regular and irregular inflection may be inherent to the design of children's language systems.

INTRODUCTION

Linguistic research during the past 25 years has sketched out the general logic by which word forms are constructed and co-ordinated with sentences (Chomsky & Halle, 1968; Aronoff, 1976; Lieber, 1980; Williams, 1981; Selkirk, 1982; Kiparsky, 1982a, 1982b, 1983; Bybee, 1985; Anderson, 1992; see Spencer, 1990, for an introduction, and Beard & Szymanek, 1988, for a bibliography). The morphological component of the human language system seems to contain a lexicon of stored word roots, a set of derivational rules that create new word forms from old ones, and a set of inflectional rules that modify a word's form according to its role in the sentence (e.g. tense and number). Derived and inflected words are mentally represented as complex data structures. These structures contain symbols that express the formal grammatical categories (noun, verb, adjective, etc.) of the roots that went into forming the word, the grammatical category of the word as a whole, and a tree structure interconnecting these symbols that reflects the rules that went into building the word form. For example, the adjective *learnable*, derived by combining the verb root *learn* with the adjectival affix *-able*, would be represented as [learn$_V$ -able$_{Adj}$]$_{Adj}$. Though the particular rules and word forms vary from language to language, the overall architecture of this system is widely seen across languages.

The organization of morphology has implications for the acquisition of morphology. Understanding language acquisition requires specifying the innate mechanisms that accomplish language learning, and the language-particular information that these mechanisms learn. It has been fruitful to posit that the universal basic organization of grammar is inherent in the learning mechanisms, which are deployed to acquire the particular words and rules in a given language (e.g. Pinker, 1984, 1989). If this is correct, one might expect that the basic design of morphology should be visible in children's linguistic behaviour as they are learning language.

But many psychologists have been reluctant to accept abstract linguistic categories and structure as part of the child's learning mechanisms and knowledge of language. Recently an alternative has become envisionable. Connectionist or Parallel Distributed Processing (PDP) models consist of networks of densely interconnected neuron-like units whose connection strengths are adjusted during an extensive training schedule (Rumelhart & McClelland, 1986). Though these models are compatible in principle with abstract grammatical categories, structured representations, and multiple components, in practice PDP language modellers (e.g. Rumelhart & McClelland, 1986; Plunkett & Marchman, 1990, 1991; MacWhinney & Leinbach, 1991; Hare & Elman, 1992; Seidenberg & Daugherty, 1992) attempt to do away with them, preferring a single, homogeneous network that maps the features of an input word form (either phonological or both phonological and semantic) to the features of an output word form. Under these proposals, any sensitivity to abstract grammatical categories and structure must either be ignored, explained away, or hoped to emerge from the patterns of acquired feature-to-feature mappings.

This paper seeks to determine what kind of information – phonological, semantic or grammatical – constitutes the input to children's inflectional system. This is a question about the global information-flow or input–output architecture of children's language system, and is relevant to any model of children's language. Note that we will NOT be testing for differences between symbolic and connectionist architectures for language, since in principle both kinds of model could feed, or sequester, various kinds of information to the mechanism that computes inflection. It does, however, speak to the style of connectionist models that is currently popular, where the modellers attempt to avoid any design that reflects abstract grammatical categories and structure, relying on networks that map only among an innate set of phonological (and possibly semantic) features.

We begin by examining the information relevant to computing past tense and plural inflections in adults. In English, there are two types of verb: those with a regular suffixed past tense form, such as *walk/walked, jump/jumped* and *open/opened,* and those with an unpredictable irregular past tense form, such as *blow/blew, sing/sang* and *break/broke.* The plural system shows a similar organization, with regular nouns like *boy/boys, cat/cats* and *hand/ hands,* and irregular nouns like *man/men, mouse/mice* and *tooth/teeth.* New verbs and nouns virtually always receive regular inflection, e.g. *He faxed the message; She received two faxes* (Prasada & Pinker, 1993). A straightforward explanation is that a rule generates the inflected forms of regular words, but irregular forms are memorized by rote. In this simple textbook model, the information fed into the inflectional system is simply whether a word is or is not on the memorized list of irregulars. If a word has an irregular inflected form listed in the mental lexicon, it is retrieved; if not, the regular rule applies.

However, this account fails to capture the fact that most irregular past tense verbs form their past tenses in ways similar to other irregular past tense verbs with similar phonological characteristics. One example is the set of irregular verbs with stems that have an /ɪ/ followed by a velar nasal consonant, such as *sing/sang, ring/rang, drink/drank, spring/sprang*, and *stink/stank*. Though this type of clustering by phonological properties is, to a large extent, a historical residue of the Old English strong verb classes, clusters and similar irregular past tense verbs may sometimes lend their patterns to phonologically similar new verbs, suggesting that a word's PHONOLOGICAL COMPOSITION is part of the input to the inflection mechanism. We see this semi-productivity in the historical record. Several verbs have been assimilated to irregular patterns within the past few hundred years under the influence of existing clusters of similar irregular verbs (Jespersen, 1942, chapter V); examples include *fling/flung, kneel/knelt, quit/quit, sling/slung, stick/stuck*, and *string/strung*. By a similar process, many dialects of English have some irregular past tense forms that differ from those in the standard dialect, like *bring/brung*, which is presumably analogized from the *sling/slung* cluster. Children also occasionally use novel irregular past tense forms, like *brang* for *brought*, *bote* for *bit*, and *truck* for *tricked* (Xu & Pinker, 1992). Finally, Bybee & Moder (1983) and Prasada & Pinker (1993) showed that when adult experimental subjects are asked to produce the past tense form of a novel verb (e.g. *to spling*), the likelihood of an irregular past tense response (e.g. *splung*) increases with the phonological similarity of the novel verb to the phonological prototype of an irregular past tense cluster.

There is general agreement that phonological information must be fed into the past tense computation, but disagreement over how this information is used. Some linguists have proposed that the redundancy and partial productivity of irregular past tense clusters be handled by subregular rules (e.g. 'change [ɪ] to [ʌ]'), some tied to specific lexical entries, others to phonological properties of classes of items (Halle & Mohanon, 1985). Others (e.g. Lieber, 1980; Pinker & Prince, 1988, 1991; Spencer, 1990; Pinker, 1991; Marcus *et al.* 1992; Prasada & Pinker, 1993) have suggested that the phonological patterns of irregular stems and their past tense forms come not from productive rules but from memory storage, where similar-sounding word pairs are superimposed in the memory representation and hence reinforce each other and enable occasional analogizing to new similar forms. In both theories, the phonological properties of a word, together with its lexical status as an irregular, are input to the inflection system. If a word is not listed as being irregular, and if it does not engage an irregular phonological pattern by virtue of its sound pattern, it is handled by the regular suffixation rule, which acts as a default, applying to any stem that slips through the irregular filter.

Rumelhart & McClelland's (1986) PDP model of past tense inflection uses the phonological properties of stems in a different way: it uses nothing but the phonological properties of the stems as input. A base form is represented by a pattern of activation within a vector of nodes each of which stands for a phonological property of the stem (e.g. a stop consonant at the beginning of the word; a high vowel between two voiced segments). The network has an output vector with a similar structure, representing the computed past tense form of the verb. Every input node is connected to every output node by a connection with a modifiable weight. In a learning phase, the network is presented with a verb stem, represented as a set of activated input nodes, and produces an inflected form by activating a set of output nodes. A 'teacher' supplies the model with the correct past tense form for the stem, and the model adjusts the strength of the connections between the input and output nodes to minimize the difference between its computed output form and the correct past tense form. After the learning phase, the network can reproduce the past tense forms of the verb stems that it was trained on, and can generalize to many novel verbs on the basis of their phonological similarity to the verbs in the training set. Thus the model performs the stem-to-past tense mapping solely on the basis of phonological information. It captures patterns of phonological similarity for regulars and irregulars alike, generalizing in similar ways from *step* to *stepped* and from *cling* to *clung*. The model makes no qualitative distinction between irregular (lexically stored) and regular (rule-generated) past tense formation, and hence needs no information in its input to indicate the irregular status of irregular verbs. Nor does it implement formal linguistic notions such as 'verb root', 'rule', and 'lexical item'. Thus the model is often characterized as an alternative to symbol-processing or rule-based accounts of the acquisition and knowledge of language.

Does the Rumelhart–McClelland model show that the only information necessary for computing past tense forms is the phonology of the stem? Pinker & Prince (1988) and Kim, Pinker, Prince & Prasada (1991) have shown why that cannot be true for adults. First, some pairs of verbs, such as *ring/rang* and *wring/wrung*, have homophonous stem forms but different past tense forms.

(1*a*)	Muddy *rang* the bell.	*ring/rang*
	Muddy *wrung* the washcloth dry.	*wring/wrung*
(*b*)	T-Bone *lay* on his bed.	*lie/lay*
	T-Bone *lied* to me again.	*lie/lied*
(*c*)	B.B. first *met* Jimmie in 1975.	*meet/met*
	B.B. gradually *meted* out favours to his roadies.	*mete/meted*

(*d*) Buddy's voice *sank* two octaves.   *sink/sank*
    Buddy *synched* his voice track to his guitar track.   *synch/synched*

Thus homophonous verbs must be given non-identical representations when they enter into the process that generates past tense forms. The representation called a 'lexical entry' captures this distinctness – each verb in the pairs above has its own lexical entry, which has the possibility of having an irregular past tense form linked to it; if not, the regular process applies.

Note that while different lexical entries are different in meaning, this does not imply that semantic information is input directly into the past tense formation process, as MacWhinney & Leinbach (1991) claimed when they redesigned the PDP past tense learning model in response to the homophone problem.[1] In fact, such a solution has additional consequences which have to be taken seriously. Hinton, McClelland & Rumelhart (1986) note what happens when features of a particular kind are input to a parallel distributed processing model: 'one of the most interesting properties of distributed representations [is that] they automatically give rise to generalizations' (p. 82); 'any subset of the microfeatures can be considered to define a type....This allows an item to be an instance of many different types simultaneously' (p. 84). But this is exactly what does not happen with homophone pairs with different past tense forms. The semantic features differentiating *wring* from *ring*, *meet* from *mete*, and so on, do not in general differentiate different types of past tense forms: Verbs with meanings similar to *wring* do not tend to have past tense forms with *-ung*, and verbs with meanings similar to *ring* do not tend to have past tense forms with *-ang*. The semantic differences between homophones with different past tense forms are haphazard and idiosyncratic to the particular pair of verbs. This shows that speakers may use semantics to tell which of two lexical entries they are dealing with, but it is the lexical entry itself that is fed into the past tense formation process, not the semantic features directly.

A second and more systematic class of homophones with different past tense forms implicates a categorical difference between regular and irregular inflection. Irregular past tense forms are stored in the mental dictionary: they are linked to the verb's ROOT – the irreducible form–meaning pairing that defines the basis of a family of verbs. Only if a verb is based on an irregular verb root will that verb have an irregular past tense form. Regular past tense formation, in contrast, has the status of a default operation – it applies in all circumstances where an irregular verb root is not available (Pinker & Prince, 1988, 1991; Pinker, 1991; Marcus, Brinkmann, Clahsen, Wiese, Woest & Pinker, 1993). Thus, the input to the past tense system must include

---

[1] In their discussion, MacWhinney & Leinbach (1991) concede the need for a lexicon with distinct entries. They do not, however, implement such a lexicon in their model, and we will discuss the model itself.

information as to whether a word is based on an irregular root – that is, information about its GRAMMATICAL STRUCTURE. This fact has several implications.

A denominal verb is a verb that is sensed by speakers to be derived from or based on a noun. Denominal verbs (and verbs based on other categories, like adjectives or prepositions) uniformly have regular past tense forms, regardless of their phonology or semantics. Indeed, even if a denominal verb is homophonous with an irregular verb, it will be regular, a phenomenon first noted by Mencken (1936) and given an explanation by Kiparsky (1982*a*, 1982*b*). Examples are shown in (2); (*a*) and (*b*) are due to Paul Kiparsky; (*c*)–(*j*) are from Pinker & Prince (1988).

(2*a*)	He *grandstanded* to the crowd.	**grandstood*
(*b*)	He *flied out* to center field.	**flew*
(*c*)	He *spitted* the pig.	**spat*
(*d*)	He *ringed* the city with artillery.	**rang*
(*e*)	Martina *2-setted* Chris.	**2-set*
(*f*)	He *righted* the boat.	**rote*
(*g*)	He *high-sticked* the goalie.	**high-stuck*
(*h*)	He *braked* the car suddenly.	**broke*
(*i*)	He *sleighed* down the hill.	**slew*
(*j*)	he *de-flea'd* his dog.	**de-fled*
(*k*)	He *steeled* himself for the ordeal.	**stole*
(*l*)	The doctor *casted* his leg.	**cast*
	(relayed by Lila Gleitman and Stephen Kosslyn)	
(*m*)	Vera *costed* out the equipment requests in the grant proposal for us.	**cost*
	(relayed by Alan Prince)	
(*n*)	I *big-ringed* it the rest of the way.	**big-rang*
	(used the big chain ring while bicycling; from a bicycle magazine).	
(*o*)	In each of the past two seasons, Cleveland State guard William Stanley has sported a self-styled, one-of-a-kind hairdo. In 1987–88 it was a half-foot-high flattop. Last season he went to a bilevel box cut. This season, as a senior, Stanley has *outdo'ed* himself. (*Sports Illustrated*, 12/6/89)	**out-done*
(*p*)	You mean this list, and you mean that list, and after you've *meaned* both lists... (from statistics lecture relayed by Annie Senghas)	**meant*
(*q*)	Most snow or sugar snap [peas] need to be '*stringed*'. To string, pinch the top and pull	**strung*

the string along the flat side to the stem end.
(from the food section of *The Boston Globe*,
26 June 1991)

(*r*) We to *be'd* or not to *be'd* for hours on end.   **were*
(Jane Austin, *Mansfield Park*, Chapter 13;
relayed by Karin Stromswold)

What these examples have in common is that the verbs are not directly constituted of verb roots; they are transparently based on nouns, adjectives, or phrases (the rough meanings in (3) correspond to the respective examples in (2)):

(3*a*) to play to the *grandstand*
  (*b*) to hit a *fly* (ball) that gets caught (in baseball)
  (*c*) to put on a *spit*
  (*d*) to form a *ring* around
  (*e*) to beat in two *sets*
  (*f*) to set *right*
  (*g*) to hit with a *high stick*
  (*h*) to apply the *brakes*
  (*i*) to travel in a *sleigh*
  (*j*) to remove *fleas*
  (*k*) to cover, point, or face with *steel*; to make as hard as *steel*
  (*l*) to put a *cast* on
  (*m*) to ascertain the *costs* of
  (*n*) to pedal with the chain on the *big ring*
  (*o*) to affect a more impressive hair-*do* than
  (*p*) to calculate the *mean* of
  (*q*) to remove the *string* from
  (*r*) to say '*to be or not to be*'

Though homophonous with irregular verbs, these verbs have regular past tense forms because irregularity is a property of verb roots, not of verbs, and these verbs have noun roots or adjective roots, not verb roots. A noun like *ring* cannot have an irregular past tense associated with it because a noun cannot have any past tense associated with it, the notion of 'past tense' making no sense for a noun. The regular inflectional rule, being the default, is the only way to inflect such derived verbs.

Regularization of denominal verbs is part of a more general phenomenon whereby the grammatical structure of a verb determines its semantic, syntactic, and inflectional properties (Williams, 1981; Selkirk, 1982; Kim *et al.* 1991; Pinker & Prince, 1991). In the constituent structure reflecting a word's derivation from more basic morphemes, one of these morphemes is generally the HEAD of the word, and its properties percolate up to the word as a whole. In English, the head of the word is generally the rightmost element. Thus the head of *overeat*, whose structure is given in (4*a*), is the verb *eat*, so *overeating* is a kind of *eating*, and it is a verb just as *eat* is a verb. Similarly, a *workman*, whose structure is given in (4*b*), is a noun referring to a kind of man, not a kind of work.

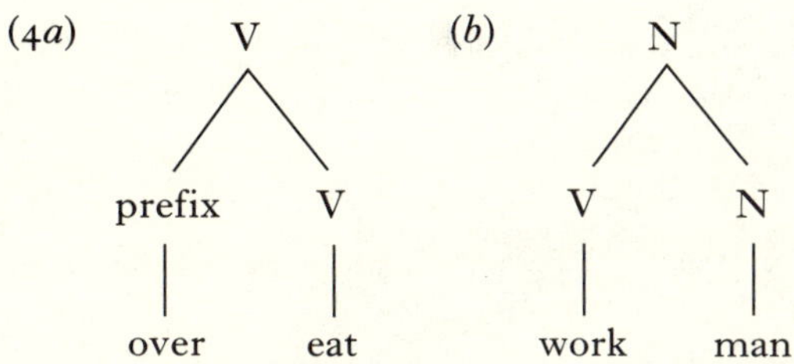

The conduit for information flow from the head to the top node of a word structure applies to ALL the information stored with the head (see Spencer, 1990, for qualifications to this statement, which are not relevant here). Not only does the grammatical category and meaning of the head percolate up (together with features like gender, humanness, animacy, and inherent aspect), but for irregular words, the irregular past tense or plural form stored with the head percolates up as well. Thus the past tense of *overeat* is *overate*, and the plural of *workman* is *workmen*. This is also why we get irregularity preserved in novel forms like *out-sang, overshot, sawteeth, oil-mice* (Chinese peasants who scavenge uncollected oil from wells), *took a leak, blew him away, came into money*, and so on. Note that neither novelty, nor, as we shall see, metaphoricity, prevents these forms from being irregular, as long as they have an irregular head.

Some words, however, are headless, or EXOCENTRIC: they differ in some property from their rightmost element, requiring that the usual pipeline of information from head to top node be blocked. For example, the structure in (5*a*), corresponding to the verb *ring* from *ringing the city*, shows a verb derived from a noun. Since the whole word, represented by its topmost label, is a verb, but the element it is made out of, *ring*, is a noun, it must be headless or exocentric – if the noun *ring* were its head, *to ring* would have to be a noun, too, which it is not. Lacking a head and its associated data pipeline, the irregular form of the verb *to ring*, namely *rang*, cannot percolate up to attach to the whole word. The regular *-ed* rule applies in its usual role as the last resort, and thus we get *ringed*.

Note that this machinery also operates in the verb *to fly out*, whose structure is given in (5*b*), even though the noun it comes from, *fly (ball)* (i.e. 'a baseball hit high in the air'), itself originally came from the verb *to fly* (i.e., 'to proceed through the air'). The step in the derivation that derives the verb (*to fly out*) from the noun (*fly ball*) yields an exocentric structure, as does the step in the derivation that derives the noun (*fly ball*) from the root verb (*fly*). Therefore, the derived verb has no head and, consequently, has no pathway for the irregularity of its root to percolate up to the top node representing the word as a whole. What kills the irregularity of *fly out*, then, is not its specialized meaning, but its being a verb based on a word that is not a verb.

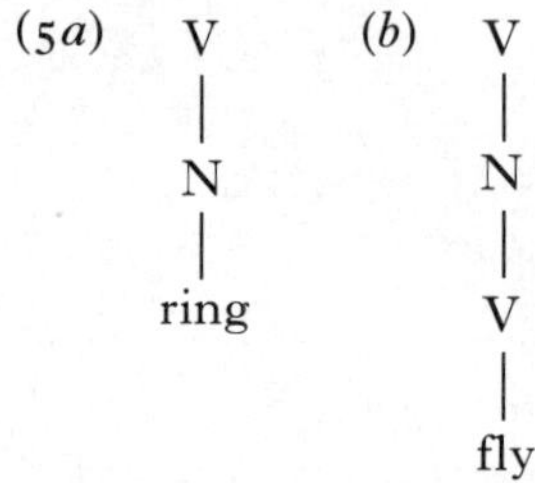

Interestingly, the theory that explains regularization by exocentrism is sufficient to explain several seemingly unrelated cases in the plural system of nouns as well, even ones where there is no category change. Consider *low-life* – not a kind of life at all, but a kind of person, namely one who leads a low life. This is an example of a BAHUVRIHI compound, a compound that refers to an object characterized by HAVING rather than BEING the referent of its rightmost morpheme. Recall that the head-to-top-node pipeline cannot be blocked for just one kind of information; if it is blocked for one thing, automatically nothing passes through. That means that there is no way for the irregularity of the root of a headless word to percolate up: if *low-life* cannot get its referent from *life*, it cannot get its plural from *life* either. When the irregular is unavailable, the all-purpose regular rule, 'add *-s*,' steps in by default. This explains why people judge its plural to be *low-lifes*, not **low-lives*. Other examples of regularized exocentric compounds (sometimes co-existing with the irregular form) include:

> (6a) We enjoyed the art gallery that displayed the *still lifes* more than any other gallery we visited.   **still lives*
>
> (b) People used to wonder if Bigfoot even existed; now they think there are several *Bigfoots*.   **?Bigfeet*
>
> (c) I used to like the police until the *flatfoots* kept pulling me over for speeding.   **?flatfeet*
>
> (d) Last year, the cub scouts went camping; but this year, the *tenderfoots* are going white water rafting.   **?tenderfeet*
>
> (e) The *goofy-foots* forgot to bring their surfboards. (slang for inexperienced or left-footed surfers; relayed by Karin Stromswold and Annie Senghas)   **?goofy-feet*
>
> (f) The *proudfoots* were creatures from Tolkien's *The Fellowship of the Ring*. (relayed by Elliza McGrand)   **?proudfeet*

(*g*) I've played a practical joke or two in my lifetime ***hotfeet**
but the greatest *hotfoots* are by my sister.

(*h*) More and more *bigmouths/loudmouths* ***/maʊðz/**
/maʊθs/ have been on television talk
shows over the past ten years.

(*i*) I have two Sony *Walkmans*; one for recording *?Walkmen*
lectures and talks and one for listening to music.

(*j*) There was a display of a family of *saber-tooths* ***saber-teeth**
at the museum.

(*k*) My favorite cartoon feline from the 1970s ***Snaggle-teeth**
was Snaggle-tooth. I wish there were more
Snaggle-tooths on TV today.

A third regularization phenomenon receives a similar explanation. Just as verbs derived from nouns are exocentric and hence take regular past tense forms even if homophonous with irregular verbs, nouns derived from verbs are exocentric and take regular plural forms even if homophonous with irregular nouns. The structure in (7) corresponds to the example in (8*a*):

(7)

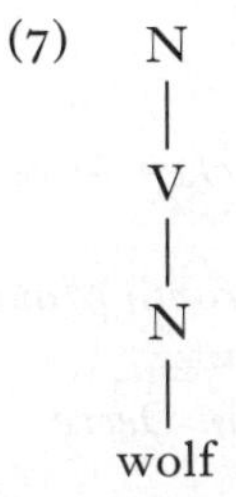

(8*a*) The boys always wolf down their food; with ***wolves**
a couple of quick *wolfs*, they consumed their
sandwiches.

(*b*) While we're at the conference in Maine I hope ***fish**
we'll have time between sessions for a couple
of quick *fishes*.

(*c*) During the last faculty meeting Harold gave ***knives**
Sam a few *knifes* in the back.

(*d*) He reached over and gave her a couple of quick ***geese**
playful *gooses*.

(*e*) I need to find some examples of splashy ***leaves**
perfume ads; can you take this magazine and
do a couple of quick *leafs* through it?

A fourth regularization phenomenon involves nouns derived from names. When a proper name (which ordinarily cannot be pluralized at all) is converted to a common noun, the result is exocentric. That is because the name of an individual is semantically ineligible to bear a plural feature, and because a noun derived from it is not an example of the kind of thing referred to by the name (see Marcus *et al.* 1993, for further explanation). The resulting N dominating a name takes a regular plural. The structures in (9*a*) and (9*b*) correspond to the examples in (10*a*) and (10*b*), respectively.

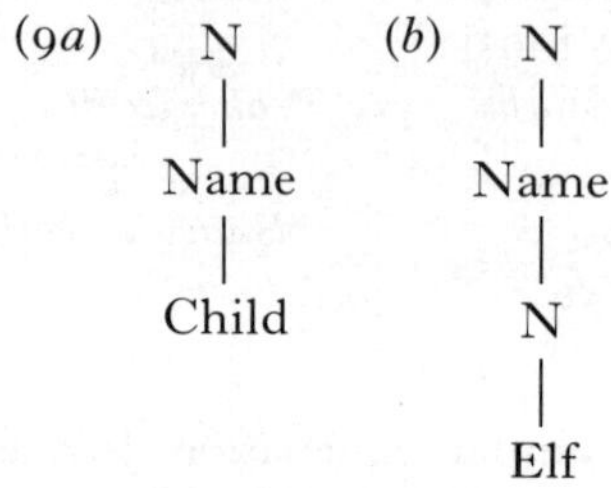

(10*a*) We're having Julia Child and her husband over for dinner. You know, the *Childs* are really great cooks.   **Children*

  (*b*) I keep telling my father to buy a Mercedes, but he insists that with that kind of money he could buy several *Renault Elfs*.   **Renault Elves*

  (*c*) I'm sick of all the *Mickey Mouses* that have been running this country for the past 12 years.   **Mickey Mice*

  (*d*) The *Toronto Maple Leafs* are sure to be one of the best hockey teams in the NHL this year again.   **Toronto Maple Leaves*

  (*e*) The number of tractors a farmer has is a good way to tell how much land he farms. We have five *John Deeres* on our farm.   **John Deere*

  (*f*) There are way too many *Thomas Manns* in the literary world today.   **Thomas Menn*

  (*g*) I like all versions of *Pretty Woman*, but Roy Orbison's original version is clearly the best of all the *Pretty Womans*.   **Pretty Women*

  (*h*) Many blues artists emulate Muddy Waters, but there aren't that many *Howlin' Wolfs* on the blues scene today.   **Howlin' Wolves*

  (*i*) He's the best of the *Mac the Knifes* in this run of Beggar's Opera.   **Mac the Knives*

  (*j*) Movie sequels are really getting out hand; there are two *Batmans* and who knows how many *Supermans* there are.   **Batmen* / **Supermen*

Other cases in English that follow this principle include nouns derived from verb phrases (e.g. *I bought two bag-a-leafs/*bag-a-leaves*) and quoted nouns (e.g. *While checking for sexist usage, I found three 'mans'/*'men' on the first page*). Indeed, the prediction of the grammatical-structure theory is that ANY circumstance in which a word is sensed not to be headed by a root in the language will cause the word to have a regular inflected form, regardless of its phonology (see Marcus *et al.* 1993).

Note that just as specific semantic features are not relevant to a word's inflectional status as either regular or irregular, the global degree of concreteness versus abstractness, literalness versus metaphoricity, or centrality versus extendedness of word sense does not predict regularization either, contrary to the suggestions of Lakoff (1987) and Harris (1992). Exocentric words are generally extended in meaning, but it is the exocentrism itself that causes regularization. Words that are extended in meaning without being exocentric do not predictably regularize, as in *chessmen/*chessmans, oilmice/ *oilmouses, sawteeth/*sawtooths, metrical feet/*foots, leaves/*leafs of the book, Freud's intellectual children/*childs*, and so on, and in verbs like *cut/*cutted a deal, blew/*blowed him off, took/*taked a leak, caught/*catched a cold, put/*putted him down, came/*comed off well, went/*goed crazy*, and hundreds of others (Pinker & Prince, 1988).

In sum, five kinds of information could, in principle, feed into the computation of a word's inflectional form: its lexical entry, phonological composition, semantic features, grammatical structure, and degree of semantic extendedness. The simplest textbook model has the lexical entry as the sole input. The Rumelhart–McClelland model has phonological composition as the sole input. The MacWhinney–Leinbach model has phonological composition and semantic features as the input. Lakoff and Harris suggest that the input includes some representation of semantic extendedness. And theories from generative linguistics have grammatical structure, which incorporates the lexical entry, as the input (with a minor role for phonological composition in analogies to novel irregular forms, though only if they involve an irregular root in head position).

Previous studies

In an experiment with 32 college students, Kim *et al.* (1991) investigated the role of phonology, grammatical structure, and semantic extendedness in adults' generalizations of past tense inflection. Subjects were asked to rate regular and irregular past tense forms of denominal and extended endocentric verbs which were homophonous with irregular verbs. An example is given in (11) and (12):

(11) DENOMINAL: It's always a good idea to relax your clients by making sure they are supplied with food and drink at all times. That's why when MacTavish arrived, I immediately snacked him, *drinked/drank* him, and fed him.

(12) EXTENDED: It's always a good idea to relax your clients by feeding them gossip and pretending to drink up the gossip they give you. That's why when MacTavish arrived, I immediately fed him lots of gossip, and *drinked/drank* up everything he said.

The findings supported the grammatical structure theory and not the phonology-only theory: subjects rated regular past tense forms as better than irregular past tense forms for denominal verbs, but irregular past tense forms as better than regular past tense forms for extended endocentric verbs. The results were replicated with non-college-educated adults, showing that the effect is not a consequence of formal language training that the college subjects might have received. Kim *et al.* also collected data showing that semantic extendedness cannot explain these results (to be discussed later).

In this paper, we present four experiments aimed to test whether children, too, are sensitive to formal grammatical structure. We look for differences in the way children inflect verbs which are homophonous with irregular verbs, and nouns which are homophonous with irregular nouns, by varying their paths of morphological derivation.

Note that we are only able to test whether children's behaviour in using inflections is SENSITIVE to grammatical structure, not whether it is DE-TERMINED by grammatical structure. Children's behaviour is the result of a multitude of factors, their knowledge of language being only one of these. In fact, Marcus *et al.* (1992) found that children's behaviour in experiments eliciting past tense and plural forms is subject to a variety of non-grammatical factors. These factors cause children to produce overregularizations like *comed* between 10 and 55% of the time, far greater than their error rate in spontaneous speech, which generally averages from 2 to 4%. Children might overregularize in experiments for several reasons: because they are under performance pressure; because they have recently been primed with the stem in the elicitation instructions (e.g. *This is a girl who knows how to **swing**; She did the same thing yesterday; Yesterday, she __*), leading them to include the stem as part of an overregularized response like *swinged*; or because they fall into a strategy of failing to attend to the word as a word to be looked up in the mental dictionary, treating it instead as a pure sound, which thereby calls for the regular rule. In the experiments we report here, attentional factors could also produce the opposite contaminant: if children are not paying attention, or if they neglect the context we provide that defines a word as exocentric for any other reason, they could treat it as the original word, and therefore fail to regularize it as its grammatical structure would demand. Because we cannot control the strategic and performance factors that can lead to regularization or lack of regularization across the board, we can only point to DIFFERENCES in regularization rates between items differing in grammatical structure, and can therefore only test whether information of a particular sort is PART of the input to the inflectional process, not whether it is the sole input.

EXPERIMENT 1

If children are designed with only phonological composition as the input to their inflectional process, as the Rumelhart–McClelland model and several of its successors assume, then all verbs that are homophonous with irregular past tense verbs will have an irregular past tense form, because there is, in principle, no way the process can distinguish among phonologically identical verbs. If children are designed with grammatical structure as the input to their past tense system, then verbs with irregular verb roots in head position will have an irregular past tense form, but denominal verbs, lacking a verbal head, will have a regular past tense form, even if they are ultimately related to some irregular verb root. The first experiment tested these predictions with six- to nine-year-old children.

METHOD

Subjects

Twelve children ranging in age from 6;8 to 8;10 (mean 7;4) were drawn from a summer day camp.

Materials

Nine irregular verbs were used: *see, buy, meet, drink, fly, stick, write, leave, ring*. Each item was used twice, once as a verb root and once as a denominal verb. The grammatical structure of the verb was indicated to the children by using the stem initially either with the usual meaning of the verb, or with the meaning of the homophonous noun. An example of the denominal and verb root pairs is shown in (13) and (14). Appendix A provides a full list of the experimental materials.

(13) (Denominal) This is a fly. Can you say 'This is a fly?' I'm going to fly this board.
(*Put flies all over the board*)
I just __.

(14) (Verb root) This airplane is going to fly. Can you say 'This airplane is going to fly?' This airplane is about to fly through the air.
(*Have the airplane fly about*)
The airplane just __.

Design and procedure

Children were presented with all 18 examples in one of four orders. The first was constructed at random. The second replaced each denominal item in the first version with its verb root counterpart, and each verb root item with its denominal counterpart. The third and fourth orders were the reverse of the first and second. Three children were presented with each of the four orders.

The children's responses were tape-recorded. Children occasionally changed their minds; their initial responses and their final ones were tallied separately. Because a child's first reaction might be based on a surface phonological association, the final response was counted as the definitive datum in the analyses reported. However, the means and the results of the significance tests are very similar in all cases when the first response rather than the final response is counted. Responses were coded as REGULAR, IRREGULAR, NO CHANGE (when the child simply repeated the stem form), or UNCODABLE (for all other response types). No-change responses were not counted as irregular, even though the past tense forms of some irregular past tense verbs involve no phonological change to the stem (e.g. *hit, cut, put, set*), because none of the verbs used in this study were of that type.

RESULTS

The data are summarized in Table 1. Two ANOVAs were performed on the final verb responses that were either regular or irregular. In the first, the random variable was subjects; the independent variables were order and grammatical structure (denominal versus verb root); the dependent variable was the proportion of the child's responses (not counting no-change and uncodable responses) that consisted of regularly inflected forms (i.e. number of regular responses/[number of irregular responses + number of regular responses]). The main effect of grammatical structure was significant: $F(1,8) = 94.75$, $p < 0.001$. The second analysis had items as the random variable, and grammatical structure as the only independent variable. Again grammatical structure exerted a significant effect: $F(1,8) = 59.07$, $p < 0.001$. That is, of the clearly regular and clearly irregular final verb responses, children responded with regular past tense forms more often than irregular past tense forms for denominal verbs, and with irregular past tense forms more often than regular past tense forms for verb roots.

Furthermore, for each subject the proportion of the regular and irregular responses that was regular was greater for denominal items than for items in the verb root condition. This was true over items as well: for each denominal/verb-root pair of items, the proportion of the regular and irregular responses that was regular was greater for the denominal item than for the verb root item.

TABLE 1. *Percentages of children's final responses in Experiment 1*

	Regular	Irregular	No change	Uncodable
Denominal verbs	66·7	17·6	11·1	4·6
Verb roots	11·1	87·0	1·9	0

DISCUSSION

Children between the ages of six and nine gave regular past tense forms for verbs that are derived from nouns even when their homophonous verb root counterparts have irregular past tense forms that the children know. The experimental results are consistent with the hypothesis that children of this age are sensitive to the morphological derivation of verbs.

As mentioned, it is not possible to determine why children provided irregular forms for denominal items 17·6% of the time. There are many possible reasons. Perhaps children's inflectional systems are inherently probabilistic; perhaps children's attention to the denominal context in this experiment was probabilistic; perhaps children were probabilistically reluctant to respond with regular past tense forms for the experimental items just because they consciously realized that the regular past tense form is incorrect for the homophonous verb root with which they are familiar (a metalinguistic process that occasionally dilutes derivation effects in adults as well; see Pinker & Prince, 1988; Kim *et al.* 1991). In any case, we see a strong effect of grammatical structure in the predicted direction above these potential sources of noise.

EXPERIMENT 2

Although Experiment 1 showed that children do not rely solely on phonology to compute past tense forms, it is premature to claim that they represent grammatical structure and a difference between regular and irregular past tense formation. First, these are school-age children, and it is possible that their grammatical systems underwent some kind of reorganization after the basis of language acquisition had been laid down, possibly in response to literacy and schooling. It is virtually certain that they did not explicitly learn in the classroom that denominal verbs have regular past tense forms, because this phenomenon is not normally included in language instruction, even for adults (Kim *et al.* 1991). But some more subtle change might occur, so it is of interest to test for the effect in children closer to the age at which most of their language is being acquired.

A second limitation is that the results from Experiment 1, though showing that children use information other than phonology, do not show that the information they use is grammatical structure. Denominal verbs, by their very nature, are extended in meaning; their meanings are based on the meanings of the nouns that they are derived from. An alternative explanation for the results of Experiment 1 is that children, for some reason, have a tendency to regularize verbs that they think are semantically 'strange' or extended, which would include all of the denominal verbs, but none of the verb roots. This interpretation is similar to a proposal made by Lakoff (1987) for adults. Lakoff suggested that if a verb has an irregular past tense form among its range of meanings, it must have an irregular past tense form in its central sense. That is, no verb will have an irregular past tense form if a more central meaning for that verb has a regular past tense form. This generally accords with the fact that denominal verbs have regular past tense forms and have relatively extended meanings, and that when a cluster of meanings of a verb has an irregular past tense form somewhere among its meanings, the most central sense is (usually) irregular. (However, Kim *et al.* 1991, note several counterexamples in which the central sense of a verb is regular and its extended sense is irregular, such as *He wetted the washcloth* vs. *The baby wet his diapers*.) Logically speaking, Lakoff's proposal that it is always the central senses that have irregular past tenses is consistent with the results of Experiment 1. But it would also be consistent with a finding of no difference, because the proposal makes no predictions for the extended senses of verbs which have irregular central senses; the past tense forms of such verbs' extended senses could be either regular or irregular, according to the literal content of the proposal. Therefore we tested a slightly stronger version of the hypothesis: if a verb is irregular in its central sense, it is likely to be regular in its extended senses.

Experiment 2, then, is similar to Experiment 1, except that it tests preschool children, and presents verb roots that, like their denominal counterparts, have extended meanings.

METHOD

Subjects

Twenty-six children ranging in age from 3;2 to 5;2 (mean 4;3) were drawn from daycare centres.

Materials, design and procedure

The design, procedure, and denominal materials from Experiment 1 were used. The verb root items were modified so that they were extended in meaning, as in (15). Appendix B presents the full list of extended verb root items.

TABLE 2. *Percentages of children's final responses in Experiment 2*

	Regular	Irregular	No change	Uncodable
Denominal verbs	64·1	5·6	20·5	9·8
Verb roots	46·6	22·6	23·5	7·3

(15) (Verb root) Mickey likes to drive really fast. Look, Mickey is going to fly down the road. Can you say 'Mickey is going to fly down the road?'
(Have Mickey drive fast down the road)
Mickey just __.

Six children participated in each of two of the versions, and seven participated in each of the other two versions.

RESULTS

The data, which are summarized in Table 2, were analysed as in Experiment 1. There was a significant main effect of grammatical structure in a two-way ANOVA (4 orders × denominal/verb root) with subjects as the random variable ($F(1,22) = 56\cdot10$, $p < 0\cdot001$), and in a one-way ANOVA with items as the random variable ($F(1,8) = 15\cdot62$, $p < 0\cdot01$). For 21 of the 26 children, the proportion of regular and irregular responses which was regular was greater for the denominal items than for the verb root items; the other five subjects gave no irregular responses and so showed no difference between denominal verbs and verb roots. For eight of the nine pairs of items, the proportion of the regular and irregular responses which was regular was greater for the denominal item than for the extended verb-root item; children never gave an irregular past tense form for the other item, *buy/bye*, and thus this item showed no difference between its denominal and verb root forms in proportion of regular responses (i.e. both were 100% regular).

DISCUSSION

This study shows that three- to five-year-old children are more likely to produce regular past tense forms for denominal verbs than for homophonous verb roots, even if those verb roots are semantically extended. These results are consistent with the hypothesis that children's inflectional systems are sensitive to grammatical structure and that they distinguish between irregular inflected forms (which are inherently bound to verb roots in memory and inherited via heads of endocentric structures), and regular forms (which are available by default). This finding replicates the results of Experiment 1 while addressing two alternative explanations. Nothing specific to schooling could have induced these results because the current subjects are preschoolers, and the extendedness of meaning for denominal items is eliminated as the factor causing the effect because here the verb roots were extended in meaning as well.

One noticeable difference between the results of this study and those from Experiment 1 is that children gave more regular responses for the extended senses of the verb roots in the present experiment (46·6%) than for the central senses of the verb roots in Experiment 1 (11·1%). Though this at first glance appears to show that extendedness itself affects regularization, there is a confound in the comparison between Experiment 1 and its replication here that prevents such a conclusion. The verb roots were extended in Experiment 2, but Experiment 2 also tested younger children (3;2–5;2, versus 6;8–8;10). Previous elicitation experiments show that the age difference itself is sufficient to account for the difference in the rates of overregularization. Kuczaj (1978) found that three- to four-year-olds overregularized 29% of the time, five- to six-year-olds 49% of the time, and seven- to eight-year olds 1% of the time. Marchman (1988) found that four-year-olds overregularized 32% of the time, five-year-olds 33%, six-year-olds 22%, seven-year-olds 10%, and nine-year-olds 5% (see Marcus *et al.* 1992, for a review). Our 47% versus 11% difference fits into this range easily, even if semantic extendedness plays no role. (We will also see in Experiments 3 and 4 that younger children overregularize more often in elicitation experiments than older children do, even when the methodology is held constant.) An across-the-board tendency for younger children to overregularize more could also explain their lower percentage of irregular responses to denominal verbs in this experiment (5·6%) than the percentage seen in their older counterparts in Experiment 1 (17·6%).

EXPERIMENT 3

Just as the phonology-only theory predicts that verbs which are homophonous with irregular past tense verbs will have irregular past tense forms, it also predicts that nouns which are homophonous with nouns with irregular plural forms will have irregular plural forms. The grammatical structure theory predicts that only nouns with nouns roots in head position can have an irregular plural form: exocentric nouns will tend to have a regular plural form, even if they are ultimately related to a noun root with an irregular plural form. This experiment tested these predictions with seven to ten-year-old children.

METHOD

Subjects

Twelve children ranging in age from 7;1 to 9;6 (mean 8;8) were drawn from after-school programs.

Materials, design and procedure

The design of this experiment parallels the design of Experiment 1. Endocentric/exocentric pairs were constructed for irregular nouns. Six of the exocentric nouns were based on proper names that were in turn based on irregular nouns: *Batman, Wonder Woman, Mickey Mouse, Mother Goose, Superchild, Mr. Tooth* (a large tooth-like figure with a face on it). The other three were bahuvrihi compounds: *brown bigfoot, pink snaggletooth* (a walrus-like animal with large teeth), *walkman* (the last is a unique compound, semantically different from standard English bahuvrihi compounds in that its referent does not possess the referent of the rightmost morpheme; the compound is a pseudo-English collocation invented in Japan). The endocentric counterparts of the exocentric nouns were common nouns with prenominal adjective modifiers that were matched with exocentric items for number of syllables: *fat man, skinny woman, fuzzy mouse, little goose, little child, purple tooth, brown big foot, yellow shark tooth, tall man.*

The experimenters suggested the derivational status of the noun to the children by using the noun initially as either a name, a bahuvrihi compound, or a common noun, using the wording in (16)–(18), respectively.

(16) (Name)   This is Mr. Tooth. Can you say 'This is Mr. Tooth?'
                (*Bring out another Mr. Tooth figure*)
                There are two __.

(17) (Bahuvrihi)   This is a pink snaggletooth. Can you say 'This is a pink snaggletooth?'
                (*Bring out another snaggletooth figure*)
                There are two __.

(18) (Noun)   This tooth is red. But this is a purple tooth. Can you say 'This is a purple tooth?'
                (*Point to another purple tooth*)
                There are two __.

RESULTS

The data, which are presented in Table 3, were analysed as in the previous experiments. There was a significant main effect of grammatical structure (endocentric/exocentric) in a two-way ANOVA (4 orders × exocentric/endocentric) with subjects as the random variable ($F(1,8) = 13.08, p < 0.01$),

TABLE 3. *Percentages of children's final responses in Experiment 3*

	Regular	Irregular	No change	Uncodable
Exocentric nouns	24·1	69·4	6·5	0
Endocentric nouns	4·6	93·5	1·9	0

and in a one-way ANOVA with items as the random variable ($F(1,8) = 18·08, p < 0·01$). For nine of the 12 subjects, the proportion of regular and irregular responses which was regular was greater for exocentric items than for endocentric items; one subject gave a greater proportion of regular responses in the endocentric condition than in the exocentric condition; the other two subjects gave no regular responses at all and so showed no difference between endocentric and exocentric conditions in the proportion of regular responses. For eight of the nine pairs of items, the proportion of the regular and irregular responses which was regular was greater for the exocentric item than for the endocentric item; one item, *skinny woman/ Wonder Woman*, had a greater proportion of regular responses for the endocentric item than the exocentric item. The tendency to regularize was approximately the same for the three bahuvrihi nouns and the six nouns derived from names (27·8 and 24·6 % of responses, respectively, excluding no-change and uncodable responses).

DISCUSSION

Children gave more regular plural responses for exocentric nouns than for endocentric nouns. This extends the evidence that children's inflection is sensitive to grammatical structure, and not just phonological composition. Children are sensitive to the derivation of nouns as well as to the derivation of verbs. They are sensitive not only to a change of grammatical category, as in the previous experiments, but to other forms of exocentrism, such as whether a nominal merely CONTAINS an irregular noun, or has the irregular noun as its head. Moreover they showed this sensitivity to the same degree when the exocentric noun referred to the same object as its root (nouns derived from names, like *Batman*) and when it referred to only a part of that object or a different object (bahuvrihi nouns, like *Snaggletooth* or *walkman*). This suggests that the children did not use some simple semantic criterion for regularization but were sensitive to exocentrism itself.

Though the rate of irregular responses for exocentric nouns was lower than for endocentric nouns (69·4 versus 93·5 %), it was fairly high, and much higher than for exocentric verbs in Experiment 1 (17·6 %). The reasons for this are unclear. Perhaps it is because the stories which were used to present the different nouns in this study were nearly identical to one another, whereas the stories from Experiments 1 and 2 varied. As a result, the children may not have paid as much attention to the context defining the items as exocentric. Another possibility is that if speakers should ever misanalyse exocentric items as endocentric (say, if they analyse *to fly out* as a metaphorical form of flying rather than one result of hitting a fly ball, or *Batman* as a kind of man rather than a name for a man) they should keep its inflected form irregular. Kim *et al.* (1991) were able to obtain independent measures of the likelihood of such reanalyses, and confirmed that they diluted the regularization of exocentric verbs. But such reanalyses are even more natural for exocentric nouns, because their rightmost noun morphemes can be interpreted as picking out some multiplicity of objects just when the exocentric nouns pick out some multiplicity of objects. That is, *two Batmans* are also two men, *pink snaggletooths* have many teeth, and so forth. So even though we designed the experiment so that children had to use the name items with the syntax appropriate for names, misanalyses may have been tempting, and they would have diluted the effects (fortunately, not completely).

EXPERIMENT 4

The goal of this experiment was to replicate Experiment 3 with preschool children. In a pilot study using the same methodology as in Experiment 3, we found that preschoolers virtually never responded with irregular plural forms in either the exocentric or endocentric conditions. As noted, this is consistent with the findings summarized by Marcus *et al.* (1992) that younger children overregularize more than older children do, and that experimental elicit-ations, in particular, exaggerate the tendency to overregularize, by an order of magnitude or greater. (It also confirms that age is sufficient to account for the difference in regularization rates in Experiments 1 and 2). To get our dependent variable of regularization rate off the ceiling for preschoolers, we had to modify the procedure to bias them to give irregular responses. Of course, this bias was introduced across the board, for both endocentric and exocentric items, so it does not confound the results obtained.

METHOD

Subjects

Twenty children ranging in age from 3;5 to 5;0 (mean 4;2) were drawn from daycare centres.

Materials, design and procedure

The design and materials from Experiment 3 were used. The only difference was that we asked the children to repeat the irregular plural form of a noun, with no context, just before presenting the relevant experimental item to

TABLE 4. *Percentages of children's final responses in Experiment 4*

	Regular	Irregular	No change	Uncodable
Exocentric nouns	50·0	17·8	24·4	7·8
Endocentric nouns	43·9	33·3	18·9	3·9

them, a manipulation that biases the children towards giving irregular plural forms, both for endocentric and exocentric items. Five children were run in each of two orders, four children were in another order, and six children were in the last order.

RESULTS

The data are presented in Table 4; they were analysed as in the previous experiments. There was a significant main effect of morphological structure (exocentric vs. endocentric) in a two-way ANOVA (4 orders × exocentric/ endocentric) with subjects as the random variable ($F(1,16) = 13·28$, $p < 0·05$), and in a one-way ANOVA with items as the random variable ($F(1,8) = 17·50$, $p < 0·01$). For 14 of the 20 children, the proportion of regular and irregular responses which was regular was greater for the exocentric item than for the endocentric item; two children gave a greater proportion of regular responses in the endocentric condition than in the exocentric condition; four children showed no difference. Of the four children that showed no difference, one gave no regular responses, and two gave no irregular responses. All nine pairs of items had a higher proportion of regular responses for exocentric items than for endocentric items. The tendency to regularize was slightly smaller for the three bahuvrihi nouns than for the six nouns derived from names (65·8 and 77·8 % of responses, respectively, excluding no-change and uncodable responses). This shows that children's tendency to regularize was not exclusively a response to nouns whose referents differed from those of their roots.

DISCUSSION

The children in this experiment gave a higher proportion of regular plural responses for exocentric nouns than for endocentric nouns. This provides further evidence that preschool children are not just sensitive to phonology in figuring out how to inflect words, but to grammatical structure as it reflects the relation between a complex word and its root.

GENERAL DISCUSSION

In the experiments reported in this paper, children were more likely to regularize denominal verbs than homophonous irregular verb roots; similarly, they were more likely to regularize exocentric nouns than homophonous irregular endocentric nouns. These results show that the input to children's inflectional systems cannot just be the phonological representations of words, as it is in the models of Rumelhart & McClelland (1986), Plunkett & Marchman (1990, 1991), Seidenberg & Daugherty (1992), and Hare & Elman (1992). Moreover, the effect cannot be due to children avoiding irregulars whenever a verb form has an unexpected meaning.

The studies reported in this paper are consistent with the hypothesis that children at an early age are sensitive to the abstract linguistic notions that underlie the linguistic knowledge of adults. It is important to note that no special theory has to be constructed to account for the phenomenon of regularization by exocentrism (for either children or adults). It falls out of the nature of irregularity and the scheme by which complex words are interpreted from the arrangement of their parts – that is, how speakers know that *breadbox* is a kind of box, not a kind of bread, and that *to brake* means to apply brakes (Lieber, 1980; Williams, 1981; Selkirk, 1982; Pinker & Prince, 1988; Spencer, 1990; Kim *et al.* 1991; Pinker & Prince, 1991). The principles are that (*i*) irregularity is a link between two word roots – a stem form and its irregularly inflected form; (*ii*) derived words are decomposed into abstract morphological structures reflecting their derivation from more basic morphemes; (*iii*) lexical features (including, but not restricted to, irregularity) are passed up to a whole word through head positions only, hence words that are headless cannot inherit grammatical features of the morphemes they are constructed out of; and (*iv*) regular past tense inflection applies by default whenever it is not specifically blocked by irregularity.

Alternative accounts

Degree of semantic extendedness. Lakoff (1987) aimed to explain regularization of denominal verbs by semantic extendedness: if a polysemous verb has an irregular past tense, its central sense will be irregular. This hypothesis, however, fails to predict any difference; it simply predicts no difference in the opposite direction. Moreover, the hypothesis that extendedness but not exocentrism causes regularization is refuted by the greater degree of regularization found for exocentric items in Experiment 2, where verb root items as well as denominal verb items were extended in meaning. But there is another conceivable hypothesis: semantic extendedness comes in degrees, and denominal verbs are more extended in meaning than extended verbs with verb roots. If so, semantic extendedness might suggest an alternative explanation for the data: if extended verbs are more likely to be regularized, and if the denominal verbs are more extended than the verb roots, denominal verbs should be regularized more often.

This explanation cannot be completely ruled out in this set of studies. However, Kim *et al.* (1991) did several statistical analyses unconfounding semantic extendedness and exocentrism, and showed that for adults, only the latter could unambiguously account for their judgements. Using a dummy variable for denominal versus verb-root structure, and a set of independent ratings of semantic extendedness, Kim *et al.* (1991) found that the unconfounded effects of exocentrism accounted for a significant 22·8% of the variance in subjects' preference for regular forms, but the unconfounded effects of semantic extendedness accounted for only 0·6% of the variance (the rest of the variance was jointly accounted for, or not accounted for by either variable). Second, the effect of semantic extendedness was entirely localized to denominal verbs, which is unexplained if there is no qualitative difference between denominal and extended endocentric verbs apart from semantic extendedness. Together with other findings, this led Kim *et al.* to conclude that the only effect of semantic extendedness is to make it more likely that subjects misanalysed denominals as being headed by an irregular verb root. Since the grammatical structure theory is consistent with data from adults and children, it offers the simplest account for all the data; if the grammatical structure theory were true for adults but the semantic extendedness hypothesis were true for children, an additional theory has to be developed that explains how children's knowledge is qualitatively reorganized when children become adults.

Reducing ambiguity. Harris (1992) suggests that speakers give regular past tense forms for denominal verbs which are homophonous with irregular verbs because doing so keeps denominal and endocentric verbs phonologically distinct. That is, some process calculates that it serves effective communication to assign a denominal verb a past tense form which is distinct from the past tense form of a homophonous endocentric verb (e.g. *I spitted/*spat a pig for the pig roast* vs. *I spat/*spitted on the ground in disgust*). This can be done because there exists a linguistic device that can signal such a distinction: the productive *-ed* past tense suffix.

The ambiguity-reduction account has some preliminary intuitive appeal because inflected exocentric forms happen to differ both in form and meaning from their homophonous endocentric irregular counterparts. But further examination shows that the ambiguity-reduction hypothesis is incorrect:

(1) Ambiguity-reduction should call for regularization whenever there is a significant meaning change in a novel verb form, not only when there is a meaning change secondary to exocentrism. But as noted at the end of the Introduction, and by Pinker & Prince (1988) and Kim *et al.* (1991), endocentric forms with irregular heads do not regularize. Pinker & Prince (1988: 112–13) note:

Verbs like *come, go, do, have, set, get, put, stand*...are magnificently polysemous (and become more so in combination with particles like *in, out, up, off*), yet they march in lockstep through the same nonregular paradigms in central and extended senses – regardless of how strained or opaque the metaphor.

The recently-popularized idiom *blow him away*, ambiguously meaning either 'overwhelm' or 'execute' but with past and participle *blew/blown*, never **blowed*, is just one out of literally hundreds of examples. Kim *et al.* (1991) also showed quantitatively that people's ratings of semantic extendedness had an unconfounded correlation of zero with their tendency to regularize verb roots (though the ratings of semantic extendedness had a small correlation with the tendency to regularize denominal verbs, reflecting subjects' tendency to misanalyse such verbs as endocentric).

(2) Most exocentric forms are not even ambiguous. Harris's theory derives from the tenets of 'functional grammar', according to which

> speakers' choice of one linguistic form over another is influenced by perceived communicative gain.... A salient task in judging novel verbs phonologically related to irregular verbs is guarding against miscommunication (Harris, 1992: 100).

Therefore her account should predict that regularization would only be a tempting option when the morphological, semantic, and syntactic context leaves the sense of a derived verb ambiguous, not when this context makes the meaning completely clear, so that the 'perceived communicative gain' is nil and 'miscommunication' impossible. But for the vast majority of denominal verbs, the meaning of the related verb root would be either ungrammatical, given their prefixes and arguments, or absurd in context. For instance, of the 18 denominals given in (2), only 4 (*brake, cast, out-do, string*) could conceivably be ambiguous in the contexts provided. Surely no speaker entertains the possibility that one can expectorate a pig (2c), levitate oneself into centre field (2b), or tap a city causing it to resonate (2d). But the denominal verbs all regularize, and apparently to the same degree.

(3) Ambiguity reduction does not predict that denominal verbs should always have a REGULAR past tense form; it only predicts that they should have a DIFFERENT past tense form from their homophonous verb roots, whenever phonologically possible. Irregular patterns like *ing-ang-ung* and *eel-elt*, though less productive than the regular suffix, can be applied to new words if they are phonologically similar to existing irregulars, like *spling* or *cleed* (Bybee & Moder, 1983; Kim *et al.* 1991; Prasada & Pinker, 1993). Therefore under the ambiguity-reduction account they, too, should be available to disambiguate derived forms. In particular, denominal verbs that are homophonous to existing REGULAR verbs and that are phonologically similar to clusters of

irregulars supporting semiproductive irregular patterns should have irregular past tense forms under this account. But no such tendency exists. For instance, though the verb *to heal* in (19*a*) has a regular past tense form, the denominal verb *to heel* in (19*b*) also has a regular past tense even though it could have been given the ambiguity-reducing past tense form *helt* by analogy to the *kneel/knelt, feel/felt* cluster of irregular past tense verbs:

(19*a*) My broken arm *healed/*helt* quite nicely.
   (*b*) I hate it when my sister stomps on my foot with her heel.
        She *heeled/*helt* me so hard yesterday that she broke my foot.

(20*a*) I nearly *keeled/*kelt* over after running the race.
   (*b*) I usually install the keels on the boats our company produces.
        But yesterday Sue *keeled/*kelt* the boats instead.

(21*a*) I *stared/*store* at him for hours.
   (*b*) For exercise, I used to bike but now it's so cold that I run stairs.
        Yesterday, I *staired/*store* for an hour.

Preference for the regular inflected form even in the face of homophony can be seen in many other examples, including ones where there are two distinct denominal senses, one established, the other novel:

(22*a*) I bought a new hoe for the garden in my backyard.
        the day I bought it, I *hoed/*hew* in the garden for hours.
   (*b*) Steve used to yell 'ho' at me for no apparent reason.
        He *ho'd/*hew* me one too many times, so I blew up.

(23*a*) Lancelot worked hard to become a knight.
        The king finally *knighted/*knit/*knought* him today.
   (*b*) I decided that my painting should depict the night rather than the day.
        So I bought some dark paints and *nighted/*nit/*nought* the painting.

Though some of these examples are strained, there is not even a hint of a tendency toward irregularization, not even if we stack the deck in favour of it. One such bias is to look for cases where there is the possibility of a regular OR an irregular form, both of which are distinct from the form of the homophonous root. For instance, though *to fling* in (24*a*) has the irregular past tense form *flung*, the denominal verb *to out-fling* in (24*b*) has no tendency to have the past tense form *out-flang* by analogy to the *ring/rang, stink/stank* cluster of irregular past tense verbs, even though this is not prevented on grounds of communicative efficacy (i.e. *flang* is phonologically different from *flung*).

(24*a*) Janet *flung/*flinged/*flang* her clothes all over the place.
   (*b*) Janet was fed up with her husband Sam's recurring flings with waitresses.

So she had more flings than Sam; she *out-flinged/*out-flang* him.

(25*a*) Boggs *swung/*swinged/*swang* and missed.
  (*b*) I have to put the swing on the tree every March.
    This year I was lazy and *swinged/*swang* the tree in April.

Note in particular that denominal verbs ending in *-ing* should be particularly liable to being irregularized if ambiguity-reduction were a factor, because the *ing/-ang* and *-ing/-ung* irregular clusters are quite distinctly irregular: there are no regular monosyllabic verb roots ending in *-ing* (Pinker & Prince, 1988). Nonetheless, denominals go regular, even when they are particularly close to the *ing-ang-ung* cluster of irregular verbs.

(4) Denominal verbs reliably take regular inflection even when there is no existing irregular that could be a source of ambiguity. For example, the very strong *ing-ang-ung* pattern is not applied to the following non-homophonous denominal verbs:

(26*a*) She *kinged/*kang/*kung* the checker piece.
  (*b*) My car *pinged/*pang/*pung* all the way home.
  (*c*) My mother *dinged/*dang/*dung* the side of my car again.
  (*d*) I forgot my slides and *winged/*wang/*wung* it.

Similarly, in the final experiment of Kim *et al.* (1991), subjects preferred a regular past tense form to an irregular past tense form more strongly for denominal verbs than for homophonous verb roots when all the verbs to be inflected were novel (each novel verb was phonologically similar to a cluster of irregulars like *to spling*, and subjects frequently did extend the *ing-ang-ung* pattern to the novel forms).

In sum, contrary to Harris (1992), denominalization reliably causes regularization, whether or not some ambiguity is eliminated, and ambiguity does not cause regularization, unless it is accompanied by denominalization.[2] Note that we are not suggesting that regularization of exocentric forms is an

---

[2] Harris (1992) presents some regression analyses designed to show that semantic relatedness of a novel form and an existing irregular predicts regularization better than grammatical structure does. But Harris's data are uninterpretable for several reasons: (1) She analysed ratings of regular and irregular forms separately, rather than the difference between them, as in Kim *et al.* (1991), so her two regression analyses reflect subjects' reactions to the overall felicity and plausibility of the derived verb meanings, rather than their relative preference for regular or irregular inflected forms. (2) She included an unexplained predictor variable ('homonym/polyseme') in the regression that was confounded with grammatical structure but that had no motivation within her theory. Indeed, her theory made two predictions, one in her Hypothesis, the other in her Conclusion, that are incompatible with the effects of that variable. (3) She did not do the crucial test, as performed in Kim *et al.* (1991), to determine whether semantic relatedness predicted regularization among the verb roots alone, the prediction that is most clearly independent of the grammatical structure hypothesis.

arbitrary quirk, unrelated to the functions of grammar. Grammatical structure, and the inheritance of grammatical features through heads, plays a crucial role in how people coin and interpret complex new words, and a default regular rule is surely useful. It is just that the phenomenon of regularization of exocentric forms is a by-product of the mechanics of this system; it is not something that speakers strive for (deliberately or not) with some immediate communicative goal in mind. (Indeed, it is of dubious functional value for people to go to such trouble in disambiguating only the past tense and plural forms of such verbs and nouns, while tolerating the ambiguity in the far more frequently used present, progressive, infinitival, and singular forms.)

Semantic features. Since verbs have meanings as well as sounds, it might seem natural to feed a verb's semantic representation into the stem-to-past-tense mapping mechanism, together with its phonological representation. That would suffice in principle to distinguish between homophonous verbs with different past tense forms. This straightforward augmentation of the Rumelhart–McClelland model was implemented by MacWhinney & Leinbach (1991) in a 'small auxiliary simulation'. Units which represent parts of the meanings of words were added to the bank of input units, supplementing the phonological input units. This allowed the model to distinguish three homophones, among a set of 10 verbs, after 2400 epochs of training.

As mentioned in the Introduction, adding semantic features to a distributed representation has the effect of defining semantic subtypes of verbs that one would expect to have similar past tense forms, just as overlap in phonological features defines clusters of verbs with similar past tense forms – but this prediction, in the case of semantic features, is not true. For instance, though *slap*, *hit* and *strike* have similar meanings, they have different past tense forms – *slap* has the regular past tense form *slapped*, *hit* has the no-change past tense form *hit*, and *strike* has the stem-changing past tense form *struck*. Conversely, though *sting*, *sing*, *swing*, and so forth form their past tenses in similar ways, they do not comprise a semantically coherent set of verbs. This is true not just of these examples, but throughout the verb lexicon. And as mentioned, if several words are sensed as having the same verb morpheme as their head, they will all have the same past tense form, no matter how semantically dissimilar they are, as in the idioms containing *take, put, give, make, have, come, go,* and *set*. Moreover inheritance of irregularity occurs not only when the verbs are used in isolation and when they are combined with particles, but even when they are combined with prefixes whose contribution to semantic composition is weak or non-existent such as *be-, for-, under-,* and *over-* as in *undertook/*undertaked, became/ *becomed, overcame/*overcomed, forgot/*forgetted,* and *understood/*understanded.*

It is also worth noting that MacWhinney & Leinbach's addition of semantic feature nodes to their past tense network amounts to a theoretically odd claim. Unlike their phonological representation, the semantic representation is not claimed to be adequate to represent the verbs' meanings. (Indeed, a rich enough set of meaning nodes, combined with reasonably-sized hidden layers of nodes, might encourage the net to develop 'grandmother cells' for the meanings of particular words, preventing desirable generalization to new, similar-sounding words altogether.) The particular semantic nodes that were used in the model were simply chosen because they were sufficient to disambiguate the homophones in MacWhinney & Leinbach's training set of 10 verbs. Furthermore, 15 of their 25 semantic features appeared only in the representation of one word in their simulation: nine of these were assigned to *wring* (a washcloth), *ring* (a bell), *ring* (a city) (an average of three semantic features each), whereas only six were assigned to the seven non-homophones (an average of less than one semantic feature each). But why should homophones be given more unique semantic features than non-homophones? Clearly this was an *ad hoc* response to the past tense homophone problem pointed out by Pinker & Prince (1988). In actuality, the 'features' that distinguish (say) *wring* from *ring* are their distinct identities as lexical items, not any particular subset of semantic features.

More generally, it is not clear what set of 'semantic features' would ever distinguish endocentric from exocentric items. A node for the feature 'exocentric' would work mechanically, of course, but would be *ad hoc* to the problem. It would not explain why words with that feature are, in particular, verbs that are derived from nouns, bahuvrihi compounds, nouns derived from names, and the other circumstances that define exocentrism. The point of the grammatical structure theory is that all exocentric words regularize FOR EXACTLY THE SAME REASON: verbs from nouns, nouns from verbs, nouns from names, nouns from verb phrases, quoted nouns, words that stand in a 'has' rather than 'is' relation to their roots, and foreign compounds like *walkman* are all represented as exocentric, and for reasons independent of their tendency to regularize (see also Marcus *et al.* 1993).

Apart from exocentrism *per se* (which goes into the scheme for determining meaning, but is not a feature of meaning itself), there is no property that exocentric items have in common semantically and that differentiates them from related endocentric items. Denominal verbs are semantically heterogeneous (Clark & Clark, 1979), as are bahuvrihi compounds and nouns-from-names. Conversely, verbs derived from nouns which are, in turn, derived from irregular verbs (i.e. V→N→V) clearly share semantic features with the irregular verb roots out of which they are built, but are regularized despite this similarity (because they are exocentric). These include not only general semantic features like 'cause' or 'punctate action' or 'animate', but specific features shared with their particular root counterparts, as in *flied out* and *costed out*. (That is, *fly out* shares features like 'involves motion through the air' with the verb root *fly*.) The same is true for bahuvrihi compounds like *bigfoots*, *flatfoots*, and *saber-tooths*, and many nouns from names like *Mickey Mouses* and *snaggletooths*. For example, *saber-tooth* shares features like 'has sharp hard white point' with *tooth*, and *Mickey-Mouse* shares features like 'rodent' with *mouse*. The necessary 'features' in fact would have to involve abstract relational notions like '*is* vs. *has* the referent of the root word', and not the binary present/absent properties that could reasonably be treated as primitive semantic features. It is hard to see how these semantic properties could be modelled without duplicating the kinds of grammatical structure and feature-percolation-through-heads that are posited by linguistic theory. Such postulates, together with the claim that irregularity involves stored roots and regularity a default rule, yield regularization of all the different kinds of exocentric forms at once, without special wiring for each one.

Learnability issues

It is not easy to see how children could learn these principles, and there is some reason to believe that they may not. That is, there may not be enough information in children's linguistic environment for them to learn that stems have an irregular inflected form only if they are headed by an irregular root, and that exocentric stems have regular inflection across the board. Marcus *et al.* (1992) showed that children hear denominal verbs that are not homophonous with irregulars, like *fish*, *plug*, *rain*, *rope* and *screw* (and probably hear at least some of them in the past tense). But this does not tell children what to do in the relatively rare conflict circumstances where a verb has a phonological representation associated with an irregular past tense form but has a grammatical structure that prevents such information from being passed upward to the word as a whole; that is, for denominals that are homophonous with irregulars. In such cases, children might simply use the verb's phonological representation and produce its irregular past tense form. The experiments reported in this paper refute this possibility. In order for children to LEARN that denominal verbs are always regular, they would have to hear the regular past tense forms of denominal verbs which are homophonous with irregular past tense verbs. But in a search of the transcripts of Adam, Eve, Sarah and Abe in the CHILDES database (MacWhinney & Snow, 1985; MacWhinney, 1990), we found no denominal verbs which are homophonous with irregular verbs in 7500 parental utterances. If this type of linguistic input is not available to children, then some endogenous mechanism must be responsible for driving them to regularize denominal verbs. The simplest account is that children's linguistic systems are inherently organized to distinguish rules from lexical storage (with regular and irregular inflection associated with these two modes of producing linguistic forms, respectively), and to use head inheritance to interpret new complex words from their familiar components. The regularization of exocentric stems, a predictable outcome in a rare circumstance, is an automatic consequence of this basic design.

Gordon (1985), using different methods and constructions, reached a similar conclusion. He conducted an experiment showing that children produce compounds that contain irregular plurals (e.g. *mice-eater*), but they never produce compounds that contain regular plurals (e.g. **rats-eater*). He discovered a fact that led him to claim that children are innately disposed to allow irregular plurals but not regular plurals inside compounds: the frequency of compounds with plurals (of any kind) as their first element is vanishingly rare in standard frequency counts (Kucera & Francis, 1967). Because children hear neither type of plural inside compounds from their parents, they could not have learned the fact that only irregular plurals can be in nonhead positions of compounds. Gordon (1985) concludes that children's lawful behaviour when confronted with such a rare linguistic circumstance reflects the basic design of morphology: irregulars (as simple words, presumably tied to the lexicon) can enter into the compounding rule, a derivational process that takes lexical stems as its input; regulars are the product of an inflectional rule that applies after morphological derivation (such as compounding) with the result that the product of the regular inflectional rule cannot enter into the compounding process. Again, there is no innate knowledge specific to the behaviour of irregular and regular forms in compounds; the interaction automatically falls out of the basic organization of the morphological system, with regular inflection as a default process applying at the end of a derivation.

CONCLUSION

The studies reported in this paper support the simple hypothesis that children are like adults, only noisier. They probably represent whether verbs (and nouns) are headed by roots using the same kinds of structured representations that adults do. Moreover they appear to distinguish irregulars (as forms that must be passed on from the lexicon) from regulars (which can be generated as a default operation). The information necessary to learn the discriminations children make is absent from parental speech, suggesting that the discriminations reflect the inherent organization of children's linguistic systems. Such conclusions, if borne out by subsequent research, have consequences for other phenomena in language acquisition. For example, insofar as the phenomena discussed in this paper implicate qualitatively different mechanisms for regular and irregular inflection, the use of such a distinction to explain overregularizations like *comed* and their

U-shaped developmental pattern receive independent support (see Marcus *et al.* 1992).

REFERENCES

Anderson, S. R. (1992). *A-morphous morphology.* Cambridge: C.U.P.
Aronoff, M. (1976). *Word formation in generative grammar.* Cambridge, MA: MIT Press.
Beard, R. & Szymanek, B. (eds) (1988). *Bibliography of morphology 1960–1988.* Philadelphia: Benjamins.
Bybee, J. L. (1985). *Morphology: a study of the relation between meaning and sound.* Philadelphia: Benjamins.
Bybee, J. L. & Moder, C. L. (1983). Morphological classes as natural categories. *Language* **59**, 251–70.
Chomsky, N. & Halle, M. (1968). *The sound pattern of English.* Cambridge, MA: MIT Press.
Clark, E. & Clark, H. (1979). When nouns surface as verbs. *Language* **55**, 767–811.
Gordon, P. (1985). Level-ordering in lexical development. *Cognition* **21**, 73–93.
Halle, M. & Mohanon, K. P. (1985). Segmental phonology of modern English. *Linguistic Inquiry* **16**, 57–116.
Hare, M. & Elman, J. (1992). A connectionist account of English inflectional morphology: evidence from language change. In *Proceedings of the Fourteenth Annual Conference of the Cognitive Science Society.* Hillsdale, NJ: Erlbaum.
Harris, C. L. (1992). Understanding English past-tense formation: the shared meaning hypothesis. In *Proceedings of the Fourteenth Annual Conference of the Cognitive Science Society.* Hillsdale, NJ: Erlbaum.
Hinton, G. E., McClelland, J. L. & Rumelhart, D. E. (1986). Distributed representations. In D. E. Rumelhart, J. L. McClelland & the PDP Research Group (eds), *Parallel distributed processing: explorations in the microstructure of cognition.* Vol. 1. *Foundations.* Cambridge, MA: Bradford Books/MIT Press.
Jespersen, O. (1942). *A modern English grammar on historical principles.* Part VI. *Morphology.* (Reprinted 1961). London: George Allen & Unwin.
Kim, J. J., Pinker, S., Prince, A. S. & Prasada, S. (1991). Why no mere mortal has ever flown out to center field. *Cognitive Science* **15**, 173–218.
Kiparsky, P. (1982a). From cyclical to lexical phonology. In H. van der Hulst & N. Smith (eds), *The structure of phonological representations.* Dordrecht: Foris.
—— (1982b). Lexical phonology and morphology. In I. S. Yang (ed.), *Linguistics in the morning calm.* Seoul: Hansin.
—— (1983). Word-formation and the lexicon. In F. Ingemann (ed.), *Proceedings of the 1982 Mid-America Linguistics Conference.* Lawrence, KS: University of Kansas.
Kucera, H. & Francis, W. N. (1967). *Computational analysis of present day American English.* Providence, RI: Brown University Press.
Kuczaj, S. (1978). Children's judgments of grammatical and ungrammatical irregular past tense verbs. *Child Development* **49**, 319–26.
Lakoff, G. (1987). Connectionist explanations in linguistics: some thoughts on recent anti-connectionist papers. Unpublished electronic manuscript, ARPAnet.
Lieber, R. (1980). On the organization of the lexicon. Unpublished Ph.D. dissertation, MIT, Cambridge, MA.
MacWhinney, B. (1990). The CHILDES Project: computational tools for analyzing talk. Version 0.88. Pittsburgh, PA: Department of Psychology, Carnegie Mellon University.
MacWhinney, B. & Leinbach, J. (1991). Implementations are not conceptualizations: revising the verb learning model. *Cognition* **40**, 121–57.
MacWhinney, B. & Snow, C. E. (1985). The Child Language Data Exchange System. *Journal of Child Language* **12**, 271–96.
Marchman, V. (1988). Rules and regularities in the acquisition of the English past tense. *Center for Research on Language Newsletter*, University of California, San Diego, **2** (4).
Marcus, G. F., Pinker, S., Ullman, M., Hollander, M., Rosen, T. J. & Xu, F. (1992).

Overregularization in language acquisition. *Monographs of the Society for Research in Child Development* **57** (4, Serial No. 228).

Marcus, G. F., Brinkmann, U., Clahsen, H., Wiese, R., Woest, A. & Pinker, S. (1993). German inflection: the exception that proves the rule. MIT Center for Cognitive Science *Occasional Paper No 47*.

Mencken, H. L. *(1936)*. *The American language*. New York: Knopf.

Pinker, S. (1984). *Language learnability and language development*. Cambridge, MA: Harvard University Press.

—— (1989). *Learnability and cognition : the acquisition of argument structure*. Cambridge, MA: MIT Press.

—— (1991). Rules of language. *Science* **253**, 530–35.

Pinker, S. & Prince, A. S. (1988). On language and connectionism: analysis of a parallel distributed processing model of language acquisition. *Cognition* **28**, 73–193.

—— & —— (1991). Regular and irregular morphology and the psychological status of rules of grammar. In L. A. Sutton, C. Johnson & R. Shields (eds), *Proceedings of the 17th Annual Meeting of the Berkeley Linguistics Society*. Berkeley, CA: Berkeley Linguistics Society.

Plunkett, K. & Marchman, V. (1990). From rote learning to system building (Tech. Rep. No. 9020). La Jolla: University of California, San Diego, Center for Research in Language.

—— & —— (1991). U-Shaped learning and frequency effects in a multi-layered perceptron: implications for child language acquisition. *Cognition* **38**, 1–60.

Prasada, S. & Pinker, S. (1993). Generalization of regular and irregular morphological patterns. *Language and Cognitive Processes* **8**, 1–56.

Rumelhart, D. E. & McClelland, J. L. (1986). On learning the past tenses of English verbs. In J. L. McClelland, D. E. Rumelhart & the PDP Research Group (eds), *Parallel distributed processing : explorations in the microstructure of cognition*. Vol. 2. *Psychological and biological models*. Cambridge, MA: Bradford Books/MIT Press.

Seidenberg, M. & Daugherty, K. (1992). Rules or connections? The past tense revisited. In *Proceedings of the Fourteenth Annual Conference of the Cognitive Science Society*. Hillsdale, NJ: Erlbaum.

Selkirk, E. O. (1982). *The syntax of words*. Cambridge, MA: MIT Press.

Spencer, A. (1990). *Morphological theory*. Cambridge, MA: Blackwell.

Williams, E. (1981). On the notions 'lexically related' and 'head of a word'. *Linguistics Inquiry* **12**, 245–74.

Xu, F. & Pinker, S. (1992). Weird past tense forms. Paper presented at the Seventeenth Annual Boston University Conference on Language Development.

APPENDIX A

Experimental items from Experiment 1

A.1 **Denominal items**

1. '*C*': This is an 'A'. I'm going to 'A' you. (*Give the letter 'A' to the child*) Now, this is a 'C'. Now I'm going to 'C' you. (*Give the letter 'C' to the child*) I just __.

2. *bye*: Kermit likes to say 'hi' and he likes to say 'bye'. Now, Kermit is saying 'hi' to you. (*Have Kermit say 'hi' to the child*) Kermit likes to 'bye' even more. (*Have Kermit say 'bye' to the child*) Now Kermit is going to 'bye' you. Kermit just __.

3. *meat*: This is a bun. This is meat and this is cheese. First, I'm going to cheese the buns. (*Put cheese on the bun*) Now I'm going to meat the buns. (*Put meat on the bun*) I just __.

4. *drink*: This is a drink. Can you say 'This is a drink?' First, I'm going to french fry you. (*Give french fries to the child*) Now I'm going to drink you. (*Give drink to the child*) I just __.

5. *fly*: This is a fly. Can you say 'This is a fly?' I'm going to fly this board. (*Put flies all over the board*) I just __.

6. *stick*: This is a stick. Can you say 'This is a stick?' I'm going to stick the cup. (*Hit the cup with the stick*) I just __.

7. *right*: Mickey likes to drive in his car. Mickey likes to go this way. (*Have Mickey go left*) See, Mickey likes to left in his car. Can you say 'Mickey likes to left?' Mickey also likes to go this way. (*Have Mickey go right*) See, Mickey likes to right in his car. Can you say 'Mickey likes to right?' (*Have Mickey go right again*) Mickey just __.

8. *leave*: These are leaves. Can you say 'These are leaves?' I like to leave the table. (*Cover the table with leaves*) I just __.

9. *ring*: This is a ring. Can you say, 'This is a ring?' I am going to ring your finger. (*Put the ring on the child's finger*) I just __.

A.2 Verb root items

1. *see*: I like to see with this telescope. Can you say 'I like to see with this telescope?' I'm going to see you through the telescope. (*Look through the telescope at the child*) I just __.

2. *buy*: (*Give the child a bell and a ring*) Kermit likes to buy things with money. First, Kermit is going to buy a bell from you. (*Have Kermit trade money for a bell*) Now Kermit is going to buy a ring from you. (*Have Kermit trade money for the ring*) Kermit just __.

3. *meet*: Mickey likes to meet people. Can you say 'Mickey likes to meet people?' He's going to meet Wonder Woman. (*Have Mickey meet Wonder Woman*) Now Mickey'll meet Batman. (*Have Mickey meet Batman*) Mickey just __.

4. *drink*: Kermit likes to drink. Can you say 'Kermit likes to drink?' Kermit is going to fill his cup with water. (*Have Kermit fill the cup with water*) Now Kermit is going to drink it. (*Have puppet pretend to drink from a cup*) Kermit just __.

5. *fly*: This airplane is going to fly. Can you say 'This airplane is going to fly?' The airplane is about to fly through the air. (*Have the airplane fly about*) The airplane just __.

6. *stick*: This putty sticks to things. Can you say 'This putty sticks to things?' I'm going to stick this putty on the ball. (*Stick putty on the ball*) I just __.

7. *write*: Kermit likes to write on the board. Can you say 'Kermit likes to write on the board?' First, Kermit is going to write 'yes'. (*Have Kermit write 'yes'*) Now, Kermit is going to write 'no'. (*Have Kermit write 'no'*) Kermit just __.

8. *leave*: Kermit wants to leave. Can you say 'Kermit wants to leave?' Kermit is going to leave the table. (*Have Kermit leave the table*) Kermit just __.

9. *ring*: I like to ring this bell. Can you say 'I like to ring this bell?' I am going to ring this bell. (*Ring the bell*) I just __.

APPENDIX B

Extended verb root items from Experiment 2

1. *see*: (*Blindfold a doll and have the doll touch a bracelet*) This doll is going to see the bracelet. Can you say that? Now, this doll is going to see the sponge. (*Have the doll touch the sponge*) Now tell Mother Goose. This doll just __.

2. *unbuy*: (*Give the child rings*) I am going to buy that ring. (*Give money to the child and take the specified ring*) Do you know what? I don't like this ring. I am going to unbuy the ring. Now tell Mother Goose. I just __.

3. *meet*: See this pen? This pen is going to meet the table. Can you say that? (*Touch the pen to the table*) Now tell Mother Goose. This pen just __.

4. *drink*: I am really thirsty. I am so thirsty I am going to drink the air. Can you say that? (*Inhale air as if drinking*) Now tell Mother Goose. I just __.

5. *fly*: See Mickey? Mickey is going fast. Mickey is going to fly down the road. Can you say 'Mickey is going to fly down the road?' (*Have Mickey drive fast down the road*) Now tell Mother Goose. Mickey just __.

6. *stick*: See the silly putty? Watch. I am going to stick the comic strip on the silly putty. Can you say that? (*Press silly putty against the comic strip, making an imprint on the silly putty*) Now tell Mother Goose. I just __.

7. *write*: Watch. I am going to write your name. (*Arrange lettered cards so they spell the child's name*) Can you say that? Now tell Mother Goose. I just __.

8. *unleave*: Superman is really busy. He's going to leave the room. (*Have Superman leave*) Oops. Superman forgot something. He better unleave the room! (*Have Superman return*) Now tell Mother Goose. Superman just __.

9. *ring*: See this stick? I am going to ring this stick against the floor. (*Bang the stick against the floor*) Watch. See I'll do it again. (*Do it again*) Now tell Mother Goose. I just __.

J. Child Lang. **21** (1994), 211–236. Copyright © 1994 Cambridge University Press

The syntax of questions in child English*

ANDREW RADFORD

University of Essex

ABSTRACT

The purpose of this article is to provide a contemporary Government-and-Binding (GB) reinterpretation and evaluation of Klima & Bellugi's classic 1966 work on the acquisition of interrogatives. I argue that the central insight of K&B's paper can be captured by positing that *wh*-questions in Child English involve a *wh*-pronoun positioned in the head complementizer (C) position within the Complementizer Phrase (CP) (so blocking auxiliary inversion if this involves positioning an inverted auxiliary in C) and that in the transition to Adult English, children come to learn that *wh*-questions involve a *wh*-phrase superficially positioned in the specifier position within CP. I argue that the *wh*-in-C analysis poses both developmental problems (in that it fails to account for child structures involving a preposed *wh*-phrase with an uninverted auxiliary) and potential theoretical problems (in that long movement of a *wh*-head may violate locality principles). I then consider two alternative accounts of *wh*-questions which posit that *wh*-movement involves movement of a *wh*-phrase from the very earliest stages of development. The first of these is an adjunction account, on which *wh*-phrases are analysed as clausal adjuncts in Child English (adjoined to the Verb Phrase (VP) in the earliest stages and to the Inflection Phrase (IP) in later stages). I note, however, that this provides no principled account of the absence of auxiliary inversion in child *wh*-questions, and poses continuity problems (especially within a framework such as that of Cinque (1990) in which it is assumed that *wh*-phrases never adjoin to VP or IP). Finally, I consider an alternative account on which initial *wh*-phrases are analysed as occupying the specifier position within CP at all stages of development. I note that the problem posed by this analysis is accounting for the absence of auxiliary inversion in early *wh*-questions, and offer an account which posits that children overgeneralize specifier-head agreement from IP to CP.

INTRODUCTION

The purpose of this article is to provide a contemporary reinterpretation and evaluation of a classic early generative work on the acquisition of English

---

[*] I am grateful to Tom Roeper and to an anonymous reviewer for helpful comments on an earlier draft of this paper.

syntax. Developmental generative syntax was firmly established as a field with the Brown project in the 1960s, which provided a rich source of longitudinal data on the grammatical development of three children (Adam, Eve and Sarah), and spawned a considerable body of descriptive developmental work. An excellent exemplar of such work is the insightful 1966 article by Edward Klima & Ursula Bellugi [henceforth *K&B*] on 'Syntactic regularities in the speech of children', looking at early stages in the acquisition of negative and interrogative sentences. This article is a tribute to their seminal paper, and the influence it has had on all subsequent work on the acquisition of negatives or interrogatives. My goal here is to look at how the developmental insights they offer into the acquisition of the syntax of questions might be captured within a contemporary theory of syntax such as the *Barriers* model developed in Chomsky's (1986) *Barriers* monograph, and revised in subsequent work such as Rizzi (1990) and Cinque (1990).

K&B discuss three main stages in the acquisition of interrogative structures, corresponding to the three earliest MLU stages posited by Roger Brown (e.g. Brown, 1968): stage I = MLU 1·75, stage II = MLU 2·25, stage III = MLU 2·75. I shall begin by looking at each of these stages in successive sections below, asking how K&B's analysis of each stage might be transposed into the *Barriers* framework, and how the children's subsequent development could be accounted for. I shall then evaluate their approach, and consider two alternative generative approaches to the acquisition of interrogatives.

THREE STAGES IN THE ACQUISITION OF INTERROGATIVES

Stage I

K&B (p. 200) provide the following examples of multiword *yes–no* questions and *wh*-questions produced by Adam, Eve and Sarah at stage I (I am excluding from consideration here potential routines such as *what dat?*):

> (1*a*)   I ride train? See hole? Have some? Sit chair? Ball go?
>   (*b*)   What cowboy doing? What doing? Where milk go? Where horse go?

The theoretical framework adopted by K&B is Chomsky's (1965) *Aspects* model, incorporating ideas from work on clause structure by Katz & Postal (1964). K&B posit that children's interrogative clauses from the very onset of multiword speech have essentially the same immediate constituent structure as adult questions and comprise an interrogative morpheme Q and a sentential nucleus. They postulate that *yes–no* questions like those in (1*a*) comprise a suprasegmental yes–no question morpheme Q (which is 'expressed as rising intonation', p. 201), and a sentential nucleus; they also note (p. 201) that 'There are no other identifying characteristics of *yes–no* questions in Adult English, since there are no auxiliaries and there is no form of subject-verb inversion'. They suggest a similar Q+nucleus structure for *wh*-questions like those in (1*b*), with the *wh*-word being positioned outside the nucleus and inside Q. Thus, they remark (in relation to questions like *Where Anne pencil?* and *Where my milk go?*) that 'One can consider the elements *Ann pencil, my milk go* in the above questions as the nucleus' (p. 200); and in addition, they suggest (p. 201) that *what* questions are of the schematic form Q[what]-NP-(doing) and *where* questions of the form Q[where]-NP-(go), where NP is the subject of the clause and the initial constituent of the nucleus, and *what* and *where* are in (or adjoined to) Q.

If we attempt to recast the K&B analysis within the *Barriers* framework, it seems natural to reanalyse their Q morpheme as an interrogative complementizer, hence a member of the category C of complementizers (following a long tradition dating back to Bresnan, 1970). If we further assume (following Chomsky, 1986) that C projects into CP, then we can capture the essential spirit of the K&B analysis by positing that the earliest multiword questions produced by young children are CP constituents comprising a head C morpheme and a clausal nucleus. Given that K&B observe (p. 201) that the nucleus 'consists primarily of nouns or verbs without indication of tense or number', and that 'there are no auxiliaries', we might analyse the nucleus as an auxiliariless VP constituent which comprises a tenseless and agreementless head V whose canonical arguments are NP constituents. This would mean that a *yes–no* question such as *I ride train?* would have the simplified structure indicated in (2) below:

(2)

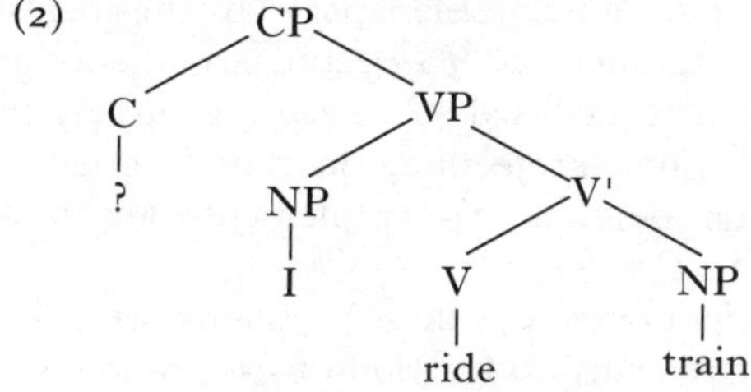

(where *?* designates a suprasegmental *yes–no* question morpheme realized as rising intonation).

It is rather less clear how we would interpret the K&B analysis of stage I *wh*-questions within the *Barriers* framework. To make our discussion more concrete, consider how we might analyse a sentence such as *What cowboy doing?* Since K&B posit that *wh*-words are base-generated *in situ* and that they are in a position outside the sentential nucleus (seemingly within Q), the apparent counterpart of their analysis would be to posit that the *wh*-pronoun *what* is positioned in C, as in (3) below:

(3)

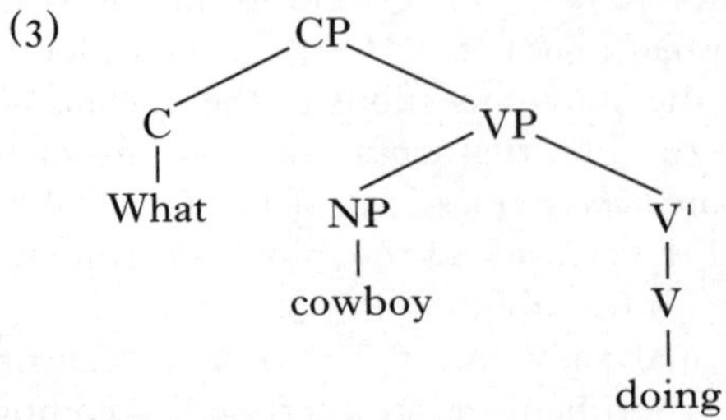

The analysis in (3) might seem appropriate if we were to assume (following a suggestion made to me by Tom Roeper) that *what* is initially used by children as 'a general question marker' (e.g. as an interrogative complementizer): Tom Roeper notes that child sentences such as 'What he saw head?' would lend empirical support to the 'question marker' analysis.

However, it is less clear that a 'question marker' analysis would be appropriate to sentences such as (3), where *what* seems to function as the internal argument (i.e. complement) of *doing*, and (if so) is assigned the thematic role PATIENT by *do*. If we make the general assumption (widespread in current theoretical work) that theta-marking (i.e. assigning thematic roles) takes place under sisterhood, then *what* cannot receive a theta-role from *doing* because it is not a sister of *doing*. An additional problem posed by the analysis in (3) is that *what* is the internal argument of *doing*, and arguments are maximal projections; yet in (3), *what* is analysed as a head (occupying the head C position in CP), not a maximal projection. So, for a variety of theoretical reasons, then, it cannot be that *wh*-complements are base-generated in the head C position of CP.

However, one way in which we might overcome these problems, while still retaining K&B's intuition that C is the surface location of *wh*-pronouns, is the following (cf. Radford 1987): we might suppose that the complement *what* originates as the head N of an NP complement of *do*, and that the N *what* is then moved from its underlying position in the head N of the complement NP into a superficial position in the head C of CP, as in (4) below:

(4)

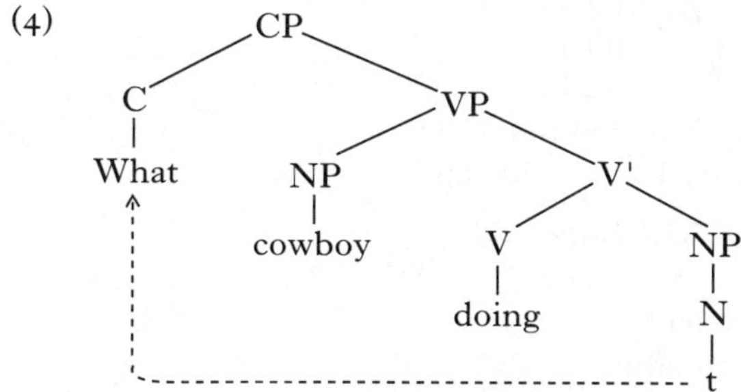

Since C is a contemporary counterpart of their Q morpheme, it seems natural
to suppose that C is interrogative, and hence that movement of *what* into C
is movement of an interrogative head (*what*) into another interrogative head
position (the head C position in CP). This type of movement would then
satisfy Emonds' (1970) STRUCTURE PRESERVING PRINCIPLE. If we posit that C
is unspecified with respect to nominal/verbal categorial properties, it follows
that a head N can move into C because C is nondistinct from N in respect of
the relevant categorial properties.

An obvious question to ask about this analysis is whether there is any
empirical evidence that natural language grammars license movement of a
wh-head in the manner represented in (4) above. One possible candidate for
a *wh*-pronoun which moves into C is the French interrogative pronoun *que*
'what'. The assumption that *que* moves into C would provide one way of
accounting for paradigms such as:

(5a) ***De que* parles-tu?
       About what speak you? ('What are you talking about?')
(b)   *Que* fais-tu?
       What do you? ('What are you doing?')
(c)   ***Qu'*est arrivé
       What is happened? ('What has happened?')

Pied piping of prepositions (as in (5a)) would be impossible since *que* must
be superficially positioned in C and cannot therefore remain inside PP (we
might assume that *que* is a clitic which must move into an interrogative head
position). Local movement of *que* 'what' from subject position – as in (5c) –
would be impossible, since the trace of *que* (in the specifier position within
IP) would not be properly head-governed, so leading to a violation of the
EMPTY CATEGORY PRINCIPLE (ECP).

A second type of construction in which we might posit that a *wh*-word
moves into C can be illustrated in relation to the following data from
Northern Norwegian given in Taraldsen, 1986: 21:

(6a) Kor   i byen *ska* [₁ₚ studentan bu]?
      Where in town will   students   stay?
      'Where in town will the students stay?'
 (b) *Kor   i byen [₁ₚ studentan *ska* bu]?
      Where in town   students   will stay?

(7a) Kor   [₁ₚ studentan *ska* bu]?
      Where   students   will stay?
      'Where will the students stay?'
 (b) *Kor   *ska* [₁ₚ studentan bu]?
      Where will   students   stay?

We might suppose that when a *wh*-phrase such as [*kor i byen*] is fronted, it
cannot move into C, since this is a head position, not a phrase position – cf.
the ungrammaticality of (6*b*): hence, it must move into the phrasal specifier
position in front of C. This leaves C empty, able to be filled by a preposed
V such as *ska*, as in (6*a*) above. But we might further suppose that *wh*-
movement may also move a *wh*-head, and that when it does – as in (7*a*) – it
moves the *wh*-head not into the specifier position within CP (since this is a
phrasal position), but rather into the head C position. This means that C is
then filled by the preposed *wh*-head, so that C can no longer serve as the
landing-site for a preposed verb like *ska* – hence the ungrammaticality of
(7*b*). Of course, this analysis crucially presupposes that preposed *wh*-heads in
Northern Norwegian are moved into C. Thus, any objection that the head-
movement analysis in (4) is an UNNATURAL one may well be unfounded.

An intriguing feature of stage I *wh*-questions is that the only questions in
which we find evidence of *wh*-movement are *wh*-complement questions (i.e.
questions in which the *wh*-constituent is the complement of a verb). We
could argue that this follows from the analysis in (4): a complement trace will
be properly head-governed, but a subject trace or adjunct trace will not.
However, this is only part of the story. K&B note that there are LEXICAL
CONSTRAINTS on the distribution of *wh*-phrases – i.e. there are restrictions on
the range of lexical items which allow *wh*-arguments. For example, *what* is
used as the complement of *doing* (but not of other transitive verbs), and *where*
occurs as the complement of *go* (but not of other intransitive verbs – cf.
K&B's remark on p. 202 in relation to questions of the form *Where NP go?*
that 'The special interrogative form is bound to the particular word *go* and
does not at all have the generality of the adult structure'). How can we
account for this?

One possible answer is to suppose that *wh*-phrases are LEXICALLY LICENSED
at this stage (via lexical selection), in the sense that a given *wh*-phrase can only
be base-generated in a position in which its predicate licenses a *wh*-phrase in
the relevant argument function. (Of course, it follows from this assumption
that all *wh*-phrases at this stage will be arguments, and that there will be no

wh-adjunct questions, if we assume that heads do not lexically select adjuncts.) We might assume, for example, that the lexical entry for *go* specifies that it selects a GOAL argument, and also that the GOAL argument may be an interrogative *wh*-phrase. If the only item in the children's lexicon which can head a GOAL *wh*-argument is *where*, this means that only *go* can take a *where*-phrase complement. Similarly, we might imagine that it is a lexical property of *do(ing)* that it selects an inanimate PATIENT as its internal argument, and also that the PATIENT argument may be an interrogative *wh*-phrase. If NP is the canonical realization of a PATIENT argument, and if the only item in the child's lexicon which can head an inanimate *wh*-NP is *what*, this in effect means that only *do(ing)* can take a *what*-phrase complement. Thus, the LEXICAL EFFECT which K&B observe in stage I *wh*-questions (to the effect that specific *wh*-items are used only as the complements of specific verbs) is accounted for in terms of lexical selection. This might be an overgeneralization of adult selection constraints on clausal complements, since in Adult English some predicates (e.g. *enquire*) select an interrogative clausal complement, and others do not (e.g. *assert*). Hence, it would not be implausible to assume that the child posits that some predicates select an interrogative phrasal complement and others do not. At any rate, the existence of lexical constraints on the range of *wh*-structures found at stage I in no way undermines a *wh*-movement analysis of initial *wh*-complements.

Stage II

K&B report that at stage II, Adam, Eve and Sarah produced *yes–no* questions such as (8*a*) below and *wh*-questions such as (8*b*) and (*c*):

   (8*a*)   Mom pinch finger? You want eat? I have it? See my doggie?
    (*b*)   What me think? What the dollie have?
    (*c*)   Where me sleep? Why you smiling? What soldier marching?

There seems to be no lexical effect at this stage, since each *wh*-pronoun can function as the complement of a range of different verbs, and since K&B note (p. 204) that the children provide 'appropriate answers to most questions'. The range of *wh*-questions produced is now extended to include not only argument *wh*-questions like those in (8*b*), but also nonargument *wh*-questions like those in (8*c*).

The analysis which K&B propose for *yes–no* questions at this stage involves the same Q+nucleus structure as at stage I, with Q containing an abstract *yes–no* question morpheme (cf. the earlier structure in (2) above). For *wh*-questions, they suggest (p. 203) that *wh*-words are base-generated *in situ* by phrase structure rules of the form: S → *what*-Nucleus; S → *where*-Nucleus; S → *why*-Nucleus. From this informal characterization of the relevant rules, it is far from clear exactly where they think *wh*-words are positioned. One possible interpretation of their rules (which would maximize continuity with stage I) is that *wh*-words are base-generated in C. This would mean that a nonargument *wh*-question such as *What soldier marching?* would have the (simplified) structure (9) below:

(9)   [CP [C What] [VP soldier [V marching]]]

However, if *wh*-constituents are positioned outside the clausal nucleus, there are obvious problems involved in handling *wh*-arguments, since in order to get a theta-role, the *wh*-constituent will have to be associated with a theta-position. K&B overcome this problem by positing that in argument *wh*-questions, there is a null interrogative N heading an argument NP which is bound by the *wh*-pronoun in C. Using *e* to denote the relevant empty interrogative N, it would seem that they envisage a structure along the lines of (10) for a sentence such as *What me think?*:

(10)

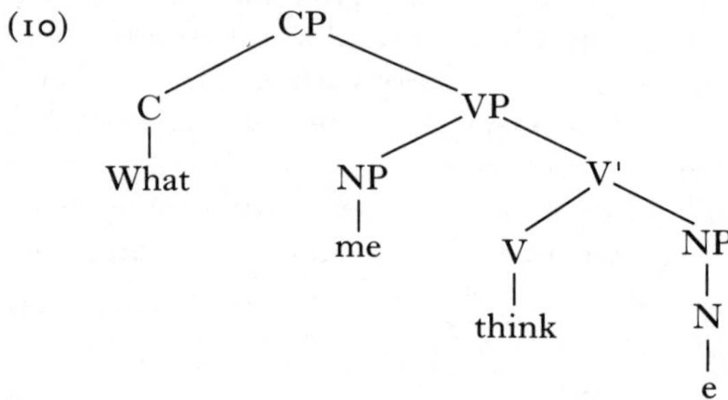

If we assume that (at the stage where they have not yet developed an Inflection (INFL) constituent which assigns nominative case to clausal subjects) the children assign objective case (perhaps by default, as suggested in Roeper & De Villiers, 1991 and Vainikka, 1992) to the subject/specifier of VP, the objective case carried by the subject *me* can readily be accounted for.

It is interesting to reflect upon the status of the empty N constituent in (10). What are we to make of K&B's designation of it as INTERROG? A natural interpretation of this designation is that the empty N is the trace of a moved interrogative N. If this is so, then K&B's analysis of *wh*-arguments amounts to the *wh*-head-movement analysis which we suggested in relation to stage I *wh*-questions: *what* in (10) would originate in the head N position of a complement NP, and then move into the head C position within CP by *wh*-head-movement – very much as in (4) above. Given this interpretation of K&B's analysis of stage II questions, the main change which comes about between stages I and II would be that *wh*-phrases are no longer lexically licensed, and that a class of *wh*-adjuncts has developed (including *what, where* and *why* as used in sentences like (8c) above) which are base-generated in C.

Stage III

K&B note that at stage III, Adam, Eve and Sarah produced *yes–no* questions such as (11*a*) below, and *wh*-questions such as (11*b*):

(11*a*)   Does the kitty stand up? Does lions walk? Is Mommy talking to Robin's grandmother? Did I saw that in my book? Oh, did I caught it? Are you going to make it with me? Will you help me? Can I have a piece of paper? Can't it be a bigger truck? Can't you work this thing? Can't you get it?

(*b*)   Where the other Joe will drive? Where I should put it when I make up? What he can ride in? Why he don't know how to pretend? Why kitty can't stand up? How he can be a doctor? How they can't talk? Which way they should go?

K&B note (p. 205) that the children now make productive use of a wide range of (positive and negative) auxiliaries, but that auxiliaries are inverted only in *yes–no* questions, not in *wh*-questions. They suggest that clauses have the same Q + Nucleus structure as at stages I and II, and that *wh*-constituents are base-generated within the sentential nucleus, and then moved into a position immediately to the right of Q; similarly, they formulate auxiliary inversion as a rule which repositions an auxiliary immediately to the right of Q.

How are we to transpose K&B's analysis of stage III questions into the *Barriers* framework? Since K&B posit that both *wh*-constituents and inverted auxiliaries are 'attracted' to C (and that *wh*-movement bleeds auxiliary inversion), we might interpret this as meaning that both are positioned in (or adjoined to) the empty head C of CP. Given this assumption, a *yes–no* question such as *Will you help me?* would be derived in the manner represented in (12) below (I assume that the clausal nucleus at this stage has the status of IP, since we find productive use of auxiliaries and tense inflections):

(12)

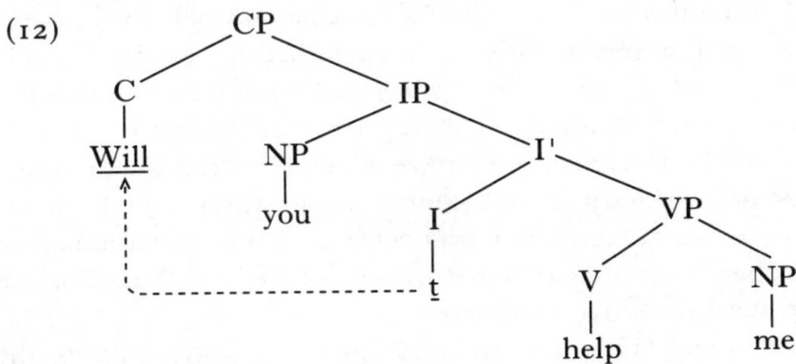

We might suppose that *wh*-argument questions like *What he can ride in?* involve (as before) movement of the pronominal *wh*-N *what* from the head N position of the NP complement of *in* into the head C position of CP, as in (13) below:

(13)

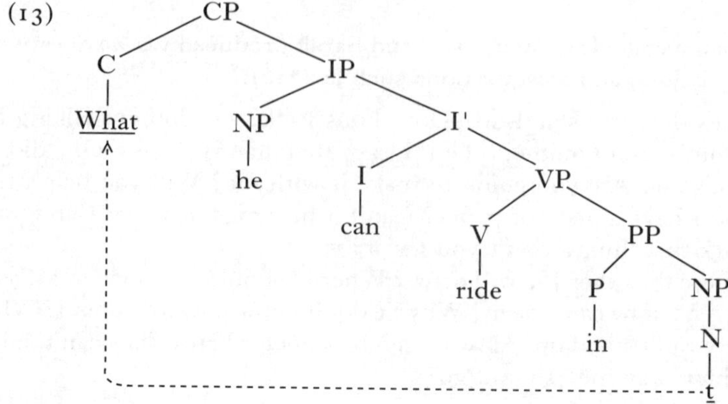

If we assume (as for stage I) that C is underspecified with respect to its (nominal/verbal) categorial features, then it follows that either a verbal constituent (like *will* in (12)) or a nominal constituent (like *what* in (13)) can be moved into C, since both will be nondistinct in categorial features from C.

We might further assume (as for our analysis of stage II) that *wh*-adjuncts like *how* and *why* continue to be base-generated in the head C position within CP: this is all the more plausible in view of the fact that *how* at this stage seems to have the interpretation of a sentential adverbial rather than a VP-adverbial; for example, in *How they can't talk?*, it is clear that *how* does not modify *talk* but rather has a sentential interpretation akin to that of *why* or *how come*. In this connection, it is interesting to note experimental evidence from de Villiers (1991: 158) that three-year-olds typically reply to *how* questions as if *how* were a sentential adverb: hence the question *How did the woman talk to her friend?* elicited a response such as *Because she didn't like that car*.

If *wh*-words and inverted auxiliaries both occupy the head C position of CP at S-structure, then it follows that the two will be mutually exclusive. If we further suppose that an interrogative C must be lexicalized (i.e. filled by an appropriate lexical item – e.g. a base-generated *wh*-adjunct, a *wh*-head moved from an argument position, or an inverted auxiliary) in order to LEXICALLY DISCHARGE the interrogative feature which C carries (or to make it VISIBLE), and that *wh*-words must obligatorily be positioned in C in *wh*-questions (perhaps to satisfy the *wh*-initial setting of the *wh*-parameter in English, or to discharge the interrogative feature carried by the *wh*-word), then the relevant word order facts fall out neatly.

The analysis of stage III questions presented here presupposes that children have a relatively well-developed C-system by this stage, in that both *wh*-pronouns and inverted auxiliaries are positioned in the head C of CP. Naturalistic evidence lends empirical support to the claim that children have indeed developed a C-system at this point. Part of the evidence comes from the fact that we find two-year-old children producing complement clauses containing (potential) complementizer constituents, as examples such as the following illustrate (where the name and age of the child producing each sample is specified in parentheses; the data are taken from the naturalistic corpus described in Radford, 1990: 11–13):

(14a)   See *if* swimming water's there (Jem 2;3)
  (b)   You know *that* the flute is in there (Hannah 2;7)
  (c)   Leave a little space *for* them to get out (Helen 2;7)

Moreover, we start to find other items seemingly miscategorized as complementizers, so that children create NOVEL COMPLEMENTIZERS of their own; for example, Ruth seems to replace the adult prepositional complementizer *for* by the preposition *in*:

(15)   Don't wait *in* me go on it (Ruth 2;6)

Many two-year-olds use *cos* (= because) to introduce main clauses, in such a way that it sometimes seems to have no causal meaning but appears to serve simply to mark the sentence as declarative in illocutionary force, e.g. sentences such as the following (none of which was used in response to a *why* question):

(16a)   *Cos* that is mine (Hannah 2;4)
  (b)   *Cos* I can't reach the Ribena (Kirsty 2;9)
  (c)   *Cos* I didn't find it. *Cos* I brought her back. *Cos* it's in the freezer. *Cos* it's not ready yet. *Cos* we don't want to go in the kitchen. *Cos* I don't like this room. *Cos* I want her (Lisa 2;10)

(See similar examples in Vainikka, 1992: 12, 28.) This might suggest that *cos* is used as a main clause declarative complementizer by the children concerned. If this is so, then it is equally plausible that its *wh*-counterpart *why* should be treated as a complementizer – especially as (unlike other *wh*-words) it is generally restricted to occurring in finite clauses in Adult English, as we see from contrasts such as:

(17a)   He asked me [*when/why* he should turn the power supply off]
  (b)   He asked me [*when/*why* to turn the power supply off]

We might suppose that *how* is initially analysed in the same way, given that children seem to treat it as a near-synonym of *why*.

An intriguing example of a novel complementizer created by a young child is noted by Akmajian & Heny (1975: 17) who report a three-year-old girl producing interrogative structures such as:

(18)   *Is* I can do that? *Is* you should eat the apple? *Is* Ben did go? *Is* the apple juice won't spill?

A similar pattern is noted by Davis (1987), who reports the following examples of child *yes–no* questions:

(19) *Are* you want one? *Are* you got some orange juice? *Are* this is broke? *Are* you don't know what Sharon's name is? *Are* you sneezed?

(For further examples, see Roeper, 1992: 341.) It seems that the children concerned have miscategorized *is* and *are* as root *yes–no* question complementizers. The assumption that adult inverted auxiliaries may be miscategorized by children as complementizers makes it all the more plausible to posit that inverted auxiliaries are positioned in C in Child English.

Moreover, there are strong theoretical arguments for claiming that auxiliary inversion involves movement from I to C. If the only type of head-movement operation licensed by universal grammar (UG) is movement into a functional head position, it follows that a preposed head I constituent can only be moved to another functional head position (and not, for example, adjoined to IP). Moreover, since head movement is a LOCAL operation in which the head of a complement phrase moves into the head position within its matrix (immediately containing) phrase, a preposed I constituent can only be moved into an immediately superordinate functional head position. If we follow Abney (1987) in positing that the only functional head which selects an IP complement is C, then it follows that the only head position which an inverted auxiliary can be moved into is C. Thus, the analysis of auxiliary inversion (as movement from I to C) sketched in (12) can be defended on both developmental and theoretical grounds.

The assumption that *wh*-words also occupy the head C position of CP makes interesting predictions about the ordering of *wh*-constituents and topic phrases in stage III questions such as *Where small trailer he should pull?* (K&B: 205). If we posit that topic phrases are adjoined to IP (as in Adult English structures such as 'I feel that *this kind of behaviour* we cannot tolerate'), then we should precisely expect that the *wh*-constituent *where* in the head C position of CP will precede the topicalized IP-adjunct *small trailer*: if *where* is a GOAL argument of *pull*, then the two types of movement paths involved in the relevant sentence would be as in (20):

(20) [CP [CP <u>Where</u>] [IP ***small trailer*** [IP he should pull *t* t]]]

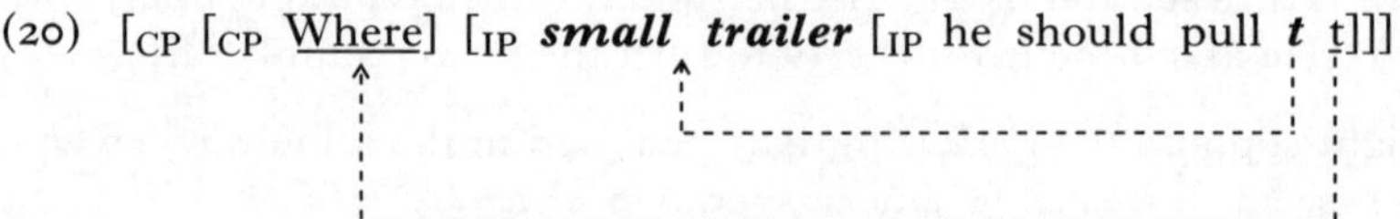

The relative ordering of the two moved constituents is exactly as predicted.

What I have argued so far is that one way of attempting to capture the spirit of K&B's analysis would be to posit that *wh*-movement at stages I, II and III involves movement of a *wh*-HEAD, rather than (as in Adult English) movement of a *wh*-PHRASE. For succinctness, I shall refer to this as the HEAD analysis of *wh*-questions. In the next section, I present a critical evaluation of the head analysis, before moving on to consider two alternative PHRASAL analyses of the syntax of *wh*-movement in Child English, in the sections headed ADJUNCTION ANALYSIS and SPECIFIER ANALYSIS.

EVALUATION OF THE HEAD ANALYSIS

Having shown how the head analysis might account for early interrogative structures produced by young children, I now turn to cast a more critical eye on the analysis – from a DEVELOPMENTAL perspective on the one hand, and a THEORETICAL perspective on the other.

Given that an explanatory model of acquisition must account for the transitions between successive developmental stages, an important question to ask is whether the head analysis provides a plausible account of the transition from Child English to Adult English. If we assume that *wh*-questions involve movement of a *wh*-head into C in Child English but movement of a *wh*-phrase into CP-specifier position in Adult English (Radford, 1988: 499–508), then the structural difference between a stage III question such as *What I can ride in?* and its adult counterpart *What can I ride in?* would be as in (21) below:

(21a) $[_{CP} [_{C} \textit{What}] [_{IP} I [_{I} can] ride in \textit{t}]] =$ stage III Child English
 (b) $[_{CP} \textit{What} [_{C} \textit{\textbf{can}}] [_{IP} I [_{I} \textit{\textbf{t}}] ride in \textit{t}]] =$ Adult English

Thus, *what* would be a moved pronominal *wh*-N head occupying the head C position in CP in the stage III question (21a), but a moved pronominal *wh*-NP occupying the specifier position within CP in the Adult English question (21b) ($t/\textbf{t}$ denote TRACES of the moved constituents). How can we account for the transition between a stage III structure like (21a) and its Adult English counterpart (21b)?

One FEATURE-BASED account which might be offered is in terms of a transition from an underspecified to a more fully specified head C constituent in clauses (consistent with the incremental feature-specification model of acquisition suggested in Radford, 1991, whereby children learn grammar 'one feature at a time'). There are two sets of C-features which are relevant to our discussion here – illocutionary features and categorial features. Let us assume that the illocutionary properties of a clause (which determine whether the clause is interrogative or noninterrogative) are canonically encoded on the functional heads within clauses – namely as a feature on the head C of CP, and (via HEAD–HEAD AGREEMENT or F-SELECTION) on the head I of IP. Transposing K&B's Q-morpheme into a binary feature-specification, we might suppose that the relevant functional heads carry the feature $[+Q]$ in interrogative clauses, and $[-Q]$ in noninterrogative clauses (though an alternative possibility would be to posit that Q is a unary feature, and any functional head not carrying the relevant Q-feature is noninterrogative by default). It seems plausible enough to posit that C carries illocutionary features, given that this would provide a straightforward account of the contrast between complementizers like *if* and *that*. The assumption that I also carries Q-features seems plausible in view of the fact that there are languages in which Q-features are morphologically realized as verbal inflections (e.g. verbs in West Greenlandic carry interrogative inflections (Sadock, 1984). Moreover, the analysis has developmental plausibility, in that it would help us to account for the observation that children sometimes restrict specific auxiliaries to either interrogative use (as claimed for early occurrences of *do* in Gruber, 1967: 42, and for early occurrences of *could* in Miller & Ervin-Tripp, 1973: 382) or noninterrogative use (as claimed in Gleitman & Wanner, 1982: 22).

The second set of C-features relevant to our discussion are the categorial features of C. Following Kayne (1982), I shall suppose that a root C has the categorial property of being an inherently VERBAL constituent in Adult English, perhaps because CP is an extended projection of a verbal predicate (the head V of VP). By contrast a complement C is intrinsically nonverbal, perhaps because it is an argument, and arguments are canonically nominal or prepositional. It will follow from this assumption that auxiliary inversion is possible in a root clause structure such as (22*a*) below, but not possible in a complement clause structure such as that bracketed in (22*b*):

(22*a*)   [$_{CP}$ *What* [$_C$ ***can***] [$_{IP}$ we [$_I$ ***t***] do *t*]]
  (*b*)   I will ask [$_{CP}$ *what* [$_C$ ***e***] [$_{IP}$ we [$_I$ can] do ***t***]]

The reason is that the root C position in (22*a*) is verbal and so can host an inverted auxiliary like ***can***, whereas the empty complement C position ***e*** in (22*b*) is nonverbal, and so cannot serve as the landing site for a preposed verbal auxiliary. If we make the reasonable assumption that overt complementizers like *that/if/for* in English are nonverbal, it will also follow that only complement clauses (not root clauses) are introduced by an overt complementizer in Adult English.

I shall make two further assumptions in my analysis here. The first is that the feature [+Q] in an interrogative clause must be IDENTIFIED (i.e. 'made visible', or 'realized', or 'discharged') in some way. One form of feature-identification is PHONOLOGICAL; compare K&B's suggestion that the interrogative nature of early *yes–no* questions is indicated by a rising intonation contour. A related form of identification is LEXICAL: for example, a *yes–no* complement C in Adult English is lexicalised as *if*. A third means of identification is MORPHOLOGICAL: for example, in West Greenlandic, verbs carry interrogative inflections (as noted earlier), and in Nonstandard Colloquial French, finite verbs may carry the interrogative suffix *-ti*. A variant of this is the MORPHOSYNTACTIC identification found in *wh-in-situ* questions in Adult English such as 'Which one has impressed you?' where *has* is morphosyntactically identified as interrogative by virtue of the fact that it stands in an agreement relation with the interrogative *wh*-NP *which one* (the agreement relation holding between the specifier and head of IP). A further type of identification is SYNTACTIC: auxiliary inversion in root *yes–no* questions like 'Is he working hard?' permits the [+Q] feature to be visible at S-structure through word order (viz. movement of an auxiliary into an interrogative C position). There is, of course, no inversion in [−Q] structures such as declaratives and exclamatives. A final type of identification is via (COMPLEMENT) SELECTION. For example, in child *yes–no* complement questions (of the type mentioned in Weissenborn, Roeper & de Villiers, 1991: 46, fn. 4) such as *I'll ask [e Daddy can do it]* (= 'I'll ask *if* Daddy can do it'), the empty complementizer *e* in the bracketed complement clause is selectionally identified as interrogative by virtue of the fact that it is the head C of a CP which is the complement of a verb *ask* which selects an interrogative complement. (It goes without saying that selectional identification of a feature is only possible in complement clauses.)

The second assumption I shall make is that a moved interrogative *wh*-constituent must be (locally) associated with an interrogative head at S-structure. One form which such 'local association' may take is an (overt or covert) specifier-head agreement relation between a *wh*-interrogative specifier and an interrogative head. Such a relation may hold in two different domains, as illustrated in (23) below:

(23a)   Which one is hurting?
   (b)   Which one do you like?

(23a) is a *wh-in-situ* question, in which the *wh*-NP *which one* is the specifier of IP, and stands in an overt (morphologically marked) specifier-head agreement relation with the interrogative auxiliary *is* in the head I position of IP. (23b) is a *wh-ex-situ* structure in which the *wh*-NP *which one* occupies the specifier position within CP, and stands in a covert (morphologically unmarked) agreement relation with the interrogative auxiliary in the head C position of CP. Thus the LOCAL ASSOCIATION between an interrogative *wh*-specifier and an interrogative head is satisfied within IP in (23a), but within CP in (23b).

Using the descriptive framework developed above, we might seek to account for the various stages which children go through in the acquisition of questions in the following terms. In keeping with the UNDERSPECIFICATION analysis of Child English alluded to above, let us suppose that children initially develop an UNDERSPECIFIED C-constituent. More specifically, let us suppose that C initially carries illocutionary features, but is unspecified with respect to (nominal/verbal) categorial features. If (as Roeper, 1992, claims), C universally carries illocutionary properties, then the Q-properties of C are determined by UG. Empirical evidence that C is initially underspecified in respect of its categorial features comes from the fact that the earliest complement clause questions produced by children often show auxiliary inversion (cf. the example 'I don't know what *are dey*' reported in Plunkett, 1991: 132). In our terms, this means that children at the relevant stage have a categorially underspecified C, and have not yet learned that a complement clause C is intrinsically nonverbal.

Given these assumptions, we might account for stage I, II and III *wh*-questions in the following terms. In all three stages, interrogative *wh*-constituents are DIRECTLY ASSOCIATED with the interrogative C heading the clause by virtue of being moved into C: moreover, the relevant Q-feature on C is thereby made visible, in that it is discharged onto the *wh*-pronoun in C. C has no intrinsic categorial features as yet, so that a pronominal *wh*-N head like *what* can move into C, since the moved *wh*-head is categorially nondistinct from C. In stage I and II *yes–no* questions, there is no I-system so that the Q-features on C cannot be made syntactically visible by movement of an interrogative auxiliary into C – hence the relevant Q-features are made phonologically visible (through rising intonation). By stage III, however, children have developed an I-system, and the Q-feature on C is made syntactically visible in *yes–no* questions by moving an interrogative auxiliary into C (thereby discharging the Q-feature carried by C onto the inverted auxiliary).

What then remains to be accounted for is the transition between stage III Child English and Adult English. Let us suppose that once children begin to master specifier-head agreement, they become (tacitly) aware that there is a second way by which a *wh*-constituent can be locally associated with an interrogative head – namely INDIRECTLY via an abstract specifier-head agreement relationship (as in Adult English structures like those in (23) above). Indirect association will involve movement of a *wh*-phrase into a phrasal specifier position within CP (it cannot involve movement of a *wh*-head into the head position within a specifier phrase, since the moved *wh*-head will not bind or antecedent-govern its trace). It may be that the child's EXPERIENCE forces this restructuring, as the child becomes tacitly 'aware' that *wh*-movement may apply to *wh*-phrases (like *which car*?) as well as to *wh*-pronouns. Given these assumptions, it would seem plausible to suppose that there might be an intermediate stage in which the requirement for a moved interrogative *wh*-constituent to be locally associated with an interrogative head could be satisfied either DIRECTLY via movement of an interrogative *wh*-head into an interrogative C, or INDIRECTLY via movement of an interrogative *wh*-phrase into the specifier position within a CP headed by an interrogative C (as in our analysis of the Norwegian data in (6) and (7) above).

We should then expect that during this transitional stage (marking the transition between stage III Child English and Adult English), children will alternate between structures like (21*a*) and (21*b*) above: that is, either they will move a *wh*-pronoun into C (so discharging the Q-feature on C and blocking auxiliary inversion), or they will move a *wh*-phrase into the CP-specifier position (with concomitant movement of an auxiliary into C in order to discharge the interrogative C-feature via specifier-head agreement). Significantly, Labov & Labov (1978) report a stage during which their daughter Jessie (between roughly three-and-a-half and four years of age) showed variable auxiliary inversion in *wh*-questions (except in *why* questions, where there was no inversion). We might suggest that in uninverted *wh*-questions like 'What I can do?', *what* is moved into C (so that *what* is directly associated with an interrogative C, the interrogative feature on C is discharged onto *what*, and auxiliary inversion is blocked). By contrast, in inverted *wh*-questions such 'What can I do?', *what* is moved into the CP-specifier position (so that *what* is indirectly associated with the head interrogative C), and the auxiliary *can* moves from I to C (to discharge the Q-feature on C). The lack of inversion after *why* might be accounted for (as earlier) by positing that *why* is miscategorized as a finite clause complementizer (the *wh*-counterpart of *cos*). If there are no categorial constraints on the range of items which may appear in C at this stage, there is no reason why a *wh*-adverbial such as *why* should not be base-generated in C.

The final stage in the acquisition of questions comes when the child masters the categorial properties of C, and 'realizes' that a root C is intrinsically verbal, and that a complement C is intrinsically nonverbal. Once the child learns that a complement clause C is intrinsically nonverbal, there will no longer be auxiliary inversion in complement clause questions (since a nonverbal complement C cannot host a verbal auxiliary). Similarly, once the child learns that a root C is intrinsically verbal, it follows that there can no longer be direct association of a *wh*-constituent with an interrogative root C via movement of an interrogative *wh*-pronoun into C, since C is now intrinsically verbal, and *wh*-pronouns are intrinsically nonverbal. The only possibility at this point is for INDIRECT association of an interrogative *wh*-constituent with an interrogative C via specifier-head agreement, in consequence of the movement of an interrogative *wh*-phrase into the specifier position of a CP headed by an interrogative C. The intrinsic Q-feature on a root C at this point can only be discharged on to an inverted auxiliary in C, given that a root C is now an intrinsically verbal constituent. Once a root C is identified as intrinsically verbal, *why* can no longer be base-generated in C, and instead is base-generated in the CP-specifier position (as Rizzi, 1990, proposes for Adult English), so leaving the head C position of CP to be filled by an inverted auxiliary which discharges the Q-feature on C.

The starting point for our discussion in this section was to examine the developmental plausibility of the HEAD analysis of early *wh*-questions. What I have suggested is that (given certain assumptions), the head analysis would enable us to put together an interesting (and by no means implausible) account of the transition from stage I Child English to Adult English – an account which minimizes developmental discontinuity. However, there are also other developmental considerations to take into account in evaluating the head analysis. One is whether the analysis attains DEVELOPMENTAL OBSERVATIONAL ADEQUACY – i.e. whether it accounts for the relevant child data at every stage of development. One potentially problematic example in this respect is the following stage III question recorded by K&B (p. 205):

(24)   Which way they should go?

If we make the (intrinsically natural) assumption that *which way* here is a *wh*-NP, then it seems clear that such questions must involve movement of a *wh*-phrase, not movement of a *wh*-head. The only way of defending the *wh*-head analysis in the face of (24) would be to make the (otherwise unsubstantiated) assumption that *which way* is a compound N, and hence can undergo movement into C. If a *wh*-head-movement analysis of stage III *wh*-questions is falsified by naturalistic data such as (24), we could argue (on the grounds of maximizing developmental continuity) that it should similarly be rejected for stage II and stage I questions, in favour of an alternative analysis which sees *wh*-movement as involving movement of a *wh-phrase* at all stages of development.

Thus far, we have examined the plausibility of the head analysis from a DEVELOPMENTAL perspective. However, the analysis should also be carefully scrutinized from a THEORETICAL perspective. A substantial question-mark which hangs over it is whether it satisfies principles of UG relating to the LOCALITY of head-movement. It is a central postulate of the theoretical framework adopted here that non-local (i.e. long-distance) movement is possible only for a constituent which is THETA-GOVERNED (in Chomsky's system) or REFERENTIAL (in Rizzi's). However, if we posit that a head cannot be theta-governed (as claimed in Chomsky, 1986: 71) or referential (as claimed in Cinque, 1990: 43), then it follows that the trace of the moved head N in a structure like (10) must be ANTECEDENT-GOVERNED. However, the relevant trace cannot be antecedent-governed in the MINIMALITY system, since the head V position in VP is a closer potential antecedent-governor for the trace (unless we assume that only C can be a potential antecedent-governor for the trace of a moved *wh*-head, in the same way as we assume that only a CP-specifier can be a potential antecedent-governor for a moved *wh*-phrase).

Thus, within the 'standard' *Barriers/Minimality* framework, a long-distance *wh*-head-movement analysis of structures like (4), (10) and (13) would violate locality principles of UG. However, one way to overcome such a violation would be to posit a two-step analysis of the movement of *what*: namely *wh*-movement of the overall *wh*-NP (either to VP-adjunct position, or to CP-specifier position), followed by head-to-head movement, moving the pronominal *wh*-N head *what* of the moved NP into the head C position in CP. This two-stage analysis would bear obvious comparison with Roberts' (1992) two-stage analysis of long clitic movement (as involving movement of a maximal projection, followed by movement of the head of the moved maximal projection). Indeed, the parallel would be even closer if interrogative pronouns in early questions were analysed (as hinted at above) as clitics needing to move into an interrogative head position. However, one of the problems posed by an analysis which sees *wh*-phrases as undergoing *wh*-movement followed by subsequent head movement is that (as we shall see below) it might be argued that a *wh*-movement analysis is in itself sufficient to account for the relevant developmental facts.

AN ADJUNCTION ANALYSIS

If *wh*-movement (from its onset) involves movement of *wh*-phrases, then an important question to ask is what is the landing-site of the moved *wh*-phrase in early stages of Child English. One possibility (discussed in this section) is that *wh*-phrases are moved into a clausal ADJUNCT position. Now, if the earliest verbal clauses produced by young children are VP structures – as argued in Radford, 1986, Guilfoyle & Noonan, 1988 and Aldridge, 1989 – and if early *wh*-movement involves adjunction to the overall clause, then it follows that *wh*-movement will involve adjunction of a *wh*-phrase to VP (as suggested in Radford, 1990: 134), so that a sentence such as *What cowboy doing?* will have the simplified S-structure (25) below:

(25)   [$_{VP}$ *What* [$_{VP}$ cowboy [$_V$ doing] t]]

Adjunction in (25) must involve movement of a *wh*-phrase (not a *wh*-head), given that principles of UG determine that only a phrase (not a head) can be adjoined to another phrase (cf. Chomsky, 1986: 88). There will be no auxiliary inversion at this stage, since there are no auxiliaries. Such an analysis would involve no developmental discontinuity if we adopt the *Barriers* analysis of *wh*-movement, whereby a moved *wh*-argument in Adult English is adjoined to VP before moving from there to its ultimate landing-site in the CP-specifier position.

At stage III (when children produce *wh*-questions with uninverted auxiliaries such as *What he can ride in?*), we might conjecture that *wh*-phrases are adjoined to IP, as in (26) below:

(26)   [$_{IP}$ *What* [$_{IP}$ he [$_I$ can] ride in t]]

(Whether or not *what* is first adjoined to VP before being adjoined to IP is a moot point which I leave aside here; the answer depends on theory-internal considerations.) We might suppose that a stage III question such as *Where small trailer he should pull?* involves adjunction to IP both of the topicalized complement NP *small trailer* and of the *wh*-moved locative NP *where*.

(Indeed, this might suggest that topicalization and *wh*-movement are not distinct at this stage, in that both involve adjunction to IP.) *Yes–no* questions like *Will you help me?* produced at the same stage might be supposed on the grounds of maximizing continuity) to involve movement of an auxiliary from I to C. However, if this is so, we must ask why the *wh*-phrase cannot move from IP-adjunct into CP-specifier position, with concomitant movement of the auxiliary from I to C, as in (27) below:

(27)   [CP *What* [C *can*] [IP *t* [IP he [I *t*] ride in *t*]]]

There are two (alternative but mutually consistent) answers which we might suggest here. One is to follow Rizzi (1990: 47) in supposing that a trace in IP-adjunct position cannot be properly head-governed (so that movement is never possible out of IP-adjunct position). Another is to suppose that the two intervening IP segments in (27) form a barrier which prevents **can** from antecedent-governing its trace. The ungrammaticality of interrogative structures such as (28) below in Adult English:

(28*a*)   *[CP [C *Will*] [IP *probably* [IP John [I *t*] arrive later]]]
  (*b*)   *[CP [C *Can*] [IP *that kind of person* [IP you [I *t*] stand *t*]]]

lends empirical support to the claim that two intervening split IP segments prevent a preposed auxiliary from antecedent-governing its trace, since an intervening sentential adverbial base-generated in IP-adjunct position as in (28*a*), or an intervening topic phrase moved into IP-adjunct position as in (28*b*) render auxiliary inversion ungrammatical.

Lest it be objected that the IP-adjunction analysis of *wh*-movement is UNNATURAL (in the sense that this type of *wh*-movement is not otherwise attested in natural language grammars), it should be pointed out that Rudin (1988) argues that *wh*-movement involves adjunction to IP in Polish in structures such as:

(29)   Maria myśli, że [IP *co* [IP Janek kupił]]
       Maria thinks that   *what*   Janek bought?
       'What does Maria think that Janek bought?'

Moreover, it might even be argued that *wh*-movement in complement clauses in Adult English may involve adjunction to IP, giving rise to structures such as:

(30)   I'm unsure about [CP [C e] [IP *how* [IP we [I should] play it *t*]]]

How cannot move directly into CP-specifier position here, if we assume (following Cinque, 1990) that a maximal projection is a barrier to government unless directly selected by a [+V] head. Since C here is clearly [−V], then IP will be a barrier and adjunction to IP is forced (a single segment of a split category is not itself a barrier) as an intermediate stage of derivation. (The possibility that a moved *wh*-phrase may be adjoined to IP is briefly discussed in Rizzi, 1990: 113, fn. 6.)

Under the ADJUNCTION analysis, the third major stage of development comes when the child learns that the ultimate landing-site for preposed *wh*-phrases is the CP-specifier position. (This is at the point where the child starts to master specifier-head agreement, and starts to differentiate *wh*-movement from topicalization.) In a main clause, the head C of CP is verbal and so can void the potential barrierhood of IP, thus allowing direct movement of the preposed *wh*-phrase into the CP specifier position (without intermediate adjunction to IP). In a complement clause, C is nonverbal, so indirect movement (via adjunction to IP) will be required if we assume that a nonverbal head cannot void the barrierhood of a maximal projection. During the transitional phase noted by Labov & Labov (1978) when children show variable inversion in *wh*-questions, we might posit that the S-structure position for the *wh*-phrase in inverted questions is CP-specifier position, while the S-structure position for the *wh*-phrase in uninverted questions is IP-adjunct position. For example, we might handle the observation by Plunkett (1991: 148) that between ages 3;9 and 4;5 Adam had auxiliary inversion after all *wh*-words except *why*, by positing that *why* is base-generated as a sentential adverb in IP-adjunct position – as also suggested by de Villiers (1991).

Overall, the adjunction analysis might be said to involve an essential continuity, in that the child is seen as gradually moving the *wh*-phrase further and further away from its extraction site – first to a position within VP, then to a position within IP, and finally to a position within CP. Moreover, developmental continuity is underlined by the fact that the positions into which the child moves the *wh*-phrase at each stage are A-bar positions which *wh*-phrases (or their traces) can occupy in Adult English S-structures (at least, given certain assumptions about how *wh*-movement operates in Adult English).

However, the adjunction analysis is problematic in certain respects. For example, it provides no straightforward account of the ultimate landing-site for moved *wh*-constituents. It is generally assumed that a moved interrogative *wh*-constituent is 'attracted' to an interrogative head in some way. However, if early child clauses at stage I are simple VP structures containing no C-system, it is not clear why moved *wh*-constituents should be adjoined to the left of VP; it cannot be that they are 'attracted' to an interrogative head, if the clause contains no abstract functional interrogative C head. Moreover, if *wh*-phrases occupy VP-adjunct position at one stage, IP-adjunct position at the next, and CP-specifier position subsequently, we have no apparent continuity in the landing-site for preposed *wh*-phrases.

Indeed, nothing in the adjunct analysis explains WHY a moved *wh*-phrase cannot simply 'skip' IP and move directly from VP-adjunct position to CP-

231

9-2

specifier position in structures like (27), with auxiliary preposing creating a verbal C constituent which will void the barrierhood of the crossed IP: this would give rise to *wh*-questions with auxiliary inversion. It is crucial to the adjunction account that we REQUIRE an intermediate stage of derivation involving IP-adjunction; yet nothing in the account ensures this. Moreover, if Cinque (1990: 42) is right in hypothesizing that *wh*-movement in adult grammars never involves adjunction to VP or to IP, there would be further discontinuity (and obvious UNNATURALNESS) involved in the adjunction analysis. Of course, all of these (potential) problems could be resolved if we were to posit that both in Child English (at all stages) and in Adult English, a moved *wh*-phrase always occupies CP-specifier position. Just how such a SPECIFIER ANALYSIS would handle the various stages in the acquisition of *wh*-questions is a question which I address in the next section.

A SPECIFIER ANALYSIS

If we follow Cinque (1990: 42) in positing *wh*-movement universally involves movement to a specifier position (NEVER to an adjunct position) and if we adopt the strongest form of continuity, it follows that the S-structure position of a moved *wh*-phrase is always the CP-specifier position. If this is so, then a stage II question such as *What me think?* might be derived in the manner suggested in (31) below:

(31)

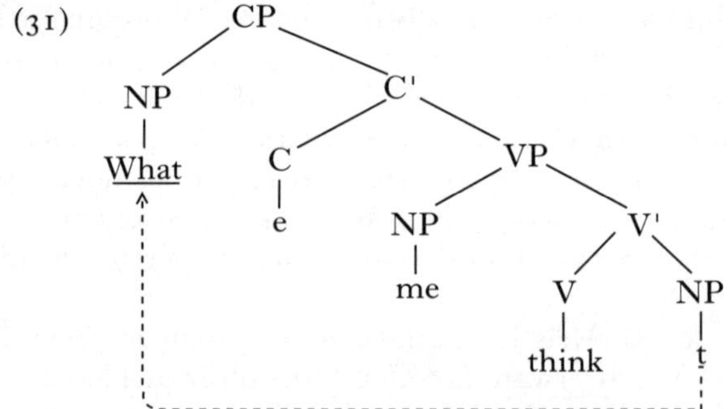

The abstract functional C head here might be argued to carry little more than the feature [+Q] to mark the overall clause as interrogative. Given the absence of canonical I properties such as nominative case and agreement, and given the assumption that CP-specifier position is always the landing-site for preposed *wh*-phrases, I assume that the root functional head here is C and not I (though see Vainikka, 1992 and Plunkett, 1992 for an attempt to argue that the root functional head is I, or a neutralized I/C constituent which – following Den Besten's 1983 analysis of German – we might call CONFL).

More problematic for the CP-specifier analysis is how we deal with stage III, when *yes–no* questions (but not *wh*-questions) show auxiliary inversion.

If we suppose that inverted auxiliaries in *yes–no* questions are in the head C position of CP, and that moved *wh*-phrases are in the CP-specifier position, then the key question to ask is what prevents the auxiliary base-generated in I (= *can*) from moving to the empty C in root *wh*-interrogative structures such as (32) below:

(32)

```
                    CP
           /              \
         NP                C'
         |            /          \
        What        C             IP
                    |          /       \
                    e        NP          I'
                    |        |        /      \
                    he     I          VP
                           |        /     \
                          can     V        PP
                                  |      /    \
                                 ride   P      NP
                                        |      |
                                        in     t
```

There are several alternative approaches which we might explore here. One is to suppose that children assume that a *yes–no* question complementizer must be filled at S-structure (either by a complementizer like *if* or by a preposed auxiliary like *can*), but that a *wh*-complementizer must be empty (as in adult *wh*-exclamatives, *wh*-relatives, and complement-clause *wh*-questions). Another possibility is to suppose that the C-feature [+Q] which (in Adult English) is directly discharged on to an inverted auxiliary in C is instead indirectly discharged (via an overgeneralization of specifier-head agreement) on to the interrogative *wh*-NP *what* in CP-specifier position. At the later stage when we find variable auxiliary inversion in *wh*-questions, we might suppose that the [+Q] feature can be discharged either directly on to an auxiliary in C, or indirectly on to an interrogative *wh*-phrase in the CP specifier position.

A third possibility would be to posit that C at stage III has no INTRINSIC categorial properties, but that C INHERITS the categorial properties of its specifier (again, via an overgeneralization of specifier-head agreement). In a *yes–no* question, C has neither intrinsic nor inherited verbal/nominal features; hence an auxiliary in I can raise to C, since C is categorially nondistinct from I. By contrast, in children's *wh*-questions at this stage, C inherits the categorial properties of its *wh*-specifier. Since the *wh*-specifier is always nonverbal (e.g. nominal in the case of *what* in (32) above), C inherits the relevant nonverbal feature, and so blocks auxiliary inversion (since an inverted auxiliary is by nature verbal, and cannot be positioned in a nonverbal C). In order to account for the transitional stage when children show variable inversion in *wh*-questions, we might suppose that categorial inheritance (i.e. agreement) is optional at the relevant point of development; this is not entirely implausible, in view of the observation in Aldridge (1989: 169) that specifier-head agreement often appears to be treated as optional by young children, e.g.

(33*a*) It goes there. Thomas go in a tent. (Thomas 2;10)
(*b*) Before he comes in. He come back. (Lisa 2;10)
(*c*) That goes with that. Round it go. (Brett 3;1)
(*d*) He wants to sit down. He want some tea. (Matthew 3;3)
(*e*) She wants to see. He want to come. (Scott 3;5)

Both approaches posit that what blocks inversion in *wh*-questions is some form of overgeneralization of specifier-head agreement within CP. In fact, there is some empirical evidence for the claim that children overgeneralize specifier-head agreement within CP, from sentences such as:

(34*a*) What's the wheels doing? (Holly 2;0)
(*b*) What's those (Alistair 2;6)
(*c*) What's you doing (Ellen 2;9)
(*d*) What's they doing? What's they called now? (James 2;10)

(35*a*) Where is his feet? (Jonathan 3;3)
(*b*) Where's me? (Michelle 2;5 = 'Where am I?')
(*c*) Where's we going tonight? (James 2;10)
(*d*) Where is you? (Elspeth 3;3 = 'Where are you?')

Under the CP-specifier analysis of *wh*-questions, the *wh*-constituents *what* and *where* would be in the CP-specifier position in (34) and (35). If this is so, then it would appear that the inverted auxiliary *is/'s* is agreeing with the specifier of CP (if we make the not unreasonable assumption that *what/where* are third person singular NPs) and not (as in Adult English) with the subject in the specifier of IP. Given that sentences like (34) and (35) provide evidence for a (morphologically) overt agreement relation between the specifier and head of CP, it seems plausible to invoke a covert specifier-head agreement relationship to account for the absence of inversion in uninverted *wh*-questions (as in the two alternative accounts offered here).

CONCLUSION

I began this paper by suggesting that one way in which K&B's analysis of *yes–no* and *wh*-questions at stages I–III could be accommodated within a contemporary GB-based model would be to suppose that *wh*-constituents are superficially positioned within the head C of CP (as indeed are inverted auxiliaries in stage III *yes–no* questions) – the HEAD ANALYSIS. I suggested that the transition between Child and Adult English could be accounted for by supposing that C is initially unspecified in respect of its categorial properties (so allowing it to host either an inverted auxiliary or a *wh*-pronoun), but that once children master the categorial properties of C (and in particular learn that a root C is intrinsically verbal), then *wh*-constituents can no longer move into C and move instead into the CP-specifier position – with the verbal C position being filled by an inverted auxiliary. I noted, however, that there are potential observational and theoretical shortcomings in the head analysis, since on the one hand the head analysis provides no natural account for stage III *wh*-phrase questions such as *Which way they should go?*, and on the other hand it involves a non-local head-movement operation which does not satisfy the MINIMALITY requirement imposed by UG (unless the class of potential antecedent governors for a *wh*-moved head is relativized and restricted to C). I suggested that one way in which both problems could be overcome would be to posit that *wh*-movement at all stages of development targets *wh*-phrases (never *wh*-heads).

I then suggested that *wh*-movement might involve adjunction to VP at stages I and II, adjunction to IP at stage III, and movement into the CP-specifier position thereafter – the ADJUNCTION ANALYSIS. I noted, however, that this analysis would provide no principled account of why *wh*-movement involves adjunction to VP in stages I and II, and would make for developmental discontinuity in the ultimate landing-site for moved *wh*-phrases. I also noted that an adjunction account would be unnatural within a model (such as Cinque's) in which *wh*-adjunction is unlicensed.

Finally, I looked at an alternative CP-SPECIFIER ANALYSIS, under which it is assumed that *wh*-movement at all developmental stages involves movement into the CP-specifier position. I noted, however, that this analysis did not automatically account for the absence of auxiliary inversion in stage III *wh*-questions, and required us to invoke an overgeneralization of specifier-head agreement to account for the relevant data.

REFERENCES

Abney, S. P. (1987). The English noun phrase in its sentential aspect. Unpublished PhD dissertation, MIT, Cambridge, MA.

Akmajian, A. & Heny, F. W. (1975). *An introduction to the principles of transformational syntax*, Cambridge, MA: MIT Press.

Aldridge, M. (1989). *The acquisition of INFL*. Indiana University Linguistics Club.

Bresnan, J. W. (1970). On complementizers: toward a syntactic theory of complement types. *Foundations of Language* 6, 297–321.

Brown, R. (1968). The development of *wh* questions in child speech. *Journal of Verbal Learning and Verbal Behavior* 7, 279–90.

Chomsky, N. (1965). *Aspects of the theory of syntax*, Cambridge, MA: MIT Press.

—— (1986). *Barriers*, Cambridge, MA: MIT Press.

Cinque, G. (1990). *Types of A-bar dependencies*. Cambridge, MA: MIT Press.

Davis, H. (1987). *The acquisition of the English auxiliary system and its relation to linguistic theory*, Unpublished PhD dissertation, University of Boulder, Colorado.

Den Besten, H. (1983). On the interaction of root transformations and lexical deletive rules. In W. Abrahams (ed.), *On the formal syntax of the Westgermania*. Amsterdam: Benjamins.

de Villiers, J. (1991). Why questions? In T. L. Maxfield & B. Plunkett (eds), *Papers in the acquisition of WH*. Amherst: GLSA Publications.

Emonds, J. E. (1970). *Root and structure-preserving transformations*. Indiana University Linguistics Club.

Gleitman, L. & Wanner, E. (1982). Language acquisition: the state of the state of the art. In E. Wanner & L. Gleitman (eds), *Language acquisition: the state of the art*, Cambridge: C.U.P.

Gruber, J. (1967). Topicalisation in child language. *Foundations of Language* 3, 37–65.

Guilfoyle, E. & Noonan, M. (1988). Functional categories and language acquisition. Paper presented to Boston University conference on language acquisition.

Katz, J. J. & Postal, P. M. (1964). *An integrated theory of linguistic descriptions*. Cambridge, MA: MIT Press.

Kayne, R. S. (1982). Predicates and arguments, verbs and nouns. *GLOW Newsletter* 8, 24.

Klima, E. S. & Bellugi, U. (1966). Syntactic regularities in the speech of children. In J. Lyons & R. Wales (eds), *Psycholinguistic papers*. Edinburgh: Edinburgh University Press.

Labov, W. & Labov, T. (1978). Learning the syntax of questions. In R. N. Campbell & P. T. Smith (eds), *Recent advances in the psychology of language*. New York: Plenum.

Miller, W. & Ervin-Tripp, S. (1973). The development of grammar in child language. In C. Ferguson & D. Slobin (eds), *Studies of child language development*. New York: Holt Rinehart & Winston.

Plunkett, B. (1991). Inversion and early *wh* questions. In T. L. Maxfield & B. Plunkett (eds), *Papers in the acquisition of WH*. Amherst: GLSA Publications.

—— (1992). Continuity and the landing site for *wh* movement. *Research Papers in Linguistics* 4, 53–77. Bangor: University College of North Wales.

Radford, A. (1986). Small children's small clauses. *Research Papers in Linguistics* 1, 1–38, Bangor: University College of North Wales (revised & extended version published in *Transactions of the Philological Society* 86, 1–46, 1988).

—— (1987). The acquisition of the complementizer system. *Research Papers in Linguistics* 2, 55–76, Bangor: University College of North Wales.

—— (1988). *Transformational syntax*. Cambridge: C.U.P.

—— (1990). *Syntactic theory and the acquisition of English syntax*. Oxford: Blackwell.

—— (1991). The nature and acquisition of grammar. Unpublished paper, University of Essex.

Rizzi, L. (1990). *Relativised minimality*. Cambridge, MA: MIT Press.

Roberts, I. (1992). Restructuring and clitic climbing in Old French. Seminar, Department of Language & Linguistics, University of Essex.

Roeper, T. (1992). From the initial state to V2: acquisition principles in action. In J. M. Meisel (ed.), *The acquisition of verb placement*. Dordrecht: Kluwer.

Roeper, T. & de Villiers, J. (1991). Ordered decisions in the acquisition of *wh*-questions. In J. Weissenborn, H. Goodluck & T. Roeper (eds), *Theoretical issues in language acquisition*. London: Erlbaum.

Rudin, C. (1988). On multiple questions and multiple *wh* fronting. *Natural Language and Linguistic Theory* 6, 445–501.

Sadock, J. M. (1984). West Greenlandic. In W. S. Chisholm (ed.), *Interrogativity* Amsterdam: Benjamins.

Taraldsen, K. T. (1986). On verb second and the functional content of syntactic categories. In H. Haider & M. Prinzhorn (eds), *Verb second phenomena in Germanic languages*. Dordrecht: Foris.

Vainikka, A. (1992). Case in the development of English syntax. Unpublished paper, University of Massachusetts.

Weissenborn, J., Roeper, T. & de Villiers, J. (1991). The acquisition of *wh*-movement in German and French. In T. L. Maxfield & B. Plunkett (eds), *Papers in the acquisition of WH*. Amherst: GLSA Publications.

J. Child Lang. **21** (1994), 237–255. Copyright © 1994 Cambridge University Press

Exploring the boundary between syntax and pragmatics: relevance and the binding of pronouns*

SUSAN H. FOSTER-COHEN
Northern Arizona University

ABSTRACT

This paper explores the interface between syntax and pragmatics, focusing on the binding of pronouns and the pragmatics of the paradigms used to test this aspect of syntactic knowledge. Reinhart's (1986) version of Binding Theory (which accords a specific role to pragmatics in processes of pronoun resolution) and Sperber & Wilson's (1986) Theory of Relevance are used to examine the syntax and pragmatics of pronoun interpretation. A set of predictions based on Relevance Theory are evaluated against published results of tests of Binding Theory. The paper concludes that Relevance Theory provides a means of understanding constraints on testing syntactic knowledge and argues that pragmatic factors must be systematically controlled in any evaluation of syntactic knowledge.

INTRODUCTION

In recent years there has been considerable discussion of modularity as a way of looking at the organization of the mind and at the ontogenetic evolution of language (Fodor, 1983; Gunnar & Maratsos, 1992). A number of possible modules have been proposed, mostly within the area of syntax. For example, Radford (1990) assumes a categorial module, a transformational module, a bounding module, a case module, a theta module, and a binding module in his discussion of children's syntax. Numerous works within theoretical accounts which assume this or a similar set of syntactic modules have explored the way these modules interact. Less well explored are the relationships between any of the syntactic modules, and what can loosely be called the pragmatic component of language and language development.

In his influential discussion of modularity, Fodor (1983) suggests that syntactic operations are fundamentally different in kind from the integrative and inferential processes which allow human beings to actually 'use' their

---

[*] I have profited greatly from discussions with Matthew Rispoli, Nina Hyams, Sharon Sabsay and Sharon Klein during the evolution of several of the ideas that appear in this paper. Particular thanks go to Matthew Rispoli for detailed comments on earlier drafts. Address for correspondence: Susan Foster-Cohen, Department of English, Box 6032, Northern Arizona University, Flagstaff, Arizona 86011, USA.

linguistic knowledge in reasoning. In Fodor's terminology, there is a difference between 'input' systems (the computational aspects of language) and integrative central processes which have access to the output of various input systems (grammatical, visual, kinesthetic, etc.). Sperber & Wilson (1986) make a similar distinction, arguing convincingly for a difference between coded communication and inferential communication. However, where Fodor argues that scientific reasoning is the classic case of inferential, central processing, Sperber & Wilson argue that normal everyday conversation reveals the operation of the central processing mechanisms *par excellence.*

In their book, Sperber & Wilson (1986) argue that pragmatics, specifically those aspects of conversation which Grice's co-operative principle and its attendant maxims are intended to cover, can best be understood in terms of the operation of a PRINCIPLE OF RELEVANCE and the processing resulting from speakers' and hearers' inevitable obedience to this innate principle. An exploration of the boundary between syntax and pragmatics can thus be seen as an exploration of the intersection and interaction between coded and inferential processes (or between input system processes and central processes), and the relation between Relevance and syntactic modules can form the basis for defining boundary issues. This paper focuses on one aspect of the boundary between syntax and pragmatics – that between the BINDING THEORY and pronoun interpretation. It will suggest that the theory of relevance, as developed by Sperber & Wilson (1986, 1987) can shed useful light on some of the problematic findings from tests of pronoun interpretation framed within the Universal Grammar (Government and Binding) approach to syntax, specifically, Reinhart's (1983, 1986) version of the binding theory.

The selection of these particular frameworks is not arbitrary. Rather, they mesh in important ways in their theoretical preconceptions, and thus facilitate discussions of the 'division of effort' between syntax and pragmatics. Firstly, as already indicated, Sperber & Wilson and Reinhart both assume a modularity thesis, and both are interested in the boundaries between syntax and pragmatics. Secondly, both approaches assume a fundamental role for innate principles. As will be detailed below, Reinhart assumes an innate principle governing coreference, along with innate syntactic principles embodied in the binding conditions. Likewise, Sperber & Wilson assume that the principle of relevance is innate since it governs not only linguistic behaviour, but all of human information processing. Thirdly, both approaches make appeal to a principle of least effort. Sperber & Wilson argue that the more effort that has to be invested in deriving an interpretation, the less relevant an interpretation it will be. Reinhart argues that the processing effort involved in interpretations that require the use of Rule I (see below) militates against children's performance being adult-like. While not sufficiently well articulated in either approach, a common appeal to processing effort nonetheless indicates that their views on human language processing assume similar strictures. Finally, both approaches share similar views of the ordered relationship between the syntactic module and pragmatic processes, i.e. that pragmatic processes operate AFTER syntactic ones in some non-trivial sense. This issue will be discussed further below.

The paper is organized as follows. First a summary of the key components of the binding theory are provided, and it is suggested that, given Reinhart's revision of the standard binding theory, the role of pragmatics in the interpretation of pronouns can be further explored in relation to a generative account of syntax. In particular, it is suggested that there is need for an account of the kind of processing that must take place, after the operation of the syntax, in order for pronoun resolution to be achieved. Moreover, without such an account, we are unable satisfactorily to account for the otherwise inexplicably uneven behaviour of young children on tests for the application of the binding theory. It is suggested that Sperber & Wilson's relevance theory provides a way to look at both adult and child processing of pronoun resolution. A series of predictions about children's behaviour with respect to binding theory is proposed in the light of relevance theory. A subset of the experimental paradigms used to test binding theory is then examined in the light of these predictions, and it is argued that the pragmatics of these paradigms do indeed suggest a confounding effect of pragmatics on children's syntactic performance. It is concluded that future research must attempt to control for pragmatics in any examination of generative theory as a viable approach to developmental syntax.

PRAGMATICS AND THE ACQUISITION OF SYNTACTIC BINDING

Over the last decade or so, there has been fairly intense interest in children's competency at interpreting both anaphoric and referential pronouns (e.g. Lust (1987), Solan (1987), Kaufman (1988), McDaniel, Cairns & Hsu (1990), Chien & Wexler (1990), Grimshaw & Rosen (1990), McKee (1992), Grodzinsky & Reinhart (1993)). Recently there has been considerable debate over why children appear to be uneven in their ability to interpret different types of pronoun. The debate has focused on binding theory, as developed by Chomsky (1981, 1986) and others. This theory attempts to capture the behaviour of different kinds of noun phrases within a set of three conditions: Principle A, governing the behaviour of anaphors such as reflexives, which must have a local (roughly speaking a clause-mate) antecedent to be interpretable; Principle B, governing the behaviour of pronouns, which must NOT have a local antecedent; and Principle C, governing full noun phrases, which must not have a syntactically-bound antecedent anywhere. The crucial notion is one of BINDING which (with some variation between formulations) amounts to a relationship between the antecedent and the NP such that the antecedent c-commands (roughly, is higher up the tree than) the relevant

NP. Thus, when an anaphor is locally c-commanded by its antecedent, the construction is predicted to be grammatical. When an anaphor is NOT locally c-commanded by its antecedent, the construction is predicted to be ungrammatical. The following sentences illustrate the grammatical contrasts that the three (standard) binding principles are designed to capture. In each case, the interpretation for consideration is the one indicated by the subscript coindexing:

Principle A
($1a$) Jon$_i$ likes himself$_i$.
  (b) *Jon$_i$ likes himself$_j$.
  (c) *Jon$_i$ thinks himself$_i$ is clever.

Principle B
  (d) *Jon$_i$ likes him$_i$
  (e) Jon$_i$ likes him$_j$
  (f) Jon$_i$ thinks he$_{i/j}$ is clever

Principle C
  (g) *He$_i$ likes Jon$_i$
  (h) He$_i$ likes Jon$_j$
  (i) *He$_i$ thinks Jon$_i$ is clever

A wide range of studies have suggested that young children do much better on tests of Principle A (anaphors) than they do on those for Principles B (pronouns) and C (referring expressions). Since binding theory is viewed as capturing a unitary cluster of syntactic properties, these differences are problematic for the binding theory account.

Researchers working in the Chomskyan generative tradition have generally been interested solely in the syntactic aspects of pronoun interpretation. However, recently, there has been serious discussion (within this tradition) of the relationship between these syntactic aspects and the pragmatic aspects of the resolution of reference of pronouns (Chien & Wexler, 1990; Grimshaw & Rosen, 1990; Grodzinsky & Reinhart, 1993). (Researchers in other frameworks have explored the pragmatics of pronoun resolution in a variety of ways, e.g. Levinson, 1987.) Grimshaw & Rosen (1990) argue that children's poor performance on Principle B tests is not due to the absence of knowledge of the binding principles but to a number of different confounding factors that add up to children knowing the binding principles but for one reason or another not obeying them. Chien & Wexler (1990), on the other hand, come to the conclusion that while children 'know' Principle B, they perform poorly on experiments designed to test it because there is some other (unitary) pragmatic principle (P) which they do not know.

In distinguishing binding and coreference, Chien & Wexler adopt a version of Reinhart's (1983, 1986) revision of the standard binding theory.

This revision (explored by Grodzinsky & Reinhart (1993) in relation to the acquisition of binding theory) reconfigures the elements involved in explaining the binding theory facts.

In the standard binding theory (as in Reinhart's revision), noun phrases are allowed to be freely coindexed. Thus, any anaphor and noun phrase, or pronoun and noun phrase (etc.) could be assigned the same index. Then, the binding theory rules out the wrongly coindexed interpretations and allows the correctly coindexed structures to be interpreted. Thus the standard Binding Theory will rule out (1*b*) above, but allow (1*a*) to be interpreted with *Jon* and *himself* as coreferential. The assumption of the standard binding theory is thus that coindexation is what allows coreference. That is, the binding theory governs both syntactic coindexation AND coreference. What Reinhart suggests is that this is an incorrect view, since coreference also occurs in cases where the binding theory has nothing to say. For example, in,

(2*a*) Before *Mickey* went to school, *he* fed the dog
(*b*) The bear near *Lucie* touched her
(*c*) Let's ask the bear that *Lucie* likes to kiss *her*
(*d*) Some of *her* friends are upset at *Lucie*

there are no binding relationships between the items interpreted as coreferential (because there are no c-command relationships between them), and yet they are interpreted as coreferential. Even more clearly, binding theory has nothing to say about coreference between items in different sentences, e.g.

(3*a*) I saw *Jon* yesterday. *He* said to say 'Hi'.
(*b*) *The man* was walking towards me. I hoped *he* wouldn't stop.

Moreover, there are pronouns in classic binding theory contexts which can either be interpreted as bound or as unbound, e.g.

(4) *Jon* thinks that *he* is crazy

in which Jon either believes himself to be crazy, or believes someone else to be crazy. When the unbound reading is taken, then determining the reference of *he* falls to the same kind of process as determining the reference of the pronouns in the non-bound intrasentential cases (2*a–d*) and the intersentential coreference cases (3*a–b*). Thus, Reinhart argues, there is clear reason to develop a pragmatic account of coreference independently of syntactic binding. Firstly, it pulls together the coreference facts both intra- and intersententially as just noted. Secondly, it allows the binding theory to apply only to anaphoric elements (i.e. bound anaphors such as reflexives, various empty elements not discussed here, and bound variable readings of pronouns) and not to referential ones.

In Grodzinsky & Reinhart (1993), the focus is on how that pragmatic account of coreference applies to INTRAsentential coreference between items not coindexed with each other. Coreference is defined as,

> the assignment of identical values to NPs with distinct syntactic indices, regardless of whether the two NPs occur in the same sentence or not. (pp. 77–78)

Rule I, which, Reinhart argues, governs intrasentential coreference, has the following formulation:

Rule I : Intrasentential Coreference
NP A cannot corefer with NP B if replacing A with C, C a variable A-bound by B, yields an indistinguishable interpretation (p. 79)

The operation of this rule requires considerable processing and it requires appeal to the pragmatic context of the utterance being interpreted. Since both these issues will be crucial in the discussion of relevance theory and its consequences on children's performance, it is worth presenting the essence of Reinhart's account in order to see the boundary between syntactic and pragmatic modules more clearly.

To see how Rule I works, suppose a child is provided with the sentence,

5.   Oscar touches him

in a context in which the interpretation of the sentence is that Oscar touches himself. That is, that the interpretation is as in (6):

6. *$Oscar_i$ touches him_i

Rule I requires that the child 'decide' if the pronoun can be replaced by a bound element, i.e. an anaphoric element c-commanded by *Oscar*. If it cannot, then the process would be finished, and the two elements would be allowed to freely corefer. However, in this case, there is such an element, namely the reflexive (*himself*). Now the child must decide if the version with the pronoun and the version with the reflexive represent distinguishable interpretations, i.e. is the context such that they could mean two different things? In this case the answer must be in the negative, and thus coreference is blocked. The child, recognizing that coreference is blocked, and the sentence thus uninterpretable, should reject the sentence.

The crucial part of this process, and the part that makes it a non-syntactic activity is that determining the distinguishability of interpretations requires checking the context of the utterance, because there ARE situations in which apparent violations of the binding theory are fully interpretable, but only because the context makes them so. For example,

7.   I dreamt that I was Brigitte Bardot and I_i kissed me_i (cited in Grodzinsky & Reinhart as being due to George Lakoff and as having been

discussed in Heim, 1991). Here, even though the *me* could be replaced by *myself*, the context makes it clear that to do so would produce a different interpretation from the *I kissed me* interpretation. One case is a reflexive interpretation. The other is not. Thus, in this context, *I kissed me* becomes interpretable and *I* and *me* must refer to the same person.

Given Reinhart's version of the binding theory and her Rule I, a rather different view of the so-called binding theory sentences tested with children appears. Under the Reinhart analysis the following types of sentences are grammatical because of the binding theory:

(8a)   Oscar$_i$ touches himself$_i$
  (b)   Bert$_i$ said that he$_{i/j}$ ran behind the box
  (c)   Bert$_i$ said that Gert touched him$_i$

The following are binding theory ungrammatical:

  (d) *Oscar$_i$ said that Bert touches himself$_i$
  (e) *Every boy$_i$ touches him$_i$

The following, however, are Rule I ungrammatical:

  (f)   *Oscar* touches *him*
  (g)   *He* touches *Oscar*
  (h)   *He* said that *Oscar* touches the box

and those sentences presented above in (2) and repeated here are Rule I grammatical:

(9a)   Before *Mickey* went to school, *he* fed the dog
  (b)   The bear near *Lucie* touched *her*
  (c)   Let's ask the bear that *Lucie* likes to kiss *her*
  (d)   Some of *her* friends are upset at *Lucie*

The crucial difference between Reinhart's analysis and those following the standard binding theory, such as Grimshaw & Rosen (1990) (whose article forms the focus of Grodzinsky & Reinhart's (1993) discussion), is that (8f–h), which, according to the standard analysis are binding theory ungrammatical, are here argued to be Rule I ungrammatical. Grodzinsky & Reinhart (1993) go on to show that under this revised view, it is the Rule I ungrammatical sentences which cause children significant difficulties, not the ones which truly test the Binding Theory. Specifically, children have a tendency to interpret pronouns as if they have a local antecedent, and this is a Rule I problem and not a binding theory problem.

So now we can see where the child's non-syntactic work lies – work which involves both processing syntactic alternatives to the sentence that has been given, and processing the context and its relevance to the two representations.

As Reinhart (1986: 79) says, 'it involves an inference based on knowledge of grammar, meaning, and appropriateness to context'. She leaves open the precise status of Rule I:

> We leave open whether Rule I is an independent principle of the coreference module of Universal Grammar or whether it may be reducible to other general principles. (p. 82)

However, the fact that Rule I crucially invokes context as a way of resolving reference means that theories of context and access to it can be brought to bear on the data she has identified. Reinhart suggests that the cost involved with the memory load required to hold representations in mind and check them against context might be sufficient to account for children's difficulties, but this would be a more powerful explanation if a more precise account of the type of processing involved could be advanced and if precise predictions about children's behaviour in certain pragmatic situations could be advanced. In the next section, I will suggest that Sperber & Wilson's relevance theory allows one to make testable predictions about children's behaviour in resolving pronoun reference.

RELEVANCE THEORY AND REFERENCE RESOLUTION

Adopting the division of labour between coded and inferential processes outlined in the introduction, relevance theory predicts that the syntactic modules provide an incomplete representation of the sentence under consideration. Assuming Reinhart's view of binding theory, this incomplete representation will be marked for syntactic coindexation, but not for pragmatic coreference. The principle of relevance may then determine the coreference interpretations for the non-coindexed noun phrases. (See Kempson's (1988) discussion of the role of the principle of relevance in completing the propositional representation of utterances in context.) Thus if *Jon said that he is crazy* comes with syntactic coindexation between *Jon* and *he*, the interpretation of coreference would be made on that basis. If *Jon* and *he* are not syntactically coindexed, the inferential processes would lead to a decision as to who exactly the *he* does refer to. In the examples from children's performance, *Oscar hit him* would exit the syntactic component without coindexation between *Oscar* and *him*, and then Rule I, operating in conjunction with the principle of relevance would act to determine the coreference, which might include coreference between *Oscar* and *him*.

Sperber & Wilson's (1987: 704) principle of relevance is,

> the thesis that every act of ostensive communication communicates the presumption of its own optimal relevance.

In other words, any communication (verbal or non-verbal) recognized as intentional by the hearer is automatically presumed to be relevant to the hearer, who must then figure out an interpretation for that communication. The interpretation is guided by the context and the effort required to process it. Specifically,

> *Extent condition* 1: An assumption is relevant in a context to the extent that its contextual effects in that context are large.
> *Extent condition* 2: An assumption is relevant in a context to the extent that the effort required to process it in that context is small.' (Sperber & Wilson, 1987: 703)

A contextual effect occurs when an assumption is added to the context via direct means (such as visual observation) or indirect means (such as verbally encoded information, or the generation of bridging assumptions), or when an assumption is either made more manifest in a context (more sure, or more noticeable) through processing the new assumption, or is eliminated from the context by being contradicted by a stronger assumption (Sperber & Wilson 1986). Thus an assumption will have greater contextual effect if it builds on previous assumptions by adding new and related information or by confirming a weakly manifest assumption in the hearer's 'cognitive environment', or if it contradicts an assumption currently in the hearer's cognitive environment. However, effect in a context must be weighed against the cost involved in processing it. Thus, if a relevant reading takes several inferential steps and involves accessing very weakly manifest assumptions, perhaps from encyclopaedic knowledge that has not been accessed for some time, the processing cost may be too great for the new material to be seen as relevant.

With respect to pronoun resolution, the two relevance conditions capture the idea that the hearer will use the context and minimal processing effort to determine how to resolve the reference and coreference of pronouns. So, just as it is for Reinhart's Rule I, understanding the context used in interpreting an utterance is vitally important to understanding how a hearer will interpret an utterance, and Sperber & Wilson devote considerable space to discussion of the types of contextual information (assumptions) the speaker and hearer have available, both individually and shared between them.

Sperber & Wilson argue that 'at any moment an individual has at his disposal a particular set of accessible contexts' (1987: 703). Specifically, there is the

> initial context consisting of the assumptions used or derived in the last deduction performed. This initial context can be expanded in three directions: by adding assumptions used or derived in preceding deductions, by adding to it chunks of information taken from the encyclopaedic entries of concepts already present in the context or in the assumption being processed, and by adding input information about the perceptual environment (ibid).

Using this information, the hearer makes the most relevant interpretation (i.e. the most richly consequential in contextual terms and least costly in processing terms) of the new material being interpreted.

With this brief overview of relevance theory, I now turn to some specific consequences for hearers placed in conversational or (as in the case of experimental testing paradigms) pseudo-conversational situations, and make some specific predictions with respect to the way children might be expected to behave in such situations. In what follows, I shall assume that children process utterances for relevance in the same way as adults do. I suggest that the difference between adults and children is not in the relevance processing they do, but in the extent to which they are able to divorce themselves from the pseudo-conversational context of the testing situation and recognize that they have been put in a truly odd situation in which the normal rules of conversational processing must be ignored. In other words, children, unlike adults, find the situation they have been placed in credible, and act accordingly. Older children and adults do not believe that the situation is credible, and so respond to the test sentences in spite of the context in which they appear. (The problems children sometimes have in school with recognizing that teachers' questions are not genuinely asked for information seems to be a continuation of the same preferences.) Clearly this distinction implies that pragmatic competence is not a unitary competence, and it will be important in further research to examine just how the aspects of pragmatic competence governed by the principles of relevance interact with other aspects of pragmatic competence.

Assuming, then, that children respond in all situations designed to test the binding theory in ways that are partially dependent on the pragmatics of the situation, we can make certain predictions about how they will behave, given the various types of information that are presented and the order in which they are presented. Binding theory studies have used two basic methodologies: 'act out' tasks and 'grammaticality judgements'. In the first, children are asked to perform or make a puppet perform a sentence provided to them. In the second, children are asked to accept or reject a sentence presented by a researcher (directly or through the mouth of a puppet) in the context of some visual stimulus. Both of these situations place considerable demands on children, and both have pragmatic consequences.

SOME PREDICTIONS

Relevance theory predicts that pure repetition of information will have low relevance because it demands processing effort for no immediately obvious increase in information. However, given the presumption of optimal relevance, the hearer will invest more processing effort to try to discover relevance when faced with a situation which is not immediately obviously relevant. Thus any situations in which there is redundant information presented in the context preceding the test sentence in a binding theory test can be expected to lead the child to further processing. Further processing, in an attempt to establish the relevance of what has been presented, will detract from the child's ability to process the test sentence and can thus be expected to lower performance on the test. Similarly, contradictory information presented by the test sentence in relation to the context will demand more processing, and therefore be more distracting, than felicitous additions of new and relevant information to the context. The first three predictions to be articulated all involve these aspects of relevance theory. They all relate to the general prediction that children will perform more poorly in experimental paradigms in which the presumption of optimal relevance is violated than they will in experimental paradigms in which the presumption of optimal relevance is respected.

> *Prediction* 1: Children will perform more poorly in situations in which there is a mismatch of information between the context and the test sentence than they will in situations in which the test sentence provides relevant information in relation to the context.
> *Prediction* 2: Children will perform worse in situations where there is a repetition of already fully manifest material in the context immediately prior to the presentation of the test sentence than they will in situations where there is a sequence of relevant additions to the context without major redundancy.

The third prediction deals with the structure of information presented in utterances provided as context for the test sentence. Sperber & Wilson argue that the familiar given/new, topic/comment structure of sentences is a result of the principle of relevance (Sperber & Wilson, 1986: 202–4). Specifically, hearers expect that information coded in the early part of an utterance will connect with information already represented in the cognitive environment, and that information coded later in the utterance will provide new and relevant information to be added to the context with a minimum of processing effort. The third prediction is thus the following:

> *Prediction* 3: Children tested using paradigms in which contextual utterances do not respect relevance-driven informational structure will perform less well on test items which immediately follow those contextual utterances than children tested using paradigms which obey the information structure strictures.

A fourth, and final, prediction comes from the assumption that there is an ordered relationship between the syntax and the pragmatics. In the preceding discussion, mention has been made of the input-output relationship between binding theory and relevance theory. Both Sperber & Wilson (1986) and Kempson (1988) have argued that the output of the syntactic modules is an incomplete specification of the 'logical form' or propositional content of a sentence. The pragmatic processes are then viewed as 'completing' these representations. Similarly, Reinhart argues that when the binding module has completed its work, Rule I completes the interpretation of coreference. The consequence of this ordering is that the processing of pronouns that are syntactically controlled is complete before the pragmatic processes set to work. It is this which allows us to account for children's much better performance on Principle A than on Principle B. Under Principle A, the interpretation of anaphors is syntactically controlled by the binding principles and there is thus no work for Rule I to do. In Principle B, on the other hand, there is considerable work for the pragmatics to do, and therein lies the problem. On the assumption that children know the binding theory, but have problems with the pragmatics, as Grodzinsky & Reinhart (1993) argue, this explains the very high rate of correct response for Principle A, and the much lower rate for Principle B.

Within relevance theory, the ordering of syntax and pragmatics, coupled with Sperber & Wilson's claims about what exactly is accessible in the context, leads to a further prediction. Recall that contexts include 'chunks of information taken from the encyclopaedic entries of concepts already present in the context or in the assumption being processed' (Sperber & Wilson, 1987: 703). This means that conceptual information may be accessed as part of the pragmatic interpretation of pronouns, which is not accessed as part of the interpretation of anaphors since the former but not the latter interpretations involve accessing conceptual information of the type stored in an individual's contexts. (These stored contexts constitute an individual's cognitive environment in Sperber & Wilson's terminology: 'A cognitive environment of an individual is a set of facts that are manifest to him' (1986: 39)). Thus the following prediction can be made:

> *Prediction* 4: Conceptual information will affect children's ability to respond to tests of Principle A of the Binding Theory differently from their ability to respond to tests of Principle B of the Binding Theory.

In the remainder of this paper I will test these four predictions against the evidence emerging from experiments designed to test the binding theory.

Testing the predictions

In this section each of the predictions will be examined in turn in the light of children's responses to experimental paradigms presented in published research. The binding theory tests of Grimshaw & Rosen (1990), Chien & Wexler (1990), and McKee (1992) – each of which uses a different testing procedure – will be used in evaluating the predictions.

The first prediction leads us to expect a difference between situations in which there is a match between the context and the test sentence and situations in which there is a mismatch. Children are predicted to do worse on the latter than on the former. This difference is widespread. Chien & Wexler (1990) use a *yes/no* judgement task in which children must look at a picture and then decide if the sentence they hear matches or does not match the picture. In tests of both Principle A and Principle B, children are routinely worse at rejecting the sentences which do not match than they are at accepting the sentences which do match the picture. McKee (1992) used a paradigm in which she asked children to watch an event staged by puppets and then either accept or reject a description of that event described by one of the puppets. Again there was a consistent and significant difference between children's ability to accept correct descriptions and their ability to reject incorrect ones. Grimshaw & Rosen (1990) in a different version of the McKee paradigm (developed by Crain & McKee 1985), found a similar systematic difference. Table 1 shows the comparisons.

TABLE 1. *Percentage correct performance on binding theory tests*

Study	Matched conditions[a]		Mismatched conditions[b]	
	A	B	A	B
McKee	99	93	84·5	28
Chien & Wexler	91·5	91·2	72·4	49
Grimshaw & Rosen	—	83	—	42

[a] Accepting grammatical sentences; [b] rejecting ungrammatical sentences.

In the studies reviewed here, the difficulty children appear to have with rejecting mismatch situations is claimed (by the authors of those studies) to be due to a difficulty in declaring something ungrammatical, or to a preference for saying 'yes' in experimental situations. However, in the light of the prediction made by relevance theory, it would seem equally likely that the problem is the relationship between the context and the test sentence in terms of relevance. If this is so, then there has been a systematic confounding in grammaticality experiments of the problem created by declaring something ungrammatical and the problem created by coping with a mismatch. The confounding may in fact be even more extensive, since the 'yes' bias is found throughout developmental psychology. It is possible that it may all reduce to a problem with relevance. Such an extension would certainly be in the spirit of Sperber & Wilson's framework since they argue that relevance guides all human processing. In the case of syntactic tests, unpacking the problem would seem to require the designing of experiments in which children must process a mismatch in order to declare something grammatical and process a match in order to declare something ungrammatical.

The second prediction leads one to expect a difference between paradigms in which redundant repetition occurs and ones in which it does not. A comparison of the three paradigms under discussion shows that there is indeed such a difference. The percentage correct responses on Principles A and B in the 'matched' situations can be seen in Table 1, and would seem to conform to prediction 2. To see this, it is necessary to describe the paradigms used by each of the research teams. I will describe only those trials in which there was a match between the context and the test sentence, since as already discussed, a mismatch appears to introduce an additional burden on the child.

McKee (whose success rates are the highest) used a paradigm (already described) in which puppets acted out a scene and then the test sentence described the scene. Here is McKee's description of a typical trial:

> A Cabbage Patch baby falls in a tub of water. A princess doll says to her, 'You're wet!', picks up a towel, and dries her. The puppet watching this event with the child then says, 'The princess dried her.' (McKee, 1992: 27)

In this paradigm, then, the non-verbal and the verbal contextual material follow natural expectations of relevance. There is little redundancy between non-verbal and verbal context, and none between the verbal context and the test sentence.

The picture-match task used by Chien & Wexler introduces a contextual problem not present in the McKee paradigm. Here is Chien & Wexler's description of a typical trial:

> suppose the name of the child being tested was Sarah. The general procedure for the task is as follows: We first presented a picture...to Sarah, then we said to her, 'Sarah, look at this picture. This is Goldilocks; this is Mama Bear. Is Mama Bear touching herself?' (Chien & Wexler, 1991: 261)

The problem introduced here is the naming of the protagonists which one may assume are already identifiable from the picture. If they are not obvious from the first picture, the fact that the trials all involve the same protagonists will quickly obviate the need to keep repeating the protagonists' identification. Thus this Chien & Wexler paradigm, while fairly felicitous, is not quite as felicitous as the McKee paradigm.

Grimshaw & Rosen's paradigm is the most problematic from a relevance point of view. In their design, they use a version of Crain & McKee's (1985) truth-value judgment task in which they show children a videotaped scenario, and then provide them with a 'context' sentence followed by the test sentence. The two sentences are 'said' by a frog puppet who, the children are told, is learning to speak English. The children are instructed to decide whether the frog has correctly described what happened in the videotape and to feed him either a rag or a cookie for either a wrong or a right description respectively. A typical trial for Principle B, using simple sentences is summarized as having the following format (Grimshaw & Rosen 1990: 219):

Principle B – Simple
Scenario: Big Bird pats Ernie
Froggie: 'I saw Big Bird doing something with Ernie. Big Bird patted him'

In fact the testing situation is more complex. The scenarios include both Big Bird and Ernie, whether or not both characters are actually doing anything. Next, 'the experimenter talked with the child about the scene (to aid in memory), without using any third person pronouns (for example, "Look who's here; Bert just hit Oscar")' (Grimshaw & Rosen, 1990: 218). Then the video-scenario was shown to the child a second time before the context sentence and the test sentence were presented.

It is clearly worrisome that Grimshaw & Rosen are not more forthcoming about what was said between trials, since whatever was said becomes part of the linguistic context which forms the background against which the test sentence must be interpreted, and it is, in fact, rather unclear how, for example, a reflexive situation can be discussed without using either a reflexive or a name. Since the former would prime the test of Principle A, and the latter would give the child evidence for a distinguishable interpretation in the terms of Rule I (see above), it becomes rather important to know what was said.

The child thus has two presentations of the video and some language between the showings which describes the same scene. A third version of the scene is presented by the context sentence, which was intended simply to provide a possible antecedent for the pronoun in the test sentence, but actually re-presents the protagonists now fully manifest from the previous context. When the test sentence is presented, then, relevance theory predicts that the child is still trying, and I hypothesize failing, to process the relevance of the context sentence, hence the lower performance on the test sentences using this paradigm.

Prediction 3 leads one to expect a problem in situations where the presentation of information within utterances fails to conform to given/new ordering predicted by relevance theory. This is precisely the case in the Grimshaw & Rosen paradigm. The position of Ernie in the focus or comment position at the end of the context sentence leads the child to expect him to be relevant to any subsequent interpretation. In the sample paradigm presented above, he is relevant (since Big Bird hit him), although weakly so, since he and Big Bird have been mentioned and re-mentioned so frequently that their relevance is now hard to process. In the cases where the child is supposed to reject a Principle B violation, the problem is acute, however. In this paradigm, we have the following set-up (recognizing that this too is not the full story, as described above):

Scenario: Big Bird hits himself
Froggie: Big Bird was standing with Ernie. *Big Bird$_i$ hit him$_i$.

Here, Ernie is not relevant. Big Bird is hitting himself and it is that interpretation that the experimenters wish the child to ascribe to *Big Bird$_i$ hit him$_i$*. The child is thus presented with information placed in such a way that it ought to be relevant. The child is thus forced by the assumption of optimal relevance to try to process an appropriate interpretation. The processing takes effort, and detracts from the ability to process the test sentence. Thus the evidence for this prediction interacts with the first prediction (of a generally lower performance on mismatch than match cases) to produce a significant problem for children. The statistics support this analysis. In the Grimshaw & Rosen paradigm, children succeed in accepting the grammatical interpretations 83 % of the time, but succeed in rejecting the ungrammatical only 42 % of the time. The difference is clearly startling.

The fourth prediction leads one to look for the influence of conceptual information when the pragmatics must be employed in the interpretation of pronominals, but not when it is not. Precisely this evidence is provided by Chien & Wexler's finding that gender aids the interpretation of pronouns but not of reflexives. In a task in which children must act-out instructions given by a puppet, such as 'Snoopy says that Adam (child's name) should point to himself', they found that when gender was a clue to the interpretation of the antecedent, as it is in 'Kitty (a clearly female puppet) says that Adam should point to himself' there was no improvement in children's performance. However, when the same paradigm was used to test pronouns there was a highly significant improvement in children's behaviour. Even the youngest children were more than 80 % correct. A sample test sentence here would be, 'Kitty says that Adam should point to her'. In the context of relevance theory, it is possible to suggest that since children recognize that the pronouns are not syntactically bound in these sentences, they move to the domain of relevance in which one of the kinds of contextual information available is the gender associated with the concepts mentioned in the context.

DISCUSSION

The preceding section has suggested that there is evidence for the effects of the principle of relevance in binding theory testing paradigms. A set of predictions, based on relevance theory, about children's behaviour in tests of the binding theory have been found to be supported by published data. The argument would clearly be strengthened, however, by evidence from deliberate manipulation of redundancy, contradictory information, conceptual information, and information structure in further experiments. Further probing of the ordering relationship between syntax and pragmatics is also necessary.

An ordering issue that arises in this connection is the preference shown in all the experiments reviewed for a local antecedent, even when Principle B allows a non-local antecedent. There is generally a preference for children NOT to go outside the sentence for an antecedent. Within this confine, the Grimshaw & Rosen paradigm shows children going outside the sentence for an antecedent more often than the other paradigms, presumably because the plethora of contextual material provided in this paradigm lures them outside the sentence in a way that the other paradigm materials do not. What might be suggested here is that, at least in languages like English which do not have long-distance anaphora binding (but see Hyams & Sigurjonsdottir's work on Icelandic (1990)), there is a locality preference both in the syntax and in the pragmatics. Perhaps this could be related to some kind of 'least effort' principle, a notion to which both Reinhart and Sperber & Wilson refer. Further study of this issue is clearly indicated.

An ordering relationship may also be needed to help explain McKee's results with Italian children in which she obtained significantly more correct responses on tests of Principle B using clitic pronouns rather than free-standing pronouns. She suggests a different configuration of Italian clitic pronouns from free-standing English pronouns. If the syntax of the construction in a particular language and/or the child's current assumptions about that syntax guide interpretations before pragmatic issues are taken into account, then in different languages, the output of the syntactic module, which is passed to the pragmatic module(s) will vary cross-linguistically. Future research would profit from examining the ways in which these inputs to the pragmatics might vary, and the consequences for the operation of the principle of relevance of the differences.

The preceding sections have attempted to show how our understanding of child language development can be enhanced by adopting a modular view of language and language development, and then probing the boundaries between the modules in order to better define each of the modules and the interactions between them in language development. The discussion has focused on one particular issue, namely pronominal binding, since this is an issue which appears to straddle the boundary between syntax and pragmatics (Levinson, 1987; Kempson, 1988). I have suggested that a Government and Binding approach to syntax plus Sperber & Wilson's approach to pragmatics can provide a starting point for evaluating our knowledge of this area of language development. (But see Levinson, 1987, for an alternative approach.)

Just as applying Chomskyan (GB) theoretical constructs to child language material has led to fairly radical changes in the theory, so applying relevance theory to acquisition data can be expected to lead to changes and refinements in that theory, too. Since the latter theory is considerably less highly articulated than current syntactic theory, it is possible for child language studies to be formative in the future development of relevance theory. Questions to be answered will include determining the precise status of the principle of relevance at various developmental stages, examining how the various aspects of context develop, and determining whether it is possible to design better tests of syntactic components such as the binding theory that take into account the pragmatic effects discussed above. While syntactic tests cannot avoid pragmatic issues, controlling for them becomes of paramount importance. Through a discussion of existing literature, this paper has attempted to take a few initial steps in the direction of articulating more clearly the insights that can be obtained by taking the modularity thesis seriously in child language research, and of attempting to bring theoretical claims from different areas into contact with each other. Such eclectic endeavour might serve us well in the next twenty years of child language research.

REFERENCES

Chien, Y.-C. & Wexler, K. (1990). Children's knowledge of locality conditions in binding as evidence for the modularity of syntax and pragmatics. *Language Acquisition* **1**, 225–95.
Chomsky, N. (1981). *Lectures on Government and Binding*. Dordrecht: Foris.
—— (1986). *Barriers*. Cambridge, MA: MIT Press.
Crain, S. & McKee, C. (1985). Acquisition of structural restrictions on anaphora. *Proceedings of New England Linguistic Society* **16**, 94–110.
Fodor, J. A. (1983). *The modularity of mind*. Cambridge, MA: MIT Press.
Grimshaw, J. & Rosen, S. (1990). Knowledge and obedience: the developmental status of the binding theory. *Linguistic Inquiry* **21**, 187–222.
Grodzinsky, J. & Reinhart, T. (1993). The innateness of binding and coreference. *Linguistic Inquiry* **24**, 69–101.
Gunnar, M. R. & Maratsos, M. (eds) (1992). *Modularity and constraints in language and cognition*. Hillsdale. NJ: Erlbaum.
Heim, I. (1991). Anaphora and semantic interpretation: reinterpretation of Reinhart's approach. Unpublished manuscript, MIT: Cambridge, MA.
Hyams, N. & Sigurjonsdottir, S. (1990). The development of 'long-distance anaphora': a cross-linguistic comparison with special reference to Icelandic. *Language Acquisition* **1**, 57–93.
Kaufman, D. (1988). Grammatical and cognitive interactions in the study of children's knowledge on binding theory and reference relations. Unpublished doctoral dissertation, Temple University, Philadelphia, PA.
Kempson, R. (1988). Grammar and conversational principles. In F. J. Newmeyer (ed.), *Linguistics: the Cambridge survey*. Vol. II. *Linguistic theory: extensions and implications*. Cambridge: C.U.P.
Levinson, S. (1987). Pragmatics and the grammar of anaphora: a partial pragmatic reduction of binding and control phenomena. *Journal of Linguistics* **23**, 379–434.
Lust, B. (ed.) (1987). *Studies in the acquisition of anaphora* (Vols 1 & 2). Dordrecht: Reidel.
McDaniel, D., Cairns, H. S. & Hsu, J. R. (1990). Binding principles in the grammars of young children. *Language Acquisition* **1**, 121–39.
McKee, C. (1992). A comparison of pronouns and anaphors in Italian and English acquisition. *Language Acquisition* **2**, 21–54.

Radford, A. (1990). *Syntactic theory and the acquisition of English syntax*. Oxford: Blackwell.
Reinhart, T. (1983). *Anaphora and semantic interpretation*. Croom Helm: London.
—— (1986). Center and periphery in the grammar of anaphora. In B. Lust (ed.), *Studies in the acquisition of anaphora*. Vol. 1. Dordrecht: Reidel.
Solan, L. (1987). Parameter setting and the development of pronouns and reflexives. In T. Roeper & E. Williams (eds), *Parameter setting*. Dordrecht: Reidel.
Sperber, D. & Wilson, D. (1986). *Relevance*. Cambridge, MA: Harvard University Press.
—— & —— (1987). Precis of relevance: communication and cognition. *Behavioral and Brain Sciences* **10**, 697–754.